Genealogical Gleanings

Abstracted from

the Early Newspapers of

Penn Yan, Yates County,

New York,

1823-1833 and 1841-1855

Compiled by Dianne Stenzel

HERITAGE BOOKS, INC.

Published 1991 By

HERITAGE BOOKS, INC.
1540E Pointer Ridge Place, Bowie, Maryland 20716
(301)-390-7709

ISBN 1-55613-528-9

TABLE OF CONTENTS

PREFACE

Yates County is located in the Finger Lake area of western New York. During the early part of the 1800's, there were two major migration trails, or roads passing through this area. The Great Genesee Road which ran from Albany, to Utica, on to Canandaigua and westward to Fort Niagara. The Catskill Road ran from Boston to Waddle's Ferry, picked up at Owego, came through the town of Penn Yan, and intersected in Canandaigua with the Great Genesee Road.

After the Revolutionary War, many families started migrating west, passing through the Finger Lake area. Some stopped briefly, while others planted their roots in the rich soil of the farm lands. Many left behind valuable records for the researcher, while others seemed to live their entire lives in obscurity.

Unfortunately, this area had few vital records prior to 1880. In my own quest for these records, I found the Yates County Office of Public History in Penn Yan to be more than helpful, but the only sources available were cemetery, church, and newspapers. Some had been micro-filmed, but as luck would have it, the church I needed had not. I could not expect a limited staff to sit down and sort through the newspapers page by page, looking for possible marriages and deaths of my ancestors. No one had yet abstracted these records into books, and the micro-films were not available outside the area. This posed a slight problem, as I live in Maryland and the records I needed were in New York state. I could not afford to travel there and spend weeks or even months, while I did the job myself. The cost for food, lodging, etc., could be very expensive.

Patience, prayers, and determination are a must for any successful researcher. I figured there had to be a way to obtain the information I was looking for. I gave the matter a lot of thought and came up with an idea that proved to be mutually beneficial. Thanks to the cooperation of Virginia Gibbs (Yates County Historian), arrangements were made for me to abstract the gleanings from the early newspapers in my own home in Maryland. In return, I would compile this book, giving the royalty to the Yates County Office of Public History. They will use the proceeds to expand their sources, while I was able to expand my own information.

The newspapers made available to me, were the "Yates County Republican", published from 1823 to 1833, and the "Yates County Whig" from 1841 to 1855, both in Penn Yan. It was from these papers that this book was compiled. They covered all of Yates County, and included news of individuals from the surrounding counties, as well as other states. Listings from other areas were printed for the benefit of family or friends, making these papers a valuable clue to migrations, as individuals moved from one location to another. Even though many papers were missing in various years, I was able to include well over 6,000 names.

The pleasure of this book was all mine, and I look forward to doing another on the Yates County newspapers dating from 1856 into the 1880's.

My hope is this book will assist people now and in the future, in finding those all important dates, and locating where their ancestors may have lived. I tried to abstract every genealogical record, or clue I could find, and copied all names as printed. Individuals are found in the index, listed by entry numbers and not by page number, making it possible to find them without reading the entire page.

I can't guarantee all information to be accurate, the newspapers could have made a mistake, and I'm sure I probably did too. Some papers were faded, blurred, torn and sometimes with an ink blot right over a name or date, but I did the best I could. There were times I had to make estimated guesses, or try to make the names out through other sources, such as the "New York Federal Census Index", or Clevelands "History of Yates County".

To assist individuals who are not familiar with the area, I added the counties to each town, unless there were multiple listings of the towns name. There are town with names like Jerusalem, Italy, Chilli, Naples, Boston, etc. that could cause confusion, if the county was not stated. And...I have included a separate index listing individuals who were mentioned with connections to the Revolutionary War.

Hopefully this book will include just the record you have been searching for.

"Happy Hunting"

Dianne Stenzel
Perry Hall, Maryland

MAP OF WESTERN NEW YORK

There were two main migration trails, or roads passing through the Finger Lake area of western New York during the early 1800's. The Great Genesee Road, which ran from Albany, to Utica, on to Canandaigua and westward to Fort Niagara. The Catskill Road, ran from Boston, MA., to Waddles's Ferry, picked up at Owego, came through Penn Yan, and intersected in Canandaigua with the Great Genesee Road.

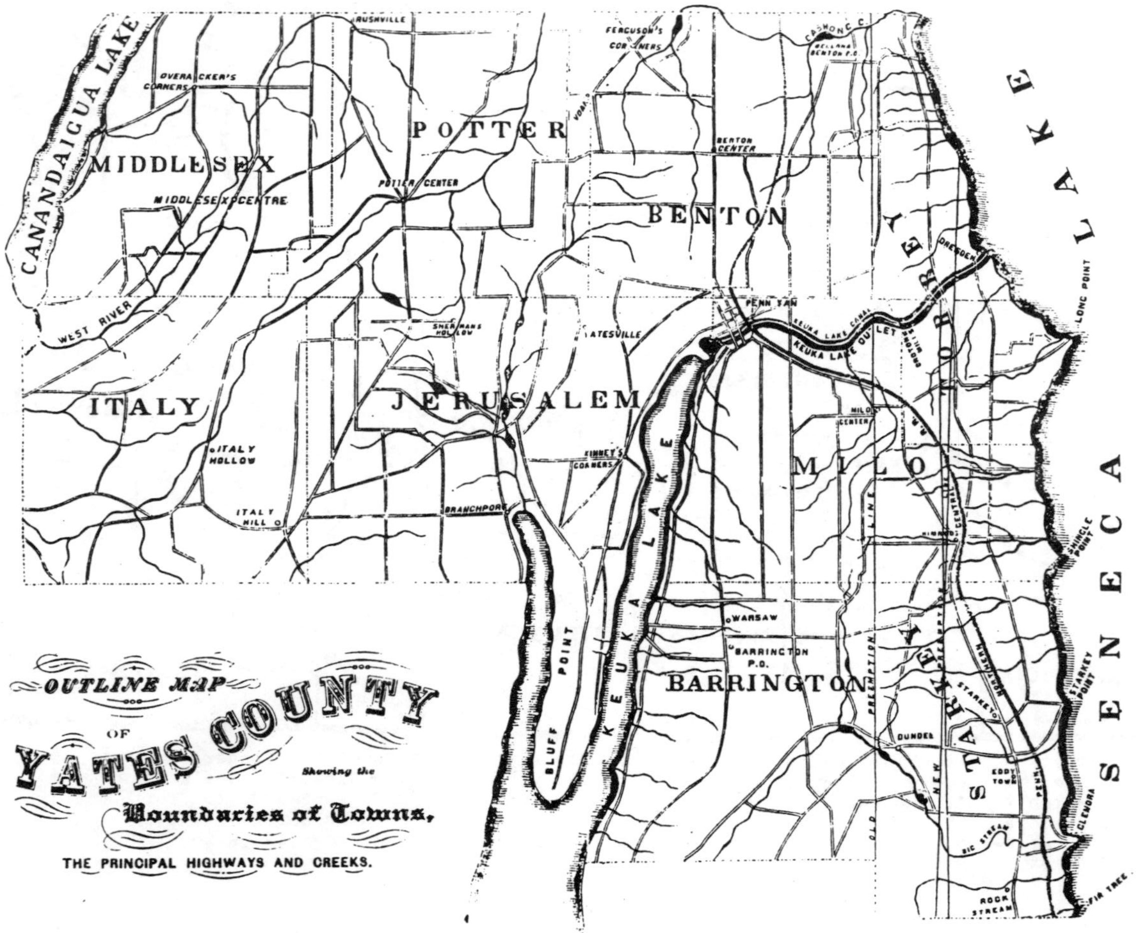
OUTLINE MAP
OF
YATES COUNTY
Showing the
Boundaries of Towns,
THE PRINCIPAL HIGHWAYS AND CREEKS.
CANANDAIGUA LAKE
MIDDLESEX
MIDDLESEX CENTRE
OVERACKER'S CORNERS
WEST RIVER
POTTER
POTTER CENTER
RUSHVILLE
BENTON
BENTON CENTER
FERGUSON'S CORNERS
BELLONA BENTON P.O.
ITALY
ITALY HOLLOW
ITALY HILL
JERUSALEM
SHERMANS HOLLOW
BRANCHPORT
KINNEY'S CORNERS
YATESVILLE
PENN YAN
KEUKA LAKE
BLUFF POINT
KEUKA LAKE OUTLET
KEUKA LAKE CANAL
MILO
MILO CENTER
TORREY
DRESDEN
BARRINGTON
BARRINGTON P.O.
WARSAW
OLD PREEMPTION LINE
NEW PREEMPTION
STARKEY
DUNDEE
EDDYTOWN
BIG STREAM
ROCK STREAM
NORTHERN CENTRAL
PENN.
STARKEY POINT
SHINGLE POINT
GLENORA
FIR TREE
LONG POINT
SENECA LAKE

DEDICATION

I wish to dedicate this book to my late Great-grand father James Steward Wilcox, born 10 Jan 1841 to Steward and Mary (Matthews) Wilcox, in Jerusalem, Yates County, New York. A man of remarkable character and strength, who earned the love and respect of everyone he met.

It was through the research of his family that this book came about.

Dianne Stenzel
Perry Hall, Maryland

SPECIAL THANKS

This book would not have been possible without the cooperation and assistance of Virginia Gibbs and Frances Dumas of the Yates County Office of Public History in Penn Yan, New York. A special thanks to David Burnisky of Southfield, Michigan for his invaluable assistance with editing, and to Kelli Hosier of Aberdeen, Maryland for her computer assistance.

My deepest thanks go to my husband William F. Stenzel for his assistance in putting entries in the computer, helping with the editing and printing, but especially for his patience. It was team work all the way around, God Bless all of you.

Dianne Stenzel
Perry Hall, Maryland

INTRODUCTION

We at the Yates County Office of Public History are delighted to have been able to supply Dianne Stenzel with the raw material for this book. The result which you now hold in your hands is due solely to her drive, initiative, and persistence. We trust you will find it as helpful as we have its generous and unpaid compiler.

Mrs. Virginia Gibbs,
Yates County Historian
Penn Yan, New York

1. Mrs. Susannah Crane age 53 yrs., died 12 Mar 1823 in Penn Yan, Yates Co. (25 Mar 1823)

2. Hon. Brockholst Livingston age 66 yrs., died 18 Mar 1823 at Washington, an Associate Judge of the U.S. Supreme Court. His remains removed to New York for interment. (8 Apr 1823)

3. FATAL ACCIDENT; news from Newburgh, NY., 30 Nov 1824. A vessel sinks on the way from New York city to Newburgh, the following individuals drowned;

Sullivan Co.....	Mrs. Couch and two children.
" "	Mr. Loveland.
" "	Mr. J. Smiley.
Crawford, NY....	Mrs. Graham and two children.
Newburgh, NY....	Samuel Carlisle.
" "	Jacob Polhemus.
" "	Mrs. M'Claughery.
Wallkill, NY....	Mrs. Rush.
Montgomery Co...	Mr. M'Curdy.
" "	Mrs. Churchill.
" "	Mr. Weed.
" "	Mrs. Cochrane.
" "	William Hensler.
Minisink, NY....	John Greenleaf.
" "	George Evertson.
" "	Matilda Helme.
" "	William Kelly and one child.
Cornwall, NY....	Mrs. Dean.
New York, NY....	F. William DeCoudres.
" " "	Mrs. Trout.
Blooming Grove..	John Leader

(16 Dec 1824)

4. Nathan Pratt age abt. 65 yrs., died 10 Dec 1824 in Gorham, Ontario Co., of apoplexy. (16 Dec 1824)

5. William Wallworth age abt. 50 yrs., died 17 Dec 1824 in Ovid, Seneca Co. (30 Dec 1824)

6. Z.A. Leland Esq. of Bath, Steuben Co., and Belinda Porter of Prattsburgh, Steuben Co., were married 30 Dec 1824 by Rev. Hotchkiss in Prattsburgh. (6 Jan 1825)

7. Samuel Ives, murdered by Robert Douglas, no date given, a trial held last week at Bath, Steuben Co. (20 Jan 1825)

8. Jason Treadwell, executed 13 Jan 1825 at Montrose, PA., for the murder of Oliver Harper last May. (26 Jan 1825)

9. Henry Fauntleroy Esq., executed recently in London, England. A late partner in the house of Marsh, Stacy, Fauntleroy and Graham, condemned to death for forgery. (2 Feb 1825)

10. Dr. Henry P. Sartwell of Bethel, Sullivan Co., and Rebecca Stewart formerly of Penn Yan, Yates Co. were married 20 Jan 1825, no pastor or town given. (2 Feb 1825)

11. Moses L. Rogers and Margaret Taylor, both of Benton, Yates Co., were married 29 Jan 1825 by Rev. Richard Williams in Benton. (2 Feb 1825)

12. Nimphus Holden and Mary Morris, both of Benton, were married 29 Jan 1825 by A. Woodworth Esq. in Benton. (2 Feb 1825)

13. L.G. Budlong of Penn Yan, Yates Co., and Calista Brownell of Ledyard, Cayuga Co., were married 14 Feb 1825 by Rev. Smith in Ledyard. (16 Feb 1825)

14. John Armistead age 17 yrs., killed by the accidental discharge of his own gun, at Alexandria VA. He had just returned from the Military School of Capt. Partridge, no date given. (22 Feb 1825)

15. William Freer of Seneca, Ontario Co., and Mabel Whitney of Benton, Yates Co., were married 6 Feb 1825 by S.G. Gage Esq. in Benton. (22 Feb 1825)

16. Richard G. Preston and Harriet Gilmore were married 17 Feb 1825 by Rev. Richard Williams in Penn Yan, Yates Co. (22 Feb 1825)

17. Jesse Layton and Abigail Tuthill, both of Reading, Schuyler Co., were married 10 Feb 1825 by Rev. Samuel White in Reading. (1 Mar 1825)

18. William Woodruff of Bridgeton, New Jersey, died 12 Feb 1825, accidentally killed by his own gun. (8 Mar 1825)

19. Stephen Wilson of Saratoga Co., and Eleanor Seeley of Ovid, Seneca Co., were married 6 Mar 1825 by Rev. Thomas Lounsbury in Ovid. (14 Mar 1825)

20. John Kown aged 35 yrs., died 20 Mar 1825 in Penn Yan, Yates Co. His death caused from injuries by the fall of a tree. (22 Mar 1825)

21. George Oxtoby and Mary Hughes, both of Benton, Yates Co., were married 17 Mar 1825 by S.G. Gage Esq. in Benton. (29 Mar 1852)

22. John Reid died 26 Mar 1825 in the Penitentiary of typhus fever. Lately convicted of an attempt to poison the Carroll family in New York city. (29 Mar 1825)

23. James Hayes aged 38 yrs., died 24 Mar 1825 in Geneva, Ontario Co. Brother of the Editor of the "Ovid Gazette", leaving a wife and several children. (5 Apr 1825)

24. Caleb Hood and Louisa Nash, both of Jerusalem, Yates Co., were married 27 Mar 1825 by N. Cothren Esq. in Jerusalem. (12 Apr 1825)

25. Gilbert Ferris of Milo, Yates Co., and Esther Hood of Jerusalem, Yates Co., were married 3 Apr 1825 by N. Cothren Esq. in Jerusalem. (12 Apr 1825)

26. General Sir Alexander Campbell, Commander in Chief of the Presidency of Madras, died 11 Dec 1824. (19 Apr 1825)

27. John L'Munyan and Gitty Gilmore were married 16 Apr 1825 by Rev. Richard Williams in Penn Yan, Yates Co. (19 Apr 1825)

28. James Richmond age 59 yrs., died 5 Apr 1825 at Bristol, Ontario Co., of injuries received from being kicked in the abdomen and back by a horse. (19 Apr 1825)

29. Hon. Return Jonathan Meigs died 25 Mar 1825 at Marietta, OH., ex-Governor of Ohio and late Postmaster General of U.S. (19 Apr 1825)

30. John Powell of Penn Yan, Yates Co., and Mrs. Emily Gilbert, daughter of Jared Patchin Esq., were married 21 Apr 1825 by A. Woodworth Esq. in Benton, Yates Co. (26 Apr 1825)

31. John Duga and Eliza Wheeler, both of Penn Yan, Yates Co., were married 21 Apr 1825 by Rev. Richard Williams in Penn Yan. (26 Apr 1825)

32. Abraham Ellsworth and Sally Clark were married 21 Apr 1825 by Rev. Kent in Reading, Schuyler Co. (26 Apr 1825)

33. William H. Sutton and Adeline Jenkins, both of Ovid, Seneca Co., were married 16 Apr 1825 by Rev. Thomas Lounsbury in Ovid. (26 Apr 1825)

34. Mrs. Joanna Ogden age 23 yrs., died 22 Apr 1852 in Penn Yan, Yates Co., wife of Mordecai Ogden. (26 Apr 1852)

35. Daniel S. Kendig of Waterloo, Seneca Co., and Sarah Maria Southwick, daughter of Major David Southwick of Junis, Seneca Co., were married 12 Apr 1825 by Rev. Lane in Junis. (26 Apr 1825)

36. Charlotte Buckbee age 2 yrs. 9 mos., died 23 Apr 1825 in Penn Yan, Yates Co., daughter of John Buckbee. (26 Apr 1825)

37. Robert Reed, killed last week in Greensburg, PA., when he was struck by lightning. (26 Apr 1825)

38. Peter Decker committed suicide several days ago at Arsenal Hill. From papers found in his pocket, it is believed he was from N.J. (26 Apr 1825)

39. John Wood, drowned 28 Apr 1825 when he upset his boat on Seneca Lake near Geneva, Ontario Co. (3 May 1825)

40. Robert Douglas, executed 29 Apr 1825, for the murder of Samuel Ives, no town given. (3 May 1825)

41. Emeline Cunningham, murdered recently in Cecil Co., MD, no date given. (3 May 1825)

42. Mrs. John Utter of Bloomfield, Oakland Co., MI, was killed 5 Apr 1825 by Imri Fish. Her daughter Cynthia Utter age 15 yrs., also killed trying to defend her mother. (10 May 1825)

43. Jones Harding of Gorham, Ontario Co., and Mary A. Rowley of Middlesex, Yates Co., were married 21 April 1825 by Chester Loomis Esq., of Gorham, no town given. (10 May 1825)

44. Russell Aldrich Esq. and Eliza Marshall, both of Middlesex, Yates Co., were married 21 April 1825 by William Bassett Esq. in Middlesex. (10 May 1825)

45. Abiel C. Canoll, Editor of the "Broome Republican", and Mary Abigail Parker, daughter of Capt. William Parker of New York, were married 21 April 1825 by Rev. Stafford in New York. (10 May 1825)

46. The body of a man named Terry, found in a distillery in the east part of town last week. The coroner stated he died from intoxication and exposure. Copied from the "Wayne Sent." 4 May 1825. (17 May 1825)

47. Elisha Delano Jr. and Sarah Andrews were married 15 May 1825 by William M. Oliver Esq. in Penn Yan, Yates Co. (17 May 1825)

48. Kirk Ireland of Benton, Yates Co., and Jemima Curtiss of Jerusalem, Yates Co., were married 19 May 1825 by Elder Potter in Jerusalem. (24 May 1825)

49. Mrs. Marcy Perry age 74 yrs., died 14 May 1825 in Jerusalem, Yates Co., widow of the late Jonathan Perry Esq. of RI., and daughter of William Potter, late of Jerusalem. (24 May 1825)

50. Eliza Ann Tuttle aged 7 yrs., died 17 May 1825 in Penn Yan, Yates Co., daughter of Benjamin Tuttle Jr. (24 May 1825)

51. Sophia Doubleday age 4 yrs., died 14 May 1825 in Italy, Yates Co., the daughter of Dr. Elisha Doubleday. (24 May 1825)

52. Henry Rosakrants and Beershaba Pardee were married 15 May 1825 by S.G. Gage Esq. in Benton, Yates Co. (31 May 1825)

53. After a long and tedious courtship of three days, Joseph Fowl and Wealthy Hall, daughter of Simon Hall Esq., of Middlesex, Yates Co., were married 1 June 1825 by Joseph Gay Esq. in Jerusalem, Yates Co. (7 June 1825)

54. Martha Reed age 11 yrs., died 6 Jun 1825 at the home of Mr. Gould in Penn Yan, Yates Co., daughter of Nathaniel Reed of Phelps, Ontario Co. (7 Jun 1825)

55. Capt. Jehial P. Parsons killed 8 June 1825 at Waterloo, Seneca Co., by the bursting of a swivel, immoderately charged. (14 June 1825)

56. Capt. Selden Williams of Middlesex, Yates Co., and Mrs. Sally Cowen of Williamson, Wayne Co., were married 2 Jun 1825 at Williamson, no pastor given. (14 Jun 1825)

57. FATAL STEAM BOAT ACCIDENT; copied from the "New York Observer" 4 Jun 1825, on Thursday morning last, the steam boat "Legislator", of the Exchange line in Philadelphia, Pa., was leaving the wharf when an explosion was heard from the steam room. Killed were;

Robert Greenleaf a fireman.
John Harris a young lad, one of the waiters.
Francis Roney age 22 yrs, a colored cook.
Thomas Williams a colored boy.
Joseph Beal a colored man, one of the waiters.
(14 Jun 1825)

58. Dr. Mason Laman and Hannah Wolcott, both of Benton, Yates Co., were married 7 June 1825 by A. Woodworth Esq. in Benton. (14 June 1825)

59. Capt. Allen Cole of Jerusalem, Yates Co., and Rosina Vickery of Penn Yan, Yates Co., were married 1 June 1825 by N. Cothren Esq. in Penn Yan. (14 June 1825)

60. William Cornwell age 75 yrs., died 11 June 1825 at his home in Jerusalem, Yates Co. A soldier of the Revolution, twice taken prisoner. Present at the fall of Oriskany, where he was wounded in the discharge of his duty as a Lieut. in the Company of Rangers, commanded by Capt. Haga. (14 Jun 1825)

61. Daniel D. Tompkins Esq. age 51 yrs., died 11 Jun 1825 at his home on Staten Island, NY., late vice-President of the U.S. (21 June 1825)

62. Nathaniel Weare age 66 yrs., died 22 June 1825 Middlesex, Yates Co. (28 June 1825)

63. Jacob VanBuskirk age 18 yrs., died 2 Jul 1825 in Penn Yan, Yates Co. (6 July 1825)

64. Elias Boudinot, a young Cherokee Indian, and Harriet R. Gold of Cornwall, Orange Co., were married, no date, pastor or town given. (12 July 1825)

65. Charles G. Haines Esq. died 3 July 1825 of consumption, the Adjutant General of New York. (12 July 1825)

66. Capt. Thomas Howard age 67 yrs., died 25 May 1825 at his home in Perryburg, Wood Co., Ohio. One of the first settlers of Benton, Yates Co. NY. (19 July 1825)

67. George W. Fenno and Phebe Waterous were married 31 Jul 1825 by James C. Robinson Esq. in Milo, Yates Co. (9 Aug 1825)

68. Paul Wheeler age 50 yrs., and Mrs. Abigail Howelage age 65 yrs., were married 1 Aug 1825 by William Bassett Esq. in Middlesex, Yates Co. (9 Aug 1825)

69. Mrs. Sarah Sears age 48 yrs., died 14 Aug 1825 in Penn Yan, Yates Co., wife of James Sears. (16 Aug 1825)

70. Jesse Ide a labouring man of Penn Yan, Yates Co., drowned 28 Aug 1826 in the Crooked Lake, when he fell from a raft while angling. (30 Aug 1825)

71. Charles Reading and Harriet Knapp were married 23 Aug 1825 by Elder John Goff in Benton, Yates Co. (30 Aug 1825)

72. Hon. Roger Skinner died 19 Aug 1825 in Albany, Albany Co., U.S. Dist. Judge for NY. (30 Aug 1825)

73. Gen. Charles Cotesworth Pinckney died 16 Aug 1825 at his home on East Bay, a veteran of the Revolution. (6 Sep 1825)

74. Newman S. Smith and Rachel Blackman, both of Benton, Yates Co., were married 4 Sep 1825 by E. Doubleday Esq. in Italy, Yates Co. (6 Sep 1825)

75. Britten M. Williams and Eliza Williams, the daughter of R.M. Williams Esq., were married by Rev. Joseph Merril in Middlesex, Yates Co., no date given. (6 Sep 1825)

76. Thomas Hilson and Eleanor Augusta Johnson, both of New York Park Theater, were married by Rev. Foster at Oyster Bay, Long Island, no date given. (6 Sep 1825)

77. Mrs. Mary Young died 22 Aug 1825 at Ballston, NY., wife of Col. Samuel Young. (6 Sep 1825)

78. Mrs. Phebe Weyburn age 41 yrs., died 5 Aug 1825 in Seneca, Ontario Co., wife of Samuel Weyburn. (6 Sep 1825)

79. Samuel Wiley of Milo, Yates Co., and Clarissa Craven of Benton, Yates Co., were married 11 Sep 1825 by Rev. M. Alverson in Benton. (13 Sep 1825)

80. Mrs. Phebe Stevens age 39 yrs. 4 mos., died 2 Sep 1825 in Canandaigua, Ontario Co. Wife of the Editor of the "Ontario Messenger", and daughter of Phineas Bates Esq. (13 Sep 1825)

81. Mrs. Naomi Curtiss died 16 Sep 1825 at Middlesex, Yates Co., wife of Pelamon Curtiss. (27 Sep 1825)

82. Asa Holmes died 27 Sep 1825 at his home in Milo, Yates Co. (4 Oct 1825)

83. Joshua Stephens died 20 Sept 1825, found in the woods near Canisteo, Steuben Co. He had been shot by Indians. (4 Oct 1825)

84. Charlotte Russell age 13 yrs., accidentally killed 22 Sep 1825 in Ovid, Seneca Co., by falling on a knife she held in her own hand, at the house of Mrs. Hogarth. (4 Oct 1825)

85. Jacob Peters, accidentally killed 23 Sep 1825 in Junius, Seneca Co., by the discharge of a rifle, carried by a hunting companion. (4 Oct 1825)

86. George H. Green Esq. died 25 Sep 1825 of consumption at York, Livingston Co., late of Penn Yan, Yates Co. (11 Oct 1825)

87. Dr. Daniel Goodwin died recently in Hamtramick, Michigan Territory, formerly of Geneva, Ontario Co. no date given. (11 Oct 1825)

88. Daniel Sutton and Anna Botsford were married 13 Oct 1825 by Elder Kent in Jerusalem, Yates Co. (18 Oct 1825)

89. Charles Lilly age 1 yr., died 11 Oct 1825 in Jerusalem, Yates Co., son of Col. William Lilly. (18 Oct 1825)

90. Gen. Daniel Shays age 84 yrs. died at Sparta, Livingston Co. An officer of the Revolution, and leader of a party in Massachusetts called "Shay's Men", no date given. (18 Oct 1825)

91. TRAGIC ACCIDENT; Messrs. Remington and Whitman killed 29 Oct 1825 at Weedsport, Cayuga Co. On the arrival of the first boat from Buffalo. An accident happened from the discharge of a twenty-four pounder. She had been discharged several times, when the man at the vent removed his thumb, due to

the heat and the charge took fire. Messrs. Remington and Whitman, mechanics of Weedsport, who were engaged in loading, were then literally blown to pieces. They both leave a wife, one had five children, and the other one child. (1 Nov 1825)

92. Elijah and Reuben Cole, twin brothers, married twin sisters, Elizabeth and Mary Jones, daughters of Edward Jones of Brunswick, on 20 Oct 1825 at the Friends Meeting House in Durham, Maine. (1 Nov 1825)

93. Charles Hubbard and Lydia Brownell were married 30 Oct 1825 by Rev. Eddy in Penn Yan, Yates Co. (1 Nov 1825)

94. Henry Plimpton of Penn Yan, Yates Co., and Marie Ann Worden of Clarkson, Monroe Co., were married 30 Oct 1825 by Rev. Hannuell in Clarkson. (15 Nov 1825)

95. Hiram Dunn and Charlotte Clark were married 17 Nov 1825 by Elder Lanning in Reading, Schuyler Co. (22 Nov 1825)

96. Thomas J. Nevins Esq., Attorney at Law in Penn Yan, Yates Co., and Minerva Loomis of Middlesex, Yates Co., were married 23 Nov 1825 by Rev. Joseph Bracketts in Middlesex. (29 Nov 1825)

97. Mr. Reynolds, executed 19 Nov 1825 in New York city for the murder of Capt. West. (29 Nov 1825)

98. Col. Sharpe, murdered recently in Frankfort, KY., no date given. (6 Dec 1825)

99. Alexander Peckens and Susan Clark were married 26 Nov 1825 by Rev. G. Lanning in Benton, Yates Co. (6 Dec 1825)

100. Zebulon Williams age 59 yrs., died 22 Nov 1825 in Palmyra, Wayne Co., his remains interred in Masonic form. (6 Dec 1825)

101. Commodore M'Donough died at sea 10 Nov 1825 of consumption. He was the hero of Champlain, forced by ill health to resign the command of the "Frigate Constitution". He embarked on board the brig "Edgar", at Gibralter on 24th of Oct, and was on his way home, when he died. (6 Dec 1825)

102. Maxmilian Joseph, the "King of Bavaria", died 12 Oct 1825 at Nymphenburg. (13 Dec 1825)

103. Brig. Gen. William Hull, late of the US Army, age 73 yrs., died 6 Dec 1825 in Newtown, Chemung Co., an officer in the Revolution. (13 Dec 1825)

104. Lord Lieut. Marquis of Wellesley of Ireland, and Mrs. Patterson of Baltimore, MD., were married 29 Oct 1825 in Dublin, Ireland. (20 Dec 1825)

105. Dr. Lewis A. Birdsall and Mary Jane Lee, the daughter of Dr. Joshua Lee, were married 18 Dec 1825 by Elder Amos Chase in Benton, Yates Co. (20 Dec 1825)

106. George D. Stewart died 15 Dec 1825 at Bethel, Sullivan Co., a merchant of that place. (20 Dec 1825)

107. Commodore David Rogers of Penn Yan, Yates Co., and Mary Ann Davis of Genoa, Cayuga Co., were married 22 Dec 1825 by Rev. Smith in Genoa. (27 Dec 1825)

108. Walter P. Hobert and Amanda Loomis, both of Middlesex, Yates Co., were married 29 Dec 1825 by Rev. Joseph Brackett at Middlesex. (3 Jan 1826)

109. John B. Townsend died 26 Dec 1825 in Benton, Yates Co. (3 Jan 1826)

110. Hiram Staunton and Betsey Earls were married 25 Dec 1825 by N. Cothren Esq. in Jerusalem, Yates Co. (10 Jan 1826)

111. Jacob Shyer of Steuben Co. and Sally S_aw ? (illegible) of Jerusalem, Yates Co., were married 1 Jan 1826 by N. Cothren Esq. at Jerusalem. (10 Jan 1826)

112. Allen Goodrich and Charity Shults, both of Jerusalem, Yates Co., were married 5 Jan 1826 by N. Cothren Esq. in Jerusalem. (10 Jan 1826)

113. Gideon Wolcott and Ann Brown were married 22 Jan 1826 by A. Woodworth Esq. in Jerusalem, Yates Co. (24 Jan 1826)

114. Timothy Jane, an elderly man, died 25 Jan 1826 in Milo, Yates Co. The Coroner stated he died from intoxication and freezing. (31 Jan 1826)

115. Willard Lucas of Middlesex, Yates Co., and Sally Gamble of Benton, Yates Co., were married 21 Jan 1826 by A. Woodworth Esq. in Benton. (31 Jan 1826)

116. John Beeden and Julia Dickerson were married 29 Jan 1826 by S.G. Gage Esq., in Benton, Yates Co. (31 Jan 1826)

117. James Lent and Catherine Lent were married in Peekskill, Westchester Co., by Rev. Hoffman, no date given. (31 Jan 1826)

118. Peter Schilderknetcht and Christina Schlechtwohl were married at Enterwalden, Delaware, no date given. (31 Jan 1826)

119. Winslow Small age 17 yrs., and weighing 99 lbs. and Polly Small age 20 yrs., and weighing 50 lbs., were married in Minot, ME., no date given. (31 Jan 1826)

120. Nathaniel Cole age 20 yrs., and Elizabeth Gardner age 12 yrs., were married in Shrewsbury, MA, no date or pastor given. (31 Jan 1826)

121. Roswell Lord of Jerusalem, Yates Co., and Huldah Graham of Italy, Yates Co., were married 29 Jan 1826 by James Fox Esq. in Italy. (7 Feb 1826)

122. Major Richard Goodell died 25 Jan 1826 at Auburn, Cayuga Co. An agent of the Auburn State Prison, former Speaker of the House, and a meritorious officer of the last War. Interred in Jefferson Co, with Military and Masonic honors. (7 Feb 1826)

123. Andrew Merrill age 35 yrs., died 25 Jan 1826 in Utica, Oneida Co., of Merrill & Hastings, publisher of the "Western Recorder". (7 Feb 1826)

124. Hiram Phinney and Peggy Morrison were married 7 Feb 1826 by Rev. G. Lanning in Tyrone, Schuyler, Co. (14 Feb 1826)

125. Melanie Delano age 26 yrs., died 25 Feb 1826 at the home of Allyn Boardman Esq. in Seneca Co. (7 Mar 1826)

126. Ralph A. Wilkoff age 20 yrs., died 13 Feb 1826 at Middletown, CT., of Capt. Partridges Military Academy, in Opelousa, LA. His funeral from the Presbyterian Church. (14 Mar 1826)

127. Abraham Stiles of Morristown, NJ., and Elizabeth Price of Fayette, Seneca Co., were married 22 Mar 1826 by Rev. C. Eddy in Penn Yan, Yates Co. (28 Mar 1826)

128. William Morris and Mary Hull were married 3 Apr 1826 by A. Woodworth Esq. in Penn Yan, Yates Co. (4 Apr 1826)

129. Henry Wisewell and Alice Whitman, both of Rushville, Yates Co., were married 19 Mar 1826 by Rev. Joseph Brackett in Rushville. (4 Apr 1826)

130. Peter Basom and Sally Wyman, both of Middlesex, Yates Co. were married 20 Mar 1826 by Charles Graves Esq. at Italy, Yates Co. (4 Apr 1826)

131. George Wheeler and Ethalinda Tubbs were married 25 Mar 1826 by S.G. Gage Esq. in Benton, Yates Co. (4 Apr 1826)

132. Samuel Weyburn of Ontario Co., and Mrs. Beeton of Benton, Yates Co., were married 25 Mar 1826 by S.G. Gage Esq. at Benton. (4 Apr 1826)

133. Joseph Shepherd and Ruth Spencer were married 4 Apr 1826 by Rev. Abner Chase in Benton, Yates Co. (11 Apr 1826)

134. Three children of Mr. Talcott of Starkey, Yates Co., burned to death 10 Apr 1826, when their log house was consumed by fire. The parents were away at the time. (18 Apr 1826)

135. Capt. Richard Whitfield aged 21 yrs., and Mary Almand age 95 yrs., were married recently in Hampton, VA. no date given. * note the ages above are as they appeared. (25 Apr 1826)

136. Isaac Voak of Benton, Yates Co., and Bersheba Paine of Middlesex, Yates Co., were married 2 May 1826 by Elder Kent in Middlesex. (9 May 1826)

137. A DREADFUL TRIP: for crew and passengers aboard the "Francis Mary" from St. Johns, N.B. to Liverpool, Eng. They experienced a horrible trip which claimed the following lives, Patrick Cooney died 5 Feb 1826, James Clark a seaman, died 12 Feb 1826, John Wilson, a seaman died 22 Feb 1826, J. Moore died 23 Feb 1826, Henry Davis a welsh boy, died 5 Mar 1826, Elex'r Kelley a seaman, died 5 Mar

1826, John Jones an apprentice and nephew of the owner, died 5 Mar 1826, James Frier a cook, died 5 Mar 1826, Daniel Jones a seaman, died 5 Mar 1826, John Hutchinson a seaman, died 5 Mar 1826.
(16 May 1826)

138. Nathaniel W. Harlow and Catherine Johnson were married 18 May 1826 by Rev. Campbell in Benton, Yates Co. (23 May 1826)

139. Pere Hazard a colored man, aged abt. 45 yrs., died 20 May 1826 at Penn Yan, Yates Co.
(23 May 1826)

140. Edward D. Denniston and Mary Jones, both of Benton, Yates Co., were married 25 May 1826 by Rev. A.E. Campbell in Benton. (30 May 1826)

141. John J. Lord Esq., an Attorney at Law, age 23 yrs., died 24 May 1826 at Penn Yan, Yates Co. His service from the Presbyterian Meeting House, burial in Benton, Yates Co. (30 May 1826)

142. Wanton Ellsworth Esq. age 62 yrs., died 25 May 1826 at Penn Yan, Yates Co. (20 Jun 1826)

143. Jackson Sutton age 13 yrs., of Yates Co., killed 9 Jun 1826. A driver for one of the freight boats, he fell from the wall of a lock, near Little Falls, while attempting to throw over a tow rope, and was drowned. (27 Jun 1826)

144. John Adams, late President of the U.S., died 4 Jul 1826 at his seat in Quincy. (18 Jul 1826)

145. Thomas Jefferson, late President of the U.S., died 4 Jul 1826 at Montecello. (18 Jul 1826)

146. Mrs. Emily Powell age 24 yrs., died 16 Jul 1826 in Penn Yan, Yates Co., wife of John Powell, and daughter of Jared Patchen Esq. Services from the Presbyterian Meeting House. (18 Jul 1826)

147. Ormond Spaulding age 24 yrs., died 25 June 1826 in the stage, while passing from Avon Springs to Rochester. One of the Editors of the "Album".
(18 Jul 1826)

148. Edwin Wisewell and Eveline Lewis, both of Rushville, Yates Co., were married 23 Jul 1826 by Rev. Joseph Brackett in Rushville. (25 Jul 1826)

149. Thomas Hathaway Jr. and Polly Headley, daughter of Samuel Headley, were married 23 Jul 1826 in Milo, Yates Co., no pastor given. (25 Jul 1826)

150. Hezekiah Niles, Editor of the "Register", and Sally Ann Warner, daughter of the late John Warner Esq., were married in Baltimore, Maryland, no date or pastor given. (25 Jul 1826)

151. Mrs. Anne Beauchamp died 20 Jul 1826 at Frankfort, KY. She had been on trial, but acquitted as an accessory with her husband in the murder trial of Col. Sharp. (1 Aug 1826)

152. Mrs. James Johnson a white woman, murdered 6 Jul 1826 by her husband, a mulatto, near Geneva, Ontario Co. Her parents reportedly lived in PA. (1 Aug 1826)

153. William F. McClean and Phebe Clements were married 18 Jul 1826 by S.G. Gage Esq. in Benton, Yates Co. (1 Aug 1826)

154. Samuel Phillips of Milo, Yates Co., and Mary Rebecca Page of Benton, Yates Co., were married 30 Jul 1826 by S.G. Gage Esq. in Benton. (8 Aug 1826)

155. Daniel Bradley age 32 yrs., died 29 Jul 1826 at Genoa, Cayuga Co., a brother of Henry Bradley Esq. of Penn Yan, Yates Co. (8 Aug 1826)

156. Major William Ray died 30 Jul 1826 in Auburn, Cayuga Co., services from the Episcopal Church. (8 Aug 1826)

157. Mrs. Susan Clark age 30 yrs., died 1 Aug 1826 in Geneva, Ontario Co., wife of Rev. Orin Clark. (8 Aug 1826)

158. John C. Shannon found drowned 10 Aug 1826 in Starkey, Yates Co. A respectable farmer, his body, wagon, and dead horses were found in the millpond of Gen. Hurd. Evidently his team had failed on a high curve above the pond, one of the horses was known to be unmanageable at times. (15 Aug 1826)

159. Gov. Shelby of Kentucky, died 18 Jul 1826, no town given. (15 Aug 1826)

160. Dr. Mason Laman died 7 Aug 1826 in Benton, Yates Co. (15 Aug 1826)

161. Jefferson Jillett age 16 yrs., died 13 Aug 1826 in Penn Yan, Yates Co., son of Capt. Jeremiah Jillett. (15 Aug 1826)

162. Adam Van Tuyl aged 23 yrs., died 13 Aug 1826 in Dresden, Yates Co. (15 Aug 1826)

163. Mrs. Eliza Manning died 6 Aug 1826 in Ovid, Seneca Co., wife of Major Rockwell Manning. (15 Aug 1826)

164. Frances Manning age 20 mos., died 11 Aug 1826 in Ovid, Seneca Co., daughter of Major Rockwell Manning, and his late wife, Eliza Manning. (15 Aug 1826)

165. Charles W. Morris age 22 yrs., died 14 Aug 1826 in Middlesex, Yates Co., son of Joseph Morris. (22 Aug 1826)

166. Jeffrey Thomas age 20 yrs., died 18 Aug 1826 in Middlesex, Yates Co., son of Abiel Thomas Esq. (22 Aug 1826)

167. Hiram T. Day died 13 Aug 1826 in Lyons, Wayne Co., late Editor and proprietor of the "Lyons Advertiser". (29 Aug 1826)

168. Isaac B. Desha died 13 Aug 1826 in jail, from self inflicted injuries several weeks past, charged with the murder of Francis Baker in Frankfort, KY. (5 Sep 1826)

169. Henry A. Wisner an Attorney at Law, and Susan Hathaway were married 31 Aug 1826 by Rev. A.E. Campbell in Milo, Yates Co. (5 Sep 1826)

170. Henry Hubbard of Penn Yan, Yates Co., and Mary Brooks of Hopewell, Ontario Co., were married 31 Aug 1826 by Rev. C. Eddy in Hopewell. (12 Sep 1826)

171. Hon. H.E. Fudger Esq. a Consul, murdered 13 Jul 1826 in Bogata. (12 Sep 1826)

172. Seth S. Brazerton age 1 mo. 6 days, died 3 Sep 1826 in Benton, Yates Co., son of Samuel Brazerton. (12 Sep 1826)

173. Major Gen. Charles Thompson age 45 yrs., died 2 Sep 1826 at his home in Ovid, Seneca Co. (12 Sep 1826)

174. Hon. William P. VanNess died 11 Sep 1826 at the home of J.O. Hoffman Esq. A U.S. District Judge for Southern New York. (12 Sep 1826)

175. Peter Blackman died 14 Jul 1826 in Dublin, Ireland. One of many who died there of starvation. (12 Sep 1826)

176. John A. Stevens, Editor of the "Ontario Messenger", and Amelia Ackley of Montreal, Canada., were married 13 Sep 1826 by Rev. B.H. Hickox in Canandaigua, Ontario Co. (26 Sep 1826)

177. Samuel Sweet of Fayette, Seneca Co., murdered 8 Oct 1826 by his wife. She then attempted to kill herself, but failed. Neighbors testify he was habitually intoxicated and very abusive to her. (10 Oct 1826)

178. Lewis Himrod and Harriet Brownell were married 5 Oct 1826 by Rev. Eddy in Penn Yan, Yates Co. (10 Oct 1826)

179. Susan Perry died 5 Oct 1826 in Middlesex, Yates Co., daughter of Captain Rowse Perry. (10 Oct 1826)

180. A child of John Plimpton died 7 Oct 1826 in Milo, Yates Co. (10 Oct 1826)

181. Noah Rockwell of Bellona, Yates Co., and Sally Marie Stevens of Sodus, Wayne Co., were married 18 Oct 1826 by Esq. Bancraft in Sodus. (24 Oct 1826)

182. Dr. Stephen Dean of Hamburgh, Erie Co., and Rachel K. Jones of Penn Yan, Yates Co., were married in Lockport, Niagara, Co., at the Friends Meeting House, no date given. (6 Nov 1826)

183. Isaac Baker of Hamburgh, Erie Co., and Elizabeth R. Jones of Penn Yan, Yates Co., were married in Lockport, Niagara Co., at the Friends Meeting House, no date given. (6 Nov 1826)

184. After a half hour courtship through the prison gates, Alfred Martin age 24 yrs., and Catharine Rumgarner age 18 yrs., were married 5 Oct 1826 in the jail at Lincoln, North Carolina. (14 Nov 1826)

185. Selleck Osborn Esq., poet and former Editor of the "Delaware Watchman", died in Philadelphia, PA., no date given. (14 Nov 1826)

186. Abel B. Buckley of Milo, Yates Co., and Catalina Bogert of Dresden, Yates Co., were married 13 Nov 1826 by Rev. Eddy in Dresden. (21 Nov 1826)

187. Dexter Stebbins of Middlesex, Yates Co., and Eliza Critterden of Gorham, Ontario Co., were married 1 Nov 1826 in Gorham, no pastor given. (21 Nov 1826)

188. Seven members of the Wylley family, and two laborer's died in an avalanche at the Notch in New Hampshire, no date given. (28 Nov 1826)

189. Hon. Nathaniel Gorham age 63 yrs., died 22 Oct 1826 in Canandaigua, Ontario Co. (28 Nov 1826)

190. Thomas Hollowell and Nancy Bateman were married Nov 1826 by Rev. M. Alverson, in Benton, Yates Co. (28 Nov 1826)

191. Col. Richard C. Anderson died 19 Oct 1826 in Jefferson Co., KY. An aid to Gen. LaFayette in the Revolution. He had been in ill health, but it is thought his death was accelerated by the news of his son's recent death, the Minister of Columbia. (28 Nov 1826)

192. Commander Oliver H. Perry died 27 Nov 1826. His remains arrived at Newport, RI. aboard the "Lexington" from Trinidad on the fifth. A 17 gun salute was fired from the sloop, and an appropriate interment followed at Newport, with numerous public and military officials. (12 Dec 1826)

193. Samuel F. Curtiss of Penn Yan, Yates Co., and Amelia Boyd of Benton, Yates Co., were married 7 Dec 1826 by Rev. Eddy in Benton. (12 Dec 1826)

194. Charles Roy and Betsey Tracy, both of Benton Yates Co., were married 7 Dec 1826 by Rev. Wilkinson in Benton. (12 Dec 1826)

195. Henry Pease of Ossian, Allegany Co., and Minerva Cornwell of Benton, Yates Co., were married 10 Dec 1826 by Rev. Alverson in Benton. (12 Dec 1826)

196. Mrs. Hannah E. Brackett age 31 yrs., died 16 Nov 1826 in Rushville, Yates Co. The wife of Rev. Joseph Brackett, and daughter of Hon. George Bliss of Springfield, MA. (12 Dec 1826)

197. Hon. Jedediah Morgan died 9 Dec 1826 at his home in Aurora, Cayuga Co. One of the first settelers of Cayuga Co., and a Senator from this 7th district, interred with Masonic honors. (19 Dec 1826)

198. Charles P. Babcock and Maria Andrews of Penn Yan, Yates Co., were married 24 Dec 1826 by Rev. M. Alverson in Penn Yan. (26 Dec 1826)

199. Lyman Dickenson and Eliza Nephins, both of Benton, Yates Co., were married 28 Dec 1826 by A. Woodworth Esq. in Benton. (2 Jan 1827)

200. Elder Thomas Simmons age 104 yrs. 5 mos. 16 days, died in Rehoboth, MA. He supplied a pulpit for about 90 yrs., and attended church until he was 100 yrs., no date given. (9 Jan 1827)

201. Capt. William Morgan abducted from the Canandaigua jail 12 Sep 1826, found murdered 14 Sep 1826 near Ft. Niagara. A native of VA., twice married, he lived in Darien, GA., and Canada, before moving to Batavia. A merchant in NY. for 5 yrs. He has grown children still living in VA. (16 Jan 1827)

202. John J. Sutton age 23 yrs., died 23 Jan 1827 at his home in Jerusalem, Yates Co. A printer with this paper. (30 Jan 1827)

203. James Williamson age 8_ yrs. (illegible), died recently at Norfolk, St. Lawrence Co., no date given. (13 Feb 1827)

204. Alexander Stewart and Harriet Runyan, both of Milo, Yates Co., were married 18 Feb 1827 by Rev. Abner Chase in Milo. (20 Feb 1827)

205. Achelles V. Brown and Lucy Ann Miller were married 13 Feb 1827 by H. Townsend Esq. in Milo, Yates Co. (20 Feb 1827)

206. Mrs. Polly Crandall age 35 yrs., died 13 Feb 1827 in Benton, Yates Co. (20 Feb 1827)

207. John King and Charlotte Wisner, both of Milo, Yates Co., were married 18 Feb 1827 by Rev. Smith in Milo. (27 Feb 1827)

208. Abraham P. Vosburgh Esq. age 36 yrs., died 1 Mar 1827 at Penn Yan. The Postmaster of Penn Yan, Surrogate of Yates Co. (6 Mar 1827)

209. James Woodruff age 50 yrs., died 11 Mar 1827 in Benton, Yates. (13 Mar 1827)

210. E.H. Trimmer and Rebecca Ellis were married 15 Mar 1827 in Benton, Yates Co. (20 Mar 1827)

211. Mrs. Mary Warner age 20 yrs. 4 mos., died 15 Mar 1827. Wife of William Warner, and daughter of Mrs. Anne Carson. (20 Mar 1827)

212. John LeFevre age 28 Yrs., died 12 Mar 1827 in Benton, Yates Co. (20 Mar 1827)

213. Joseph Degolier age 46 yrs., died 21 Mar 1827 in Penn Yan, Yates Co. (27 Mar 1827)

214. Josiah Chapman Esq. died 21 Mar 1827 in Ovid, former Sheriff of Seneca Co. (27 Mar 1827)

215. Jacob Keyser and his wife, Sally Keyser, were drowned 31 Mar 1827 in the Crooked Lake. They were crossing the West Branch in a canoe, and were within a few rods of the shore, when they capsized. Their bodies found Sunday. (3 Apr 1827)

216. Jesse Smith of Goshen, Orange Co., and Emeline Tusten of Barrington, Yates Co., were married 31 Mar 1827 by Rev. C. Eddy in Barrington. (3 Apr 1827)

217. David Wagener and Maria West were married 1 Apr 1827 by George Youngs Esq. in Milo, Yates Co. (3 Apr 1827)

218. Joseph Merrit of Barrington, Yates Co., and Amanda Townsend of Benton, Yates Co., were married 7 Apr 1827 by Rev. Alverson in Benton. (10 Apr 1827)

219. Mrs. Margaret Babcock age 78 yrs., died 4 Apr 1827 in Milo, Yates Co. The mother of William Babcock Esq. of Penn Yan. (10 Apr 1827)

220. Capt. Benjamin Shaw age 50 yrs., died 6 Apr 1827 in Benton, Yates Co. His death caused from injuries received when he fell from a wagon. He was interred with Masonic honors. (10 Apr 1827)

221. Mrs. Jane Hall died 4 Apr 1827 in Seneca, Ontario Co., wife of Edward Hall. (17 Apr 1827)

222. J.W. Cornwell and Maria Youngs, both of Benton Yates Co., were married 17 Apr 1827 by A. Woodworth Esq. in Benton. (24 Apr 1827)

223. William Hilton age 85 yrs., and Mrs. Sally Barber age 50 yrs., were married 17 Apr 1827 by A. Woodworth Esq. in Benton, Yates Co. (24 Apr 1827)

224. A son and daughter of Adam Timmerman Jr., died 11 Apr 1827 at Manheim, Herkimer Co. One 6 yrs., and the other 4 yrs., both were poisoned by eating the root of the American Hemlock found in a field where they had played. (1 May 1827)

225. The 5 yr. old daughter of Isaac Smith, died 11 Apr 1827 at Manheim, Herkimer Co., poisoned by eating the root of the American Hemlock found in a field where she was playing. (1 May 1827)

226. Hon. Rufus King aged 73 yrs., died 19 Apr 1827 in New York city. Late Minister of the U.S. to the Court of St. James. (8 May 1827)

227. Hon. William Tilghman aged 71 yrs., died 29 Apr 1827 at Philadelphia, PA. A Chief Justice of the Supreme Court. (8 May 1827)

228. Capt. Duffy of the brig "Laura", and Miss Hamilton, the noted sailoress, were married in Liverpool, Eng., no date given. (8 May 1827)

229. Mrs. Minerva Nevins age 22 yrs., died 2 May 1827, wife of T.J. Nevins Esq. of Penn Yan, Yates Co. She died at the home of her father, Nathan Loomis Esq., of Middlesex, where she was confined for several months by illness. (8 May 1827)

230. John Whipples of Albany, NY., murdered 14 May 1827 in Albany, Albany Co. (15 May 1827)

231. Mrs. Deborah Gannett died 19 Apr 1827, the wife of Benjamin Gannett of Sharon, MA. Enlisted in the army in MA., during the Revolution, dressed as a male, served 3 yrs. performing the duties of a soldier, wounded twice, yet her sex undiscovered. She received an honorable discharge, and when her case was made known, her full wages were paid, and a considerable bounty added. (22 May 1827)

232. John Powell and Jane Bellows were married 19 May 1827 by Rev. Alverson in Penn Yan, Yates Co. (22 May 1827)

233. Uriah T. Arnout of Jerusalem, Yates Co., and Catharine Townsend of Milo, Yates Co., were married 16 May 1827 by Rev. Chase in Milo. (22 May 1827)

234. Alonzo Laman of Dresden, Yates Co., drowned 21 May 1827. When he fell from a canal boat, lying at Pattisons and Harts dock in Troy, Rensselaer Co. (29 May 1827)

235. Jacob C. Abel and Mary Chase were married 27 May 1827 by Rev. M. Alverson in Milo, Yates Co. (29 May 1827)

236. Sarah Parsons age 17 yrs., died in New Haven, CT. Returning home after dark, she was seized and carried a short distance by her brother, who wore a frightful looking mask. The prank proved to be his sisters death, no date given. (29 May 1827)

237. Elijah S. Gregory and Fanny Fenno were married 31 May 1827 by Rev. Abner Chase in Milo, Yates Co. (5 Jun 1827)

238. John Buckbee age 33 yrs., died 29 May 1827 in Penn Yan, Yates Co. (5 Jun 1827)

239. James Fanning, accidentally killed 9 Jun 1827 at Gorham, Ontario Co. while assisting in raising a barn frame. He was crushed under falling timber and died instantly. (12 Jun 1827)

240. William A. Crittenden and Lydia P. Smith were married 13 Jun 1827 by Rev. Joseph Merrill in Gorham, Ontario Co. (18 Jun 1827)

241. Mrs. Mary Willson age 34 yrs., died 18 Jun 1827 in Penn Yan, Yates Co., wife of John Willson. (26 Jun 1827)

242. Col. Gideon Fairman died in New York city. An engraver and artist, no date given. (26 Jun 1827)

243. Hugh King, a soldier, executed 27 May 1827 in St. Louis, for the murder of Sgt. Martin Green. (26 Jun 1827)

244. Delight Wire age 26 yrs., died 27 Jun 1827 in Middlesex, Yates Co., of consumption. (3 Jul 1827)

245. Eliah Scudder age 24 yrs., died 5 Jul 1827 in Geneva, Ontario Co., of consumption. A student of law. (17 Jul 1827)

246. Daniel Norris and Julia Ann Stoddard were married 21 Jul 1827 by James C. Robinson Esq. in Milo, Yates Co. (24 Jul 1827)

247. Samuel S. Clark died 28 Jul 1827 in Benton, Yates Co. (31 Jul 1827)

248. Dr. William Chambers age 30 yrs., died 21 Jul 1827 in New York. Born in County Donegal, Ireland, and educated at Rephow Academy. He studied medicine in Glasgow and Edinburgh before migrated to this country in 1815. He lived 4 yrs. in Westchester Co., before moving to New York city. (7 Aug 1827)

249. Cyrenus Sawdy and Pamela Burdick, both of Benton, Yates Co. were married 5 Aug 1827 by N. Cothren Esq. in Pulteney, Steuben Co. (21 Aug 1827)

250. John Parish age 15 yrs., and Lebins Goodwin age 16 yrs., were married 10 Jun 1827 in Montgomery Co., Illinois, no pastor given. (21 Aug 1827)

251. Jessie Strang, alias Joseph Orton, age 30 yrs., executed 24 Aug 1827 in Albany, Albany Co., for the murder of John Whipple. (28 Aug 1827)

252. Levi Lyman, Attorney at Law in Penn Yan, Yates Co., and Betsey Buckbee were married 26 Aug 1827 by Rev. James H. Hotchkin in Prattsburgh, Steuben Co. (4 Sep 1827)

253. John Hall and Nancy Payne were married 30 Aug 1827 by A. Woodworth Esq. in Middlesex, Yates Co. (4 Sep 1827)

254. Rufus McIntire accidentally killed 25 Aug 1827 in New Berlin, Chenango Co., when Chauncy Lewis, a powder peddler from Suffield, CT., stopped at his blacksmith shop. McIntire approached in the course of his work and somehow a spark communicated to the powder, exploding about five kegs. McIntire was so badly burned, he survived only five hours. The recovery of Lewis is doubtful. (11 Sep 1827)

255. Lorenzo Pratt of Geneva, Ontario Co., and Betsey Lee of Milo, Yates Co., were married 12 Sep 1827 by Rev. M. Alverson in Milo. (18 Sep 1827)

256. Margaret Winters, a colored woman, died 17 Sep 1827 from internal hemmoraging, no town given. (18 Sep 1827)

257. Hon. George Canning died 8 Aug 1827 at Chiswick, Eng. A noble Statesman who earned many Royal titles. Born 11 Apr 1770, and married in 1799 to the daughter of Gen. Scott. He has one son who is a Captain in the Navy, another a student at Eton and his daughter married to the Marquis of Clanricarde. (18 Sep 1827)

258. Joseph C. Williams died 23 Jul 1827 at Galena, MS. A young man accused of pilfering the mail at Canadaigua, Ontario Co., NY. (25 Sep 1827)

259. Stephen Hollarday and Betsey Wilkalow were married 16 Sep 1827 by S.G. Gage Esq. in Benton, Yates Co. (2 Oct 1827)

260. Timothy Monro found drowned 20 Oct 1827 in the Niagara River near Orchard Creek. His body mistakenly identified as that of Capt. William Morgan. His wife, Sarah Monro of Clark township, New Castle District, Canada. Upon hearing the news, claimed she was 44 yrs., and had been married 24 yrs. She stated her husband had left their home about six weeks ago, bound for Newark. She also identified his clothing, which she claims to have made for him. (5 Nov 1827)

261. Henry Runyan and Laura Shaw, both of Jerusalem, Yates Co., were married 4 Nov 1827 by Rev. Alverson in Jerusalem. (13 Nov 1827)

262. John Watson died 7 Nov 1827 in Benton, Yates Co. (13 Nov 1827)

263. The wife of Jeremiah Edwards died 15 Nov 1827 in Benton, Yates Co., at an advanced age. (20 Nov 1827)

264. George C. Arnold and Charlotte Crafts were married 15 Nov 1827 by Phillip Robinson Esq. in Middlesex, Yates Co. (20 Nov 1827)

265. Hon. Thomas Addis Emmet died 14 Nov 1827 in New York city. Services from the Episcopal Church, and his remains conveyed to the burial grounds of St. Marks Church. (27 Nov 1827)

266. Horace B. Miller and Olive Stokes were married 19 Nov 1827 by Rev. M. Alverson in Penn Yan, Yates Co. (27 Nov 1827)

267. Willis Pearce and Elsie Sprague, both of Ben-

ton, Yates Co., were married 15 Nov 1827 by Rev. Southerland in Jerusalem, Yates Co. (27 Nov 1827)

268. Delila Lowrey age 9 yrs., died 26 Nov 1827 in Jerusalem, Yates Co. (27 Nov 1827)

269. W.G. Graham, killed 28 Nov 1827 in a duel on the Jersey shore. An Editor of the "New York Enquirer". The dispute originated at a card table. (4 Dec 1827)

270. Earnest A. Dunlap Esq. died 30 Nov 1827 in Ovid, Clerk of Seneca Co. (4 Dec 1827)

271. M.M. Noah and Rebecca Jackson, daughter of Daniel Jackson, were married 28 Nov 1827 in New York, by Rev. Hart, all of New York. (4 Dec 1827)

272. Eli Spencer and Ann Hogeboom were married 6 Dec 1827 by Rev. Bennet in Windham, Greene Co. (25 Dec 1827)

273. Mrs. Ann Little age 109 yrs., died recently at Lowbyer near Alston, no date given. (1 Jan 1828)

274. Jacob Colver of Milo, Yates Co., and Hannah Potter of Benton, Yates Co., were married 30 Dec 1827 by S.G. Gage Esq. in Benton. (1 Jan 1828)

275. Levi Kelley, executed 4 Jan 1828 at Cooperstown, Otsego Co., for the murder of Abraham Safford. (8 Jan 1828)

276. Elisha C. Tracey, accidentally killed 4 Jan 1828 at Cooperstown, Otsego Co., when the platform erected for the hanging of Levi Kelley collapsed. (8 Jan 1828)

277. Daniel Williams, accidentally killed 4 Jan 1828 at Cooperstown, Otsego Co., when the platform erected for the hanging of Levi Kelley collapsed. (8 Jan 1828)

278. James Merry of Leroy, Genesee Co., poisoned to death. His wife is in the Batavia Jail on suspicion of murder, no date given. (15 Jan 1828)

279. Major James Smith Jr. age 40 yrs., died 4 Jan 1828 in Geneva, Ontario Co. Born in Gloucester, MA, he leaves a wife and 4 children. A book dealer, he came to Geneva about 3 yrs. ago. (15 Jan 1828)

280. Mrs. Anne Woodworth age 74 yrs., died 15 Jan 1828 in Benton, Yates Co. (22 Jan 1828)

281. Andrew Rector and Betsey Coon were married 22 Jan 1828 by Peleg Briggs Jr. Esq. in Benton, Yates Co. (29 Jan 1828)

282. Ezekial Clark of Jerusalem, Yates Co., and Polly Youngs of Benton, Yates Co., were married 24 Jan 1828 by Rev. Alverson in Benton. (29 Jan 1828)

283. Mrs. Grace Webster died 28 Jan 1828 in New York city. Wife of the Hon. Daniel Webster, a Senator from MA., buried in Boston. (29 Jan 1828)

284. Ward Nicholas Boylston Esq., age 78 yrs., died at his home in Roxbury, Delaware Co. It is said President John Quincy Adams received no less than $4000,000,00 of the estate, no date given. (29 Jan 1828)

285. A daughter of Henry Eckford Esq. of New York city, age 19 yrs., burned to death on 23 Jan 1828. She was watching her younger sister and fell asleep in a chair, when a burning coal ignited her garment. (5 Feb 1828)

286. William Shultz and Jemima Collver, both of Milo, Yates Co., were married 2 Feb 1828 by Elder Simon Southerland in Milo. (5 Feb 1828)

287. George Caward Jr. and Hannah Clark were married 24 Jan 1828 by Rev. Abner Chase in Seneca, Ontario Co. (5 Feb 1828)

288. FATAL ACCIDENT: On 26 Jan 1828 the following were drowned, when their sleigh fell through the ice, while they were crossing the Schorrie Creek, all of Florida, Orange Co. William C. Newkirk and his daughter, the daughter of John I. Newkirk, and the daughter of widow Malatt. (12 Feb 1828)

289. John Freer and Delana Haunsom were married 31 Jan 1828 by S.G. Gage Esq. in Benton, Yates Co. (12 Feb 1828)

290. Coe B. Sayre and Mrs. Pamela Worden were married 9 Feb 1828 by Rev. Eddy in Milo, Yates Co. (12 Feb 1828)

291. The son of Peter A. Schuyler was accidentally killed 18 Jan 1828. When he jumped from a hay-mow,

onto a pitchfork in the barn near Danube, Herkimer Co., copied from the "Albany Argus". (12 Feb 1828)

292. Gov. DeWitt Clinton age 58 yrs. 11 mos., died 11 Feb 1828 in Albany, Albany Co. (19 Feb 1828)

293. John H. Eckford age 22 yrs., died 18 Feb 1828 in New York, son of Henry Eckford Esq. He was badly burned, trying to extinguish the flames which proved fatal to his sister 23 Jan 1828. The skill of his physician has been unable to save his life. Sadly, another daughter of Mr. Eckford lies at the point of death from the same incident. (19 Feb 1828)

294. Franklin Thomas of Jerusalem, Yates Co., and Lucinda Hobart of Middlesex, Yates Co., were married 13 Feb 1828 by Rev. Sylvester Cary in Middlesex. (19 Feb 1828)

295. Henry R. Coleman of Benton, Yates Co., and Caroline Squier of Seneca, Ontario Co., were married 7 Feb 1828 by Rev. Gilmore in Seneca. (19 Feb 1828)

296. Ephriam Lord and Emeline Secor were married 12 Feb 1828 by Rev. Alverson in Benton, Yates Co. (19 Feb 1828)

297. Isaac Youmans age 37 yrs., died 8 Feb 1828 in Penn Yan, Yates Co. (26 Feb 1828)

298. Dr. Augustus Aspenwall age 21 yrs., died 19 Feb 1828 in Genoa, Cayuga Co., of typhus fever, son of Dr. Aspenwall. (26 Feb 1828)

299. Thomas Tudor Tucker Esq. died 8 Feb 1828 in Washington, Treasurer of the U.S. (26 Feb 1828)

300. James Cooley and Mary Bruyn were married 26 Feb 1828 by Rev. C. Eddy in Milo, Yates Co. (4 Mar 1828)

301. Jeremiah Edwards and Mrs. Martha Clark were married 21 Feb 1828 by Rev. Alverson in Benton, Yates Co. (4 Mar 1828)

302. John S. Sheppard age 21 yrs., died 2 Feb 1828 at the home of his father. Second son of Morris F. Sheppard Esq. of Penn Yan, Yates Co. Services from the Presbyterian Meeting House. (4 Mar 1828)

303. Jacob Cronk age 24 yrs., died 29 Feb 1828 in Jerusalem, Yates Co. His death occasioned by the falling of a tree. (4 Mar 1828)

304. Rev. Orin Clark age 40 yrs., died 24 Feb 1828 in Geneva, Ontario Co. The Rector of the Trinity Church in Geneva. (4 Mar 1828)

305. The funeral of Major Gen. Brown held 27 Feb 1828 in Washington. Attended by numerous public and military officials. (11 Mar 1828)

306. Capt. Ebenezer Crowell of the brig "Ann Maria", sailing from St. Johns, New Brunswick, and James W. Wright a passenger, drowned 27 Feb 1828, when it sank off the coast of Maine, near Matinic Rock. (18 Mar 1828)

307. Thomas C. Sutton of Jerusalem, Yates Co., and Betsey Barrett of Benton, Yates Co., were married 16 Mar 1828 by Ezra Rice Esq. in Jerusalem. (25 Mar 1828)

308. Warren Barrett of Benton, Yates Co., and Phebe Ann West of Jerusalem, Yates Co., were married 16 Mar 1828 by Ezra Rice Esq. in Jerusalem. (25 Mar 1828)

309. William Hilton age 86 yrs., died 18 Mar 1829 in Benton, Yates Co. A patriot of the Revolution, he fought at the Battle of Bunker Hill. (25 Mar 1828)

310. Levi Wheeler of Jerusalem, Yates Co., and Margaret Moon of Benton, Yates Co., were married 23 Mar 1828 by Peleg Briggs Jr. in Benton. (1 Apr 1828)

311. Peter Raywalt and Ann Hallowell were married 27 Mar 1828 by Rev. A. Chase in Milo, Yates Co. (1 Apr 1828)

312. Hon. Donald Cameron of Bath, Steuben Co., age 52 yrs., died 30 Mar 1828 at his lodgings in Albany, Albany Co. A member of the Assembly from Steuben Co. His remains conveyed to his home, for interment in the vault of the Dudley Walsh family, services from the Presbyterian Church. (8 Apr 1828)

313. Samuel Finch and Lorany Green, both of Milo, Yates Co., were married 10 Apr 1828 by Elder Simon Southerland in Milo. (15 Apr 1828)

314. Samuel Brown and Letty Rogers were married 12 Apr 1828 by Ira Cushman Esq. in Jerusalem, Yates Co. (15 Apr 1828)

315. John Van Pelt age 70 yrs., died 22 Apr 1828 at his home in Milo, Yates Co. A veteran of the Revolution, wounded three times. He was with General Washington when he forded the Delaware. Fought in the Battles of Long Island, White Plains and Short Hills. Interred at the Methodist Chapel in Penn Yan, Yates Co. (29 Apr 1828)

316. Lewis Sutton age 20 yrs., died 25 Apr 1828 in Jerusalem, Yates Co. (6 May 1828)

317. Mrs. Rebecca Winants age 76 yrs., died 29 Apr 1828 in Benton, Yates Co. (6 May 1828)

318. Rev. William W. Bostwick of Bath, Steuben Co. and Mary Lewis, daughter of Ozias Lewis Esq., were married in Litchfield, CT., no date or pastor given. (13 May 1828)

319. Peter Miller and Lydia Kronck were married 17 May 1828 by Peleg Briggs Jr. Esq. in Benton, Yates Co. (20 May 1828)

320. Peter Betts and Anne Sisson were married 17 May 1828 by Ezra Rice Esq. in Benton, Yates Co. (20 May 1828)

321. Robert Brown and Temperance Dorman were married 17 May 1828 by Rev.Alverson in Milo, Yates Co. (20 May 1828)

322. Reuben P. Lamb of Penn Yan, Yates Co., and Diana Roots of Prattsburgh, Steuben Co., were married 19 May 1828 by Rev. James H. Hotchkin in Prattsburgh. (27 May 1828)

323. Mrs. Sarah Magee died 16 May 1828 at the home of her father, Judge M'Burney, at Painted Post, Steuben Co. Wife of Hon. John Magee, who was in Washington at the time of her death. He arrived home on the day of her interment. (27 May 1828)

324. Isaac Van Wart died 22 May 1828 at Greenburgh, near Tarrytown, Westchester Co. One of the captors of Major Andre' in the Revolution. (3 Jun 1828)

325. Joseph Voak and Abigail Walling were married 26 May 1828 by Rev. Smith in Middlesex, Yates Co. (3 Jun 1828)

326. Mrs. Nancy Rice age 43 yrs., died 29 May 1828 in Jerusalem, Yates Co., wife of Ezra Rice Esq. (3 Jun 1828)

327. Elizabeth Ballard age 18 yrs., died 29 May 1828 in Seneca, Ontario Co., daughter of William Ballard, late of Genoa, Cayuga Co. (3 Jun 1828)

328. Sylvanus Rice of Prattstown, and Harriet Shaw of Jerusalem, Yates Co., were married 1 Jun 1828 by Rev. Alverson in Jerusalem. (10 Jun 1828)

329. Elijah G. Simons and Eliza Shaw were married 1 Jun 1828 by Rev. Ackley in Benton, Yates Co. (10 Jun 1828)

330. David G. Allen and Betsey Maria Winans, both of Benton, Yates Co., were married 8 Jun 1828 by Rev. Alverson in Milo, Yates Co. (10 Jun 1828)

331. Hon. Nathan Sanford of this state, and Mary Buchanan, daughter of the late Andrew Buchanan Esq., of Baltimore, MD., were married 27 May 1828 by Rev. Wyatt in Baltimore. (17 Jun 1828)

332. Sargent Baker age 83 yrs., killed by lightning 24 Jun 1828 at his home in Hector, Tompkins Co. A veteran of the Revolution, and member of the Methodist Episcopal Church. (1 Jul 1828)

333. Joseph T. Briggs of Benton, Yates Co., and A. Andrews of Middlesex, Yates Co., were married 28 Jun 1828 by Peleg Briggs Jr. Esq. in Middlesex. (1 Jul 1828)

334. Col. Jonathan Brooks, killed 25 Jun 1828 near Belmont, Orange Co., NY. (8 Jul 1828)

335. Rufus Edson age 64 yrs., killed by lightning 23 Jun 1828. A member of the M.E. Church in Italy, Yates Co., leaving a wife and ten Children. He was born at Bridgeport, MA. in 1764, and married at 19 yrs. He lived a few years in Vermont before immigrating in 1814 to Penn Yan, Yates Co. (22 Jul 1828)

336. Caleb Clark and Elizabeth Taylor were married 17 Jul 1828 by William Bassett Esq. in Rushville, Yates Co. (22 Jul 1828)

337. Daniel Wright, killed 20 Jul 1828 at Nares, Seneca Co., by George Chapman. (29 Jul 1828)

338. John Thompson a black man, killed 19 Jul 1828 by his brother Jecobus Thompson in Victor, Ontario Co. (29 Jul 1828)

339. General Philetus Swift died 24 Jul 1828 in Phelps, Ontario Co. A patriot of the Revolution. (29 Jul 1828)

340. The body of Soloman Jones age 30 yrs., found 17 Aug 1828 in the woods near Thomas' Tavern, at Rose, Wayne Co. He had been murdered, and dead about 10 days. (19 Aug 1828)

341. Elias Gilbert age 80 yrs., died 20 Jul 1828 in Middlesex, Yates Co. Born in Brookfield, MA. He was a patriot of the Revolution, and one of the first settlers in Genesee Co., having migrated 40 yrs. ago. (26 Aug 1828)

342. John M. Brown and Mary Dickerson were married 28 Aug 1828 by S.G. Gage Esq. in Milo, Yates Co. (2 Sep 1828)

343. Judas Conkling and Sarah Jones were married 28 Aug 1828 by Rev. Alverson in Milo, Yates Co. (2 Sep 1828)

344. Mrs. Mary Van Pelt age 30 yrs., died 1 Sep 1828 in Penn Yan, Yates Co., wife of Capt. John VanPelt. (2 Sep 1828)

345. Timothy Soper died 25 Aug 1828 in Benton, Yates Co. (2 Sep 1828)

346. Mrs. Elizabeth Oliver age 71 yrs., died 23 Aug 1828 at Springfield, Otsego Co. The wife of Rev. Andrew Oliver, and mother of W.M. and A.F. Oliver of Penn Yan, Yates Co. (2 Sep 1828)

347. Allen Tu_lls (illegible) died 20 Aug 1828 at Sackett's Harbour, Jefferson Co., formerly of Penn Yan, Yates Co. (2 Sep 1828)

348. Jeremiah H. Stark and Anna Fowler were married 3 Sep 1828 by Rev. D. Page in Middlesex, Yates Co. (9 Sep 1828)

349. Hon. Thomas M'Burney died 30 Aug 1828 at Painted Post, Steuben Co. (9 Sep 1828)

350. William Pratt of Deerfield, Oneida Co. lost his family to dysentery. His wife, Mrs. Catherine

Pratt age 23 yrs., died 6 Aug 1828, and children Joel Pratt age 5 yrs., died 7 Aug 1828, Charlotte Pratt age 1 yr., died 9 Aug 1828, and William Jackson Pratt died 17 Aug 1828. (9 Sep 1828)

351. William E. Sawyer and Mary Bellows were married 4 Sep 1828 by Rev. John B. Alverson in Penn Yan, Yates Co. (16 Sep 1828)

352. Russell Fargo of Benton, Yates Co., and Mary Chapman, eldest daughter of the late Josiah B. Chapman Esq. of Ovid, Seneca Co., were married 10 Sep 1828 by Rev. Lounsbury in Ovid. (16 Sep 1828)

353. John Hewey and Mrs. Elizabeth Ginner were married 14 Sep 1828 by Elder John Goff in Seneca, Ontario Co. (16 Sep 1828)

354. Gen. Theodorus Bailey age 70 yrs., died 6 Sep 1828 in New York, the Postmaster of that city. (16 Sep 1828)

355. Col. Jaspar C. Moon and Lydia Lothrap were married 7 Sep 1828 by A. Woodworth Esq. in Milo, Yates Co. (23 Sep 1828)

356. William Ketchum age 36 yrs., died 17 Sep 1828 in Starkey, Yates Co. A member of the Methodist Episcopal Church. (23 Sep 1828)

357. Hon. Richard Trimble died at his home in Bourbon, KY. A Justice of the U.S. Supreme Court, no date given. (23 Sep 1828)

358. Harvey Harrison and Catherine Bohall were married 24 Sep 1828 by Rev. C. Eddy in Benton, Yates Co. (30 Sep 1828)

359. Mr. Rogers a merchant, died 23 Sep 1828 at Weedsport, Cayuga Co. (30 Sep 1828)

360. James Sears age 48 yrs., died 30 Sep 1828 in Penn Yan, Yates Co., leaving a wife and 8 children. (7 Oct 1828)

361. Thomas H. Smith Esq. age 49 yrs., died 23 Sep 1828 in New York, a merchant of that city. (7 Oct 1828)

362. Henry Miller of Rensselear Co., and Mrs. Polly Stokes of Penn Yan, Yates Co., were married 11 Oct 1828 by Rev. John B. Alverson in Penn Yan. (14 Oct 1828)

363. Samuel Stewart age 36 yrs., died 14 Oct 1828, a merchant in Bethel, Sullivan Co. (21 Oct 1828)

364. Daniel Brown died last week in Jerusalem, Yates Co., at an advanced age, no date given. (21 Oct 1828)

365. Isaac Bishop of Darien, CT., committed suicide 3 Oct 1828 in the Danbury jail. (28 Oct 1828)

366. James McAuley of Seneca, Ontario Co., and Mrs. Hannah Laman of Benton, Yates Co., were married 22 Oct 1828 by A. Woodworth Esq. in Benton. (28 Oct 1828)

367. Abraham Steler and Susan Shepherd were married 25 Oct 1828 by A. Woodworth Esq. in Benton. (28 Oct 1828)

368. John Hewlett of Onondaga Co., and Angeline Wilson of Penn Yan, Yates Co. were married 20 Oct 1828 by S.G. Gage Esq. in Seneca, Ontario Co. (28 Oct 1828)

369. Johnson Willson of Penn Yan, Yates Co., and Susan Dyer of Middlesex, Yates Co., were married 6 Nov 1828 by Rev. Ackley in Middlesex. (11 Nov 1828)

370. Mrs. Fleming, killed 9 Nov 1828 in Shrewsbury, NJ. Stabbed in the chest by her husband, Joseph Fleming, she leaves 3 children. (11 Nov 1828)

371. James Barr a native of Scotland, drowned 8 Nov 1828 in the Crooked Lake. The coroner stated his death was suicide, due to insanity. (11 Nov 1828)

372. Rev. Smith and Rev. Alice M. Miller, a lady known for her talents as a preacher, were married at the home of Lawther Layton Esq. in Milford, Otsego Co., no date or pastor given. (11 Nov 1828)

373. Mrs. Mary Rogers age 26 yrs., died 10 Nov 1828 at Weedsport, Cayuga Co. A sister of E. Sheldon of Penn Yan, Yates Co., her husband died six weeks ago. (18 Nov 1828)

374. Caleb West Bradley and Clarissa Bradley, both of Genoa, Cayuga Co., were married 16 Nov 1828 in Genoa, no pastor given. (25 Nov 1828)

375. Sylvester Cole of LaFayette, Ontario Co., age 45 yrs., killed 21 Nov 1828 in the woods near his

home. He had gone for saw logs, and while loading, one slipped and rolled on him. He was found some hours after, lifeless. (25 Nov 1828)

376. Truman Matthews, executed 24 Oct 1828 at Bethany, Wayne Co. PA., for the murder of Col. Brooks of Orange Co. NY., last June. (25 Nov 1828)

377. Mrs. Montgomery age 86 yrs., died 6 Nov 1828 at her home on North River, Dutchess Co. The widow of Gen. Montgomery, she survived her husband by 53 yrs. (2 Dec 1828)

378. Mrs. Ursula Newman killed 20 Nov 1828 in New York, by Richard Johnson, a printer, and boarder of Mrs. Newman. (2 Dec 1828) * additional information From the "NY Com. Adv." dated Nov 24th, a statement of Johnson claims he was 26 yrs., last January. Born in Virginia, he became acquainted with Mrs. Newman at the New England hotel in Philadelphia, where they had lived together about three yrs. They moved to New York last May, and Mrs. Newman ran a boarding house, while he worked as a printer. Mrs. Newman refused to marry him, as she had remarried a second man named Lattell, and believed he had died at sea, but she wasn't sure. She leaves several children. (9 Dec 1828)

379. William E. Beeden and Sarah Taylor were married 27 Nov 1828 by S.G. Gage Esq. in Benton, Yates Co. (9 Dec 1828)

380. John Thomas a merchant, and Ann Lawrence, both of Penn Yan, Yates Co., were married 9 Dec 1828 by Rev. John B. Alverson in Penn yan. (16 Dec 1828)

381. Jacob Baldwin died 9 Dec 1828 in Benton, Yates Co., at an advanced age. (16 Dec 1828)

382. Nathan Wheeler aged abt. 50 yrs., died 12 Dec 1828 in Benton, Yates Co. (16 Dec 1828)

383. Caleb Legg of Benton, Yates Co., and Elizabeth Henderson of Milo, Yates Co., were married 25 Dec 1828 by Rev. John B. Alverson in Milo. (30 Dec 1828)

384. Horace Stebbins of Middlesex, Yates Co., and Helena Lewis of Seneca, Ontario Co., were married 25 Dec 1828 by Rev. John B. Alverson in Seneca. (30 Dec 1828)

385. Morris Earl of Penn Yan, Yates Co. and Emeline Clark of Rushville, Yates Co., were married 23 Dec 1828 by William Bassett Esq. in Rushville. (30 Dec 1828)

386. Mrs. Rachel Jackson, the wife of Gen. Andrew Jackson, died 22 Dec 1828 at Hermitage. (13 Jan 1829)

387. Joseph P. Owen of Seneca, Ontario Co., and Dorcas Crafts of Middlesex, Yates Co., were married 22 Jan 1829 by Rev. Ackley in Middlesex. (27 Jan 1829)

388. Mrs. Hannah Allen age 39 yrs., died 9 Jan 1829 in Scipio, Cayuga Co. The wife of Gideon Allen of Jerusalem, Yates Co. (27 Jan 1829)

389. Rev. Chester died 12 Jan 1829 in Philadelphia. Pastor of the Second Presbyterian Church in Albany, Albany Co., NY. (27 Jan 1829)

390. Four children of William Lewis Jr., burned to death in Monroe, Orange Co. When their home was consumed by fire, no date given. (27 Jan 1829)

391. Stephen Earl and Ann Eliza Evans, both of Benton, Yates Co., were married 28 Jan 1829 by S.G. Gage Esq. in Benton. (3 Feb 1829)

392. Henry Bryan Esq. of Cattaraugus Co. and Clarissa L. Fobes of Canandaigua, Ontario Co., were married by Rev. Eddy, no date given. (3 Feb 1829)

393. Major Jarvis L. Smith age 38 yrs., died 24 Jan 1829 in Geneva, Ontario Co. (3 Feb 1829)

394. Deacon Elkanah Wilmarth age 100 yrs., died in Attleborough. He breathed his last breath beneath the same roof he inhaled his first, no date given. (3 Feb 1829)

395. James C. Brooks Esq., Editor of the "Morning Courier", and Mary Elizabeth Aiken, formerly of Geneva, Ontario Co., were married in New York, no date given. (10 Feb 1829)

396. Alman Hopkins and Susan Sawdy were married 1 Feb 1829 by Peleg Briggs Jr. Esq. in Benton, Yates Co. (10 Feb 1829)

397. Jeremiah Nichols age 44 yrs., killed 21 Jan

1829 at Italy, Yates Co. While cutting ice from a water wheel at the grist mill of Abraham Maxfield Esq. He was suddenly precipated from his position by the unexpected revolution of the wheel, and literally crushed to death. (10 Feb 1829)

398. Timothy Pickering age 84 yrs., died in Salem, Washington, Co., no date given. (10 Feb 1829)

399. Jeremiah VanResselner Esq. died 26 Jan 1829 in Canandaigua, Ontario Co., formerly of Utica, Oneida Co. (10 Feb 1829)

400. Asler C. Thompson and Abigail Durkee were married 14 Feb 1829 by Elder Simon Southerland Esq. in Milo, Yates Co. (17 Feb 1829)

401. Rev. Henry Axtell died 12 Feb 1829 in Geneva, Ontario Co., services from the Presbyterian Church. (17 Feb 1829)

402. Major Robert Lewis age 60 yrs., died in Fredericksburg, VA., a nephew to Gen. Washington, no date given. (17 Feb 1829)

403. Gen. Mack, who surrendered Ulm, and an army of 60,000 to Bonaparte, died in Germany, no date or town given. (17 Feb 1829)

404. Rebecca Axtell died 19 Feb 1829 in Geneva, Ontario Co., daughter of the late Rev. Henry Axtell. It seemed a mysterious providence, while the funeral of her father had been delayed five days, so people living at a distance could attend. She died the morning of his funeral, both buried in the same grave, on the same day. (24 Feb 1829)

405. Edward Perry of Middlesex, Yates Co., and Harriet Woodworth of Benton, Yates Co., were married 15 Feb 1829 by Rev. Ackley in Benton. (24 Feb 1829)

406. Thomas F. Westcott and Mrs. Sarah Soper were married 28 Feb 1829 by Peleg Briggs Jr. Esq. in Benton, Yates Co. (3 Mar 1829)

407. Edmund Jones of Cumberland Co. PA., and Theodosia Conkling of Barrington, Yates Co., were married 1 Mar 1829 by Peleg Briggs Jr. Esq. in Barrington. (3 Mar 1829)

408. George W. Prentis age 37 yrs., died at Keene,

NH. An Editor of the "New York Statesman", no date given. (17 Mar 1829)

409. Conrod Rector and Mary Wheeler were married 13 Mar 1829 by Peleg Briggs Jr. Esq. in Benton, Yates Co. (24 Mar 1829)

410. __anias Carey (illegible) aged abt 70 yrs., died 18 Mar 1829 in Benton, Yates Co. (24 Mar 1829)

411. Hon. John Tayler died 19 Mar 1829 in Albany, former Lieut. Governor of New York. (24 Mar 1829)

412. Benjamin Remer and Ann Townsend were married 29 Mar 1829 by Rev. Alverson in Milo, Yates Co. (31 Mar 1829)

413. James Norman age 62 yrs., drowned 29 Mar 1829 near Dresden, Yates Co., in the raceway leading to the mills of Mr. Bogert. (7 Apr 1829)

414. Nicholas McNeer of Genesee Co., age 28 yrs., and Eunice Brown age 14 yrs., of Seneca, Ontario Co. were married 26 Mar 1829 by S.G. Gage Esq. in Seneca. (7 Apr 1829)

415. Hon. Ezra C. Gross died 9 Apr 1829 in Albany, Albany Co. A member of the Assembly from Essex Co. (14 Apr 1829)

416. Dr. Edward Augustus Holyoke age 101 yrs., died 7 Apr 1829 in Salem, MA. (14 Apr 1829)

417. Mrs. Ford died 24 Apr 1829 at Dresden, Yates Co., wife of Dyer Ford, a merchant. (28 Apr 1829)

418. Nathaniel Morril and Eliza Gile were married at Hopkinton, RI., by Elder A. Caveron, no date given. (5 May 1829)

419. James Parker Esq. age 86 yrs., died 24 Apr 1829 in Benton, Yates Co. Born in Rhode Island, one of the first settlers of Genesee Co. An officer of the Revolution, and member of the M.E. Church. (12 May 1829)

420. Thomas Ruger of Benton, Yates Co. and Margaret Briggs of Middlesex, Yates Co., were married 9 May 1829 by P. Briggs Jr. Esq. in Benton. (12 May 1829)

421. Mrs. Elizabeth Randall age 80 yrs., died 8 May 1829 in Benton, Yates Co. (12 May 1829)

422. Mrs. Catharine Auten died 7 May 1829 in Dresden, Yates Co. (12 May 1829)

423. John Metcalf Esq. died 8 May 1829 at Bath, NY., a clerk of Steuben Co. (12 May 1829)

424. Richard Johnson, executed 7 May 1829 at Blackwell Island, NY., for the murder of Mrs. Ursula Newman. (19 May 1829)

425. Catharine Cashiere a colored woman, executed 7 May 1829 at Blackwell Island, NY., for murdering Susan Anthony. (19 May 1829)

426. James Hewey, son of Major John Hewey, and Mary Jackson, daughter of Gen. William Jackson, were married 7 May 1829 by A.A. Post Esq. in Seneca, Ontario Co. (19 May 1829)

427. Mrs. Amelia Curtiss age 25 yrs., died 14 May 1829 at Penn Yan, Yates Co. The wife of Samuel Curtiss. (19 May 1829)

428. William Ellis and Rachel Davis, both of Seneca, Ontario Co., were married 17 May 1829 by S.G. Gage Esq. in Seneca. (26 May 1829)

429. John N. Rose of Jerusalem, Yates Co., and Jane Eliza Navarre of New York city, were married 26 May 1829 by Rev. John Clark in New York. (2 Jun 1829)

430. Harriet Cole age 17 yrs., died 30 May 1829, daughter of Smith M. Cole of Penn Yan, Yates Co. (2 Jun 1829)

431. John Newhall and Mary E. Underhill, both of Phelps, Ontario Co., were married 4 Jun 1829 by Rev. Eddy in Penn Yan, Yates Co. (9 Jun 1829)

432. Lewis H. Sandford of Skeneateles, Onondaga Co., and Laura Porter, daughter of the late Dr. Alanson Porter of Williamstown, MA., were married 4 Jun 1829 by Rev. Williams in the Third Presbyterian Church at Albany, Albany Co. (9 Jun 1829)

433. Col. William King died 28 May 1829 at his home near Fort Niagara, NY. (9 Jun 1829)

434. Mr. Chapman, executed 4 Jun 1829 at Waterloo, Seneca Co., for the murder of Dan Wright, near Geneva, Ontario Co. (9 Jun 1829)

435. DREADFUL ACCIDENT; On 4 Jun 1829 a terrible fire aboard the steamship "Fulton" at the navy dock in Albany, injured and killed many passengers. Most of the bodies were interred at Wallabout. However Lieut. Breckenridge was interred at the Episcopal Burying Ground on Fulton Street. Known dead are:

Lieut. Breckenridge of the "Fulton",

"Marines"	"Seamen"
Sylvester O'Halloran	James Livingston
Alexander Comeron	Thomas Walton
Robert M. Peck	John Brown
Otto E. Furgustine	Jacob Boise
William Kemp	James D. Burgher
John McKeever	John Pierce
Corp. Henry Logan	J.T.D. Burger
Charles Williamson	
Henry McGraw	
Franklin Ely	

Peter Gillen a landsmen, Thomas Williams a gunner, John Delos Rayes a barber, Mr. and Mrs. William Brown, Mr. Stockwell, A. Lehman, Mrs. Neilson, and Harmen Vatel. (9 Jun 1829 and 16 Jun 1829)

436. Oliver Warner of Ontario Co., killed by lightning 20 May 1829 while on a visit at Conway, CT. (16 Jun 1829)

437. Charles Baker Esq. of Ontario Co., killed by lightning 20 May 1829 while on a visit at Conway, CT. (16 Jun 1829)

438. Mrs. Mary Baldwin age 29 yrs., died 1 Jun 1829 at Benton, Yates Co. The wife of Alfred Baldwin. (16 Jun 1829)

439. Mrs. Margaret Oliver age 36 yrs., died 13 Jun 1829 in Penn Yan, Yates Co., wife of Dr. Andrew F. Oliver. (16 Jun 1829)

440. Capt. John Cleves Symmes died 19 May 1829 at Hamilton, Butler Co., Ohio, a native of New Jersey. (16 Jun 1829)

441. George Washington Adams died 17 Jun 1829 at City Island, NY, son of the late president. (23 Jun 1829)

442. Mrs. Maria Josefa Amalla, "Queen of Spain", died 24 May 1829 in Madrid. The daughter of the Duke of Saxon, she was about 23 yrs., and married Ferdinand when she was 15 yrs. (7 Jul 1829)

443. John Kinney of Benton, Yates Co., and Sally Lane of Middlesex, Yates Co., were married 23 Jun 1829 by S.G. Gage Esq. in Benton. (7 Jul 1829)

444. Mary Riley, killed 25 Jun 1829 by lightning in Savannah, GA. (14 Jul 1829)

445. George Blacknull, killed 8 Jun 1829 by lightning, while sitting in the counting room of a store at Haysville, NC. (14 Jun 1829)

446. John Van Pelt of Penn Yan, Yates Co., and Eliza Ann Cheever of New Haven, Oswego Co., were married 6 Jul 1829 by Rev. Russell Smith in New Haven. (14 Jul 1829)

447. Cyrus Miller and Margaret Larzelere, both of Benton, Yates Co., were married 16 Jul 1829 by Rev. Abner Chase at Benton. (21 Jul 1829)

448. William Coleman Esq. died 13 Jul 1829 at his home in New York city. For 23 yrs. Editor of the "New York Post". (21 Jul 1829)

449. Silas Beers died 22 Jul 1829 in Starkey, Yates Co. A respectable farmer of that town. (28 Jul 1829)

450. Silas Hemmingway of Geneva, Ontario Co., and Mary Ottly, daughter of Capt. William Ottly of Phelps, Ontario Co., were married Monday, (date illegible) by Rev. M.P. Squier in Phelps. (4 Aug 1829)

451. Malancton Smith Esq. died at Rochester, Monroe Co., a merchant there for 12 yrs., no date given. (4 Aug 1829)

452. Margaret Bloodgood age 18 yrs., drowned while on a visit to Buttermilk Falls, near Ithaca, Tompkins Co., daughter of Francis A. Bloodgood Esq. of Ithaca, no date given. (11 Aug 1829)

453. Walter Bullock and Mary Scutt were married 26 Jul 1829 by S.G. Gage Esq. in Benton, Yates Co. (11 Aug 1829)

454. Russell Twist of West Troy, killed 9 Aug 1829 by lightning. On observing the approaching storm, he entered a room to close a window, when he was struck and killed instantly. He leaves a wife and two children. (18 Aug 1829)

455. Curtis Chatfield of Middlesex, Yates Co., died 16 Aug 1829. He was driving a one horse wagon at a fast rate of speed, and furiously hit the sign post of Mr. E. Palmer's Tavern. He fell out, landing upon his head, the wagon tipped over and fell upon him, he died the next day from his injuries. (18 Aug 1829)

456. Richard C. Delamater age 36 Yrs., died 10 Aug 1829 at Dresden, Yates Co., after a short illness. Lately of Hudson, Columbia Co., where he united with the Presbyterian Church. He leaves a wife and 2 children. Interred in Geneva, Ontario Co., services from the residence of his father in-law, H.H. Bogert Esq. (18 Aug 1829)

457. Conrad Gansevoort Esq. of Albany, age 70 yrs., died 9 Aug 1829 at Bath, Steuben Co, where he had come to settle the estate of his recently deceased son. He was preparing to return to Albany, when he was seized with dysentery and died. His remains and his son, are to be disinterred and removed to Albany. (18 Aug 1829)

458. Richard Lyon Esq. and Aravesta Lamb were married at Sullivan Co. Ohio, by Rev. Child, no date given. (25 Aug 1829)

459. William Southerland and Roxanna Henry, both of Geneva, Ontario Co., were married 27 Aug 1829 by A. Woodworth Esq., at the "Franklin House" in Penn Yan, Yates Co. (8 Sep 1829)

460. Alexander H. Cole and Eliza Way were married 3 Sep 1829 by Rev. Abner Chase in Milo, Yates Co. (8 Sep 1829)

461. A daughter of John Adams, age 13 yrs., killed instantly by lightning 31 Aug 1829 at her home in Richland, Ontario Co. Her two sisters, ages 18 yrs., and 5 yrs., were sleeping in the same bed, which was set a fire by the lightning. The 18 yr. old, so badly burned she survived but 5 days. The younger was not seriously hurt. Two sons sleeping in the same room were not injured. (15 Sep 1829)

462. Mrs. Sarah Supplee age abt. 60 yrs., died 11 Sep 1829 in Milo, Yates Co. (15 Sep 1829)

463. Henry M'Causland age 70 yrs., died 11 Sep 1829 in the jail at Augusta, Maine, imprisoned 35 yrs. for murder. (15 Sep 1829)

464. Elisha Lee died in Waterloo, Seneca Co., no date given. (15 Sep 1829)

465. Ellena Cross age 26 yrs,. died 15 Sep 1829 in Middlesex, Yates Co., daughter of Edward Cross. (22 Sep 1829)

466. Burage Smith of Rochester, Monroe Co., died in New Orleans. One of the persons suspected of kidnapping Capt. Morgan in 1826, no date given. (6 Oct 1829)

467. Major Jonathan Perry and Theoda Brown were married 1 Oct 1829 by Rev. Abner Chase in Milo, Yates Co. (6 Oct 1829)

468. Thomas J. Nevins Esq. and Cornell S. Clark, were married 3 Oct 1829 by Rev. Eddy in Penn Yan, Yates Co. (6 Oct 1829)

469. Thomas Dunn and Rachel Saterlee, both of Newtown, Chemung Co., were married 4 Oct 1829 by Rev. Barton in Newtown. (13 Oct 1829)

470. Lawrence Remer of Benton, Yates Co. and Sarah Sears of Elmira, Chemung Co., formerly of Penn Yan, Yates Co., were married 4 Oct 1829 by Rev. Barton in Elmira. (13 Oct 1829)

471. J.D. Haviland and Harriet Tuthill, both of Newtown, Chemung Co., were married 6 Oct 1829 by Rev. Barton in Newtown. (13 Oct 1829)

472. Samuel F. Curtiss of Penn Yan, Yates Co., and Emily Lewis of Benton, Yates Co., were married 8 Oct 1829 by Rev. Todd in Benton. (13 Oct 1829)

473. Phelps Moultroup and Catharine Ward were married 4 Oct 1829 by Rev. Abner Chase in Benton, Yates Co. (13 Oct 1829)

474. Eliza Degolier age 22 yrs., died 10 Oct 1829 of consumption, in Penn Yan, Yates Co. (13 Oct 1829)

475. Hon. Enoch Lincoln died 8 Oct 1829 in Augusta, Maine, Governor of that state. (20 Oct 1829)

476. Richard Francis Jr. of Hammondsport, Steuben Co., and Lydia Wilkinson of Penn Yan, Yates Co., were married 19 Oct 1829 by Rev. Chase in Penn Yan. (20 Oct 1829)

477. John Connelly and Sally Ann Ellsworth, both of Milo, Yates Co., were married 11 Oct 1829 by S.G. Gage Esq. in Benton, Yates Co. (20 Oct 1829)

478. Charles Wickliffe, killed 9 Oct 1829 in Lexington, KY. Shot in a duel by Mr. Trotter, Editor of the "Kent Gazette". (27 Oct 1829)

479. Josiah H. Young of Penn Yan, Yates Co., and Julia Ann Marther of Bath, Steuben, Co., were married 28 Oct 1829 by Rev. W.W. Bostwick in Bath. (3 Nov 1829)

480. Hon. John V. Henry died 22 Oct 1829 in Albany, Albany Co. (3 Nov 1829)

481. Hon. Peter Derbigny died 6 Oct 1829, Governor of Louisiana. (10 Nov 1829)

482. William Judd and Susannah Wood of Milo, Yates Co., were married 11 Nov 1829 by Rev. Abner Chase in Milo. (17 Nov 1829)

483. Phineas Bates age 81 yrs., died 23 Nov 1829 at Canandaigua, Ontario Co. (1 Dec 1829)

484. Mrs. Hannah Wyman, a widow age 78 yrs., died 5 Nov 1829, no town given. (1 Dec 1829)

485. Hon. Bushrod Washington died 26 Nov 1829 in Philadelphia, PA., a Judge of the U.S. Supreme Court. His wife, Mrs. Washington, died suddenly 28 Nov 1829 in a stagecoach near Philadelphia. (8 Dec 1829)

486. Gideon Allen of Yates Co. and Sally Larrowe of Wheeler, Steuben Co., were married 1 Dec 1829 by Levi Gray Esq. in Wheeler. (15 Dec 1829)

487. Allen Cole Esq. died 8 Dec 1829 in Jerusalem, Yates Co. (15 Dec 1829)

488. Hon. Daniel Webster of the U.S. Senate and Caroline Leroy, youngest daughter of Herman Leroy Esq., were married 12 Dec 1829 in New York city. (29 Dec 1829)

489. Ira Barber of Middlesex, Yates Co., and Lydia Belknap of Benton, Yates Co., were married on 24 Dec 1829 by Peleg Briggs Jr. Esq. in Benton. (29 Dec 1829)

490. Isaac Nichols age 82 yrs., died 23 Dec 1829 in Milo, Yates Co. A member of the Friends Society, and one of the first settlers of Genesee Co. (29 Dec 1829)

491. Sylvester Nichols and Susan Crane, both of Milo, Yates Co., were married 27 Dec 1829 by Rev. Abner Chase in Milo. (5 Jan 1830)

492. Delausun Latimer of Penn Yan, Yates Co., and Abigail Smith of Italy, Yates Co., were married 3 Jan 1830 by Esq. Fox in Italy. (12 Jan 1830)

493. John Mitchell of Benton, Yates Co. and Merinda Sherwood of Seneca Falls, Seneca Co., were married 31 Dec 1829 by Rev. Barton in Seneca Falls. (12 Jan 1830)

494. Elisha Gleason and Christena Finger, both of Benton, Yates Co., were married 1 Jan 1830 by Peleg Briggs Jr. Esq. in Benton. (12 Jan 1830)

495. Benjamin P. Prosser and Mary Jane Arnout, both of Milo, Yates Co., were married 7 Jan 1830 by Rev. Abner Chase in Milo. (12 Jan 1830)

496. Loring Arnold age 21 yrs., died 5 Jan 1830 in Penn Yan, Yates Co. He has no relatives here, but is believed to be from PA. (12 Jan 1830)

497. The son of John Powell, age 2 mos., died 5 Jan 1830 in Penn Yan, Yates Co. (12 Jan 1830)

498. Mr. Smith, killed 4 Jan 1830 at Danville, Livingston Co., by Ashly Millard. (12 Jan 1830)

499. Mr. Davis a tavern keeper at Le Roy, Genesee Co., killed 3 Jan 1830 by Mr. Gray. (19 Jan 1830)

500. John Coykendall and Susan Baldwin, both of Milo, Yates Co., were married 16 Jan 1830 by Rev. Abner Chase in Milo. (26 Jan 1830)

501. Wakeman Burr died 30 Jan 1830 in Benton, Yates Co. (2 Feb 1830)

502. Alvy Taylor of Benton, Yates Co., and Ardelisa Genung of Jerusalem, Yates Co., were married 8 Feb 1830 by A. Brown Esq. in Jerusalem. (9 Feb 1830)

503. Henry B. Ferris and Dolly Ann Townsend, both of Jerusalem, Yates Co., were married 4 Feb 1830 by

Rev. Abner Chase in Milo. (9 Feb 1830)

504. Gen. Peter Vosburgh age 80 yrs., died 29 Jan 1830 at Stuyvesant, Columbia Co. A soldier of the Revolution. (9 Feb 1830)

505. Col. Sherman Lee age 42 yrs., died 2 Feb 1830 at Milo, Yates Co. An active, meritorious officer during the last war. (9 Feb 1830)

506. Mrs. Amelia Curtiss age 22 yrs., died 6 Feb 1830 in Penn Yan, Yates Co., wife of Samuel F. Curtiss. * Note their marriage appearing 13 Oct 1829, gave her name as Emily. (9 Feb 1830)

507. Mrs. Abigail Thompson died 7 Feb 1830 in Milo, Yates Co., wife of Asler C. Thompson. (9 Feb 1830)

508. Lewis Smith and Lydia Ackley, both of Bath, Steuben Co., were married 25 Jan 1830 by A. Brown Esq. in Jerusalem, Yates Co. (16 Feb 1830)

509. Joseph Dikeman and Amanda Rouse, both of Jerusalem, Yates Co., were married 4 Feb 1830 by A. Brown Esq. in Jerusalem. (16 Feb 1830)

510. Mrs. Parthenia Marble age 34 yrs., died 1 Feb 1830 in Benton, Yates Co., at the residence of E. Delano. (16 Feb 1830)

511. John C. Montgomery Esq. of Danville, Livingston Co., and Debra Kerr, youngest daughter of Jacob Kerr of Turbut Township, Northumberland Co., were married 18 Feb 1830 by Rev. Bryson. The next day, they started in a sleigh from the residence of her father, and had proceded but a short distance, when the horses took fright and upset the sleigh. Mrs. Montgomery was thrown against a fence and killed. (23 Feb 1830)

512. Several family members drowned 10 Feb 1830 in the Crooked Lake when Mr. Goodwin, of Goodwin's Ferry on Seneca Lake, took his wife and infant for a social visit with Mr. and Mrs. Gibson (a sister of his wife) and their infant, to see another of her sisters, Mrs. Gleason, who lived on the other side of lake. They set out across the ice, with the women and infants riding in the cutter, while Mr. Goodwin and Mr. Gibson guided the horses. They had almost reached their destination, when the ice broke. Drowned were Mrs. Goodwin, her infant, and the infant of Mr. and Mrs. Gibson. (23 Feb 1830)

513. Capt. Elijah Kinne age 87 yrs., died in Ovid, Seneca Co. The first militia officer commissioned between Cayuga and Seneca Lakes, no date given. (23 Feb 1830)

514. Mrs. Brown, mother of the late Major Gen. Jacob Brown, died in Brownville. The first white woman to set foot on the soil of Jefferson Co., NY. no date given. (23 Feb 1830)

515. Col. Henry Rutgers age 85 yrs., died 24 Feb 1830 in New York city. A soldier of the Revolution and philanthropist, who devoted a large portion of his income to charity. (2 Mar 1830)

516. Nathaniel Carter Esq. of New York city, died 2 Jan 1830 at Marseilles, France. (2 Mar 1830)

517. William Comstock died last week in Steuben Co. from poisoning. His wife, Eliza Comstock, has been charged with his murder. A peddler named Mr. Allen has been charged as an accessary to the crime, no date given. (2 Mar 1830)

518. William Coons and Sally Wheeler, both of Benton, Yates Co., were married 27 Feb 1830 by Peleg Briggs Jr. in Benton. (9 Mar 1830)

519. John L. Marriner of Benton, Yates Co., and Elizabeth C. Raywalt of Milo, Yates Co., were married 12 Mar 1830 by Rev. Abner Chase in Milo. (23 Mar 1830)

520. A FATAL STEAMBOAT ACCIDENT near Memphis, TN., on 24 Feb 1830 killed or critically wounded are the following:

from Hardin Co., TN...	A. VanMeter, killed.
" "	Z. Bailey, wounded.
Tipton Co., TN...	George Frey, wounded.
east TN..........	J. Dunn, killed.
Madison Co., TN..	H. Heldredth, wounded
Wilson Co., TN...	Thomas Bernard, wounded.
Louisville, KY...	Richard Hancock, killed.
Long Reach, OH...	Mr. Talbot, killed.
Cincinnati, OH...	Mr. Carroll, killed.
" "	C.B. Giles, killed.
Union Co., OH....	J. Suggs, wounded.
Indiana..........	Joshua Richardson, wounded.
Clark Co., IN....	Edward Beadles, killed.
" "	William Ewing, killed.
" "	John Cameron, wounded.
Brookville, IN...	Ephraim Coble, killed.

Salem, Co., IN... William Stockwell, killed.
Harrison Co., IN. J. Reaves, killed.
Lawrence Co., IN. J. Swan, wounded.
Kentucky......... James Bledsoe, killed.
Philadelphia, PA. Mr. DeHaven, wounded.
Massachusetts.... John Valentine, wounded.
New York......... William Case, wounded.
Shippingport..... J. Tenyck, wounded.
Delany a free black man, killed.
Lewis Young a free black man, killed.
John Leland one of the pilots, wounded.
John Addison one of the crew, wounded.
(30 Mar 1830)

521. The body of Samuel Patch, found where it had floated ashore, near the mouth of the Genesee, seven miles from Rochester, Monroe Co., no date given. (30 Mar 1830)

522. Hon. Herman M. Hardenburgh age 53 yrs., died 21 Mar 1830 at his lodging in Albany, Albany Co. A member of the Assembly from Sullivan, Co. (30 Mar 1830)

523. Rev. Joseph S. Christmas died 14 Mar 1830 at Utica, Oneida Co. He began his parochial labour in Montreal, Canada. (6 Apr 1830)

524. Rev. Daniel McDonald age 44 yrs., died 25 Mar 1830 at his home near Geneva, Ontario Co. A proffesor of languages at Geneva College. (6 Apr 1830)

525. William Miller Jr., killed in a duel 4 Apr 1830 at Naaman's Creek, near the mouth of the Delaware River. A member of the Philadelphia bar, killed by Lieut. Charles G. Hunter of the U.S. Navy. (6 Apr 1830)

526. James Armstrong and a son, killed 22 Mar 1830 when a tornado hit their home near Peters Township, OH. The entire family wounded in the incident. (13 Apr 1830)

527. Ludlow E. Lapham a merchant of Penn Yan, Yates Co., and Reliance W. Townsend of Milo, Yates Co., were married 8 Apr 1830 by Rev. Abner Chase in Milo. (13 Apr 1830)

528. Joseph White Esq. age 82 yrs., murdered 6 Apr 1830 at Salem, MA. (13 Apr 1830)

529. Aaron and Moses Wilcox, twins, died in Twinsburgh, OH., Born in Connecticut, they married sisters on the same day. Employed as teachers in their early life, but later merchants in Middletown, before moving to Ohio. Taken sick on the same day, they died the same day, and are buried in the same grave, no date given. (20 Apr 1830)

530. Hiram S. Fargo age 30 yrs., died 13 Apr 1830 in Benton, Yates Co. (20 Apr 1830)

531. Corey Clark age 99 yrs., died 17 Apr 1830 in Middlesex, Yates Co. (20 Apr 1830)

532. The wife of David Mills died 12 Apr 1830 in Benton, Yates Co. (20 Apr 1830)

533. Gen. Alexander Smyth died near Washington. Late of the US Army, a member of the House from Virginia, no date given. (27 Apr 1830)

534. A STEAMBOAT DISASTER near Newburgh, Orange Co., NY., 23 Apr 1830 when the boiler on the "Chief Justice Marshall" burst. The following died;
Mr. Volant of New York, an engineer,
James Cassidy age 16 yrs., a waiter of Albany,
Peleg Moore a fireman of Troy,
Thomas Diamond a blackman and cook of Troy.
(4 May 1830)

535. John Black died 22 Apr 1830 in the Auburn State Prison, a convict from Yates Co. (4 May 1830)

536. Cyrus Jones drowned last week, his body found 9 May 1830. It appeared he had fallen from a rail laid across the small brook and hit his head. A soldier of the Revolution and member of the Friends Society, no town given. (11 May 1830)

537. Hiram Raplee and Ann Headley were married 2 May 1830 by Rev. John B. Chase, no town given. (11 May 1830)

538. Thomas Franklin died 30 Apr 1830 in New York, the Register of that city. (11 May 1830)

539. Joseph E. Morris age 45 yrs., died 5 May 1830 in Pulteney, Steuben Co. (11 May 1830)

540. Mrs. Joanna Beasley died 18 May 1830 in Boston, Massachusetts, wife of Antonio Beasley. (25 May 1830)

541. Mrs. Susan Peckins age 24 yrs., died 21 May 1830 in Benton, Yates Co. (25 May 1830)

542. David Mills and Mrs. Betsey Gregory were married 7 Jun 1830 by Elder John Goff in Benton, Yates Co. (8 Jun 1830)

543. Moses Shepherd age 30 yrs., died 4 Jun 1830 in Benton, Yates. (8 Jun 1830)

544. Mrs. Eliza Comstock, sentenced to be executed 23 Jul 1830 in Steuben Co. for murdering her husband, William Comstock, in February. (15 Jun 1830)

545. Reuben Sanborn, found dead last week, at his home in Steuben Co. He was suspended by the neck, it appeared to be a suicide. (15 Jun 1830)

546. Joseph H. Beaumount and Ann Meriah Brown, both of Benton, Yates Co., were married 19 Jun 1830 by Rev. Abner Chase in Benton. (22 Jun 1830)

547. Jane Castine age 119 yrs., died 1 Jun 1830 at the poor house in Erie Co. A colored woman, born 1711 at Nine Partners, Dutchess Co. (22 Jun 1830)

548. Richard Crowninshield Jr. age 26 yrs., hung himself 22 Jun 1830 in the jail at Salem, MA. A suspect in the murder of Joseph White. (29 Jun 1830)

549. James Porter, executed 2 Jul 1830 in Philadelphia, Pa., for mail robbery. (13 Jul 1830)

550. Samuel M. Warner of Penn Yan, Yates Co., and Eveline Chase of Benton, Yates Co., were married 18 Jul 1830 by Rev. Abner Chase in Benton. (20 Jul 1830)

551. Henry Robbins of Bridgewater, Oneida Co., and Jerusha Kinney of Penn Yan, Yates Co., were married 15 Jul 1830 by Rev. Eddy in Penn Yan. (20 Jul 1830)

552. John Johnson of Olean, Cattaraugus Co., and Jane Cook of Middlesex, Yates Co., were married 12 Jul 1830 at the Penn Yan Hotel by Rev. Eddy in Penn Yan, Yates Co. (20 Jul 1830)

553. Edwin W. Lewis and Relief P. Holden, both of Starkey, Yates Co., were married 17 Jul 1830 by Rev. White in Starkey. (20 Jul 1830)

554. Charles Hutchins age 74 yrs., died 2 Jul 1830 at Italy, Yates Co., a soldier of the Revolution. (20 Jul 1830)

555. Reuben Crawford of Benton, Yates Co., and Nancy Dorman of Jerusalem, Yates Co., were married 12 Aug 1830 by Rev. Abner Chase in Jerusalem. (17 Aug 1830)

556. Joseph Jones died 21 Aug 1830 in Jerusalem, Yates Co., at an advanced age. (24 Aug 1830)

557. Richard Francis died 26 Aug 1830 at Sodus, Wayne Co. A merchant of that place, formerly of Hammondsport, Steuben Co. (31 Aug 1830)

558. William A. Thurston and Una L. Pratt, daughter of Ebenezer Pratt of CT., were married 25 Sep 1830 by Rev. Eddy in Penn Yan, Yates Co. (28 Sep 1830)

559. Jacob Thayer and Sarah Ann M'Intire were married married 26 Sep 1830 by George Youngs Esq. in Milo, Yates Co. (28 Sep 1830)

560. Sophronia Gould age 25 yrs., died 23 Sep 1830 in Penn Yan, Yates Co. (28 Sep 1830)

561. John Francis Knapp, executed 28 Sep 1830 in Salem, MA., for the murder of Capt. White. (12 Oct 1830)

562. Anthony Swarthout and Maria Lilly, both of Junuis, Seneca Co., were married 2 Oct 1830 by S.G. Gage Esq. in Benton, Yates Co. (12 Oct 1830)

563. Silas Spinks aged between 70 and 80 yrs., died 9 Oct 1830 in Milo, Yates Co., one of the earliest settlers there. (12 Oct 1830)

564. Cranston Hewett and Maria Dunning, both of Jerusalem, Yates Co., were married 13 Oct 1830 by Rev. Eddy in Jerusalem. (19 Oct 1830)

565. Charles G. Tuthill of Starkey, Yates Co., and Elizabeth Casner of Milo, Yates Co., were married 14 Oct 1830 by Rev. Abner Chase in Milo. (19 Oct 1830)

566. Mrs. Sally Colburn age 23 yrs., died 17 Oct 1830 in Milo, Yates Co., the wife of Sylvenus Colburn. (19 Oct 1830)

567. Willet Gardiner age 23 yrs., accidently killed 19 Oct 1830 from being thrown off a horse. He lived in Milo, Yates Co., his parents still live in Rhode Island. (26 Oct 1830)

568. James Gray, executed 5 Nov 1830 in Batavia, Genesee Co., for the murder of Samuel Davis. The son of Elijah Gray, who was also accused, but pardoned in the same murder. (16 Nov 1830)

569. Alexander Bassett and Cynthia Parkman, both of Middlesex, Yates Co., were married 2 Dec 1830 by Rev. Joseph Brackett in Middlesex. (7 Dec 1830)

570. George W. Harris Esq. and Mrs. Lucinda Morgan, widow of the late Captain William Morgan, were married 23 Nov 1830 by S. Cummings Esq. in Batavia, Genesee Co. (7 Dec 1830)

571. Sexton Mount of Buffalo, Erie Co., and Lucretia Kendig, daughter of Martin Kendig Esq. of Milo, Yates Co., were married 29 Nov 1830 by Rev. A.D. Lane at Waterloo, Seneca Co. (7 Dec 1830)

572. Jewett Marriner and Nancy N. Gage, both of Benton, Yates Co., were married 24 Dec 1830 by Peleg Briggs Jr. Esq. in Benton. (4 Jan 1831)

573. Jacob Stewart and Lester Ann Osborn, both of Barrington, Yates Co., were married 28 Dec 1830 by Rev. Bignall in Barrington. (4 Jan 1831)

574. Christopher Houghtailing and Betsey Jolly were married 30 Dec 1830 by Miles Terrill Esq. in Barrington, Yates Co. (4 Jan 1831)

575. Mrs. Abser Ferris age 35 yrs., died 27 Dec 1830 in Barrington, Yates Co., wife of Nicholas Ferris. (4 Jan 1831)

576. George Tassels an indian, executed 24 Dec 1830 (copied from the "George Anthenian" 28 Dec 1830), no town given. (18 Jan 1831)

577. Marcus Wilmouth of Victor, Ontario Co., and Susan Latham of Middlesex, Yates Co., were married 4 Jan 1831 by Elder Smith in Middlesex. (18 Jan 1831)

578. William Denning a blacksmith, age 94 yrs., died recently at his residence in Muffing Township, PA. An artificer in the Army of the Revolution, he

manufactured wrought iron canons for the war. Two canons are at Middlesex, a larger one at Mt. Holly and another at the Carlisle Barracks. One taken by the British at the Battle of Brandywine, now stands in the Tower of London. The British Government offered him a large ammount of money, and a stated annuity, if he would instruct them in the manufacturing of that article, but the patriotic blacksmith preferred obscurity and poverty in his own country. His health and strength continued till near his last. He was able to walk to the village of Newville, two miles from his residence, until about 6 mos. ago, no date given. (18 Jan 1831)

* * * MANY PAPERS MISSING * * *

579. Hon. William Ramsey died 6 Oct 1831 at his home in Carlisle, PA., a member of Congress. (12 Oct 1831)

580. Alanson Potter and Nancy Johnson, both of Rushville, Yates Co., were married 7 Oct 1831 by by William Bassett Esq. in Rushville. (12 Oct 1831)

581. Asa Colvard Esq. age 64 yrs., died 11 Oct 1831, the high sheriff of Albany. (12 Oct 1831)

582. Dr. Alfred Baldwin and Nancy Whited of Saratoga, Saratoga, Co., were married 15 Oct 1831 by S.G. Gage Esq. in Benton, Yates Co. (19 Oct 1831)

583. Lieut. Hayne died 18 Sep 1831 of yellow fever at the Naval Hospital near Pennsacola, of the ship "U.S. Vincennes". (19 Oct 1831)

584. William H. Lamport a merchant in Barrington, Yates Co., and Mary E. Townsend of Milo, Yates Co., were married 23 Nov 1831 by Rev. Chester V. Adgate in Milo. (23 Nov 1831)

585. Jedediah Smith a fur trader, killed 27 May 1831 by the Cormurek Indians, west of the Rocky Mountains. (30 Nov 1831)

586. Rev. Statham Clary died 25 Nov 1831 at Hopewell, Ontario Co., pastor of the Presbyterian Church in Benton. (30 Nov 1831)

587. Samuel W. Scott age 38 yrs. or 88 yrs.?(blurred), died 15 Nov 1831 in Benton, Yates Co. (30 Nov 1831)

588. Dibdell Holt, executed 18 Nov 1831 at Buffalo, Erie Co., for the murder of his wife. (30 Nov 1831)

589. Jacob P. Dickerson and Sally Ann Garrison, both of Benton, Yates Co., were married 21 Dec 1831 by S.G. Gage Esq. in Benton. (21 Dec 1831)

590. William Holden and Eliza Ann Nichols were married 14 Dec 1831 by Elder Amos Chase in Milo, Yates Co. (21 Dec 1831)

591. Alexander Nichols Jr. and Deborah Gardiner, both of Milo, Yates Co., were married 15 Dec 1831 by Elder Simon Southerland in Milo. (21 Dec 1831)

592. Stephen Girard Esq. age 85 yrs., died 27 Dec 1831 in Phila. A native of Bordeaux, France, he came to this country years before the Revolution, engaged in commerce, and died one of the wealthest men in the world, * brief biography printed. (4 Jan 1831 and 11 Jan 1831)

593. Jacob M. Woodruff of Penn Yan, Yates Co., and Maria Cushman of Benton, Yates Co., were married 9 Jan 1831 by Samuel G. Gage Esq. in Benton. (11 Jan 1832)

594. James H. Gallagher of Penn Yan, Yates Co., and Clarrisa Dunning of Jerusalem, Yates Co., were married 9 Jan 1832 by Rev. Chester V. Adgate in Jerusalem. (11 Jan 1832)

595. James Taylor age 82 yrs., died in Benton, Yates Co., a soldier of the Revolution, no date given. (11 Jan 1832)

596. William Brooks of Penn Yan, Yates Co., and Louisa A. Swan of Onondaga Hollow, Onondaga Co., were married 10 Jan 1832 by Rev. Thatcher in Onondaga Hollow. (18 Jan 1832)

597. William A. Way and Rebecca Alfred, both of Milo, Yates Co., were married 16 Jan 1832 by Rev. Abner Chase in Milo. (18 Jan 1832)

598. Dr. Harvey Burnett and Annie Babcock, both of Campbell, Steuben Co., were married 13 Dec 1831 by Rev. Smith in Campbell. (18 Jan 1832)

599. Cornelius Warren and Sally Emery were married 16 Jan 1832 by J.M. Lean Esq. in Benton, Yates Co. (18 Jan 1832)

600. Abraham Hymen age 70 yrs., and Mrs. Catharine Jenkins age 75 yrs., a widow, married at Nautwich. A fourth marriage for the groom, who had been a widower only 4 weeks. He married first at 17 yrs., but his wife soon died. At 19 yrs., he married again, this wife lived only 6 weeks. At her funeral, he made acquaintance with his third wife. He was her third husband, and is the third husband of his present wife, no date given. (25 Jan 1832)

601. Guy C. Clark, executed 3 Feb 1832 at Ithaca, Tompkins Co., convicted for the murder of his wife. (8 Feb 1832)

602. Samuel W. Journey age 12 yrs., accidentally hung himself 6 Feb 1832 at his home in Canandaigua, Ontario Co. He was kidding his sister, pretending to hang himself. She repeatedly tried to get him to stop his foolishness, but he persisted. So she simply ignored him. About fifteen minutes later, she found him hanging. (15 Feb 1832)

603. William Gage of Penn Yan, Yates Co., and Abigail Fargo of Benton, Yates Co., were married 9 Feb 1832 by A. Woodworth Esq. in Benton. (15 Feb 1832)

604. Nathan Dunning of Ithaca, Tompkins Co., and Maria Sprague of Jerusalem, Yates Co., were married 7 Feb 1832 by Rev. Chester V. Adgate in Penn Yan, Yates Co. (22 Feb 1832)

605. Amos C. Clark and Clarrisa C. Cody were married 14 Feb 1832 by Rev. Chester V. Adgate at Benton, Yates Co. (22 Feb 1832)

606. Benedict Robinson age 74 yrs., died 18 Feb 1832 in Milo, Yates Co. (29 Feb 1832)

607. Abraham V. Remer of Dresden, Yates Co., and Sarah A. Olney of Benton, Yates Co., were married 29 Feb 1832 by Rev. Adgate in Benton. (7 Mar 1832)

608. Charles G. Judd, a Counselor at Law in Penn Yan, Yates Co., and Amelia Hart Goodrich, daughter of Rev. Charles Goodrich of Havana, Schuyler Co., lately of Pittsfield, MA., were married 22 Feb 1832 in Havana, no pastor given. (7 Mar 1832)

609. Robert Norman and Sarah M. Willis, both of Benton, Yates Co., were married 6 Mar 1832 by Rev. Chester V. Adgate in Benton. (7 Mar 1832)

610. Mrs. Elizabeth Johnson age 25 yrs., died 3 Mar 1832 in Milo, Yates Co., wife of William G. Johnson. (7 Mar 1832)

611. Jerome B. Cole age 14 yrs., died 23 Mar 1832 in Penn Yan, Yates Co., from lock-jaw. An apprentice for William Gardner of Penn Yan. (28 Mar 1832)

612. Three daughters of James Kent Esq. were killed 28 Mar 1832, when their home in Piermont, NH., was consumed by fire. (4 Apr 1832)

613. Joseph M. Pratt age 20 yrs., died 3 Mar 1832 at Amherst, Erie Co. (11 Apr 1832)

614. Silas Folsom Sr., Editor of the "Antimasonic Intelligencer" and Mary E. Taylor were married 28 Mar 1832 in Hartford, CT. (11 Apr 1832)

615. William McCauley of Seneca, Ontario Co., and Sarah Bugby of Penn Yan, Yates Co., were married 9 Apr 1832 by Rev. Adgate in Penn Yan. (11 Apr 1832)

616. Benjamin Loomis age 22 yrs., died 13 Apr 1832 in Middlesex, Yates Co., of consumption, son of Nathan Loomis Esq. (18 Apr 1832)

617. Hon. William B. Rochester of Buffalo, Erie Co. and Mrs. Eliza Powers, widow of the late Gershom Powers of Auburn, Cayuga Co., were married 9 Apr 1832 by Rev. Rudd in Auburn. (18 Apr 1832)

618. Catharine C. Wheeler age 6 yrs., died 11 Apr 1832 in Penn Yan, Yates Co. (18 Apr 1832)

619. Lieut. A.B. Foster, stationed at Green Bay, killed by a soldier named Doyle, no date given. (18 Apr 1832)

620. William S. Hudson of Benton, Yates Co., and Rebecca Malen of Jerusalem, Yates Co., were married 21 Apr 1832 by Rev. Crosby in Jerusalem. (25 Mar 1832)

621. William Jackson and Sarah Lacy, both of Seneca, Ontario Co., were married 12 Apr 1832 by S.G. Gage Esq. in Seneca. (25 Apr 1832)

622. Mrs. Amy Fowle age 43 yrs., died 30 Apr 1832 in Seneca, Ontario Co. (2 May 1832)

623. Anson Benjamin of Chatham, Columbia Co., and Lucia Smith of Penn Yan, Yates Co., were married 27 Apr 1832 by Rev. Todd in Penn Yan. (2 May 1832)

624. Mrs. Robert P. Walker of New York city, and her child, were killed 9 Apr 1832 near Memphis, TN. When the steamboat they were riding on had an explosion. (2 May 1832)

625. Asa Martin died 18 Apr 1832. He was found frozen to death by the roadside in Attlebourgh. A bottle of gin in his pocket. (2 May 1832)

626. Robert Strothart of New York city, killed 9 Apr 1832 near Memphis, TN. When the steamboat he was riding, had an explosion. (2 May 1832)

627. DEADLY CATASTROPHE; A corner of the new six story building in New York city, occupied by Messrs. Phelps and Peck, collasped 4 May 1832. Killed were: Thomas H. Goddard a book keeper, Josiah Stokes a clerk, Alfred K. Seymour a clerk, and Mr. Pitkin a clerk. (9 May 1832)

628. David Peck and Catharine Hughes, both of Benton, Yates Co., were married 28 Apr 1832 by S.G. Gage Esq. in Benton. (9 May 1832)

629. David Schaeffer, executed 16 Apr 1832 in Lancaster, PA. for the murder of Bowers. (16 May 1832)

630. Eli Terry Jr., a solicitor of Alabama, killed 19 Apr 1832 near Selena, Alabama by Mr. Reed. (16 May 1832)

631. Henry C. Wheeler of Penn Yan, Yates Co., and Mary Ann Spencer, daughter of Hon. E. Spencer of Benton, Yates Co., were married 10 May 1832 by Rev. Chester V. Adgate in Benton. (16 May 1832)

632. Ransford Whitting and Alma Crane, both of Benton, Yates Co., were married 10 May 1832 by Rev. Chester V. Adgate in Benton. (16 May 1832)

633. George W. Clinton Esq. and Laura Catharine Spencer, daughter of Hon. John C. Spencer, were married 15 May 1832 by Rev. Kearney in Canandaigua, Ontario Co. (23 May 1832)

634. Oliver Wolcott of Barrington, Yates Co., and Sophia Stewart of Penn Yan, Yates Co., were married 5 Jun 1832 by Rev. Crosby in Penn Yan. (6 Jun 1832)

635. John McCreey a well known printer, died in in Paris of cholera, no date given. (13 Jun 1832)

636. William S. Gregory of Bethany, Genesee Co., committed suicide 11 May 1832 by shooting himself. (13 Jun 1832)

637. FATAL SHIPWRECK; The brig "Edwins" capsized 2 Jun 1832 near Cape Hatteras during a squall and the following drowned; Mrs. G. Champlin of Georgia, Mrs. Cohen and two of her children of Santee, S.C., Mr. J. Brack from Germany. (20 Jun 1832)

638. STEAMBOAT DISASTER; A tornado struck the steamboat "Hornet" on the way from Cincinnati to Kanawha 2 Jun 1832. Drowned were Capt. John Sullivan the ship captain, of Kanawha, Mr. Garrett of Greensburg, Mr. Duvall, John Johnson the ship pilot, and the chambermaid. (20 Jun 1832)

639. Morris Clarke of Seneca, Ontario Co., and Elizabeth Vorce, daughter of Judge Vorce of Milo, Yates Co., were married 14 Jun 1832 by Rev. Chester V. Adgate in Milo. (20 Jun 1832)

640. Col. John O. Cook age 43 yrs., died 13 Jun 1832 in Starkey, Yates Co. (13 Jun 1832)

641. Josiah Page age 72 yrs., died 15 Jun 1832 in Benton, Yates Co. (20 Jun 1832)

642. Hon. Charles C. Johnson, drowned 17 Jun 1832. A member of the House from Virginia. His body was found in the Potomac River near Alexandria, on the 18th. It is believed he accidentally fell into the water, while boarding a boat in the dark. (27 Jun 1832)

643. Gen. Joseph Heister age 82 yrs., died 23 Jun 1832, ex-Governor of PA. (27 Jun 1832)

644. Carolina Mina, executed 21 Jun 1832 at Erie, PA. for the murder of Mr. Chapman at Doylestown, PA. Mina, a Spaniard, stated he was born Oct 1809 at Trinidad, near the island of Cuba. Soon after Mr. Chapman's death, he married Mrs. Chapman who was also charged with the murder, but acquitted. Mina leaves behind a 4 yr. old daughter. (4 Jul 1832)

645. John O'Brine aged abt. 65 yrs., died 4 Jul 1832 in Penn Yan, Yates Co. (11 Jul 1832)

646. MORTALITY TABLE OF 1831 FOR TOWN OF BENTON; prepared for the "Yates County Whig" by Samuel G. Gage Esq.:

Jan...6	Buel Mariner on his 77th birthday.
" 9	Peter Bain age 66 yrs.
" 17	Abigail Burgduff age 23 yrs.
Feb...5	Frances M. Moon age under 1 yr.
" 19	Mary Nichols age 71 yrs.
" 23	Thomas Chrysler age over 60 yrs.
" 29	Jane E. Coddington age 26 yrs.
Mar..15	Sylvester N. Ketcham age 37 yrs.
" 19	Ann M. Scott age 38 yrs.
" 23	John Powell age 58 yrs.
Apr...1	Margaret Earl age 18 yrs.
" 17	Sarah Brown age 88 yrs.
May...2	Julia Fowle age 7 yrs.
" 23	Martha Beard age 62 yrs.
Jun...1	Nathan P. Cole Esq. age over 70 yrs.
" 1	Henry Andrews age 35 yrs.
" 2	Harriet Moon age 3 yrs.
" 7	Caroline Townsend age 31 yrs.
" 21	Andrew Griffin age 24 yrs., killed by lightning.
" 22	Eliza Hicks age 45 yrs.
Jul..20	Garret E. Crank age 11 yrs.
" 28	Charles R. Kelsey age 31 yrs.
Aug..14	Elizabeth Meeker age 66 yrs.
Oct..15	Mary S. Gage age 4 yrs.
" 15	Jesse F. Gage age 5 yrs.
" 16	Eleanor M. Gage age 15 yrs.
" 24	Mary H. Gage age 16 yrs.
Nov...2	Nancy Patchen age 74 yrs.
" 24	son of D. Feagles, age under 1 yr.
" 28	DeWitt C. Chrysler age 37 yrs.
Dec..15	Hon. Elijah Spencer age 76 yrs.
" 20	Eva Finger age 59 yrs.
" 31	Ann King age 24 yrs.

(11 Jul 1832)

647. Alexander M. Muir Esq. of New York city, died 13 Jul 1832 of cholera. The ex-Commissary General of New York. (18 Jul 1832)

648. Michael Swift age 22 yrs., killed 13 Jul 1832 on the Erie Canal. He had left Buffalo on a heavy laden boat, about 6 miles below Black Rock. While attempting to pass another boat, they struck and he was crushed to death instantly. (18 Jul 1832)

649. Michael Drugan a workman on the PA Canal near Columbia, Lancaster Co., killed 12 Jul 1832. By Theophilus Hughes, a constable, who had attempted

to arrest him on a debt suit. Drugan resisted and struck Hughes with a mason's hammer. Hughes then drew a pistol and shot Drugan. (18 Jul 1832)

650. Cornelius Garretson a fireman, killed 4 Jul 1832 in New York city, when a chimney fell at a fire on Elm St. (25 Jul 1832)

651. Malachi Davis aged abt. 90 yrs., died 30 Jul 1832 in Milo, Yates Co. One of the earliest settler's in this part of the country. (1 Aug 1832)

652. Mrs. Steeprock an Indian, killed 24 Jul 1832 by her husband John Steeprock at their home near Batavia, Genesee Co. He beat her with his fist, until she died. (1 Aug 1832)

653. Mrs. Eliza Freeman, executed 27 Jul 1832 at Mt. Holly, NJ., for the murder of her husband. (8 Aug 1832)

654. Rev. Calvin S. Coats and Mary Jane Dorman, daughter of Joel Dorman Esq., were married 7 Aug 1832 by Rev. Abner Chase in Jerusalem, Yates Co. (8 Aug 1832)

655. Margaret Boyd age 22 yrs., died 2 Aug 1832 in Jerusalem, Yates Co. (8 Aug 1832)

656. David Gilbert age 47 yrs., died 2 Aug 1832 in Jerusalem, Yates Co. (8 Aug 1832)

657. Mrs. Nancy Collins died 4 Aug 1832 in Benton, Yates Co., wife of Henry Collins. (8 Aug 1832)

658. Elias Steenburgh and George Kidney, both of Poughkeepsie, Dutchess Co., drowned 19 Jul 1832 on the Hudson River, when the sailboat they were in upset. (8 Aug 1832)

659. Mr. Pearce, with his wife and child, were killed 24 Jul 1832 aboard the steamboat "Phoebus" at Cincinnati, OH. When the boat suddenly burst into flames. (8 Aug 1832)

660. CHOLERA VICTIMS; This deadly disease is taking it's toll in New York city. Word has reached us of the following victims; (no dates given), Aldermen Strong and Alderman Smith of the 4th ward of New York, Dr. John C. Vought formerly of Rochester, Monroe Co., and the son-inlaw of the late Thomas

Mumford of Cayuga, Cayuga Co., and Rev. Hinton of the Episcopal Church at Harlem, with his wife and child. (8 Aug 1832)

661. Hon. Thomas D. Arnold and Luritta Rose were married 27 Jul 1832 in Tazewell, Tennessee by Rev. Charles McAnally. (15 Aug 1832)

662. Capt. Thomas L. Stevens and Martha J. Farley, daughter of James Farley, were married 25 Jul 1832 in Milton, NC., by Rev. Penick, all of that town. Two days later, his bride awoke at 5 o'clock in the morning to find him suffering in pain. She immediately summoned a doctor, who did everything he could, but Capt. Stevens died 27 Jul 1832. He was 36 yrs. old. (21 Aug 1832)

663. Cyrus McCollister and Marion K. Stanton, both of Penn Yan, Yates Co., were married 21 Aug 1832 by Rev. C.V. Adgate in Penn Yan. (22 Aug 1832)

664. Russell S. Streeter age 20 yrs., died 15 Aug 1832 in Rochester, Monroe Co. A printer, formerly of Rushville, Yates Co. (21 Aug 1832)

665. Horatio Gates Spafford Esq. died 7 Aug 1832 in Lansingburgh, Rensselaer Co., of cholera. Author of the "New York Gazeteer". (22 Aug 1832)

666. Anna Marie Potter died 21 Jun 1832 near Bristol, Canada, a well known novelist. (29 Aug 1832)

667. Samuel Cobb age 41 yrs., died 3 Sep 1832 in Penn Yan, Yates Co. Of the American Hotel, he leaves a large family. (5 Sep 1832)

668. Hon. William H. Maynard died 1 Sep 1832 in New York city. Former Editor of the "Utica Sentinel", and a Senator of New York. (12 Sep 1832)

669. Glen Cuyler Esq. died 1 Aug 1832 in Aurora, Cayuga Co. An early settler of Yates Co., and member of the bar. (12 Sep 1832)

670. Rev. Michael MacNamara died 30 Aug 1832 in Chili, Monroe Co. The late Roman Catholic Pastor of Rochester, Monroe Co. (12 Sep 1832)

671. John Renwick died 7 Aug 1832 at his home near Beardstown, Illinois. Late Editor and proprietor of the "Beardtown Chronicle", former Editor of the "Penn Yan Enquirer". (12 Sep 1832)

672. Napoleon Bonaparte died 22 Jul 1832 in Vienna, at the Palace of Schoenburn. (19 Sep 1832)

673. Henry Lathrop age 54 yrs., died 16 Sep 1832 in Penn Yan, Yates Co. (19 Sep 1832)

674. Andrew Dunn Jr. and Elizabeth Davis, both of Milo, Yates Co. were married 16 Sep 1832 by Elder Steed in Benton, Yates Co. (26 Sep 1832)

675. George Lowrey of Penn Yan, Yates Co., and Hester Reeder of Cold Springs, Erie Co., were married by Rev. W.W. Bostwick at Hammondsport, Steuben Co., no date given. (26 Sep 1832)

676. Calvin Edson died at the home of Dr. Scudder in Randolph, Vermont. He was known as the living skeleton, and put himself on exhibition to earn a living for his family. He died from tapeworm, no date given. (3 Oct 1832)

677. Ray C. Wait of Jerusalem, Yates Co. and Phebe Remer of Benton, Yates Co., were married 24 Sep 1832 by Rev. Phelps in Geneva, Ontario Co. (3 Oct 1832)

678. Benjamin E. Kidder and Anne Brown were married 2 Oct 1832 by Rev. Abner Chase in Penn Yan, Yates Co. (3 Oct 1832)

679. Charles Williams of the General Post Office, and Mary E. Hamilton, daughter of Col. William Hamilton of Charles Co., MD., were married 18 Sep 1832, no date or town given. (3 Oct 1832)

680. Samuel Ovenshire of Barrington, Yates Co., and Sophia Beebe of Junius, Seneca Co., were married 10 Oct 1832 by Rev. Abner Chase in Penn Yan, Yates Co. (17 Oct 1832)

681. James Johnson and Sally Coleman, both of Bellona, Yates Co., were married 14 Sep 1832 by Rev. Abner Chase in Bellona. (17 Oct 1832)

682. Marcus Jackson and Mrs. Usebe Rosecrants were married 14 Sep 1832 by Rev. Abner Chase in Bellona, Yates Co. (17 Oct 1832)

683. Warren Mills and Lovina Barse, both of Penn Yan, Yates Co., were married 13 Oct 1832 by Rev. Chester V. Adgate in Starkey, Yates Co. (17 Oct 1832)

684. Rev. Adam Clarke died 18 Oct 1832 at Bayswater. Present at his death were his wife, a daughter, and sons Theodore and John Clarke. (24 Oct 1832)

685. James Dalliba died in Utica, Oneida Co., no date given. (24 Oct 1832)

686. Uzziah B. Owens and Rhoda Pruden were married 25 Oct 1832 by S.G. Gage Esq. in Bellona, Yates Co. (14 Nov 1832)

687. Sir Walter Scott died 22 Sep 1832 at Abbotsford, England. (14 Nov 1832)

688. Norman Snider of Jerusalem, Yates Co., and Sally Vanscoy of Milo, Yates Co., were married 15 Nov 1832 by Rev. Hurlburt in Milo. (21 Nov 1832)

689. William Baxter and Mary White, both of Benton, Yates Co., were married 8 Nov 1832 by S.G. Gage Esq. in Benton. (21 Nov 1832)

690. Hon. Charles Carroll age 96 yrs., died 14 Nov 1832 in Baltimore, MD. The last surviving signer of the Declaration of Independence. (28 Nov 1832)

691. Hon. Phillip Doddridge of VA., died 19 Nov 1832 at Washington city. (28 Nov 1832)

692. Hon. Silas Halsey age 90 yrs., died 19 Nov 1832 in Ovid, Seneca Co. (5 Dec 1832)

693. Joel G. Simmonson and Julia Demmory, both of Geneva, Ontario Co., were married 4 Dec 1832 by Rev. Adgate in Penn Yan, Yates Co. (12 Dec 1832)

694. John Coleman age 63 yrs., died 11 Dec 1832 in Bellona, Yates Co. (19 Dec 1832)

695. Henry C. Wiley and Sarah Peck, daughter of Abel Peck Esq., were married 22 Dec 1832 by Rev. C.V. Adgate in Benton, Yates Co. (26 Dec 1832)

696. John Simms of Seneca, Ontario Co., and Lorietta Olney of Benton, Yates Co., were married 23 Dec 1832 by Rev. Chester V. Adgate in Jerusalem, Yates Co. (26 Dec 1832)

697. Joel Burtch and Clamania Hulburd, both of Jerusalem, Yates Co., were married 23 Dec 1832 by Elder R.P. Lamb in Jerusalem. (26 Dec 1832)

698. Gilbert A. Laton and Mary Baskin were married 18 Dec 1832 by Elder Martin at Starkey, Yates Co. (26 Dec 1832)

699. Josiah Bates and Harriet Hopkins, both of Benton, Yates Co., were married 19 Dec 1832 by S.G. Gage Esq. in Benton. (26 Dec 1832)

700. Mrs. Susan Willson age 37 yrs., died 20 Dec 1832 in Penn Yan, Yates Co., wife of Johnson Willson. (26 Dec 1832)

701. Mrs. Julia Huntington age 34 yrs., died 31 Dec 1832 in Starkey, Yates Co. The wife of James Huntington, a merchant there. (9 Jan 1833)

702. Henry Halloway of Ovid, Seneca Co., and Lydia Johnson of Benton, Yates Co., were married 8 Jan 1833 by Rev. C.V. Adgate in Benton. (16 Jan 1833)

703. John McFarrin and Caroline Johnson, both of Benton, Yates Co., were married 8 Jan 1833 by Rev. Chester V. Adgate in Benton. (16 Jan 1833)

704. Sarah M. Cornell found murdered 21 Dec 1832 near Tiverton, RI. (16 Jan 1833)

705. Jesse Genung age 30 Yrs., committed suicide 17 Jan 1833 by hanging himself. A respectable farmer of Milo, Yates Co. (23 Jan 1833)

706. Jonathan Botsford age 91 yrs., died 19 Jan 1833 in Milo, Yates Co. (30 Jan 1833)

707. Mr. Eckford Esq. died 12 Nov 1832 at Constantinople. (6 Feb 1833)

708. Major Stephen Rice of Geneva, Ontario Co., and Jane Bates of Benton, Yates Co., were married 30 Jan 1833 by Rev. Todd in Benton. (6 Feb 1833)

709. Rev. Chester V. Adgate age 37 Yrs., died 4 Feb 1833 in Penn Yan, Yates Co., pastor of the Methodist Episcopal Church. (6 Feb 1833)

710. Milton H. Curtiss of Penn Yan, Yates Co., and Deborah Mallory of Benton, Yates Co., were married 14 Feb 1833 by Rev. Carpenter in Benton. (20 Feb 1833)

711. Dewey Willever and Phebe Rodman, both of Ben-

ton Yates Co., were married 2 Feb 1833 by S.G. Gage Esq., in Benton. (20 Feb 1833)

712. John B. Carter age 25 yrs., and Mary A. Bradlee age 20 yrs., both found Monday, where they had hung themselves in the second story of the hardware owned by her father Samuel Bradlee in Boston. From the letters both left, it was a mutual decision. Her parents had objected to their marriage, services for both, from the Trinity Church, no date given. (27 Feb 1833)

713. George Garside died about a fortnight at York, U.C. Formerly of Niagara, he was killed instantly, when he was thrown from an unruly horse against a wagon, no date given. (27 Feb 1833)

714. Thomas Utter and Laura Davis, both of Penn Yan, Yates Co., were married 28 Feb 1833 by Rev. Crosby at the Penn Yan Hotel. (6 Mar 1833)

715. Rev. George Whitfield age 79 yrs., died 24 Dec 1832 at Tottenham, Eng., the celebrated Methodist preacher. (6 Mar 1833)

716. Mrs. Cordelia Scofield died 5 Mar 1833 in Penn Yan, Yates Co., the wife of Rufus Scofield. (6 Mar 1833)

717. Hon. Walter Cornell died 4 Mar 1833 at his lodging in Albany, Albany Co. A member of the Assembly from Washington Co. (13 Mar 1833)

* * * NOTE, MANY PAPERS MISSING * * *

718. William VanDeventer of Benton, Yates Co., and Elizabeth Durry, daughter of John Durry of Jerusalem, Yates Co., were married 17 Dec 1840 by Rev. Ovid Miner at Jerusalem. (1 Jan 1841)

719. Thomas Draper died recently in Salisbury, Eng. during a prize fight. The bout lasted over two hours, and he was beaten to his death, by a man named Skinner, no date given. (1 Jan 1841)

720. Hon. William Henry Harrison died 4 Apr 1841 at Washington, late president of the U.S. (13 Apr 1841)

721. Dr. E. Potter and Rebecca T. Secer, both of Benton, Yates Co., were married by Rev. Parker, no date given. (13 Apr 1841)

722. Charles E. Silsbe and M_?_ Dewey (illegible), both of Geneva, Ontario Co., were married 9 Apr 1841 by Rev. Ovid Miner in Penn Yan, Yates Co. (13 Apr 1841)

723. James E. __?__ey (illegible) and Elizabeth P. Fitzhugh, were married _?_ Mar 1841 (blurred) at Groveland, Livingston Co., no pastor named. (13 Apr 1841)

724. GUNPOWDER EXPLOSION; in Syracuse, Onondaga, Co. 27 Aug 1841. The gunpowder shop of Mr. Goings exploded, causing shock waves 20 miles away. Many buildings were blown apart and others burned to the ground. The Syracuse and Auburn Railroad Co. ran extra lines, to bring in extra physicians and surgeons as so many people were seriously injured.
Killed were;

Hugh T. Gibson	Ezra H. Hough
Thomas Betts	Elijah Jones
Zebina Dwight	William Conklin
Horace T. Goings	Loren L. Cheney
Joel Kohlhamer	Benjamin F. Johnson
Horatio N. Cheney	Elisha Ladd
George W. Burdick	Isaac Stanton
William B. Close	George Gorman
Charles A. Maffitt	John Durnford Jr.
Noah Hoyt	Hanson Maynard
Matthew Smelt	Charles Miller
James M. Barker	Charles Austin
Benjamin Baker	

Seriously wounded;

Elisha George	D.C. Leroy
Luther Gifford	S.W. Cadwell
David Myers	Z. Robinson
W. Deiorant	

(31 Aug 1841)

725. John Rodman age 57 yrs., died 27 Aug 1841 at his home in Benton, Yates Co. His death caused by injuries received, when his horse took fright and over turned his carriage 3 days ago. (31 Aug 1841)

726. William H. Watson and Sabrina Holmes, both of Penn Yan, Yates Co., were married 26 Aug 1841 at St. Marks Church in Penn Yan, no pastor named. (7 Sep 1841)

727. Charles Turner Risdon age 4 yrs. 20 days, died 15 Aug 1841 in Penn Yan, Yates Co., son of Charles and Jane E. Risdon. (14 Sep 1841)

728. John Spangler and Jane Conklin, both of Jerusalem, Yates Co., were married 18 Oct 1841 by Rev. James Richards in Jerusalem. (19 Oct 1841)

729. Mrs. Rebecca W. Wise age 28 yrs., died 15 Oct 1841 in Milo, Yates Co., wife of Zenus P. Wise. (19 Oct 1841)

730. Richard M. Smith and Elizabeth A. Beach, both of Penn Yan, Yates Co., were married 22 Aug 1841 by Rev. W.M. Davis in Penn Yan. (2 Nov 1841)

731. Josiah Strong age 83 yrs., died 14 Nov 1841 at the home of his son in Fayette, Seneca Co., a soldier of the Revolution. (30 Nov 1841)

732. Col. Charles Downing died 24 Oct 1841 at St. Augustine, FL. A native of VA., and early emigrant to FL., a delegate to Congress. (30 Nov 1841)

733. Hon. Thomas Buchanan died 3 Sep 1841 at Bassa, the Governor of Liberia. (7 Dec 1841)

734. Josiah H. Youngs and Abigail T. Rugg, both of Benton, Yates Co., were married 28 Nov 1841 by Rev. Robert Parker in Benton. (7 Dec 1841)

735. Stephen N. Davis and Hannah Briggs, both of Benton, Yates Co., were married 23 Dec 1841 by Rev. W.M. Parker in Benton. (28 Dec 1841)

736. Ephraim Sanford of Steuben Co., and Betsey Crawford of Seneca, Ontario Co., were married 28 Dec 1841 by Rev. William H. Delano in Seneca. (4 Jan 1841)

737. Samuel F. Beyea and Edna Bardeen, both of Branchport, Yates Co., were married 30 Dec 1841 by Elder William Frary in Branchport. (4 Jan 1842)

738. William Whipple and Luna Hanchet, both of Groton, Tompkins Co., were married 2 Jan 1842 by Rev. S.M. Plumb in Fleming, Cayuga Co. (18 Jan 1842)

739. Mrs. Taylor, drowned 13 Jan 1842 in the canal at Rochester, Monroe Co. (25 Jan 1842)

740. Hon. Nathan F. Dixon died 4 Feb 1842 at his lodging in Washington, a member of the bar, and Senator from Rhode Island. (8 Feb 1842)

741. Isaac Haight and Mrs. Lydia Arnet, both of Jerusalem, Yates Co., were married 8 Feb 1842 by Elder William Frary in Jerusalem. (15 Feb 1842)

742. Henry Adams Esq., drowned 11 Feb 1842 while fishing near his home in Litchfield, CT., Editor of the "Litchfield Enquirer". (22 Feb 1842)

743. Thomas Veazie and Julia Ann Yates, both of Dresden, Yates Co., were married 15 Feb 1842 by Rev. O. Montague in Dresden. (22 Feb 1842)

744. David Mills died 17 Feb 1842 in Benton, Yates Co., at an advanced age. (22 Feb 1842)

745. MARINE DISASTER; The bargue "William Fales" of Portland, ME., Lost in Wellis Bay during a storm on 22 Mar 1842, drowned were; Capt. William Thomas age 45 yrs., master, Martin Gilpatrick 1st. officer, Ephraim Littlefield 2nd officer, Thomas McLellan, John R. Plummer, William Dempsey, all of Portland, ME., and Capt. Perry of Warren, RI. (8 Mar 1842)

746. John G. Boyd committed suicide 17 Feb 1842 in Philadelphia, PA. (8 Mar 1842)

747. Hon. Lewis Williams died 23 Feb 1842 at Washington. A Congressman for 26 yrs., for the state of N.C. (8 Mar 1842)

748. Mrs. Sophia H. Sheldon age 29 Yrs., died 5 Mar 1842 in Penn Yan, Yates Co., wife of Eli Sheldon. (8 Mar 1842)

749. Mr. White was killed 16 Mar 1842 by his son Benjamin T. White, no town given. (22 Mar 1842)

750. Alexander H. Dey and Augusta Stewart, both of Penn Yan, Yates Co., were married in the Congregational Church at Penn Yan, by Rev. Ovid Miner. (22 Mar 1842)

751. The only child of Steward Hotchkiss, died 3 Mar 1842 at Nelson, Portage Co., Ohio. Then, Steward Hotchkiss was killed 7 Mar 1842, by the fall of a tree, when he went for firewood. (22 Mar 1842)

752. John Jones, murdered 13 Jun 1841 in Ithaca, Tompkins Co., by John Graham. * per the trial of Mr. Graham. (29 Mar 1842)

753. Tragedy hit the family of Eben Smith of Penn Yan, Yates Co., taking the lives of 3 daughters, Harriet Smith age 18 mos., died 13 Mar 1842, Catharine Smith age 5 yrs., died 19 Mar 1842, and her twin Caroline Smith age 5 yrs., died 24 Mar 1842. (29 Mar 1842)

754. William J. Fuller age 33 yrs., died 31 Mar 1842 at Rushville, Yates Co., a merchant of that place. (5 Apr 1842)

755. MORTALITY TABLE FOR THE TOWN OF BENTON 1841; furnished for the "Yates County Whig", by Samuel G. Gage Esq.

Jan..14	Eugene Clark age 1 yr.
" 20	Lucy Barden age 17 yrs.
" 22	Hannah Porter age 81 yrs.
" 26	Hon. Aaron Remer age 60 yrs.
Feb...4	Caroline J. Eddy age 1 yr.
" 4	Albert Maynard age 1 yr.
" 14	Jane Mitchell age 46 yrs.
Mar...1	Dea. David Holmes age 56 yrs.
" 2	Martha Cole age 75 yrs.
" 14	Jane Lapham age 9 yrs.
" 24	Huldah Baldwin age 25 yrs.
" 25	Nicholas Chrysler age 40 yrs.
" 25	Richard D. Finger age 1 yr.
Apr..18	Bethiah Bates age 76 yrs.
" 24	Caroline Canfield age 11 yrs.
May...6	Matthew Cole age 66 yrs.
" 8	William Sturges age 58 yrs.
" 11	Hiram T. McCorwell age 1 yr.
" 12	Fanny Hazen age 23 yrs.
Jun..13	Angeline Canfield age 7 yrs.
" 18	George W. Everest age 1 yr.
" 19	Elizabeth Speelman age 94 yrs.
" 28	Jane M. Veazie age 26 yrs.
" 28	Catherine Kelsey age 87 yrs.
" 28	Mary Briggs age 76 yrs.
Jul...7	Jacob Sutton age 73 yrs.
" 13	Martin Gage Esq. age 51 yrs.
" 21	Richard Veazie age 2 yrs.
Aug...8	John McLean age 93 yrs.
" 11	Peleg Hoard age 66 yrs.
" 26	Jerusha Benjamin age 54 yrs.
" 28	John Rudman age 57 yrs.
" 31	Phebe Ann Ellis age 2 yrs.
Sep...3	Sarah McLean age 88 yrs.
" 7	Dennis Tubbs age 23 yrs.
" 8	John Teter age 2 yrs.
" 28	Ezekial B. Holmes age 29 yrs.
Oct...2	Alfred T. Jackson age 1 yr.

Oct...4 Moses St. John age 66 yrs.
Nov..10 Editha Belt age 73 yrs.
" 22 Ruth Hall age 22 yrs.
Dec...5 Esther Nichols age 42 yrs.
" 9 Phebe Janes age 17 yrs.
" 23 _ ? _ Curby age 4 yrs.
Mrs. Baker, a colored woman aged over 100 yrs., no date given. (5 Apr 1842)

756. Hon. Jesse L. Holman died a few days past, a U.S. District Judge in Indiana, no date or town given. (12 Apr 1842)

757. Seth B. Briggs and Mary Jane Davis, both of Benton, Yates Co., were married 7 Apr 1842 by Rev. O. Montague in Benton. (12 Apr 1842)

758. Sarah L. Waite age 16 yrs., died 30 Mar 1842 in Jerusalem, Yates Co., daughter of B. and Elizabeth Waite. (12 Apr 1842)

759. A boat crew of the steam frigate "Missouri" lost their lives 17 Apr 1842 on the Potomac River near Washington. The ship having deviated from the channel, grounded on a shoal. The boat referred to, having cut with an anchor and chain cable to get the ship off. The anchor got overboard, carrying with it the chain cable, which running out, carried overboard every person in the boat, dead are;

Lieut. John Borden
Iram Lord
Joseph Webster
John Murphy
F.A. Gill
James May
R. Ehricks
E. Fellows
Peter Hanson
T. Willis
James White
Charles Gibbs
Joseph Nicholls
Simon Spero
C. Simpson
B. Dimmock

(19 Apr 1842)

760. Hon. Joseph Lawrence died 24 Apr 1842 at his lodging in Washington, a member of the House from PA. (26 Apr 1842)

761. Roswell Jones of Milo, Yates Co., late of Cortlandville, Cortland Co., and Phebe Ann Bell of Benton, Yates Co., were married 26 Apr 1842 by Rev. O. Montague in Benton. (3 May 1842)

762. William K. Ackley of Milo, Yates Co., and Emeline Barrett of Jerusalem, Yates Co., were married 28 Apr 1842 by Rev. O. Montague in Penn Yan, Yates Co. (3 May 1842)

763. James Moffitt and Mrs. Clarissa Curtis, both of Jerusalem, Yates Co., were married 17 Apr 1842 by Rev. Decker in Jerusalem. (3 May 1842)

764. Mrs. Louisa H. Prosser age 24 yrs., died 4 May 1842 in Penn Yan, Yates Co., the wife of David B. Prosser. (10 May 1842)

765. Abraham H. Bennett Esq. age 46 yrs., died 12 May 1842 in Penn Yan, Yates Co. He published the first Penn Yan newspaper, the "Penn Yan Herald", then the "Penn Yan Democrat", and served as county clerk and postmaster. (17 May 1842)

766. John Graham, executed 12 May 1842 at Ithaca, Tompkins Co., for the murder of John Jones. (17 May 1842)

767. Daniel Conger of Penn Yan, Yates Co., and Caroline Darling of Peruville, Tompkins Co., were married 12 May 1842 by Rev. Scovel in Peruville. (17 May 1842)

768. Nathan C. Cass and Marilla Stevens, both of Groton, Tompkins Co., were married 11 May 1842 by Rev. J. Backus in Groton. (17 May 1842)

769. Nathan Brand and Martha B. Andridge, formerly of Penn Yan, Yates Co., were married 21 Apr 1842 in Scipio, Michigan, by Rev. Paige. (17 May 1842)

770. John D. Kritzer age 47 yrs., died 9 May 1842 at his home in Benton, Yates Co. (17 May 1842)

771. John Watson and Nancy Wheeler, both of Penn Yan, Yates Co., were married 21 May 1842 by Rev. O. Montague in Penn Yan. (24 May 1842)

772. Timothy Brigden and Cornelia D. Hickox, both of Penn Yan, Yates Co., were married 30 May 1842 at the Congregational Church in Penn Yan, by Rev. Ovid Miner. (31 May 1842)

773. Lewis P. Holmes and Helen M. Gage, eldest daughter of Samuel G. Gage Esq., both of Benton Yates Co., were married 26 May 1842 by Rev. William H. Delano in Benton. (7 Jun 1842)

774. Uriah Coffin and Catharine Fisher, both of Bellona, Yates Co., were married 16 Jun 1842 by Rev. Eddy in Benton, Yates Co. (21 Jun 1842)

775. Margaret Malin died 23 Jun 1842 in Jerusalem, Yates Co., at an advanced age. (28 Jun 1842)

776. Hon. Samuel L. Southward died 3 Jul 1842 at Fredericksberg, VA., a Senator from New Jersey. (5 Jul 1842)

777. Mrs. Sarah Randolph age 32 yrs., died 22 Jun 1842 in Potter, Yates Co., wife of Selah Randolph, daughter of Ichabod Buel of Potter. (5 Jul 1842)

778. Morris F. Herrington age 23 yrs., died 27 Jun 1842 in Potter, Yates Co. (5 Jul 1842)

779. Mrs. Hannah Davidson a widow, age 70 yrs., died 30 Jun 1842 at her residence in Jerusalem, Yates Co. (12 Jul 1842)

780. Joseph D. Fulton, killed 4 Jul 1842 at Geneva, Ontario Co., during the Independence Day fireworks celebration. Mr. Fulton was standing near a box of fireworks, which was somehow ignited by a spark. When box exploded and Mr. Fulton was so badly burned, he died within a few hours. (12 Jul 1842)

781. Capt. Joseph L. Savage and Lucy Jane Waring, both of Milo, Yates Co., were married 11 Jul 1842 by J. Holmes Esq. in Barrington, Yates Co. (19 Jul 1842)

782. Mrs. Susan Cole age 30 yrs., died 28 Jul 1842 at Benton, Yates Co. The wife of Myron Cole, a merchant in Benton, and daughter of Morris F. Sheppard Esq. of Penn Yan, Yates Co. (2 Aug 1842)

783. Mrs. Lovina Phelps age 71 yrs., died 29 Jul 1842 in Benton, Yates Co. (2 Aug 1842)

784. Mrs. Harriet S. Dusinbury age 24 yrs., died 18 Jul 1842 in Benton, Yates Co., wife of Lancaster Dusinbury. (2 Aug 1842)

785. Briggs Belknap age 60 yrs., died 2 Aug 1842 in Benton, Yates Co. (9 Aug 1842)

786. Charles C. Casner age 6 yrs., died 2 Aug 1842 in Penn Yan, Yates Co., son of Ezekial Casner Esq. (9 Aug 1842)

787. John Spaulding died 7 Aug 1842 in Jerusalem, Yates Co., a farmer there. (9 Aug 1842)

788. William Stewart died 9 Aug 1842 in Milo, Yates Co., at an advanced age. (16 Aug 1842)

789. A.A. Woodworth and Margaret Worden were married 30 Aug 1842 by Rev. James Richards in Penn Yan, Yates Co. (6 Sep 1842)

790. Josephus Barrett and Amelia Danes, both of Jerusalem, Yates Co., were married 30 Aug 1842 by Rev. O. Montague in Jerusalem. (6 Sep 1842)

791. Mrs. Rebakah Cook age 94 yrs., died 22 Aug 1842 at Starkey, Yates Co. The widow of Major Daniel Cook, formerly of Mendham, NJ. She survived her husband by 50 yrs. (6 Sep 1842)

792. James Finn age 39 yrs., died 31 Aug 1842 in Milo, Yates Co. (6 Sep 1842)

793. George P. Monell of Carbondale, PA., and Henrietta J. Wagener, youngest daughter of Abraham Wagener Esq. of Penn Yan, Yates Co., were married 13 Sep 1842 by Rev. B.W. Stone in Penn Yan. (20 Sep 1842)

794. J.C. Minor a printer, formerly of Auburn, Cayuga Co., and Harriet Newton, daughter of Col. A. Newton of Rochester, Monroe Co., were married 12 Sep 1842 by Rev. Shaw in Rochester. (20 Sep 1842)

795. Martin S. Roat, accidently killed 24 Sep 1842 on his farm in Jerusalem, Yates Co., while pitching off a load of hay. The oxen started suddenly with the wagon, and in an effort to stop them, as he jumped off the wagon, one of the pitch fork tines, entered his breast, piercing his heart. He leaves a wife and 5 children. (27 Sep 1842)

796. Richard Jones age about 50 yrs., found drowned 2 Oct 1842 in Penn Yan, Yates Co. (4 Oct 1842)

797. Mrs. Mary J. Whitman age 35 yrs. 9 mos., died 29 Sep 1842 at Rushville, Yates Co., wife of Samuel Whitman. (4 Oct 1842)

798. John Finger age 60 yrs., died 1 Oct 1842 in Benton, Yates Co. (4 Oct 1842)

799. John Miller and Mary E. Davis were married 5 Oct 1842 by Rev. Hibbard in Jerusalem, Yates Co. (11 Oct 1842)

800. Archibald Millspaugh and Sarah Drew, both of Milo, Yates Co., were married 5 Oct 1842 by Rev. O. Montaque in Milo. (11 Oct 1842)

801. Peter Sutpin of Hunterdon, NJ., and Mary Schenck of Jerusalem, Yates Co., NY., were married 5 Oct 1842 by Rev. James Richards in Jerusalem. (18 Oct 1842)

802. John Gardner of Penn Yan, Yates Co., and Sarah Malin of Jerusalem, Yates Co., were married 11 Oct 1842 by Rev. James Richards in Jerusalem. (18 Oct 1842)

803. Bartlett Nye a merchant, and Laura M. Moore, daughter of N. Moore Esq., both of Champlin, Clinton Co., were married 31 Oct 1842 by Rev. Ovid Miner in Penn Yan, Yates Co. (1 Nov 1842)

804. Herman H. Cole a merchant, and Emeline Johnson, daughter of the late Col. John Johnson of Ithaca, Tompkins Co., were married 9 Oct 1842 by Levi Patchen Esq. in Benton, Yates Co. (1 Nov 1842)

805. Daniel Marsh Jr. a merchant, and Sophia H. Peck, both of Penn Yan, Yates Co., were married 17 Nov 1842 by Rev. Miner in Penn Yan. (22 Nov 1842)

806. Stephen Gilbert and Margaret Jane Hallett, both of Penn Yan Yates Co., were married 17 Nov 1842 by Rev. Richards in Penn Yan. (22 Nov 1842)

807. Castle Dains age 96 yrs., died 11 Nov 1842 in Jerusalem, Yates Co. One of the first settlers of Milo, Yates Co., he moved there in 1788 or 1789, a soldier of the Revolution. (22 Nov 1842)

808. Mary Smith age 17 yrs., died 24 Nov 1842 in Penn Yan, Yates Co. The eldest daughter of Eben Smith Esq., who lost 3 daughters, but a few months past. (29 Nov 1842)

809. David Hathaway age 76 yrs., died 20 Nov 1842 at Starkey, Yates Co. (29 Nov 1842)

810. Mrs. Phebe Ann Hathaway age 22 yrs. 27 days, died 21 Nov 1842 in Italy, Yates Co., the wife of Frederick S. Hathaway. (29 Nov 1842)

811. John McIntyre of Milo, Yates Co., and Eliza Ellis of Barrington, Yates Co., were married 15 Dec 1842 by Rev. Spencer at Barrington. (20 Dec 1842)

812. Edward Hoogland Esq. and Eliza Huson, eldest daughter of Dr. Richard Huson, both of Dundee, Yates Co., were married 24 Dec 1842 by Rev. Seth Marvin in Dundee. (27 Dec 1842)

813. Joseph Church of Benton, Yates Co., and Betsey Sherwood of Potter, Yates Co., were married 11 Dec 1842 by Rev. Matison in Bellona, Yates Co. (27 Dec 1842)

814. Fitch Shaw of Gorham, Ontario Co., and Mari Kinney of Benton, Yates Co., were married 15 Dec 1842, no pastor or town given. (27 Dec 1842)

815. Abel Briggs age 60 yrs., died 21 Dec 1842 in Potter, Yates Co. (27 Dec 1842)

816. Joshua Lee age 60 yrs., died 29 Dec 1842 at his home in Milo, Yates Co. He lived in this part of the country for over 40 yrs., serving in the Legislature, and Congress. (3 Jan 1843)

817. Rowland Champlin died 10 Jan 1843 in Milo, Yates Co., at an advanced age, a farmer there. (17 Jan 1843)

818. Orin Robinson of Warsaw, Wyoming Co., and Eliza Ann Bellows, daughter of Peter Bellows, were married 19 Jan 1843 by Rev. James Richards in Penn Yan, Yates Co. (24 Jan 1843)

819. Malin W. Hobart of Athens, Greene Co., and Eunice L. Pierce of Leonidas, St. Joseph Co., MI., were married 3 Jan 1843 by Rev. William Hobart at Leonidas. (24 Jan 1843)

820. John Hallowell of Milo, Yates Co., and Mercy Sprague of Benton, Yates Co., were married 23 Jan 1843 by Elder Southerland in Benton. (31 Jan 1843)

821. Benjamin Watroube age 82 yrs., died 21 Jan 1843 at Pulteney, Steuben Co., a soldier of the Revolution. (31 Jan 1843)

822. Elijah Malin age 9 yrs., died 26 Jan 1843 in Jerusalem, Yates Co., of scarlet fever, son of George W. Malin Esq. (31 Jan 1843)

823. Adam Sawyer Esq. of Starkey, Yates Co., and Elizabeth Masten of Penn Yan, Yates Co., were married 31 Jan 1843 by Rev. James Richards in Penn Yan. (7 Feb 1843)

824. James Stout and Sarah Ann Comstock, both of Potter, Yates Co., were married 29 Jan 1843 by Rev. Calvin Coats in Rushville, Yates Co. (7 Feb 1843)

825. Mrs. Rachel L. Holmes died 10 Feb 1843 in Benton, Yates Co., widow of Ezekial B. Holmes. (14 Feb 1843)

826. Mrs. Calista Booth died 11 Feb 1843 at Branchport, Yates Co. Wife of Spencer Booth, a merchant of Branchport, leaving 5 children. (14 Feb 1843)

827. Silas Rushmore and Hannah Baker, both of Barrington, Yates Co., were married 16 Feb 1843 by Rev. Horace Spencer in Barrington. (21 Feb 1843)

828. Harriet Dean age 11 yrs., died of scarlet fever at the home of A. Bridgewater, daughter of Freeman Dean, no town or date given. (21 Feb 1843)

829. Clement C. Bennett of the "Penn Yan Democrat", and Margaret Goundry of Dresden, Yates Co., were married 21 Feb 1843 by Rev. B.W. Stone at St. Mark's Church in Penn Yan, Yates Co. (28 Feb 1843)

830. Mrs. Phila Robinson died _1 Feb 1843 (blurred) at Potter, Yates Co., wife of James Robinson Esq. (28 Feb 1843)

831. Capt. Joseph Owens shot and killed by his son, at their home near Annapolis, MD., no date given. (28 Feb 1843)

832. Joel Burtch age 30 yrs., died 21 Feb 1843 at his home in Jerusalem, Yates Co. (14 Mar 1843)

833. Samuel Keeler and Delight Gallery, both of Jerusalem, Yates Co., were married 8 Mar 1843 by John Gallet Esq. in Jerusalem. (21 Mar 1843)

834. George Wilber of Penn Yan, Yates Co., and Susan Charlesworth of Wheeler, Steuben Co., were married 8 Mar 1843 by Rev. Schultz at Wheeler. (21 Mar 1843)

835. Hiram Vescelius age 24 yrs., died 25 Mar 1843 in Dresden, Yates Co. (28 Mar 1843)

836. Oscar Knapp of Saunder Hill ? (blurred) and Ariette Terry, youngest daughter of the widow Mrs. Betsey Terry of Aurelius, Cayuga Co., were married 21 Mar 1843 by Elder Barrell at Aurelis. (28 Mar 1843)

837. John Vaughn and Mariah Bates, both of Potter, Yates Co., were married 19 Mar 1843 by Rev. Gillman in Rushville, Yates Co. (28 Mar 1843)

838. P.P. Wells committed suicide 11 Mar 1843 at Honeoye, Ontario Co. (4 Apr 1843)

839. Sylvester Pew and Electa Fox, daughter of William Fox Esq., were married 7 Apr 1843 by Rev. Pinney at Jerusalem, Yates Co. (18 Apr 1843)

840. Cyrus W. Weed age 47 yrs., died 7 Apr 1843 in Jerusalem, Yates Co., of consumption. (18 Apr 1843)

841. Elias VanCourt and Elizabeth N. Hopkins, daughter of Jeremiah Hopkins of Barrington, Yates Co., were married 19 Apr 1843 by Rev. Sunderlin at Barrington. (25 Apr 1843)

842. Dresden McCarty of Dresden, Yates Co., and Eunice Olney of Kellogsville, Cayuga Co., were married 27 Apr 1843 by Rev. Moore at Kellogsville. (2 May 1843)

843. Joseph Stow Jr. and Mary Robinson Bouns, daughter of Peter Bouns, were married 29 Apr 1843 by Rev. Irving in Geneva, Ontario Co. (2 May 1843)

844. Alanson M. Clark and Sarah Comstock, both of Fleming, Cayuga Co., were married 20 Apr 1843 by Rev. Plumb in Fleming. (2 May 1843)

845. Theron G. Tuthill age 48 yrs. 6 mos., died 19 Apr 1843. His funeral held at Starkey, Yates co., on the 21st. (2 May 1843)

846. Daniel Comstock age 37 yrs., died 16 Apr 1843 at Fleming, Cayuga Co. (2 May 1843)

847. William Roy age 65 yrs., died 26 Apr 1843 at his home in Benton, Yates Co. (2 May 1843)

848. Benjamin White, executed at Batavia, Genesee Co., last week, for the murder of his father, no date given. (9 May 1843)

849. Charles Bellis of Starkey, Yates Co., and Sophronia Cowing of Jerusalem, Yates Co., were married 4 May 1843 by Rev. Wheeler in Jerusalem. (9 May 1843)

850. Mortimer J. Smith, late Editor of the "Seneca

Falls Democrat", and Mary Ogden, daughter of the Hon. Mordecai Ogden, were married 5 May 1843 by Rev. Fowler at Elmira, Chemung Co. (9 May 1843)

851. Hon. Hodijah Baylie age 87 yrs., died 25 Apr 1843 at Dayton, MA. Educated at Harvard, in 1777 he joined the Army of the Revolution, served as an aid to Gen. Lincoln and Gen. Washington, present at both the surrender at Saratoga and Yorktown. For many years a judge of the Probate Court of Bristol, MA. (16 May 1843)

852. Rev. Leonard McClasham of Warwick, Canada, and Margaret Oliphant, daughter of the late John Oliphant of Auburn, Cayuga Co., were married 16 May 1843 by Rev. Hopkins in Auburn. (23 May 1843)

853. Hon. William Ruger died recently at Watertown, Jefferson Co., a Senator of the 5th District. (30 May 1843)

854. Dr. Barnet N. Wisner age 24 yrs., died 27 May 1843 at Penn Yan, Yates Co. (30 May 1843)

855. Henry A. Hawes a printer, and Elizabeth Stone, both of Auburn, Cayuga Co., were married 18 May 1843 by Rev. Montgomery in Auburn. (6 Jun 1843)

856. William N. Cole a printer in Lyons, Wayne Co., and Emily Smith, daughter of the late Col. Ovid Smith of New York city, were married 15 May 1843 by Rev. Cheever in New York. (6 Jun 1843)

857. F. Cowbert a printer, and Mrs. Sarah S. Wolcott, were married 14 May 1843 by Rev. Passet in Rochester, Monroe Co. (6 Jun 1843)

858. Mrs. Eliza Cheever age 39 yrs., died 30 May 1843 at Starkey, Yates Co., wife of Benjamin Cheever. (6 Jun 1843)

859. Noah Webster age 85 yrs., died 28 May 1843 at New Haven, CT. (6 Jun 1843)

860. A. McFarren and Mary Huner were married 1 Jun 1843 by Rev. Charles Eddy in Bellona, Yates Co., at the Presbyterian Church. (13 Jun 1843)

861. Philo P. Rounds and Harriet A. Pacey were married 5 Jun 1843 by Rev. Charles Eddy at the home of E. Deyo in Bellona, Yates Co. (13 Jun 1843)

862. Asahel H. Savage, a merchant at Benton, Yates Co., and Olivia L. Dorman of Penn Yan, Yates Co., were married 14 Jun 1843 by Rev. G.W. Townsend in Penn Yan. (20 Jun 1843)

863. Augustus Winegof of Kingston, Ulster Co., and Anna Whiting of Penn Yan, Yates Co., were married 15 Jun 1843 by Rev. B.W. Stone at St. Mark's Church in Penn Yan. (20 Jun 1843)

864. Major Gen. A.F. Whitaker and Louise P. Torrance, daughter of Richard Torrance Esq., were married 20 Jun 1843 by Rev. Appleton at East Avon, Livingston Co. (4 Jun 1843)

865. Horace Kingsley and Mrs. Mary Jones, both of Milo, Yates Co., were married 4 Jul 1843 by Robert Buel Esq. in Milo. (11 Jul 1843)

866. George D.W. Griswold age 3 yrs., died 11 Jun 1843 at Benton, Yates Co. (11 Jul 1843)

867. Needham Maynard, born 1746 at Farmington, MA. A veteran of the Revolution, now a resident of this state, and father of our late Whig Representative in Congress from the Seneca and Wayne District.
* a brief biography printed. (11 Jul 1843)

868. Sylvester Barden and Jane S. Hedges, both of Barrington, Yates Co., were married 9 Jul 1843 by Rev. Horace Spencer in Barrington. (18 Jul 1843)

869. Jane Milligan age 15 yrs., died recently in Philadelphia, PA. She entered a store to inquire the cost of lemons, when seized with a coughing fit and died within ten minutes. Her mother, unaware of her daughters distress, was waiting outside the door for her return, no date given. (18 Jul 1843)

870. Mrs. Abigail Town gave birth to triplets on 13 Jun 1843 at Ontario, Wayne Co., NY. (25 Jul 1843)

871. Judge Joseph Eve died 16 Jun 1843 from consumption at Galveston, Texas, of the American Charge to Texas. (25 Jul 1843)

872. Garnelin Chase age 2 yrs. 2 mos., died 15 Jul 1843 at Geneva, Ontario Co., only daughter of Dr. Robert and Hannah Chase of St. Louis, Mo. (25 Jul 1843)

873. John Griswold age 1 yr., died 28 Jul 1843 at

Benton, Yates Co., * note this is clearly the date given, even though the paper is dated on the 25th. (25 Jul 1843)

874. Jacob Conklin and Mrs. Hannah Anderson, both of Jerusalem, Yates Co., were married 18 Jul 1843 by Rev. Horace Spencer at Barrington, Yates Co. (1 Aug 1843)

875. Rev. James Richards Sr. age 75 yrs., died 2 Aug 1843 in Auburn, Cayuga Co. A professor of Christian Theology at the Theological Seminary. (8 Aug 1843)

876. John Owen died in Corsa Co., AL. He had killed a man in the Pinetimber Precinct. A number of persons were in pursuit of Owen, who refused to be taken alive. He was eventually killed by his own knife, while being wrestled to the ground, no date given. (15 Aug 1843)

877. Henry Bowers of Manchester, Washtenaw Co, MI. and Margaret Chase of Benton, Yates Co., were married 8 Aug 1843 by Rev. E.G. Townsend at Benton. (22 Aug 1843)

878. Hannah R. Davis age 26 yrs., died 18 Aug 1843 in Benton, Yates Co. The wife of Stephen N. Davis, and only daughter of the late Peleg Briggs Esq. (22 Aug 1843)

879. Hannah Beard age 33 yrs., died 26 Aug 1843 in Milo, Yates Co., wife of Allen Beard of Shiawassee Co., Michigan. (29 Aug 1843)

880. Rev. Harvy age 107 yrs., a Baptist preacher of Frankfort, Herkimer Co., exhorts religious meetings to which he walks, a mile and a half distant. He reads fine print without glasses, and remembers events of 90 yrs. ago as well as 90 days. (5 Sep 1843)

881. Robert Kenady, killed last week in Hector, Schyler Co., by a man named Swick, no date given. (5 Sep 1843)

882. Theodore B. Hamilton, an Attorney at Rochester, Monroe Co., and Emily Welles, eldest daughter of Hon. Henry Welles of Penn Yan, Yates Co., were married 29 Aug 1843 by Rev. James Richards Jr. in Penn Yan. (5 Sep 1843)

883. David D. Prosser, a Councelor at Law, and Mrs. Maria Root, both of Penn Yan, Yates Co., were married 31 Aug 1843 by Rev. Ovid Miner in Penn Yan. (5 Sep 1843)

884. James Miller formerly of Steuben Co., and Hannah Benedict of Jerusalem, Yates Co., were married 32 Aug 1843 by Elder Lamb in Jerusalem. (5 Sep 1843)

885. Saunders Crane of Penn Yan, Yates Co., and Caroline Olmstead of Attica, Wyoming Co., were married 4 Sep 1843 by Rev. Preston in Attica. (5 Sep 1843)

886. Sarah J. Turner age 18 yrs., died 28 Aug 1843 in Owego, Tioga Co. The daughter of the late David Turner, her funeral from the Presbyterian church. (5 Sep 1843)

887. Hon. Lewis Summers died 9 Sep 1843 at the White Sulphar Springs. (12 Sep 1843)

888. Miles Benham of Penn Yan, Yates Co., and Mrs. Cynthia Maro of Elbridge, Onondaga, Co., were married 3 Sep 1843 by Rev. Pomeroy at East Cayaga, Cayuga Co. (12 Sep 1843)

889. Eli Sheldon Esq. and Sarah F. Sheppard, daughter of M.F. Sheppard Esq., both of Penn Yan, Yates Co., were married 14 Sep 1843 by Rev. Ovid Miner in Penn Yan. (19 Sep 1843)

890. Samuel L. Sheldon and Hannah Burr, both of Penn Yan, Yates Co., were married 31 Aug 1843 by Rev. Day at Ensfield, Tompkins Co. (19 Sep 1843)

891. Stephen Baker and Mary Ann Vanzant, both of Benton, Yates Co., were married 16 Sep 1843 by Levi Patchen Esq. in Benton. (19 Sep 1843)

892. Harrison Gregory of Bethany, PA., and Isabella Sloan of Benton, Yates Co., were married 19 Sep 1843 at the home of A. Woodworth in Benton, by Rev. James Richards. (26 Sep 1843)

893. W.G. Breck, a merchant of the firm "Breck and Co." in Vienna, Ontario, Co., and Mary VanDeventer of Benton, Yates Co., were married 20 Sep 1843 by Rev. James Richards in Benton. (26 Sep 1843)

894. George Lord and Mary Ann Bishop, both of Barrington, Yates Co., were married 29 Sep 1843 by Rev. Bracely in Barrington. (3 Oct 1843)

895. Henry Clark age 60 or 69 yrs. (blurred), died 30 Sep 1843 in Penn Yan, Yates Co. (30 Oct 1843)

896. Hon. James Vanderpoel died 3 Oct 1843 at his home in Albany, Albany Co., a Circuit Judge for this state. (10 Oct 1843)

897. Thomas Pier Turner age 9 mos., died 18 Sep 1843 at Dundee, Yates Co., only child of Y.E. and M. Pier Turner. (10 Oct 1843)

898. Mrs. Susan Snook age 26 yrs., died 5 Aug 1843 at Barrington, Yates Co., wife of James Snook, formerly of New Jersey. (10 Oct 1843)

899. Oliver Youngs of Benton, Yates Co., and Elizabeth Scott of Seneca, Ontario Co., were married 5 Oct 1843 by Elder Pease in Seneca. (17 Oct 1843)

900. Mrs. Bacon age 50 yrs., killed 15 Oct 1843 at Middletown, CT. Mr. Bacon and the children had gone to church. Upon their arrival home, they found her murdered, and their home in shambles, about eighty dollars had been stolen. (17 Oct 1843)

901. Daniel Hedges of Milo, Yates Co., and Elizabeth Emory of Seneca, Ontario Co., were married 17 Oct 1843 by Elder Pease in Seneca. (24 Oct 1843)

902. Hon. Lewis F. Linn died 3 Oct 1843 at St. Genevieve, MO., a Senator from that State. (31 Oct 1843)

903. Nelson Aubrey and Eliza Little were married 28 Sep 1843 at Palmyra, MO., by Squire J.F. Mahan. The couple plans to live in Illinois. (31 Oct 1843)

904. James Travis of Milo, Yates Co., and Caroline Stamp of Benton, Yates Co., were married 26 Oct 1843 by J. McCain Esq. in Barrington, Yates Co. (31 Oct 1843)

905. W.M. Patchen and Lydia M. Hopkins, both of Penn Yan, Yates Co., were married 24 Oct 1843 by Rev. Abner Chase in Penn Yan. (31 Oct 1843)

906. John Breed Dwight, a tutor at Yale University, died from wounds inflicted by one of his students, no date given. (7 Nov 1843)

907. Orem Curtis of Lexington, Illinois and Pheobe A. Moore of Jerusalem, Yates Co., were married 30 Sep 1843 by Rev. Simon Southerland in Jerusalem. (7 Nov 1843)

908. D.W.C. Stamford of Penn Yan, Yates Co., and Rosamond _?_elman (illegible) of Benton, Yates Co., were married 1 Nov 1843 by Rev. Braine in Benton. (7 Nov 1843)

909. John Lightfoot of Canandaigua, Ontario Co., and Jane Gravil of Yorkshire, Eng., were married 1 Nov 1843 by Rev. James Richards in Penn Yan, Yates Co. (7 Nov 1843)

910. Bill Johnson died in the New Purchase, County of Makaska, directly west of Washington. A hero of the Thousand Isles, during the rebellion in Canada. He and his daughter Kate Johnson, left Marion, Linn Co., Iowa, supposedly bound for Oregon, after he had swindled a number of people, out of a considerable amount of goods and money. He settled instead, in the New Purchase, where Kate met a man by the name of Mr. Peck. Her father disapproved of a marriage, so the couple eloped, and moved to Jefferson Co. Johnson later found out their residence, and went after his daughter, confronting Peck with a gun, and took his daughter home. Peck followed, and through the chinking of Johnson's cabin, leveled his rifle, and shot Johnson through the heart. Peck was arrested and awaits trial in the Washington Co. jail. no date given. (7 Nov 1843)

911. William H. Reddy age 3 yrs., died 5 Nov 1843 in Penn Yan, Yates Co. (7 Nov 1843)

912. John Brigden age 8 mos., died 9 Nov 1843 in Penn Yan, Yates Co., son of Timothy and Cornelia Brigden. (14 Nov 1843)

913. Mrs. Olivia Savage age 21 yrs., died 13 Sep 1843 at her home in Benton, Yates Co. The wife of Ashael H. Savage, daughter of the late Joel Dorman Esq. and Olivia Dorman of Penn Yan, Yates Co., she was married but 3 mos. (14 Nov 1843)

914. The death of Hon. Edward P. Livingston, was announced last Sat., in the "NY Commercial". A

Senator of this state nearly 40 years ago, and Lt. Governor in 1830, no date given. (14 Nov 1843)

915. Isaac Penfield of Catskill, Greene Co., age 89 yrs., showed his patriotic voting spirit last Tuesday, when he walked nearly two miles, to cast his vote. He returned again by foot, through a snow storm. Mr. Penfield is a genuine "Whig". (21 Nov 1843)

916. After an extensive courtship of one hour, Joseph Barto of Fairhaven, VT., and Filena Gilmore of Whitehall, Washington Co., were married 9 Nov 1843 by Rev. Webster in Whitehall. (21 Nov 1843)

917. Mr. Doyle, a saddler of Little Rock, Arkansas, killed his wife 20 Oct 1843 by pouring a boiling pot of rosin and grease over her head. The poor woman's screams were heard half a mile away. The husband escaped, but was pursued, and later found laying dead with his face in a little riverlet, his throat cut from ear to ear, and a bloody jack knife clasped tightly in his hand. (28 Nov 1843)

918. Peter Masten Esq. of Penn Yan, Yates Co., and Jane Bentley of Clear Creek, were married 2 Oct 1843 by I.H. Clary Esq. in Elliottville, Cattaraugus Co. (28 Nov 1843)

919. Alexander Bixby age 20 yrs., died 24 Nov 1843 in Penn Yan, Yates Co. From Ohio, he was buried among strangers. He had been here but a few weeks, with his parents unaware of his death. (28 Nov 1843)

920. Col. John Trumball age 87 yrs., died in New York city. (5 Dec 1843)

921. Mrs. Sarah Clausen age 22 yrs., died 1 Dec 1843 in Penn Yan, Yates Co., of consumption, wife of William Clausen. (5 Dec 1843)

922. William S. Briggs and Elizabeth S. Dorman, both of Penn Yan, Yates Co., were married 11 Dec 1843 by Rev. Ovid Miner in Penn Yan. (12 Dec 1843)
j

923. Capt. Fay of Rochester, Monroe Co., a captain of a canal boat, drowned 6 Dec 1843 while breaking ice from in front of his boat. He slipped into the canal, the boat passed over his body, which was badly bruised, and before it could be recovered, life was extinct. (12 Dec 1843)

924. Lewis File died 24 Dec 1843. Employed in the glue factory at Lansingburgh, Rensselaer Co. He fell head first into a large cauldron of boiling glue. He was pulled out immediately, but burned so badly, he died within a few hours. (26 Dec 1843)

925. Samuel Rail of Benton, Yates Co. and Catherine Titsworth of Milo, Yates Co., were married 24 Dec 1843 by Rev. O. Montaque at Milo. (26 Dec 1843)

926. Friend James Brown and Maria Clark were married by John A. Gallett Esq. in Jerusalem, Yates Co., no date given. (2 Jan 1844)

927. Ephraim Baker and Mrs. Mary Haytt were married 28 Dec 1843 by Robert Buel Esq. in Penn Yan, Yates Co. (2 Jan 1844)

928. William Purchase age 14 yrs., left home last April. Any person knowing his whereabouts, please write, or contact Eratus Purchase, Phelps, Ontario Co. (9 Jan 1844)

929. Ambrose Stark of Penn Yan, Yates Co., and Harriet A. Brown of Jerusalem, Yates Co., were married 20 Dec 1843 by Rev. Willson at Hammondsport, Steuben Co. (9 Jan 1844)

930. Seth Haight, proprietor of the "Cortland Democrat", and Calista Merrick, daughter of Danforth Merrick Esq., both of Cortland, Cortland Co., were married 20 Dec 1843 by Rev. Whitecomb in Cortland. (9 Jan 1844)

931. Leander Spooner and Mary Ann Nichols, both of Milo, Yates Co., were married 1 Jan 1844 by Rev. Alonzo Sunderline at Milo. (9 Jan 1844)

932. Lorenzo Botsford and Betsy Wheeler were married 28 Dec 1843 by Rev. William Wheeler in Potter, Yates Co. (9 Jan 1844)

933. Robert N. McFarren and Harriet A. Bates, both of Benton, Yates Co., were married 28 Dec 1843 by Rev. Eddy in Benton. (9 Jan 1844)

934. Charles A. Bogert and Susan Remer, both of Dresden, Yates Co., were married 27 Dec 1843 by James Young Esq. in Dresden. (9 Jan 1844)

935. John Wentworth, the tallest member of Congress, is a printer, 7 ft. 2 inches tall. (16 Jan 1844)

936. Amassa Sprague Esq. of Cranston, RI., murdered 31 Dec 1843, of the firm "Messrs. A & W. Sprague". His partner is Hon. William Sprague, a Senator. Two Irish brothers, Nicholas Gordon and John Gordon, have been arrested. (16 Jan 1844)

937. Henry Thompson of Bradford, Steuben Co., and Mrs. Rachel Flemming of Barrington, Yates Co., were married 7 Jan 1844 by P.A. Crosby Esq. in Barrington. (16 Jan 1844)

938. The steamboat "Sheppardess" out of Cincinnati, Ohio, under Capt. A. Howell, struck a snag in the Mississippi River, about 3 miles below St. Louis, tearing several planks from the boat. The accident occurred 31 Dec 1843, known dead include; 3 children of Levi Craddock of Davidson Co. TN., Mrs. Green and her 3 children of Davidson Co. TN., a son and daughter of Mr. Snell of Louisville, KY., Mr. Wright and 2 of his children of Mecklenburg Co., VA., and Capt. Howell of Covington, KY., who leaves a wife and 11 children. Several passengers showed an utter disregard for their own safety to secure that of others. Special thanks and honors go to; Robert Bullock of Maysville, KY., Dr. Massy of St. Charles, MO., and Mr. Irwin of Pittsburg, PA. (23 Jan 1844)

939. Mr. Lanchner age 29 yrs., committed suicide 22 Jan 1844 in the city prison, at New York, where he was being held for robbing the Pomeroy Express. Of swiss birth, he was just married 18 Dec 1843, but no name given for his wife. (23 Jan 1844)

940. Mrs. Fox died in a fire that consumed their home, and Mr. Fox is so badly burned, he is not expected to live. The home situated on the Southern Railroad, about seven miles west of Adrian. They were both young and very recently married. Taken from the "Adrian Watch-Tower". (23 Jan 1844)

941. Polly Bodine has been charged with the murder of Mrs. Houseman, no date or town given. (30 Jan 1844)

942. John J. VanVoast of Schenectady, NY., just celebrated his 104th birthday, no date given. (30 Jan 1844)

943. Hon. Alexander Porter died 18 Jan 1844 at his home in the Parish of St. Mary, LA., a Senator and Judge from that state. (6 Feb 1844)

944. Roscius Ensign Morse age 3 yrs. 2 mos. 24 days, died 31 Dec 1843 in Penn Yan, Yates Co., of croup. The second son of Dr. and Mary A. Morse. (6 Feb 1844)

945. Thomas H. Bassett, an associate Editor of the "Michigan City Gazette", and Mrs. Julia Ann Woodbury of Penn Yan, Yates Co., were married 1 Feb 1844 by Rev. Williams in Penn Yan. (6 Feb 1844)

946. Charles Dake of Nunda, Allegany Co., and Polly Gillett, daughter of Jeremiah Gillett Esq. of Penn Yan, Yates Co., were married 22 Jan 1844 by Rev. O. Montague in Penn Yan. (13 Feb 1844)

947. Caroline Olive Coleman age 3 yrs., died 9 Feb 1844, daughter of Samuel T. Coleman, no town given. (13 Feb 1844)

948. George H. Wood Esq. age 38 yrs., died 5 Feb 1844 in Auburn, Cayuga Co., a Surrogate of that county. (13 Feb 1844)

949. Hon. Esen Cowen died 11 Feb 1844 at his lodggings at Albany, Albany Co. A Justice of the NY. Supreme Court, interred at Saratoga Springs. (20 Feb 1844)

950. Mr. Cornell killed his wife last February at Jamestown, Chatauque Co., by cutting her throat with a razor. He tried to do the same to himself, but was unsuccessful. Tried at Maysville, and sentenced to be executed 14 Mar 1844. (20 Feb 1844)

951. M.J. Francisco of Middlesex, Yates Co., and Sarah M. French of Jerusalem, Yates Co., were married 15 Feb 1844 by Rev. Lamb in Jerusalem. (20 Feb 1844)

952. William Duel of Marion, Wayne Co., and Nancy Keeler of Penn Yan, Yates Co., were married 14 Feb 1844 by Rev. Decker at Italy Hill, Yates Co. (20 Feb 1843)

953. Joseph Cochrane age 18 yrs., died 18 Feb 1844 in Washington, from a wound received in a duel on the 16th. (27 Feb 1844)

954. John Fiero a merchant, and Mary Ann Aspell, both of Milo, Yates Co., were married 14 Feb 1844 by Rev. J.K. Tinkham in Milo. (27 Feb 1844)

955. Henry Underwood and Eliza Welles Catlin were married 15 Feb 1844 by Rev. Hayward in Auburn, Cayuga Co. (27 Feb 1844)

956. T. Campbell and Jane Angus were married 14 Feb 1844 by Rev. Hotchkiss in Bellona, Yates Co. (27 Feb 1844)

957. James C. Deyo and Hester A. Sands were married 13 Feb 1844 by Rev. Eddy, no town given. (27 Feb 1844)

958. David Prosser and Miss Youngs were married 15 Feb 1844 by D.S. Mathers Esq., no first name for the bride, and no town given. (27 Feb 1844)

959. Mr. Hall of Starkey, Yates Co., and Mrs. Hall of Benton, Yates Co., were married 15 Feb 1844 by Rev. Eddy, no first names, and no town given. (27 Feb 1844)

960. Caleb Briggs age 80 yrs.,of Benton, Yates Co., and Mrs. Hannah Briggs of Potter, Yates Co., were married 21 Feb 1844 by Israel Comstock Esq. in Potter. Both heros of the Revolution. This is the 3rd husband for the bride, with the name of Briggs. (27 Feb 1844)

961. James M. Lockwood and Emily Gilbert, late of Penn Yan, Yates Co., and now of Pontiac, Michigan, were married 8 Feb 1844 by Rev. Harris, no town given. (27 Feb 1844)

962. Gov. Reynolds committed suicide 9 Feb 1844 at Jefferson City, MO. (5 Mar 1844)

963. A catastrophe occurred aboard the U.S. "Princeton" on 28 Feb 1844, near Alexandria, VA., when Capt. Stockton's big gun "Peace Maker" burst during a demonstration for the President, and other heads of state. The vessel was moving down the Potomac, just below Ft. Washington, among the dead were; Mr. Upsher, Secretary of State, Mr. Gilmer, Secretary of the Navy, Mr. M'Kennon, Commander of the Navy, Hon. Virgil Maxey of Maryland, Hon. David Gardiner of Gardiner Island, late Senator of New York, Joseph Armistead, the President's mulatto servant. (5 Mar 1844 and 12 Mar 1844)

964. James G. Baley and Eleanor Guthrie were married 2_ Feb 1844 (blurred) by Rev. Horace Spencer at Barrington, Yates Co. (5 Mar 1844)

965. Mrs. Teresa A. Elmore age 29 yrs., died 17 Feb 1844 at North Bergen, Genesee Co. The wife of Albert Elmore, daughter of the late Moses Whitney. (5 Mar 1844)

966. A WHALING CREW LOST AT SEA; off the coast of Kamschata last June 1843, from the bark "Elizabeth", under Capt. Winslow, out of Fall River. A boat crew made fast to a whale, when it commenced running to windward, and was soon lost sight of. Two days later the boat was found, detached from the whale, but the crew missing. Lost at sea are the following; Capt. Bradford W. Winslow, George Evans, Daniel Reed, Benjamin Hall, all of Freetown, and David Hathaway boat steerer of Fall River. (12 Mar 1844)

967. Marcus Beebe of Cuba, Allegany Co., and Betsey Young, eldest daughter of Abram Young, were married 7 Mar 1844 by Rev. William Wheeler in Jerusalem, Yates Co. (12 Mar 1844)

968. Nicholas Biddle Esq. died yesterday at his home "Andalusia" on the Delaware. Born 8 Jan 1783 in Philadelphia, PA. At age 15 yrs., he graduated from Princeton, and has served in numerous public offices. * brief biography printed. (12 Mar 1844)

969. William H. Stark and Julia Clark, daughter of Roswell Clark, were married 14 Mar 1844 by Rev. Conable in Jerusalem, Yates Co. (19 Mar 1844)

970. Erastus Cole Jr. and Sarah A. Larzelere, only daughter of H. Larzelere, were married 13 Mar 1844 by Rev. Wheeler in Jerusalem, Yates Co. (19 Mar 1844)

971. Eliza Drew died 18 Mar 1844 in Benton, Yates Co., her funeral from the Congregational Meeting House. (19 Mar 1844)

972. Lydia Bates age 19 yrs., died 12 Mar 1844 in Benton, Yates Co., daughter of Linus Bates. (19 Mar 1844)

973. George W. Hazard Esq. age 43 yrs., died 22 Mar 1844 at Milo, Yates Co. (26 Mar 1844)

974. Charles Monell died 18 Mar 1844 at Angelica, Allegany Co., son of Hon. Robert Monell of Greene, Chenango, Co. (26 Mar 1844)

975. Gen. Peter B. Porter died 27 Mar 1844 at his residence at Niagara Falls. (2 Apr 1844)

976. Henry N. Lewis of Penn Yan, Yates Co., and Marietta Beard of Milo, Yates Co., were married 27 Mar 1844 by Rev. O. Montaque in Milo. (2 Apr 1844)

977. Peter Seeley of Arcadia, Wayne Co., and Mary Elizabeth Hunt, daughter of Abel B. Hunt of Milo, Yates Co., were married 4 Apr 1844 by Rev. Chase in Milo. (9 Apr 1844)

978. W.H. Ongley and Mary B. Silversides were married 24 Mar 1844 by Rev. Chapman in Orange, Steuben Co. (9 Apr 1844)

979. Josiah Gaylord of Benton, Yates Co., and Matilda Seeley of Ovid, Seneca Co., were married 26 Mar 1844 by Rev. Lounsbury in Ovid. (9 Apr 1844)

980. Gen. Morgan Lewis died 15 Apr 1844 in New York city. Honorably connected with the history of New York, while it was yet a colony. An officer of the Revolution, a Senator, and Governor for NY., and in the late War, served as a Major-General. (16 Apr 1844)

981. John Johnson and Amanda Ward, both of Barrington, Yates Co., were married 4 Apr 1844 by J. McCane Esq. in Barrington. (16 Apr 1844)

982. Zephaniah Lockwood of Geneva, Walworth Co., Wisconsin, and Rebecca Ellis of Barrington, Yates Co., were married 12 Apr 1844 by Rev. Spencer in Barrington. (23 Apr 1844)

983. Henry Shaw of Kingston, Ulster Co., and Sabra Arnold, late of Penn Yan, Yates Co., were married 15 Apr 1844 in Kingston, no pastor named. (23 Apr 1844)

984. Elijah G. Brown age 27 yrs., died 18 Apr 1844 in Penn Yan, Yates Co. (23 Apr 1844)

985. Hon. Henry Baldwin died 28 Apr 1844 at his lodging in Phila. PA., a Judge for the U.S. Supreme Court. (30 Apr 1844)

986. H.L. Winants, Editor of the "Democratic Organ" and Cornelia Elmendorf, both of Penn Yan, Yates Co., were married 23 Apr 1844 by Rev. Ovid Miner in Penn Yan. (30 Apr 1844)

987. Daniel Fowle age 65 yrs., died 23 Apr 1844 in Bellona, Yates Co. (30 Apr 1844)

988. The son of James Fowle, age 10 wks., died 23 Apr 1844 in Bellona, Yates Co. The grandson of Daniel Fowle who died the same day. The two funeral processions met on the way to church, two coffins laid before the same altar, and laid side by side in the same grave. (30 Apr 1844)

989. Mrs. Betsey West, murdered 18 Apr 1844 in New Orleans, by her husband George B. West, who stated he killed her out of jealousy. Both natives of Philadelphia, PA., and married about 8 years. (7 May 1844)

990. John B. Cummings killed his wife 15 Apr 1844 in New Orleans. He cut his own throat 17 Apr 1844 in the Parish Prison, and died. (7 May 1844)

991. Hon. Isaac Lacey died 5 May 1844 at his home in Chilli, Monroe Co., a former Senator of NY. (7 May 1844)

992. Hon. Henry Baldwin died 21 Apr 1844 in Philadelphia, PA. (7 May 1844)

993. Hon. Bossiere a member of Congress from LA., died 1 May 1844 at Washington. (7 May 1844)

994. Death struck the children of Alfred and Emily Valentine of Milo, Yates Co. Carl Valentine age 6 yrs. 3 mos., died 26 Nov 1843 of dropsy of the brain, Iantha Walters Valentine age 2 yrs. 8 mos., died 8 Apr 1844 of scarlet fever, Sarah Elizabeth Valentine age 8 mos., died 12 Apr 1844 of scarlet fever, Phebe Elizabeth Valentine died 18 Apr 1844 of scarlet fever. (7 May 1844)

995. Isaac Overshire and Matilda Snook, both of Barrington Yates Co., were married 1 May 1844 by Rev. Foot in Barrington. (7 May 1844)

996. Marther E. Skinner of Grand Rapids, Michigan, and Eunice Edwards Huntington, second daughter of Hon. Israel Huntington of Geneva, Ontario Co., were married 1 May 1844 by Rev. Hay, no town stated for the marriage. (14 May 1844)

997. Silas Champlin of Potter, Yates Co., and Maria Odell of Penn Yan, Yates Co., were married 22 Feb 1844 by Rev. O. Montaque in Penn Yan. (14 May 1844)

998. Stimson Gardner and Nancy Bonny, both of Milo, Yates Co., were married 1 May 1844 by Rev. Montaque in Milo. (14 May 1844)

999. A riot in Philadelphia, started over a meeting called by the Native American Party, and supposedly cast a slanderous attack on those of Irish birth, and their religion. Killed were the following; George Shieffler, William Wright, Nathan Ramsey, and George Young. (21 May 1844)

1000. Harrison Youmans and Sophia A. Pierce were married 15 May 1844 at Penn Yan, Yates Co., by Rev. Braine. (21 May 1844)

1001. Benjamin Hobart and Jane Sutherland, both of Potter, Yates Co., were married 19 May 1844 by Rev. O. Montaque in Penn Yates Co. (21 May 1844)

1002. Robert Buel Esq. of Benton, Yates Co., and Phebe Ann Drew of Milo, Yates Co., were married 12 May 1844 by Rev. Barr in West Bloomfield, Ontario Co. (21 May 1844)

1003. Daniel D. Burtch and Hannah Russell were Married 14 May 1844 by Robert Buel Esq. in Jerusalem, Yates Co. (21 May 1844)

1004. Mrs. Mary Brown who was indicted last summer, for the murder of her son, aged 2 yrs., had her trial at the "Oyer and Terminer" last week. Her defense was insanity caused by the brutal treatment from her husband, she was acquitted. (28 May 1844)

1005. David C. Hyatt and Ann E. Misner, both of Penn Yan, Yates Co., were married 15 May 1844 by Rev. Braine in Penn Yan. (28 May 1844)

1006. George Goodwin age 87 yrs., died 13 May 1844 at Hartford, CT. A founder of the "Connecticut Courant" in Hartford. (4 Jun 1844)

1007. John M. Rumney a merchant, and Mary Smith, both of Penn Yan, Yates Co., were married 28 May 1844 by Rev. James Richards in Penn Yan. (4 Jun 1844)

1008. Richard Danes and Sarah Tucker, both of Penn Yan, Yates Co., were married 21 May 1844 by Robert Buel Esq. in Penn Yan. (4 Jun 1844)

1009. Francis Danes and Mary Jane Lewis, both of

Penn Yan, Yates Co., were married 2 Jun 1844 by Rev. Montaque in Penn Yan. (4 Jun 1844)

1010. Sarah Elizabeth Vanderlip age 21 yrs. 4 mos., died 7 Jun 1844, no town given. (11 Jun 1844)

1011. James C. Welles of Rochester, Monroe Co., and Julia A. Hampshie, only daughter of Henry Hampshie of Seneca, Ontario Co., were married 11 Jun 1844 by Rev. Cook in Seneca. (18 Jun 1844)

1012. E.P. McAllister and Sarah Banks, only daughter of Judge Banks of Millport, Chemung Co., were married 6 Jun 1844 by Rev. VanZandt in Millport. (18 Jun 1844)

1013. Mrs. Theoda Bissell age 77 yrs., died 14 Jun 1844 at the home of D. Bissell in Genesee, Livingston Co. Buried beside her late husband, Daniel Bissell Esq. in Allen's Hill, at Richmond, Ontario Co. (18 Jun 1844)

1014. Mrs. Emeline Ellis age 26 yrs., died 9 Jun 1844 at Milo, Yates Co. Wife of William S. Ellis, and oldest daughter of Orange Hollister of Starkey, Yates Co. A member of the Milo Baptist church. (25 Jun 1844)

1015. Almon H. Read a member of Congress in the 12th district of PA., has died, no date given. (25 Jun 1844)

1016. Josiah Morse age 25 yrs., committed suicide 27 Jun 1844 at Sterling, Cayuga Co., by taking a large dose of opium. Married about 2 yrs, he leaves a wife and infant. (2 Jul 1844)

1017. The eldest son of William Thorton of Fleming, Cayuga Co., died 25 Jun 1844, when fire consumed their home. (2 Jul 1844)

1018. Lor Howell and Isabel Coolbough were married 3 Jul 1844 by Rev. Horace Spencer in Barrington, Yates Co. (9 Jul 1844)

1019. Robert Dale, arrested for the murder of his wife, this past April, in Boston. (9 Jul 1844)

1020. Lucien Hall age 26 yrs., executed 5 Jul 1844 for the murder of Mrs. Bacon in New Haven. Mr. Bacon, his two sons and four of Mrs. Bacon's brothers were present at the execution. (9 Jul 1844)

1021. Samuel Sprague age 91 yrs., died recently at Boston, MA., no date given. (9 Jul 1844)

1022. Joseph Smith, the Mormon Prophet and his brother Hiram Smith, killed 27 Jun 1844 in the jail at Carthage, Illinois. (16 Jul 1844)

1023. Helen Maria Potter age 4 yrs., died 4 Jul 1844 in Penn Yan, Yates Co., from scarlet fever, daughter of Dr. F.M. Potter. (16 Jul 1844)

1024. Harrison Youmans age 25 yrs., died 4 Jul 1844 in Penn Yan, Yates Co. (16 Jul 1844)

1025. J. Hunt Jr., Editor of the "Tompkins Democrat" at Ithaca, Tompkins Co., and Jane Ann Scott of South Bainbridge, Chenango Co., were married 10 Jul 1844 by Rev. Okill, no town given. (23 Jul 1844)

1026. Samuel R. Fish Esq. and Janet A. Lee, daughter of the late Dr. Joshua Lee, both of Penn Yan, Yates Co., were married 25 Jul 1844 by Rev. B.W. Stone at St. Mark's Church in Penn Yan. (30 Jul 1844)

1027. Byron Andrews and Caroline Holmes, both of Milo, Yates Co., were married 7 Jul 1844 by Rev. Spencer at Pulteney, Steuben Co. (30 Jul 1844)

1028. Stephen Angell of Sparta, Livingston Co., and Almira Weston of Penn Yan, Yates Co., were married 12 Jul 1844 by Rev. Tinkham in Milo, Yates Co. (30 Jul 1844)

1029. A.M. Harris, drowned 23 Jul 1844 while bathing in the lake, a printer with the "Buffalo Gazette", in Erie Co. (6 Aug 1844)

1030. William Henry Hopkins age 12 yrs., drowned 1 Aug 1844 at Seneca Falls. Unknown to his family, he had gone to bath alone. The son of Ebenezer Hopkins Esq., formerly of Penn Yan, Yates Co., his funeral held 4 Aug 1844 at the Presbyterian Church. (6 Aug 1844)

1031. Zachariah Poulson age 83 yrs., died 31 Jul 1844 at Philadelphia, PA., Editor of the "Poulson's Daily Advertiser". (13 Aug 1844)

1032. Ebenezer Cornish and Mary Ann Thomas, both of Pulteney, Steuben Co., were married 7 Aug 1844 by

Rev. O. Miner in Penn Yan, Yates Co. (13 Aug 1844)

1033. Catharine Woodruff age 69 yrs., died 8 Aug 1844 in Penn Yan, Yates Co., member of the Baptist Church of Penn Yan. (13 Aug 1844)

1034. Col. William L. Stone age 52 yrs., died 15 Aug 1844 at Saratoga Springs, Saratoga Co. He was born in CT., the son of Rev. William Stone. * brief biography printed. (20 Aug 1844 and 27 Aug 1844)

1035. Rev. Dyer drowned 1 Aug 1844 near Keeseville, Essex Co., of the Episcopal Church, late of Whitehall, Washington Co. (20 Aug 1844)

1036. William Walter Scott, late of Van Dieman's Land, where he was sent for his participation in the Patriot War, and Nancy Egbert of this city were married 16 Aug 1844 by Judge Wentworth. They first became acquainted about fifteen minutes before the ceremony, * from the "Rock Democrat", no town given. (20 Aug 1844)

1037. Mrs. Mary Richards age 31 yrs., died 3 Aug 1844 in Springport, Cayuga Co., sister of N.D. Sutdam of Penn Yan, Yates Co. (3 Sep 1844)

1038. Nicholas D. Sutdam, Editor of the "Yates County Whig", and Roxanna Legg, both of Penn Yan, Yates Co., were married 27 Aug 1844 by Rev. Montaque in Penn Yan. (3 Sep 1844)

1039. Samuel B. Hyatt and Sarah Ann Hagerman, both of Jerusalem, Yates Co., were married 1 Sep 1844 by Rev. O. Montaque in Penn Yan. (3 Sep 1844)

1040. Rosetia Willey age 19 yrs., died 1 Sep 1844 at the home of S. Beck in Penn Yan, Yates Co., formerly of Dansville, Livingston Co. (3 Sep 1844)

1041. Mrs. Mary Smith died 30 Aug 1844 in Jerusalem, Yates Co., the wife of Benjamin Smith. (3 Sep 1844)

1042. C.S. Underwood, a printer in Auburn, Cayuga Co., and Cornelia M. Russell of Dansville, Livingston Co., were married 2 Sep 1844 by Rev. Walker in Dansville. (10 Sep 1844)

1043. Rodney Taylor of Penn Yan, Yates Co., and Elizabeth Beers of Jerusalem, Yates Co., were married 4 Sep 1844 by Rev. Burnett in Jerusalem. (10 Sep 1844)

1044. Daniel B. Tuttle of Ohio, and Rachel Chissom of Jerusalem, Yates Co., were married 7 Sep 1844 by Rev. James Richards in Jerusalem. (10 Sep 1844)

1045. Philo Barnum a printer, age 39 yrs., died 31 Aug 1844 at Auburn, Cayuga Co. (10 Sep 1844)

1046. Manassah Knox age 39 yrs., died 21 Aug 1844 in Scipio, Cayuga Co. (10 Sep 1844)

1047. Abraham Miller of Auburn, Cayuga Co., and Mary Ann Winants of Penn Yan, Yates Co., were married 11 Sep 1844 by Rev. Ovid Miner at the Congregational Church in Penn Yan. (17 Sep 1844)

1048. Col. E.M. Whitaker a merchant, and E.W. Bates, both of Bellona, Yates Co., were married 12 Sep 1844 by Rev. Eddy in Benton, Yates Co. (17 Sep 1844)

1049. Joseph C_otch ? (illegible) and Susan N. Harris, both of Penn Yan, Yates Co., were married 15 Sep 1844 by Rev. James Richards in Penn Yan. (17 Sep 1844)

1050. Rev. James Blake Howe died at Albany, on his way to Indiana. He had purchased his train ticket, sat down in the seat, and just before the cars started, he was seized with apoplexy, and died instantly. The Rector of the Episcopal Church at Claremont, NH., he seemed to be abt. 65 yrs. old, no date given. (24 Sep 1844)

1051. James Haggerty Esq. a U.S. Consul, age 54 yrs., died 24 Aug 1844 in Liverpool, Eng. (24 Sep 1844)

1052. Rev. L. Smith Hobart of Union City, Michigan, and Jane Louisa Goodrich, daughter of Andrew M. Goodrich Esq. of New York city, were married 9 Sep 1844 by Rev. Jacobus in New York. (1 Oct 1844)

1053. Amasa Tuell a merchant in Penn Yan, Yates Co., and Susan Southerland of Seneca, Ontario Co., were married 24 Sep 1844 by Rev. Delano in Seneca. (1 Oct 1844)

1054. Henry A. Bennett of Geneva, Ontario Co., and Mary Ann King of Barrington, Yates Co., were married 29 Sep 1844 by Rev. Spencer in Barrington. (1 Oct 1844)

1055. Mrs. Sally Cole age 61 yrs., died 29 Sep 1844 at Benton, Yates Co., wife of Nathan P. Cole. (8 Oct 1844)

1056. Alexander Butler of Jerusalem, Yates Co., and Phebe Stoddard of Potter, Yates Co., were married 8 Oct 1844 by Robert Buel Esq. in Benton, Yates Co. (15 Oct 1844)

1057. Peter B. Millis of Barrington, Yates Co., and Jane Vance of Starkey, Yates Co., were married 13 Oct 1844 by Rev. O. Montaque, no town given. (15 Oct 1844)

1058. George A. Sheppard of Penn Yan, Yates Co., and Jane Black of Seneca, Ontario Co., were married 1 Oct 1844 by Rev. Ovid Miner at Seneca. (15 Oct 1844)

1059. John Gordon, tried and sentenced to die 14 Feb 1845 in Rhode Island, for the murder of Amasa Sprague. (22 Oct 1844)

1060. John Daines and Alice Ann Watkins were married 21 Oct 1844 by Rev. McMahon in Penn Yan, Yates Co. (22 Oct 1844)

1061. Virginia Scott, daughter of Col. Scott has taken the veil as a nun in one of the Baltimore Convents, and assumed the name of "Sister Mary Emanuel", no date given. (29 Oct 1844)

1062. William Parsons, attorney in Yates Co., and Catharine Day, daughter of Judge Day of Orleans, Orleans Co., were married 17 Oct 1844 in Holley, no pastor given. (29 Oct 1844)

1063. Gen. H.G. Runnels ex-Governor of Mississippi, assassinated in that state, no date or town given. (12 Nov 1844)

1064. James M. Hartshorne Esq. age 27 yrs., died 4 Nov 1844 at Freehold, Greene Co. A lawyer and member of the New Jersey Legislature. (12 Nov 1844)

1065. Rev. Wilson Conner, a Baptist minister in Georgia, fell dead in the pulpit on the fifth Sunday of June last. (12 Nov 1844)

1066. Rev. Benjamin Hovey age 110 yrs., preached recently at the Utica Baptist Church in Oneida Co. (12 Nov 1844)

1067. James H. Neal hung himself recently in the jail at Ripley, MS., where he was confined for negro stealing. (12 Nov 1844)

1068. George Graves age 4 yrs., son of Rev. Josiah Graves of Middletown, CT., fell into the well of Rev. Goodwin, but kept his head above water, by hanging onto the stones. The alarm reached his mother, who immediately descended the well, secured him to a bucket and rescued him. (19 Nov 1844)

1069. Rev. Abel Brown died 8 Nov 1844 in Canandaigua, Ontario Co., at the home of John Mosher Esq. (19 Nov 1844)

1070. James C. Longwell of Hammondsport, Steuben Co. and Rachel A. Henderson, youngest daughter of Richard Henderson Esq., were married 13 Nov 1844 by Rev. Richards in Milo, Yates Co. (19 Nov 1844)

1071. Dr. William Welch of Norfolk, CT., and Emeline Collin, daughter of the late Henry Collin of Yates Co., were married 7 Nov 1844 by Rev. Himrod at Hillsdale, Columbia Co. (19 Nov 1844)

1072. Miles Gould of Gorham, Ontario Co., and Martha Scott, were married 16 Nov 1844 by Elder Tozer in Geneva, Ontario Co. (19 Nov 1844)

1073. Luewillen Delano age 2 yrs., died 14 Nov 1844, of injuries caused by a burn, son of Elisha Delano of Penn Yan, Yates Co. (26 Nov 1844)

1074. The death notice of Hon. Needham Maynard was given in "Seneca County Courier". He died at the home of his son John Maynard, no town or date given. (3 Dec 1844)

1075. Elisha D. McAllister age 18 yrs. 8 mos., died 1 Dec 1844 in Penn Yan, Yates Co. (3 Dec 1844)

1076. Samuel P. Cowles age 53 yrs., died 5 Dec 1844 in Syracuse, Onondaga Co., of apoplexy. (24 Dec 1844)

1077. William Blanchard and Sarah Secor, both of Penn Yan, Yates Co., were married 12 Dec 1844 by Rev. Montaque in Penn Yan. (24 Dec 1844)

1078. Elijah Smith, killed last week at Grafton, Rensselaer Co., in a dispute with some Indians, over the cutting of timber, no date given. (31 Dec 1844)

1079. Charles G. Stocking of Penn Yan, Yates Co., and Mary Woodhull of Seneca Falls, Seneca Co., were married 25 Dec 1844 by Rev. Fegler in Seneca Falls. (31 Dec 1844)

1080. Mrs. Almira Chidsey age 26 yrs., died 4 Jan 1845 in Milo, Yates Co. (7 Jan 1845)

1081. On 14 Dec 1844 the steamboat "Belle of Clarkville" collided with the "Louisanna" about 25 miles below Helena, Arkansas. Many lives are lost, most of west Tennessee, including:

William Tabb	P. Linn	W. Linn,
J. Ryan	R. Malisle	N. Sills
William Jones	T. Whitley	N.T. Allen
G. Hyer	A. Kirklan	J. Askew
son of J.W. Hull	J. Peay	Jno. Holliday

(7 Jan 1845)

1082. Col. Benjamin Fowler died 1 Jan 1845 at his home in Georgetown, D.C. One of the gallant defenders of Baltimore, and Commander of the 39th Reg., at the Battle of North Point, his remains taken to Annapolis for interment. (21 Jan 1845)

1083. Platt Cole and Martha Scott, both of Benton, Yates Co., were married 16 Jan 1845 by Rev. Parsons in Benton. (21 Jan 1845)

1084. Mrs. Oliver age 25 yrs., wife of T.G. Oliver of Albany, died in a shocking accident on the Troy Road. Two men were shouting in a cutter, coming in the opposite direction at full speed, and sheered across the road, colliding with the sleigh of Mrs. Oliver and upsetting it. One of the cutter's shafts pierced the temple of Mrs. Oliver, killing her instantly, no date given. (28 Jan 1845)

1085. Hon. Roger M. Shearman age 72 yrs., died 21 Jan 1845 at his home in Fairfield, CT. (28 Jan 1845)

1086. James Cary an Irishman, was killed 8 Jan 1845 at Bath, Steuben Co. He had been cutting a Hemlock tree, which first lodged in another, then broke away and fell upon the youth, killing him instantly. (28 Jan 1845)

1087. Robert Lantz and Rhoda Ann Baley were married 16 Jan 1845 by Rev. Horace Spencer at Barrington, Yates Co. (28 Jan 1845)

1088. Ruth Antoinette McAlpine age 4 yrs. 9 mos., died 20 Jan 1845 in Benton, Yates Co., only child of Deacon John W. and Cordelia McAlpine. (28 Jan 1845)

1089. Ambrose Chidsey age 30 yrs., died 26 Jan 1845 in Milo. (28 Jan 1845)

1090. Mrs. Polly Vorce died 24 Jan 1845 in Milo, Yates Co., wife of Volney Vorce. (28 Jan 1845)

1091. Mrs. Rhoda Amesbury age 66 yrs., died 21 Jan 1845 in Penn Yan, Yates Co. (28 Jan 1845)

1092. Henry E. Benson of Montreal, Canada, and Helen Stewart of Penn Yan, Yates Co., were married 22 Jan 1845 by Rev. Miner in the Congregational Church at Penn Yan. (4 Feb 1845)

1093. Rawson H. Murdock a merchant, and Eliza Welch both of Rushville, Yates Co., were married 24 Jan 1845 By Rev. M. Ghelston in Rushville. (4 Feb 1845)

1094. Levi Dildine and Mary Boyd, both of Pulteney, Steuben Co., were married 23 Jan 1845 by Rev. Olney, no town given. (4 Feb 1845)

1095. Mrs. Sarah S. Briggs age 27 yrs., died 31 Jan 1845 in Milo, Yates Co., wife of Thomas Briggs. (4 Feb 1845)

1096. John Devil a butcher, and Elizabeth Shad, both of Milton, PA. were married 25 Dec 1844 by Rev. Stoever in Milton. (11 Feb 1845)

1097. William Miller, a German, executed 28 Jan 1845 at Sand Lake, Rensselaer Co., for the murder of George West, a German, in May of 1842. Miller was a Catholic, and was attended by Rev. Peter Haversman of St. Mary's Church, who received the body and placed it in a vault at the burying ground. (11 Feb 1845)

1098. Israel Skinner age 41 yrs., committed suicide 4 Feb 1845 at Elmira, Chemung Co., he leaves a wife and child. (11 Feb 1845)

1099. Elisha W. Fargo and Harriet N. Wise, both of Penn Yan, Yates Co., were married 9 Feb 1845 by Rev. Ovid Miner in the Congregational Church at Penn Yan. (11 Feb 1845)

1100. Mrs. Lydia Haight died 5 Feb 1845 at Bluff Point, Yates Co. (11 Feb 1845)

1101. Amos C. Leach and Louisa Carpenter, were married 10 Jul 1845 by Rev. James Richards Jr. in Penn Yan, Yates Co. (5 Aug 1845)

1102. Caroline Cole age 34 yrs. 1 mo. 14 days, died 1 Aug 1845 at Benton, Yates Co., eldest daughter Nathan P. Cole Esq. (5 Aug 1845)

* * * MANY PAPERS MISSING * * *

1103. Ezra Watrous and Catherine Groesbeck, both of Honeoye Falls, Monroe Co., were married 31 Dec 1845 by Rev. Briggs in Honeoye Falls. (6 Jan 1846)

1104. John H. Bruen and Lucy Wright, both of Penn Yan, Yates Co., were married 8 Jan 1846 by Rev. Ovid Miner in Penn Yan. (13 Jan 1846)

1105. J.N. Gillett of Benton, Yates Co., and H.C. Newman of Bloomfield, Ontario Co., were married 31 Dec 1845 by Rev. Hill in Bloomfield. (13 Jan 1846)

1106. Mrs. Eunice McCarty age 27 yrs., died 5 Jan 1846 at West Dresden, Yates Co., wife of Dresden McCarty. (13 Jan 1846)

1107. THE DEAD OF 1845; the year just closed has witnessed the following deaths;

Gen. Andrew Jackson, ex-President of the U.S., age 78 yrs., died 8 Jun 1845.
Hon. Joseph Story, Justice of the Supreme Court, age 65 yrs., died 10 Sep 1845.
Hon. Isaac C. Bates, Senator from MA., age 65 yrs., died 16 Mar 1845.
Hon. Douglas Houghton, General Elect of MI., drowned, no age or date given.
Hon. Leverett Saltonstall, ex-Congressman from MA., age 64 yrs., died 8 May 1845.
Rev. H. Ware, D.D., Professor at Harvard, age 81 yrs. died 12 Jul 1845.
Rev. J. Milnor, D.D., from New York city, age 70 yrs., died 8 Mar 1845.
Hon. G. Morell, Chief Justice from MI., age 59 yrs., died __ Mar 1845.
Hon. Roger M. Sherman, from CT., age 71 yrs., died 30 Dec 1845.
Hon. Joseph L. Tillinghast, from RI., no age given, died 30 Dec 1845.

(20 Jan 1846)

1108. John Carroll age 86 yrs., died 9 Jan 1846 at New London, CT., a Patriot of the Revolution. (20 Jan 1846)

1109. Thomas Russell died 20 Jan 1846 in Albany, Albany Co. (27 Jan 1846)

1110. William Gould died 20 Jan 1846, the eminent Law Book seller, no town given. (27 Jan 1846)

1111. Hon. Augustus Torrey died 21 Jan 1846 in Rushville, Yates Co., a Judge of the County Court. (27 Jan 1846)

1112. Hon. William Taylor of VA., funeral held 19 Jan 1846 in Washington. (27 Jan 1846)

1113. Morris Ford and Laura Spencer, both of Penn Yan, Yates Co., were married 14 Jan 1846 by Rev. Horace Spencer in Bath, Steuben Co. (27 Jan 1846)

1114. Mathew C. Patterson a district attorney, died in New York city, no date given. (30 Jan 1846)

1115. Hugh Ellison found dead on the Mohawk and Hudson Railroad, near Albany, Albany Co., a bottle of whiskey by his side, no date given. (3 Feb 1846)

1116. Sarah Carns age 22 yrs., died 28 Jan 1846 at Bluff Point, Yates Co. (3 Feb 1846)

1117. William Davis an Englishman, employed by Avery & Howlett, butchers, found dead in a canal boat near Syracuse, Onondaga Co., a whiskey bottle by his side. (10 Feb 1846)

1118. Dr. Daniel Johnson, killed in a duel 2 Feb 1846 at Bladenburgh, MD., near Washington, DC, by Thomas F. Jones, both of Elizabeth City, NC. (10 Feb 1846)

1119. Patrick Walker, killed 30 Jan 1846 in the Carbondale, PA. mines. (10 Feb 1846)

1120. Mark Brennan, killed 30 Jan 1846 in the Carbondale, PA mines. (10 Feb 1846)

1121. Ashley Birney Sutton age 4 yrs. 6 mos., died 20 Feb 1846 in Penn Yan, Yates Co., of croup, son of John and Catherine Sutton. (24 Feb 1846)

1122. Elizabeth Wintergreen Watersnake died 16 Feb 1846 in Syracuse, Onondaga Co., a member of the Onondaga Tribe. (3 Mar 1846)

1123. H.H. Winants of Penn Yan, Yates Co., and Sarah A. Bannister of Newark, Wayne Co., were married 25 Feb 1846 by Rev. Kellogg at Newark. (3 Mar 1846)

1124. DeWitt C. Gage of Benton, Yates Co., and Catharine Glover of Auburn, Cayuga Co., were married 25 Feb 1846 by Rev. James Richards at the home of J.S. Glover in Penn Yan, Yates Co. (3 Mar 1846)

1125. Tippett Sunderlin a farmer, died 9 Mar 1846 in Barrington, Yates Co. Just two weeks ago, he was a member of the Grand Jury in Penn Yan, Yates Co. (10 Mar 1846)

1126. William Fullagar age 3 yrs., died 4 Mar 1846 in Benton, Yates Co., son of Samuel Fullagar. (10 Mar 1846)

1127. Dr. Bradlee, convicted of mail robbery in 1841, died last week in the Pittsburgh jail. (10 Mar 1846)

1128. HORRID MURDER NEAR AUBURN; on 12 Mar 1846 in Fleming, Cayuga Co. John VanNess, his wife and child were found murdered. Mrs. Wyckoff, the mother in-law, and Mr. C. VanArsdall were dangerously wounded. William Freeman a mulatto, is suspected of the murder. (17 Mar 1846)

1129. Rahab Marchell died 10 Mar 1846 at Louisville. He left $2000.00 in gold, and at least $20,000.00 worth of property. All of which will go to his wife in Cincinnati, whom he abandoned 20 yrs. ago, and his son an actor, who goes by the name of Williams. (17 Mar 1846)

1130. H. Easton of Wayne, Steuben Co., and Eliza Banks of Benton, Yates Co., were married on 3 Mar 1846 by Rev. Ferris in Benton. (17 Mar 1846)

1131. Caroline Augusta Townsend age 4 yrs. 6 mos. 2 days, died 12 Mar 1846 in Penn Yan, Yates Co., the daughter of Homer and Caroline A. Townsend. (17 Mar 1846)

1132. Catherine Knickerbacker age 17 yrs., died 11 Mar 1846 in Benton, Yates Co., at the home of C.J. Legg. (17 Mar 1846)

1133. Mrs. Mary Welles age 56 yrs., died 3 Mar 1846 at Wayne, Steuben Co., wife of James N. Welles. (17 Mar 1846)

1134. Robert Patterson age abt. 65 or 85 yrs. ? (blurred), died 4 Mar 1846 in Benton, Yates Co. (17 Mar 1846)

1135. Mr. Haywood age 22 yrs., drowned 21 Mar 1846 near Geneva, Ontario Co. The son of Mr. Haywood the hotel keeper, in Canandaigua, Ontario Co. He was visiting relatives, went hunting and shot a muskrat near the Jones Bridge. When he stepped out on the ice to get it, the ice broke and carried him beneath to his death. (24 Mar 1846)

1136. Josephine Amelia Goodrich age 1_ yrs.? (blurred) died 22 Mar 1846 in Penn Yan, Yates Co. The adopted daughter of Charles G. Judd Esq., funeral from the Presbyterian Church. (24 Mar 1846)

1137. Mrs. Jane Isabella Simmons age 44 yrs., died 15 Feb 1846 at her home in Benton, Yates Co., wife of James Simmons. (24 Mar 1846)

1138. Mrs. Charity Fowler age 39 yrs., died 8 Feb 1846 in Starkey, Yates Co., wife of Ira Fowler. (24 Mar 1846)

1139. Hon. John Miller died 19 Mar 1846 at St. Louis, MO. A late member of Congress, and ex-Governor of that state. (7 Apr 1846)

1140. Luther Spaulding age 20 yrs., died 4 Apr 1846, while driving a team. The end board of the wagon gave way, causing him to fall off. The wheels passed over his head, and injured him to the point, he died within 2 hrs. Employed by Mr. Root in Penn Yan, Yates Co. He had no relatives living here, except one brother. (7 Apr 1846)

1141. Norman Holmes and Emily Stanton, both of Benton, Yates Co., were married 28 Mar 1846 by Rev. Rev. Baker in Benton. (7 Apr 1846)

1142. Reuben L. Cory and A___ide Harvey (illegible) both of Penn Yan, Yates Co., were married 31 Dec 1845 by Rev. Tinkham in Geneva, Ontario Co. (7 Apr 1846)

1143. Palmer Bassett of Barrington, Yates Co., and Susan Jane Smith of Troy, Rensselaer Co., were married 8 Apr 1846 at the home of William Root Esq. in Penn Yan, Yates Co., by Rev. Powell of Dundee. (14 Apr 1846)

1144. Mary Wait age 43 yrs., died 6 Apr 1846 at the home of her father Benjamin Wait in Bluff Point, Yates Co. (14 Apr 1846)

1145. Mrs. Betsey Torrance age 26 or 36 yrs. (blurred), died 8 Apr 1846 at East Avon, Livingston Co., wife of Richard Torrance Esq. (21 Apr 1846)

1146. Mrs. Mary Coffin age 37 or 57 yrs. (blurred), died 12 Apr 1846 in Bellona, Yates Co. (21 Apr 1846)

1147. Mrs. Limara Boyd age 47 yrs., died 15 Apr 1846 in Benton, Yates Co., wife of Robert Boyd. (21 Apr 1846)

1148. Robert Calvin Hamilton died 15 Apr 1846 at Rochester, Monroe Co., infant son Theodore S. and Emily Hamilton. (21 Apr 1846)

1149. Amzi Bruen of Milo, Yates Co., and Mrs. Abby Ann Burrows of Ohio City, Ohio, were married 16 Apr 1846 by Rev. Watson at Oswego, Oswego Co. (28 Apr 1846)

1150. Jasper Moon age 55 yrs., died 21 Apr 1846 at Penn Yan, Yates Co. (28 Apr 1846)

1151. Joshua Landon age 36 or 56 yrs., (blurred) died 23 Apr 1846 at Barrington, Yates Co. (28 Apr 1846)

1152. Mrs. Elizabeth Casner died 28 Apr 1846 in Penn Yan, Yates Co., wife of Hon. Emanuel Casner, funeral from the Presbyterian Church. (5 May 1846)

1153. Mrs. Caroline Raplee died 29 Apr 1846 in Milo, Yates Co., wife of John Raplee, and daughter of Thomas Hathaway of Milo. (5 May 1846)

1154. Alice Little age 78 yrs., died 7 May 1846 in Cherry Valley, Otsego Co. A native of Williamstown, MA., she married there about 54 years ago to the late Dr. David Little. They lived in Springfield, MA., where she remained until the death of her husband in 1832. She then moved with her son D.W. Little Esq. to Cherry Valley, were she lived out her life. (12 May 1846)

1155. James Henry R__?__son (illegible) of Arcadia, Wayne Co., and Nancy Louisa __?__ (illegible) of Milo, Yates Co., were married 8 May 1846 by Rev. J.K. Tinkham in Milo. (12 May 1846)

1156. Mrs. Eleanor Campbell died 7 Apr 1846 on the day of her 88th birthday at Cherry Valley, Otsego Co. She married Capt. Samuel Campbell 1 Jan 1782, and was a daughter of the late John Campbell. (12 May 1846)

1157. Mrs. Ann Potter died 11 May 1846 in Penn Yan, Yates Co., wife of Dr. Francis M. Potter. (12 May 1846)

1158. John VanBuren age _ mos. 12 days, (illegible) died 12 May 1846 in Penn Yan, Yates Co., youngest son of Evert and Catharine VanBuren, funeral from the Episcopal Church. (12 May 1846)

1159. Dr. Partridge Parsons age 83 yrs., died 9 May 1846 of consumption, at the home of his son in Penn Yan, Yates Co. Formerly of Litchfield, CT., he removed to Dundee, Yates Co., where he lived until 8 mos. ago, when he became ill. A member of the Episcopal Church. (12 May 1846)

1160. Mrs. Elizabeth Casner age 39 yrs., died 4 May 1846 in Penn Yan, Yates Co. wife of Ezekial Casner. She came with her husband in 1825, from Allentown, Pa. (12 May 1846)

1161. The daughter of J.S. Lambright age 12 yrs., drowned 11 May 1846 in the canal at Lyons, Wayne Co. She was crossing the canal on a lock gate, when she fell in. (19 May 1846)

1162. Hon. Robert Wickliffe Jr., Charge d'Affaires of the U.S. at Turin, and Josephine Van Houton of Rotterdam, were married 7 Apr 1846 at Turin by Rev. Bert, pastor of the Protestant Legations, marriage witnessed by Chevalier Biscarra for the bride, and G.J. Crafts for the groom. (19 May 1846)

1163. Mrs. Ann Potter age 33 yrs., died 5 May 1846 in Penn Yan, Yates Co., wife of Dr. Francis M. Potter. (19 May 1846)

1164. Mary Caroline Wheeler age 2 yrs. 1 mo. 29 days, died 17 May 1846 in Benton, Yates Co., of croup, daughter of Henry C. and Mary Wheeler. (19 May 1846)

1165. Nathan P. Cole Esq. and Charlotte Shay were married 28 May 1846 by Rev. Baker in Benton, Yates Co. (2 Jun 1846)

1166. Rev. C.T. Torrey died 9 May 1846 in Baltimore, MD. (2 Jun 1846)

1167. Gasevoort Melville age 30 yrs., died 12 May 1846 in London, Eng. The Secretary of American Legation at the Court of St. James. (9 Jun 1846)

1168. Rufus S. Reed died 8 Jun 1846 at Erie, Erie Co. For nearly 50 yrs., he was identified with the commerce and business of the lakes. (9 Jun 1846)

1169. Jared Hubbard age 26 or 36 yrs. (blurred), murdered 25 May 1846 at Burlington Flatts, Otsego, Co., he leaves a wife and 2 children. (9 Jun 1846)

1170. Rufus Kingsley age 84 yrs., died 26 May 1846 at his home in Hartford, Susquehanna Co. PA. Born 1 Feb 1763 at Windham, CT., he entered the service at age 13 yrs., and was a drummer boy at the Battle of Bunker Hill. His wife of 60 yrs. survived her husband by 3 days, and died on the 29 May 1846, no name given for the wife. (16 Jun 1846)

1171. George A. ---G (illegible) of Penn Yan, Yates Co., and Jane N. Wright of Avon, Livingston Co., were married 7 Jun 1846 at the Universalist Church in C___?___, (illegible) by Rev. Hammond. (16 Jun 1846)

1172. John Burnet Esq. of Syracuse, Onondaga Co., and Cynthia M. Munro, were married 7 Jun 1846 by Rev. Lathrop in Elbridge, Onondaga Co. (16 Jun 1846)

1173. Mrs. Elizabeth Richards age 22 yrs., died 16 Jun 1846 at Penn Yan, Yates Co. Wife of Rev. James Richards of the Presbyterian Church in Penn Yan, and daughter of Thomas B-?-- Esq. (illegible) of Canandaigua, Ontario Co. (16 Jun 1846)

1174. Mary Wheeler age 19 yrs., died 15 Jun 1846 in Benton, Yates Co., eldest daughter of George S. Wheeler of Benton. (16 Jun 1846)

1175. Abner Gilbert of Elmira, Chemung Co. and Rhoda Maria Hathaway of Starkey, Yates Co., were married 1 Jun 1846 by Rev. Wollage at Rock Stream, Yates Co. (23 Jun 1846)

1176. Jacob F. Bridgeman of Penn Yan, Yates Co., and Lucy A. Sheppard of Jerusalem, Yates Co., were married 13 Jun 1846 by Rev. Creamer in Jerusalem. (23 Jun 1846)

1177. James Whitfield of Pontiac, MI., and Jane Buck of Penn Yan, Yates Co., NY., were married 21 Jun 1846 by Rev. McMahon in Penn Yan. (23 Jun 1846)

1178. John P. Scofield and Deborah L. Townsend, both of Benton, Yates Co., were married 25 May 1846 by Rev. Baker in Benton. (30 Jun 1846)

1179. Peter G. Lawson of Albany, Albany Co., and Susan Dox, eldest daughter of Abramham Dox of Benton, Yates Co., were married 25 Jun 1846 by Rev. Norton at Hopeton, Yates Co. (30 Jun 1846)

1180. Walter J. Sherwood of Manlius, Onondaga Co., and Sarah E. Edmonds of Benton, Yates Co., were married 8 Jul 1846 by Rev. Baker in Benton. (14 Jul 1846)

1181. Rebecca Crawford age 38 or 58 yrs. (blurred), died 7 Jul 1846 at the home of Morris Sheppard in Penn Yan, Yates Co. (14 Jul 1846)

1182. Henry Livingston of Irondequoit, Monroe Co., died 17 Jul 1846 from drinking too freely of cold water from a spring, when too heated. (21 Jul 1846)

1183. H.B. Stiles and Mary Babcock, daughter of the late Hon. William Babcock, were married 20 Jul 1846 by Rev. Silas Hawley at Penn Yan, Yates Co. (21 Jul 1846)

1184. Mrs. Maria Critterden age 50 yrs.? (blurred), died 11 Jul 1846 at Starkey, Yates Co., wife of Rev. J. Critterden. (21 Jul 1846)

1185. Charles K. Morris age 25 yrs., died 23 Jul 1846. Employed as a clerk by Moses Yeamans, in Manchester, Ontario Co. He was found lying upon the west bank of Canandaigua Outlet, where he had gone to bath, gasping for breath and unable to speak before he expired. It is believed he became ill while bathing, as there were no sign of violence on his body. (28 Jul 1846)

1186. Hon. Caleb J. M'Nulty died 1 Jul 1846 at Memphis, TN., of apoplexy. Late clerk of the House of Representatives, he was there with the Ohio Volunteers, and was buried in Memphis, with military honors. (28 Jul 1846)

1187. DREADFUL ACCIDENT ON THE ERIE RAILROAD; the train left Middleton 28 Jul 1848 bound for New York, and ran off the track near Monroe Village, killing two passengers and seriously injuring about thirty others. The accident was caused, when the wheel broke on the second car and the train was thrown off. Killed were, Dr. Crane of Goshen, Orange Co., and Charles Stevens a grocer of New York city. (28 Jul 1846)

1188. William Freeman, sentenced to be executed 16 Sep 1846 for the murder of the VanNess family, no town given. (28 Jul 1846)

1189. A daughter of Orren Hoyt of Lansingburgh, Rensselaer Co., died last week from eating the phosphorus from a bunch of matches, no date given. (28 Jul 1846)

1190. Mr. VanBenthuysen died 25 Jul 1846, Postmaster at Poughkeepsie, Dutchess Co. (28 Jul 1846)

1191. Mathew Henry Webster died in New York city, well known in the science field, formerly of Albany, Albany Co., no date given. (11 Aug 1846)

1192. Mrs. Desdamona E. Bennett age 45 yrs. 10 mos. 10 days, died 6 Aug 1846 in Penn Yan, Yates Co. Wife of the late Abraham M. Bennett, and mother of the junior proprietor of this paper. A member of the Baptist Church for 18 yrs. (11 Aug 1846)

1193. Lewis Harris Esq. formerly of Penn Yan, Yates Co., and Jane E. Wilson, daughter of the late Dr. Wilson of East Bloomfield, Ontario Co., New York, were married 19 Jun 1846 in Houston, Texas, at the home of Dr. Birdsall. (18 Aug 1846)

1194. William M. Price buried 24 Aug 1846 in Penn Yan, Yates Co., funeral from the Episcopal Church, burial at St. Mark's burying ground. (25 Aug 1846)

1195. William Mathews age 113 yrs., lives in the Parish of Beguildy, Radnorshire. He retains the full power of his natural faculties, walks at the rate of three miles an hour, and commonly journeys 20 miles a day. (25 Aug 1846)

1196. Gov. Henderson of Texas, died recently. He has been ill since his arrival on the Rio Grande, no date given. (25 Aug 1846)

1197. Col. Samuel Humphrey died 23 Aug 1846 at Georgetown, Chief Naval Constructor of the U.S. Navy. (25 Aug 1846)

1198. William Clark of Dayton, Ohio and Mary Ann Boilean of Penn Yan, Yates Co., were married 26 Aug 1846 by Rev. Adoit in Penn Yan. (1 Sep 1846)

1199. John R. Brown age 36 yrs., died 11 Aug 1846 at Catlin, Chemung Co. formerly of Penn Yan, Yates Co. (1 Sep 1846)

1200. Ketchel Birdseye age 37 or 57 yrs. (blurred), died 21 Aug 1846 at Havana, Chemung Co. (1 Sep 1846)

1201. Edward Simonds formerly of Walpole, NH., and Emily Capell of Milo, Yates Co., were married 3 Sep 1846 by Rev. Sunderlin in Milo. (8 Sep 1846)

1202. Jonathan G. Baker of Milo, Yates Co., and Miriam B. Ellis of Starkey, Yates Co., were married 20 Aug 1846 by Rev. West in Starkey. (8 Sep 1846)

1203. The boiler on the steamboat "Excelsior" under Capt. Nelson, exploded off the Jersey shore 10 Sep 1846 killing Daniel Slosson age 78 yrs. He was the father in-law of Alderman Gilbert of the first ward. (15 Sep 1846)

1204. George D. Stewart age 20 yrs. 9 mos., died 8 Sep 1846 in Penn Yan, Yates Co., son of the late George D. Stewart. (15 Sep 1846)

1205. Hon. Samuel Foot died 15 Sep 1846 at his home in Cheshire, CT. He has served the state of CT. in the House, Senate, as Governor, and other public offices. (22 Sep 1846)

1206. S.E. Watkins a merchant in Waterloo, Seneca Co., and Eliza B. Taylor, eldest daughter of James Taylor Esq. of Penn Yan, Yates Co., were married 22 Sep 1846 by Rev. James Richards in Penn Yan. (22 Sep 1846)

1207. Thomas Hure age 3 yrs. 6 mos., died 25 Jul 1846 in Union City, Michigan, only child of W.P. and Catharine E. Hure. (22 Sep 1846)

1208. Pitts Hudson of Scipio, Cayuga Co., committed suicide 28 Sep 1846 by hanging himself, he leaves a wife and large family. (29 Sep 1846)

1209. Patrick Chushing age 30 yrs., murdered 23 Sep 1846 at Buffalo, Erie Co. (29 Sep 1846)

1210. Capt. John Spering age 89 yrs., died recently at his home in Spring Gardens, PA. A soldier of the Revolution, no date given. (29 Sep 1846)

1211. Gen. Vincent Mathews age 80 yrs., died 23 Sep 1846 at his home in Rochester, Monroe Co. (29 Sep 1846)

1212. Amelia Elizabeth Gillett age 3 yrs., died 3 Oct 1846 at Penn Yan, Yates Co., daughter Ansen C. and Amelia Gillett. (6 Oct 1846)

1213. Smith Scudder Esq. of the New Jersey bar, died recently in court. He was observed with his head hanging back, his wig falling off and a mist covering his eyes. He was pronounced dead by Dr. T.B. Gauntier, no date given. (6 Oct 1846)

1214. Charles Crocker of LeRoy, Genesee Co. and Angeline Burgess of Dresden, Yates Co., were married 4 Oct 1846 by S.G. Gage Esq. in Benton, Yates Co. (13 Oct 1846)

1215. Oliver Teft of Penn Yan, Yates Co., and Catharine Moulthrope of Dresden, Yates Co., were married 4 Oct 1846 by A. Veazie Esq. in Dresden. (13 Oct 1846)

1216. Aaron McLean of Dresden, Yates Co., and Elizabeth Rider of Branchport, Yates Co., were married 11 Oct 1846 by A. Veazie Esq. at Dresden. (13 Oct 1846)

1217. Charles E. Seymour age 23 yrs., died 8 Oct 1846 at Jackonsonville, FL., of the firm "W.H. Seymour" of Penn Yan, Yates Co. (27 Oct 1846)

1218. Hon. Jonas Earl Jr. age 61 yrs., died 2 Nov 1846 in Syracuse, Onondaga Co. A canal commissioner of this state, and Senator. (3 Nov 1846)

1219. Samuel Whitehorn of Penn Yan, Yates Co., and Sally Ann Evens of Cayuga, Cayuga Co., were married 23 Oct 1846 by Rev. Warren in Penn Yan. (3 Nov 1846)

1220. Edwin Goodrich of Milwaukee, Wisconsin, and Mary S. Robinson, daughter of James C. Robinson of Penn Yan, Yates Co., were married 28 Oct 1846 by Rev. James Richards in Penn Yan. (3 Nov 1846)

1221. George Wagener age 2 yrs., died 27 Oct 1846 in Jerusalem, Yates Co., son of George and Adelia Wagener. (3 Nov 1846)

1222. Calvin Fargo age 2 yrs. 10 mos. 29 days, died 14 Oct 1846 at Jackson's Mills, Lenawee Co., MI., only son of J.C. and Ermine Fargo. (3 Nov 1846)

1223. Mrs. Mary Lewis age 63 yrs., died 23 Oct 1846 in Benton, Yates Co., wife of Barnet Lewis. (3 Nov 1846)

1224. John J. Wise and Mariah M. Stark, both of Benton, Yates Co., were married 4 Nov 1846 by Rev. Silas Hawley in Benton. (10 Nov 1846)

1225. Dr. William Cornwall of Penn Yan, Yates Co., found drowned in the outlet Friday. He went fishing in a skiff 11 Nov 1846, and had not been seen since. (17 Nov 1846)

1226. Mrs. Betsey Nichols died 16 Nov 1846 at Pultney, Steuben Co. Wife of Josiah G. Nichols of Milo, Yates Co., her funeral from the M.E. Church in Penn Yan, Yates Co. (17 Nov 1846)

1227. Hon. Samuel Benton age 60 yrs. died at San Augustine, Texas, no date given. (24 Nov 1846)

1228. Mrs. Olivia Dorman age 54 yrs., died 25 June 1846 last, in Bainbridge, MI., formerly of Penn Yan, Yates Co., wife of the late Joel Dorman. She left here about a year ago to visit and tend to an afflicted family living there, when she herself was taken ill, of the well known John Lawrence Family. (24 Nov 1846)

1229. Azariah Smith Esq. of Onondaga Co. died recently, a member of the Assembly, no date given. (24 Nov 1846)

1230. Hon. Morris F. Sheppard age 72 yrs., died 23 Nov 1846 in Penn Yan, Yates Co. One of the founders of Penn Yan over 50 yrs. ago, he spread his tent in the wilderness, not far from the spot his remains now lie. He served in the Legislature and other public offices. (24 Nov 1846)

1231. Phillip Pulver of Milo, Yates Co., and Caroline Boardman of Barrington, Yates Co., were married 27 Nov 1846 by Elder Sunderlin in Barrington. (1 Dec 1846)

1232. Charles Winants of Penn Yan, Yates Co., and Mary Gay of Auburn, Cayuga Co., were married 23 Nov 1846 by Rev. Mathews in Auburn. (1 Dec 1846)

1233. Joel W. Crane of Penn Yan, Yates Co., and Mariette C__?__, eldest daughter of Jno. C__?__ of C__?__ville, MA. or PA., (illegible), were married 26 Nov 1846, no town or pastor given. (8 Dec 1846)

1234. Henry Wood and Perces G. Babcock, both of Penn Yan, Yates Co., were married 9 Dec 1846 by Rev. Silas Hawley in Penn Yan. (15 Dec 1846)

1235. James McLean and Sarah Jane Winants, both of Penn Yan, Yates Co., were married 9 Dec 1846 by Rev. Silas Hawley in Penn Yan. (15 Dec 1846)

1236. Charles Wheeler of Auburn, Cayuga Co., and Mary B. E_?__, (illegible) daughter of Artemas E_?__, (illegible) of Rochester, Monroe Co., were married 3 Dec 1846 by Rev. Thompson in Rochester. (15 Dec 1846)

1237. Samuel W. Spencer Esq. age 76 yrs., died 28 Nov 1846 in Geneva, Ontario Co. (15 Dec 1846)

1238. William Goundry age 62 yrs. 6 mos., died 17 Dec 1846 in Benton, Yates Co. (22 Dec 1846)

1239. Thomas Emory and Charlotte West, both of Penn Yan, Yates Co., were married 31 Dec 1846 by Rev. James Richards in Penn Yan. (5 Jan 1847)

1240. Seth J. Gemung and Sarah Williams, both of Penn Yan, Yates Co., were married 30 Dec 1846 by Rev. Goodwin in Penn Yan. (5 Jan 1847)

1241. Harvy Eartin and Mrs. Mary Pratt, both of Milo, Yates Co., were married 27 Dec 1846 by Rev. Evans in Milo. (5 Jan 1847)

1242. Rachel Malin died 5 Jan 1847 in Jerusalem, Yates Co., at an advanced age. (5 Jan 1847)

1243. Isaiah Youngs and Sabella Mathias, daughter of the late John Mathias, were married 28 Dec 1846 in Milo, Yates Co., by Rev. Adoit, all of Milo. (12 Jan 1847)

1244. Ambrose Stark and Elsie Sheppard, both of Penn Yan, Yates Co., were married 24 Dec 1846 by Rev. Silas Hawley in Penn Yan. (12 Jan 1847)

1245. Dwight Wells age 13 yrs., died 14 Dec 1846 in Jerusalem, Yates Co., The son of Walter and Susan Wells, formerly of Madison Co. (12 Jan 1847)

1246. Mrs. Sarah Morgan age 70 yrs., died 2 Jan 1847 in Jerusalem, Yates Co., mother of James D. Morgan of Penn Yan, Yates Co. (12 Jan 1847)

1247. Fancelia Vincent age 2 yrs., died 2 Jan 1847 in Jerusalem, Yates Co., daughter of Cornelius and Marelis Vincent. (12 Jan 1847)

1248. Charles Comstock and Catharine __?__ (illegible), both of Benton, Yates Co., were married 21 Jan 1847 by Rev. James Richards in Penn Yan, Yates Co. (26 Jan 1847)

1249. Mr. _?_ Fowler (illegible) and Cynthia Clark were married 24 Jan 1847 by Rev. Silas Hawley in Penn Yan, Yates Co. (26 Jan 1847)

1250. Andrew H. Waterman of Penn Yan, Yates Co., and Sarah Quick of Hammondsport, Steuben Co., were married 27 Jan 1847 by Rev. Watson in Hammondsport. (2 Feb 1847)

1251. Mrs. Ann Potter age 75 yrs., died 23 Jan 1847 at Milo, Yates Co. The wife of Edward Potter, and mother of Dr. F.M. Potter of Penn Yan, Yates Co. She was born in Rhode Island. (2 Feb 1847)

1252. Spencer Boyd Armstrong age 5 yrs., died 21 Jan 1847, and James Frank Armstrong age 3 yrs., died 3 Feb 1847, sons of James and Mary Jane Armstrong of Penn Yan, Yates Co. (9 Feb 1847)

1253. John Waterman age 30 or 50 yrs. (blurred), died 12 Jan 1847 in Athens, Calhoun Co, Michigan, formerly of Yates Co. (9 Feb 1847)

1254. Henry N. Wagener Esq. of Jerusalem, Yates Co., and Mary A. Laman, niece of Hon. George W. Wolcott of Barrington, Yates Co., were married 10 Feb 1847 by Rev. James Richards at the Hermitage in Barrington. (16 Feb 1847)

1255. Charles Strobridge and Hannah Josephine Slitor, both of Potter, Yates Co., were married 4 Feb

1847 in Potter, by Rev. Wilkinson. (16 Feb 1847)

1256. Watkins Davis of Benton, Yates Co., and Emeline Beard, daughter of Joshua Beard of Milo, Yates Co., were married on 10 Feb 1847 by Rev. Sunderlin in Milo. (16 Feb 1847)

1257. John B. Robertson and Sophia J. Flowers, both of Benton, Yates Co., were married 11 Feb 1847 by Rev. Ferris in Benton. (16 Feb 1847)

1258. Isaac Hartshorn and Sarah A. Beers were married 9 Feb 1847 by Rev. Adoit in Jerusalem, Yates Co. (16 Feb 1847)

1259. Jay L. Mariner and Emeline Quick, both of Benton, Yates Co., were married 2 Mar 1847 by Rev. Baker in Benton. (9 Mar 1847)

1260. Andrew F. Chapman and Mary E. Hicks, both of Benton, Yates Co., were married 4 Mar 1847 by Rev. Spencer in Benton. (9 Mar 1847)

1261. Thomas Fairbrother and Lois Houghtailing, were married 5 Mar 1847 by Robert Buel Esq. in Penn Yan, Yates Co. (9 Mar 1847)

1262. Robert Fairbrother and Mary Houghtailing, were married 5 Mar 1847 by Robert Buel Esq. in Penn Yan, Yates Co. (9 Mar 1847)

1263. Lewis Mandeville age 40 yrs., died 17 Dec 1846 at the home of his father, Henry Mandeville in Ulysses, Tompkins Co. (16 Mar 1847)

1264. John W. Williamson and Mary Lane, both of Penn Yan, Yates Co., were married 2 Mar 1847 by Rev. Silas Hawley in Penn Yan. (16 Mar 1847)

1265. L.N.B. VanDerlip age 25 yrs., died 18 Mar 1847 in Benton, Yates Co. (23 Mar 1847)

1266. Mrs. Elizabeth Jane Taylor age 2_ yrs.? (illegible) died 20 Mar 1847 in Penn Yan, Yates Co., wife of Rodney Taylor. (23 Mar 1847)

* * * MANY PAPERS MISSING * * *

1267. Hiram DePew and Cornelia Jane Purdy both of Milo, Yates Co., were married 7 Oct 1847 at Milo, by Rev. Hancock. (12 Oct 1847)

1268. Joseph Levert, to be executed 16 Nov 1847 in Plattsburgh, Clinton Co., for the murder of his wife last Dec 1846. (19 Oct 1847)

1269. William Eastman of Milwaukee, Wisconsin, and Sarah J. Bacon of Ottawa, Illinois, were married 21 Sep 1847 by Rev. Barrell in Ottawa. (19 Oct 1847)

1270. David Lacy of Penn Yan, Yates Co. and Deborah Middleton of Williamson, Wayne Co., were married 10 Nov 1847 by Rev. Goodwin in Penn Yan. (23 Nov 1847)

1271. Rev. James Richards Jr. and Sarah Wisner, only daughter of the late Henry A. Wisner of Hempstead, Nassau Co., were married by Rev. Geiston in Hempstead, no date given. (23 Nov 1847)

1272. Judge Timothy Childs died a few weeks ago, while on his way to a warmer climate for his health. The brother of Col. Childs, his 89 year old mother attended the funeral, buried 10 Dec 1847 at Pittsfield, MA., no date given.
(14 Dec 1847) and (21 Dec 1847)

1273. William J. M---berg (illegible) of Benton, Yates Co., and Esther Torrey of Middlesex, Yates Co., were married 8 Dec 1847 by William S. Bestwick Esq. in Middlesex. (14 Dec 1847)

1274. Dr. A.F. Wainwright died the week before last. An English professor of chemistry, at a medical college in NY. He was bitten by a rattlesnake while exhibiting it to some friends and died in about five hours, no town or date given.
(21 Dec 1847)

1275. Dr. Edwin G. Munn died 12 Dec 1847 at his home in Gates, Monroe Co. Widely known as a medical man, more extensively as a optician, in this practice he probably had no equal in western New York. (21 Dec 1847)

1276. Stephen Williams age 60 yrs.? (blurred), died _?_ Dec 1847 (illegible) in Penn Yan, Yates Co., services from the Methodist Chapel. (21 Dec 1847)

1277. Deloam Wood age 22 yrs., died 8 Dec 1847 at Potter, Yates Co. (21 Dec 1847)

1278. William A. Vanderlin, convicted at Detroit, MI., 21 Nov 1847 for murdering Thomas Bingham, and sentenced to life in prison. (4 Jan 1848)

1279. Dr. Charles Townsend age 69 yrs., died in Albany, Albany Co. One of the oldest physicians there, no date given. (4 Jan 1848)

1280. Joel Siples died a few days ago from small pox, at Shoemakers Corner, Allegany Co., formerly of Jerusalem, Yates Co. He had several wives, and was about to marry another at the time of his death, no date given. (4 Jan 1848)

1281. Senator Fairchild of Maine died, no date or town given. (4 Jan 1848)

1282. David P. Page age 37 yrs., died 1 Jan 1848 in Newburyport, Principal of the Normal School, a citizen of MA. (11 Jan 1848)

1283. Malinda Kinney age 27 yrs., died 10 Jan 1848 in Penn Yan, Yates Co. (11 Jan 1848)

1284. Samuel Cole of Milo, Yates Co., and ___?___ Feagles (illegible) of Benton, Yates Co., were married 8 Jan 1848 by S.G. Gage in Benton. (18 Jan 1848)

1285. Gen. George P. Barker died 27 Jan 1848 in Buffalo, Erie Co., one of the most prominent public men in western New York. (1 Feb 1848)

1286. Charles Scott age 38 yrs., died 25 Jan 1848 at Penn Yan. (1 Feb 1848)

1287. Agnes Maria Sawyer age 5 mos., died 28 Jan 1848 at Starkey, Yates Co., daughter of Adna and E. Sawyer. (1 Feb 1848)

1288. John Jacob Astor age 85 yrs., said to be in dangerously ill health. Born Jul 1763 at Waldrop, near Heidelberg, in the Duchy of Baden. (8 Feb 1848)

1289. 1847 MORTALITY TABLE FOR THE TOWN OF BENTON; prepared for the " Yates County Whig" by S.G. Gage.

Jan...	1	Miss __?__ Wixon age 20 yrs.
"	1	Myron Winters age 12 yrs.
"	29	William Silvernail age 74 yrs.
Feb...	7	Elizabeth Brown age 41 yrs.
"	10	Elizabeth Ladue age 42 yrs.
Mar..	__	Gideon Sprague age 26 yrs.
"	18	L.N.B. Vanderlip Esq. age 25 yrs.
"	23	Froanna Allen age 78 yrs.
"	23	Olive Barden age 35 yrs.

Mar..23	Amelia Taylor age 26 yrs.
" 27	Marsena E. Wheat age under 1 yr.
Apr...8	Bradner B. Robinson age 2 yrs.
" 26	Clark Smith age 39 yrs.
" 28	Jane Sheppard age 38 yrs.
" 29	Dorinda Hughes age 67 yrs.
" 29	Sarah Remer age 29 yrs.
" __	Inf' of J. Hood age under 1 yr.
May..10	Charles Halsted age 3 yrs.
" 28	Maria B. Gilderslieve age under 1 yr.
" 29	Mabel Whitney age 83 yrs.
Jun...1	Hannah J. Smith age under 1 yr.
" 24	Abigail Gage age 27 yrs.
" 28	Dudley Brown age 68 yrs.
Jul...3	Dr. Nathan L. Kidder age 67 yrs. died
" 3	Rebecca B. Hudson age 39 yrs.
" __	Mrs. Smith age 28 yrs.
Aug..16	Alice E. Deyo age under 1 yr.
" 18	Mary A. McAlpine age 3 yrs.
" 19	Hester A. Deyo age 21 yrs.
Sep...3	Mary Earl age 22 yrs.
" 6	Inf' son of J.M. Gage age under 1 yr.
" 20	Mary Hotchkiss age 77 yrs.
" 23	Harriet N. Hudson age under 1 yr.
" __	Ann Grinnell age 30 yrs.
Oct..__	John Agar age 16 yrs.
" 5	John Cronk age 22 yrs.
" 11	William Goundry age 22 yrs.
" 29	Mary E. Owston age 3 yrs.
Nov...8	Mary Ann Pressler age 27 yrs.
" 9	John Conklin age 45 yrs.
" 15	Olive E. Coffin age 3 yrs.
" 17	Inf'of R. Tompkins age under 1 yr.,
Dec..__	Inf'of S. Austin age under 1 yr.,
" __	Obediah Dennis age 41 or 44 yrs. ?
" 27	Joseph D. Pembroke age 48 yrs.

(29 Feb 1848)

1290. Hon. John Quincy Adams died 21 Feb 1848 in Washington, late U.S. President, statesman and patriot. (29 Feb 1848)

1291. Mrs. Leafe Simonds died 20 Feb 1848 in Milo, Yates Co., wife of William Simonds, formerly of Walpole, NH. (Printers in Bellows Falls, VT., Keene and Claremont, NH., please copy). (29 Feb 1848)

1292. Hon. Henry W. Strong age 38 yrs., died 28 Feb 1848 at his residence in Troy, Rensselaer Co. The Recorder of Troy, an ex-Senator, and Secretary of the late Constitutional Convention. (7 Mar 1848)

1293. John M. Landon died 26 Feb 1848 at Millport, Chemung Co., NY, of small pox, formerly of Penn Yan, Yates Co. (7 Mar 1848)

1294. Hon. Chief Justice Ambrose Spencer died 12 Mar 1848 at his home in Lyons, Wayne Co. * a brief biography printed. (14 Mar 1848)

1295. Hon. John M. Holley died 9 Mar 1848 at Jacksonville, FL., an ex-member of Congress from the Wayne and Seneca Dist's of New York. (14 Mar 1848)

1296. Martin Quick age 63 yrs., died 12 Mar 1848 at his home in Branchport, Yates Co. (14 Mar 1848)

1297. Mrs. Andeline VanDerlip age 48 yrs., died 24 Apr 1848 in Penn Yan, Yates Co. (27 Apr 1848)

1298. Gen. Ashley, a Senator for Arkansas, died last week in Washington, a native of Columbia Co., New York, no date given. (11 May 1848)

1299. Azariah Crandall and Mary Jane Page, both of Dundee, Yates Co., were married 30 Apr 1848 by Rev. Boyer at Rock Stream, Yates Co. (11 May 1848)

1300. Richard H. Toler age 49 yrs., died 23 May 1848 at Richmond, VA. The Sr. Editor of the "Richmond Whig", and for 22 yrs. Editor of the "Lynchburg Virginian". (25 May 1848)

1301. James E. Scott of Penn Yan, Yates Co., and Mary Playsted of Milo, Yates Co., were married 24 May 1848 by Rev. Starkey in Milo. (25 May 1848)

1302. Milton B. Barden and Susan Coffin, both of Benton, Yates Co., were married 17 May 1848 by Rev. Hotchkiss in Bellona, Yates Co. (25 May 1848)

1303. John V. Masten, killed 12 Mar 1848 at Santa Cruz, son of Hon. C. Masten of Penn Yan, Yates Co. (1 Jun 1848)

1304. Benjamin Perry and Mrs. Sarah E. Buck, both of Rushville, Yates Co., were married 28 May 1848 by Rev. H. Townsend in Rushville. (1 Jun 1848)

1305. Dr. Stephen P. Choate and Susan Ann Cole, daughter of Rev. E. Cole formerly of Benton, Yates Co., were married 14 May 1848 at Three Rivers, MI., by Rev. S. Steele. (1 Jun 1848)

1306. John Havens of Lyons, Wayne Co., and Cornelia Haught, daughter of D.C. Haught of Rochester, Monroe Co., were married 25 May 1848 by Rev. Stanwood in Rochester. (1 Jun 1848)

1307. Mrs. Maria Graham age 23 yrs., died at Italy Hollow, Yates Co., wife of Lewis B. Graham, no date given. (1 Jun 1848)

1308. Edward S. Burton and Ann Eliza Laferge, both of Prattsburg, Steuben Co., were married 8 Jun 1848 by Rev. Smith in Prattsburg. (15 Jun 1848)

1309. Dr. M. Caldwell of Phelps, Ontario Co., and Olive S. Noble, formerly of Canandaigua, Ontario Co., were married 8 Jun 1848 by Rev. Mervin in Victor, Ontario Co. (15 Jun 1848)

1310. Charles Gillett age 66 yrs., died 5 Jun 1848 in Benton, Yates Co. (15 Jun 1848)

1311. Mrs. Mary M. Stebbins age 31 yrs., died 28 Jun 1848 at Penn Yan, Yates Co., of apoplexy, wife of Fitz A. Stebbins. (29 Jun 1848)

1312. Hiram Kenyon of Penn Yan, Yates Co., and Sarah Ann Northrup of Potter, Yates Co., were married 3 Jul 1848 by Rev. Goodwin in Penn Yan. (6 Jul 1848)

1313. Mrs. Sarah Lamb age 49 yrs., died 23 Jun 1848 at Branchport, Yates Co., wife of Dexter Lamb Esq. (6 Jul 1848)

1314. Rev. Gilbert Crawford died 29 Jun 1848, pastor of the Presbyterian Church in Leroy. Genesee Co. (13 Jul 1848)

1315. Rev. William R. Weeks age 66 yrs., died 7 Jul 1848 at Newark, New Jersey. (13 Jul 1848)

1316. Dr. H.R. Foote of Penn Yan, Yates Co., and Caroline Durry of Jerusalem, yates Co., were married 5 Jul 1848 by Rev. Robinson in Jerusalem. (13 Jul 1848)

1317. Dr. Stephen G. Lombard of Aurelius, Cayuga Co. and Cordelia Nutt of Benton, Yates Co., were married 11 Jul 1848 by Rev. Daniel W. Litchfield in Benton. (13 Jul 1848)

1318. Rodney L. Taylor formerly of Penn Yan, Yates Co., and Amelia Graham of Jefferson, Schoharie Co., were married 11 Jul 1848 at Jefferson, no pastor given. (13 Jul 1848)

1319. Benjamin Cole age 30 yrs., died 14 Jul 1848 from injuries received on the 4th in Penn Yan, Yates Co., formerly of NJ. (20 Jul 1848)

1320. Prof. Edmund Chadwick, principal of Starkey Seminary, at Starkey, Yates Co., and Cassandra Deplacey Hobart of Potter, Yates Co., were married 1 Aug 1848 by Rev. Goodwin in Potter. (3 Aug 1848)

1321. Harriet Stewart Conlee age 2 yrs., died 24 Jul 1848, youngest daughter of A.H. and Caroline Conlee of Dresden, Yates Co. (3 Aug 1848)

1322. Frank Richards Durry age 5 yrs., died 5 Aug 1848 in Jerusalem, Yates Co., youngest son of John and Margaret Durry. (10 Aug 1848)

1323. Martin B. Lewis of Penn Yan, Yates Co., and Emma Harriet Williams, daughter of the late B.M. Williams of Potter, Yates Co., were married 1 Aug 1848 in Cambridge, MA. by Rev. Laury. (10 Aug 1848)

1324. B.R. Clark of Penn Yan, Yates Co., and Emily Rathburn of Centre Almond, Allegany Co., were married 26 Jul 1848 at Mount Morris, Livingston Co., by Rev. Bacon. (10 Aug 1848)

1325. Mary Elizabeth Ellsworth age 11 yrs., died 3 Aug 1848 in Milo, Yates Co., only daughter of Hon. Samuel S. Ellsworth. (10 Aug 1848)

1326. Ephraim N. Wheeler and Sarah Briggs, both of Penn Yan, Yates Co., were married 17 Aug 1848 by Rev. Silas Hawley in Penn Yan. (24 Aug 1848)

1327. Albert Henry Bohall age 8 yrs., died 8 Aug 1848 in Benton, Yates Co., son of A.A. and Betsey Bohall. (24 Aug 1848)

1328. Ashbel Hollister, a merchant at Dundee, Yates Co., and Abigail Smith were married 30 Aug 1848 by Rev. Smith in Penn Yan, Yates Co. (31 Aug 1848)

1329. Lewis S. Rhoda and Helen McLane married 30 Aug 1848 by Rev. Smith at Penn Yan, Yates Co. (31 Aug 1848)

1330. Thomas M. Craft of Cincinnati, Ohio, formerly of Penn Yan, Yates Co., and Jane Snodgrass, youngest daughter of the late William Snodgrass of Cincinnati, formerly of Baltimore, MD., were married 10 Aug 1848 by Rev. Robert Spencer in Cincinnati. (31 Aug 1848)

1331. Nancy R. Lewis age 22 yrs., died 24 Aug 1848 in Penn Yan, Yates Co., daughter of George and Elizabeth Lewis. (31 Aug 1848)

1332. William Parkinson age over 60 yrs., died 2 Sep 1848 in the state prison at Sing Sing. He was convicted 15 yrs. ago of robbery. For years he kept a looking glass store in New York city, and owned a farm at Woodbridge, NJ. A few months past his wife remarried. His brother in-law James Honeyman, alias James Smith is also in prison. (7 Sep 1848)

1333. Thomas Powers died 31 Aug 1848 in the state prison at Sing Sing. (7 Sep 1848)

1334. Lucius Hiram Gr__?__ (illegible) age 1 yr. 3 mos., died 30 Aug 1848 at Waterloo, Seneca Co., son of Seth J. and Sarah A. Gr__?___. (7 Sep 1848)

1335. Oliver Hazzard Perry age 15 yrs., died 28 Aug 1848 at the home of A. Russell in Milo, Yates Co., son of Jonathan Perry. (7 Sep 1848)

1336. Grison E. Graham age 22 yrs., died 28 Aug 1848 at Italy, Yates Co. (7 Sep 1848)

1337. George D.A. Fridgman a printer, and Saphronia E. Ackley, both of Penn Yan, Yates Co., were married last 5 Jul 1848 by Rev. McMahon in Milo, Yates Co. (14 Sep 1848)

1338. Elisha Luther and Lucretia Alvord were married 4 Sep 1848 by Rev. Robinson in Jerusalem, Yates Co. (14 Sep 1848)

1339. Asa Bennett and Eliza Ann Place were married 9 Sep 1848 by Samuel G. Gage Esq. in Benton, Yates Co. (14 Sep 1848)

1340. Lewis Owen and Sophronia Hyatt, both of Starkey, Yates Co., were married 13 Sep 1848 by Rev. Brown in Starkey. (28 Sep 1848)

1341. John Jenkins, Editor of the "Vicksburg Sentinel" killed 15 Sep 1848 at Vicksburg, MS. by H.A. Crabb. (5 Oct 1848)

1342. James Simons of Benton, Yates Co., and Wilhelmina Verveer of New Haven, daughter of the late Gen. Verveer of Holland, were married 28 Sep 1848 by Rev. Cooke at New Haven. (5 Oct 1848)

1343. Samuel H. Wheaton of Prattsburgh, Steuben Co. and Susan K__?__ey (illegible) of Penn Yan, Yates Co., were married 3 Oct 1848 by Thomas H. Locke Esq. in Penn Yan. (5 Oct 1848)

1344. John Earl of Michigan, and Orrlesa Lane of Potter, Yates Co., were married 5 Oct 1848 by Rev. Townsend in Potter. (19 Oct 1848)

1345. Daniel S. Marsh Jr. age 30 yrs., died 16 Oct 1848 in Penn Yan, Yates Co., a merchant of that place. (19 Oct 1848)

1346. John M. Oliver and Joanna Wagener, only daughter of David Wagener, were married 23 Oct 1848 by Rev. Starkey at St. Mark's Church in Penn Yan, Yates Co. (26 Oct 1848)

1347. Jeremiah S. Jillett of Penn Yan, Yates Co., and Flora Spence, the daughter of Dr. Spence of Starkey, Yates Co., were married 23 Oct 1848 by Rev. Pratt in Starkey. (26 Oct 1848)

1348. Ephriam C. Fletcher of Bath, Steuben Co., and Maria M. Winants of Penn Yan, Yates Co., were married 24 Oct 1848 by Rev. Silas Hawley in Penn Yan. (26 Oct 1848)

1349. James H. Whitney formerly of Penn Yan, Yates Co., and Mary Scott of Elizabethtown, NJ., were married 4 Oct 1848 by Rev. Moore in Elizabethtown. (26 Oct 1848)

1350. Mrs. Anna Barber age 51 yrs., died 18 Oct 1848 in Potter, Yates Co., wife of Jeremiah Barber Esq., daughter of Nicholas and Ida VanZant. (26 Oct 1848)

1351. Mrs. Sarah Ann Winants age 27 yrs., died 23 Oct 1848 at Newark, Wayne Co. The wife of H.H. Winants, and daughter of Howard Bannister. (26 Oct 1848)

1352. George E. Chapine of Glasgow, Scotland, and

Martha Ann Bellows of Charlestown, NH., were married 29 Oct 1848 by Rev. Starkey in St. Mark's Church in Penn Yan, Yates Co. (2 Nov 1848)

1353. Almond Beal and Martha A. Smith, both of Jerusalem, Yates Co., were married 30 Oct 1848 in by Rev. Abner Chase in Penn Yan. (2 Nov 1848)

1354. Lt. Christopher H. Perry, son of Commodore Perry, died on the ship "Suvich" 8 Oct 1848, from New Orleans to New York. (9 Nov 1848)

1355. Harrison Gray Otis age 85 yrs., died 28 Oct 1848 in Boston, MA. A descendant of John Otis, who came from England in 1630, and settled at Hingham, MA. A nephew of the celebrated James Otis, the noted Revolutionary Patriot. Mr. Otis was born 8 Oct 1765 in Boston, graduated from Harvard in 1783 and filled many public offices. * brief biography printed. (9 Nov 1848)

1356. Dr. C.C. Yates died in Nova Scotia, at an advanced age. Formerly of New York city and Albany, husband of Mrs. Willard, the celebrated teacher of Troy, Rensselaer Co., who he had married only a short time before his death, no date or town given. (9 Nov 1848)

1357. Miss Susannah Laurent age 150 yrs. 5 days, died in Montreal,Canada, no date given. (9 Nov 1848)

1358. Mr. McNutt, Ex-Governor of Mississippi, died 23 Oct 1848 at Memphis, TN. (9 Nov 1848)

1359. Mrs. Mary Shearman age 33 yrs., died 8 Nov 1848 in Penn Yan, Yates Co. The wife of Bradley Shearman, daughter of the late Hon. Aaron Remer. (23 Nov 1848)

1360. Caroline Lucretia Miner age 11 yrs. 15 days, died 19 Nov 1848 in Syracuse, Onondaga Co., eldest daughter of the Rev. Ovid Miner. (23 Nov 1848)

1361. Mrs. Mary Leonard a widow, drowned 26 Nov 1848 in the canal at Penn Yan. She leaves a son, and a daughter abt. 12 yrs. old. (30 Nov 1848)

1362. Thomas M. Townsend of Benton, Yates Co., and Sarah M. Rappleye, daughter of Abram Rappleye of Farmersville, Cattaragus Co., were married on 21 Nov 1848 by Rev. Bessler at Farmersville. (30 Nov 1848)

1363. Amanda M. Ackley age 3 yrs. 4 mos. 6 days, died 25 Nov 1848 in Penn Yan, Yates Co., daughter of William and Emily Ackley. (30 Nov 1848)

1364. Rufus Allen and Mary Ann Spooner were married 29 Nov 1848 by Rev. Chase in Milo, Yates Co. (7 Dec 1848)

1365. Charles E. Kelsey of Bellona, Yates Co., and Mary E. Sawyer of Milo, Yates Co., were married 22 Nov 1848 by Rev. Hotchkiss in Milo. (7 Dec 1848)

1366. Laura Kelsey age 17 yrs., died 23 Nov 1848 in Benton, Yates Co., of consumption. (7 Dec 1848)

1367. Rev. Howell Smith of Penn Yan, Yates Co., and Frances Degolia of Prattsburgh, Steuben Co., were married 12 Dec 1848 by Rev. Parington in Prattsburgh. (14 Dec 1848)

1368. A son born 19 Dec 1848 to Benjamin Cook in Penn Yan, Yates Co. (21 Dec 1848)

1369. Mrs. Malinda B. Hawley age 31 yrs., died 23 Dec 1848 in Penn Yan, Yates Co. The wife of Rev. Silas Hawley, and daughter of Stephen Benedict. Married in 1836, she gave birth to two boys and one daughter. The oldest son died at the age of five. (28 Dec 1848 and 4 Jan 1849)

1370. Edwin Goodrich Weaver age 9 mos. 17 days, died 25 Dec 1848 at Branchport, Yates Co., only son of Myron H. and Mary Weaver. (4 Jan 1849)

1371. Richard L. Benedict age 9 yrs. 7 mos., died 14 Dec 1848 in Jerusalem, Yates Co., son of Nathan G. Benedict. (4 Jan 1849)

1372. Alexander Millspaugh of Penn Yan, Yates Co., and Sophia E. Elwood of Jerusalem, Yates Co., were married 17 Jan 1849 by Rev. Silas Hawley in Jerusalem. (18 Jan 1849)

1373. John Summers of Woodford Co. IL, and Lydia B. Moore, late of Jerusalem, Yates Co., were married 31 Oct 1848 at Washington, Tazewell Co. IL., by Rev. D. Chase. (25 Jan 1849)

1374. John D. Hotchkin and Esther A. Wheaton, the daughter of John M. Wheaton, both of Prattsburgh, Steuben Co., were married 17 Jan 1849 by Rev. Hotchkin in Prattsburgh. (25 Jan 1849)

1375. Mary J. Herrington age 4 yrs. 11 mos. 10 days died last 15 Oct 1848 in Jerusalem, Yates Co., only child of James and Elizabeth Herrington.
(25 Jan 1849)

1376. Dr. John Loffland died 22 Jan 1849 at Wilmington, Delaware. (1 Feb 1849)

1377. George Allen of Redford, Wayne Co. MI. and Emily S. Cornwell of Penn Yan, Yates Co., NY., were married 31 Dec 1848 by Rev. Curtis in Redford.
(1 Feb 1849)

1378. The wife of the Hon. Robert L. Rose died 3 Feb 1849 at the family home in Allen's Hill, Ontario Co. (8 Feb 1849)

1379. 1848 MORTALITY TABLE FOR THE TOWN OF BENTON; prepared for the "Yates County Whig" by Samuel G. Gage Esq.:

Jan...7	Inf' of S. Austin age under 1 yr.
" 8	Inf' of L. Harris age under 1 yr.
" 11	Chris. G. Mitchell age under 1 yr.
" 16	Harriet B. Griffin age 30 yrs.
" 19	Joseph F. Pembrook age under 1 yr.
" 20	Sabrina Carr age 14 yrs.
Feb...5	Remember L. Freeman age 50 yrs.
" 6	Bethia Sutton age 30 yrs.
" 8	Melissa Carr age under 1 yr.
" 17	Colbourn H. Scoonmaker age 2 yrs.
" 29	David Lain age 82 yrs.
Mar...9	Dr. Abijah E. Perry age 53 yrs.
" 13	Alice V. Gage age 1 yr.
Apr...7	Charles Moon age 4 yrs.
" 11	Richard Owston age 37 yrs.
" 21	Elizabeth Griswold age 56 yrs.
May..13	Mary D. Parsons age 3 yrs.
" 18	Wilhelmus Bookstaver age 76 yrs.
Jun...3	Ann Newsom age 84 yrs.
" 5	Capt. Charles Gillett age 56 yrs.
" 10	Robert Tiff age 4 yrs.
" 14	Edward Carr age 18 yrs.
" 17	George E. Brizzee age 36 yrs.
" 23	Franklin J. Day age 29 yrs.
Jul..24	Harriet S. Condit age 2 yrs.
" 26	Joseph Whally age 45 yrs.
" 30	Theodore Graves age 5 yrs.
Aug...3	Ciprian Carr age 16 yrs.
" 4	Edwin Willis age under 1 yr.
" 5	Edmond Graves age 6 yrs.
" 6	Rynard Rush age 78 yrs.
" 8	Albert H. Bohall age 8 yrs.

Aug..11 Adelia Townsend age 7 yrs.
" 13 Lewis A. McLean age 2 yrs.
" 16 Milan Eaton age 2 yrs.
" 25 Nancy Buckbee age 56 yrs.
" 25 Sarah L. Adams age 32 yrs.
" 25 Inf'of Sarah L. Adams age under 1 yr.
Sep...7 Catharine E. Swarthout age 3 yrs.
" 15 George Stonice age 6 yrs.
" 24 Smith Peck age 56 yrs.
Oct..12 Barney Geldon age 80 yrs.
" 15 Sarah L. Abel age 7 yrs.
" 25 William Varick age under 1 yr.
" 25 Michael Francisco age 87 yrs.
" 26 Augusta Swarthout age 4 yrs.
" 28 Phebe J. Briggs age 3 yrs.
Nov...9 Eliza Titus age 19 yrs.
" 15 Mary Eldridge age 32 yrs.
" 15 Inf'of H. Eldridge age under 1 yr.
" 20 Inf'of E.D. Gage age under 1 yr.
" 23 Laura Kelsey age 17 yrs.
" 25 Mary A. Pearce age 75 yrs.
" 27 Amanda M. Ackley age 4 yrs.
Dec..11 Alfred Ackley age 5 yrs.
" 26 Darwin Litchfield age 6 yrs.
(15 Feb 1849)

1380. Joseph Kelsey a tavern owner, died 23 Feb 1849 in Buffalo, Erie Co. Upon his death bed, he confessed to numerous crimes, including a murder of which he was a suspect, and several other charges, one of which he had been tried for, but acquited. (1 Mar 1849)

1381. A.F. Tyler, executed 16 Feb 1850 at Bryan, Williams Co. Ohio, convicted of a murder, he professed to the last his innocence. (1 Mar 1849)

1382. Jonathan B. Tombs formerly of Penn Yan, Yates Co., and Bethi Ann Averett, niece of Hon. Thomas Averett, married 14 Feb 1849 by Rev. Longanere in Halifax Co. VA. (8 Mar 1849)

1383. Calvin R. Way and Caroline M. Hellems, daughter of Isaac Hellems, both of Rochester, Monroe Co., were married 1 Mar 1849 by Rev. Montgomery in Rochester. (8 Mar 1849)

1384. Hon. Timothy S. Williams died 11 Mar 1849 at his home in Ithaca, Tompkins Co., a Senator of this state. (15 Mar 1849).

1385. Mrs. Mary Scott age 29 yrs., died 14 Mar 1849

in Penn Yan, Yates Co., wife of James E. Scott, the daughter of John Playsted of Milo, Yates Co., married but 2 months ago, her funeral from the Episcopal Church. (15 Mar 1849)

1386. Edgar Hyatt and Mary A. Wise, daughter of Samuel Wise, were married 7 Mar 1849 by Rev. Knox in New York city. (22 Mar 1849)

1387. A building at the powder mill of Marshfield Parsons in Brighton, Monroe Co., exploded 29 Mar 1849, killing Archibald Ross, who was blown abt. 35 to 40 feet across the creek. (5 Apr 1849)

1388. Amos C. West age 25 yrs., died 7 Mar 1849 at Ottawa, Illinois, formerly of Penn Yan, Yates Co. (5 Apr 1849)

1389. James Savage and Fidelia A. Simmons, both of Penn Yan, Yates Co., were married 24 Mar 1849 by Rev. Robinson in Penn Yan. (12 Apr 1849)

1390. Rev. William J. Popham died 5 Jan 1849. He was lost at sea, while on a schooner in which he had taken passage for Hong Kong. It wrecked two days from its point of destination. A missionary on the board of the Reformed Dutch Church. (19 Apr 1849)

1391. Mrs. Lucinda G. Martin age 31 yrs., died 6 Apr 1849 in Penn Yan, Yates Co., wife of D. Martin. (19 Apr 1849)

1392. Mrs. Cassandra D. Chadwick age 25 yrs. 8 mos. died 14 Apr 1849 in Starkey, Yates Co., wife of Rev. Edmund Chadwick. (19 Apr 1849)

1393. Mr. C.H. Langley age 23 yrs., died in New York city. One of the publishers of the "Western Literary Emporium". He had gone to the roof of his boarding house, to observe a fire and passed over, to an adjoining building, to get a better view. In returning, he stumbled in the dark and fell through a glass sky-light, striking his head and dying instantly, a brother in-law of Rev. A. Wright of Penn Yan, Yates Co. (3 May 1849)

1394. Joseph Jones age 78 yr., died 12 May 1849 in Penn Yan, Yates Co. A native of PA., brought up in the Society of Friends. He moved to Penn Yan over 50 yrs. ago. (17 May 1849)

1395. Mary Elizabeth Jewitt age 15 yrs. 6 mos. 13 days, died 3 May 1849 in Bellona, Yates Co. (31 May 1849)

1396. George Buckhart age 114 yrs., is now living in Harlan Co., KY. Born in Germantown, PA., he has lived for years in a hollow sycamore tree, of such dimensions as to contain his family, consisting of a wife and 5 or 6 children, bed and bedding, cooking utensils, etc. He professes to hold to the Lutheran faith, being of a German family. (7 Jun 1849)

1397. Daniel Baldwin age 36 or 56 yrs. (blurred), died 2 Jun 1849 in Italy, Yates Co. (7 Jun 1849)

1398. Sewals Vaughn of Jackson, Michigan, and Helen A. Billings, daughter of Hon. B.J. Billings of Elma, Erie Co., were married 26 May 1849 by Rev. Parsons in Elma. (14 Jun 1849)

1399. Mrs. VanWormer age 45 yrs., died of injuries received on a boat, in the canal about a mile from Rochester. She attempted to cross the deck of the boat from one cabin to the other, but being too near a bridge to accomplish it. She hit her head on the timber, making a ghastly wound, and rupturing the ligaments of her neck, which caused her to die almost instantly. She was traveling from the east to meet her husband Mr. VanWormer, had been boarding at the Clinton House. Every day he had checked the arriving boats, waiting anxiously for her arrival, only to be rewarded with her bleeding corspe, no date given. (21 Jun 1849)

1400. Hon. James Polk died 15 Jun 1849 at Nashville, Tennessee. The ex-President of the U.S., he was born 2 Nov 1795 at Mecklenberg, North Carolina. (21 Jun 1849)

1401. Samuel P. Carray and Fear Youngs, were married 10 Jun 1849 by Rev. Decker in Jerusalem, Yates Co. (21 Jun 1849)

1402. Two sons of H.C. Sheppard of Concord, Wisconsin, one age 12 yrs., and the other 10 yrs., were in the field hunting chipmunks. The elder loaded a gun, applied the hammer, and the piece exploded as he was in the act of handing it to his brother, the latter shot in the head, died instantly, no date given. (28 Jun 1849)

1403. A son of Mr. Duell of Burnett, Dodge Co. WI., was accidently killed by his brother, as they were shooting blackbirds, one age 9 yrs., and the other 12 yrs., no date given. (28 Jun 1849)

1404. A group of young people were enjoying an evening at Lunar Island, near Niagara Falls. When Charles Addington age 21 yrs., playfully threatened to throw Annette DeForrest age 9 yrs., into the river. He picked her up, and swung her back and forth several times, then his foot slipped, and they both fell into the rapids. Addington tried desparately to save the girl, who was fighting his efforts, and in a few minutes, they were both swept over the falls and drowned. She was the daughter of Charles H. DeForrest of Buffalo, Erie Co. (28 Jun 1849)

1405. Rev. Timothy Wardwell of Lyons, Wayne Co., and Mary Blair Day, daughter of Abraham Day of Hopeton, Yates Co., were married 19 Jun 1849 by Rev. DeLancey in Hopeson. (28 Jun 1849)

1406. Hon. George W. Peck, Secretary of State of Lansing, MI., and Sophia E. Lee, daughter of Daniel S. Lee of Brighton, MI., were married 31 May 1849 in Brighton, by Rev. Hollister. (28 Jun 1849)

1407. Seymour Scutt and Mary Ann Fitzwater, both of Milo, Yates Co., were married 21 Jun 1849 by Rev. Sunderline in Milo. (28 Jun 1849)

1408. James Jamacia Collins age 102 yrs., died 18 Jul 1849 in Penn Yan, Yates Co., a colored man and patriot of the Revolution. (26 Jul 1849)

1409. Jay S. Mariner died 23 Jul 1849 in Milo, Yates Co., leaving a wife and 2 children. (26 Jul 1849)

1410. Henry B. Clarke Esq. age 48 yrs., died 21 Jul 1849 near Chicago, Illinois. (2 Aug 1849)

1411. Miles Thomas age 19 yrs., died 24 Jul 1849 in Potter, Yates Co. (2 Aug 1849)

1412. Alice Holmes age 3 yrs. 7 mos. 28 days, died 24 Jul 1849 in Benton, yates Co., only daughter of Lewis P. and Helen Holmes. (2 Aug 1849)

1413. William D. Anderson died 30 Jun 1849 at Rochester, son of Hixon Anderson of Jerusalem, Yates Co. (2 Aug 1849)

1414. William T. Lawrence of Milo, Yates Co., died 25 Jun 1849 at Troy, Rensselaer Co., while he and his wife were visiting friends. (2 Aug 1849)

1415. David Anderson and his infant son, died 7 Jun 1849 in Albany, Albany Co. Owner of a cargo boat the "Young Fox", which ran between Wayne and New York city. (2 Aug 1849)

1416. Prof. Rev. Edmund Chadwick, principal of Starkey Seminary, Yates Co., and Adeline Ward of Jefferson, Schoharie Co. were married 31 Jul 1849 by Elder Marvin at Jefferson. (9 Aug 1849)

1417. William Turner of Potter, Yates Co., and Thankful Galusha, daughter of Simeon Galusha of Middlesex, Yates Co., were married 29 Jul 1849 by J.J. Johnson Esq. in Middlesex. (9 Aug 1849)

1418. Hon. Albert Gallatin age 89 yrs., died 12 Aug 1849 in Astoria, Queens Co. * A brief biography printed. (16 Aug 1849)

1419. John Rogers of Penn Yan, Yates Co., and Catharine Evans of Hammondsport, Steubens Co., were married at Avon, Steuben Co., by Rev. Spencer, no date given. (21 Aug 1849)

1420. John _?_ (illegible) of Penn Yan, Yates Co., and Catharine A. Ryan of Branchport, Yates Co., were married in Avon, Steuben Co., no date or pastor given. (16 Aug 1849)

1421. George Wheeler age 21 yrs., died 7 Aug 1849 in New York city, son of Mrs. Pauline Wheeler of Penn Yan, Yates Co. (16 Aug 1849)

1422. The daughter of Peter Carvey of Italy, Yates Co., age 4 yrs., accidently fell in a bucket of boiling water a few days ago. She was so badly scalded, she lived but a few hours. This is the third death in his family in less than two years. A little over a year ago, he lost his wife and another child, no date given. (23 Aug 1849)

1423. William B. Shaw age 19 yrs., died in Benton, Yates Co., of typhus fever, the eldest son of Owen Shaw, no date given. (23 Aug 1849)

1424. Aaron Henries of Benton, Yates Co., died 16 Aug 1849 at Buffalo, Erie Co., from cholera. (23 Aug 1849)

1425. Edward Potter age 81 yrs., died 14 Aug 1849 in Milo, Yates Co., at the home of Samuel J. Potter. (23 Aug 1849)

1426. Edward Franklin Holbrook age 18 yrs. 6 mos., died 23 Aug 1849, youngest son of Galen Holbrook of Rushville, Yates Co. (30 Aug 1849)

1427. Mrs. Mary Jane Hunt age 23 or 25 yrs. (blurred), died 25 Aug 1849 in Milo, Yates Co., wife of Adam Hunt. Their son Adalbert M. Hunt age 1 yr. 9 mos. 17 days, also died on the 25th. (30 Aug 1849)

1428. Rev. Henry Coleman of Boston, age 65 yrs., died 17 Aug 1849 near London. (6 Sep 1849)

1429. George M. Chase age 30 yrs., died 2 Sep 1849 in Penn Yan, Yates Co., a resident of Penn Yan for two and a half yrs. (6 Sep 1849)

1430. Mrs. Sarah L. Wells age 23 yrs., died 3 Sep 1849 in Penn Yan, Yates Co., wife of George D. Wells, daughter of Willis Newman of East Bloomfield, Ontario Co. (6 Sep 1849)

1431. Henry Rosakrants age 35 yrs., died 28 Aug 1849 at Troy, Rensselaer Co., his wife Cornella Rosakrants age 23 or 33 yrs. (blurred), died the day before, both of cholera, leaving 4 children, formerly of Penn Yan, Yates Co. (6 Sep 1849)

1432. Harvey Eggleston died 23 Aug 1849 at Milan, Ohio., of cholera, the son of Allen Eggleston of Potter, Yates Co. (6 Sep 1849)

1433. John Cromwell age 18 yrs., died 4 Sep 1849 in Benton, Yates Co., of consumption. (13 Sep 1849)

1434. Benjamin Cook died 11 Sep 1849 in Potter, Yates Co. * Age given, but paper very blurred on film. (13 Sep 1849)

1435. Ransom Olney age 65 yrs., died 16 Aug 1849 in Benton, Yates Co. (13 Sep 1849)

1436. George Winters and Mary Shuett, both of Seneca, Ontario Co., were married 21 Sep 1849 by Rev. Daniel W. Litchfield in Seneca. (27 Sep 1849)

1437. Salley Barden age 50 yrs., died 22 Sep 1849 at her home in Benton, Yates Co. (27 Sep 1849)

1438. James Beamount Spencer age 23 or 33 yrs.? (blurred), died 18 Sep 1849 in Benton, Yates Co. (27 Sep 1849)

1439. William T. Remer and Mary Trimmer, both of Benton, Yates Co., were married 1 Oct 1849 by Rev. Warner in Benton. (4 Oct 1849)

1440. George Bruen and Anna Henry, daughter of William D. Henry, both of Penn Yan, Yates Co., were married 4 Oct 1849 by Rev. Silas Hawley in Penn Yan. (11 Oct 1849)

1441. William McAllister of Penn Yan, Yates Co., and Ruth Ward of Barrington, Yates Co., were married 7 Oct 1849 by Elder Olney in Barrington. (11 Oct 1849)

1442. Mrs. Sarah S. Sheldon age 56 yrs., died 5 Oct 1849 in Penn Yan, yates Co., wife of Eli Sheldon. (11 Oct 1849)

1443. Mary E. Hammond age 24 yrs., died 5 Sep 1849, eldest daughter of Oliver Hammond of Rushville, Yates Co. (18 Oct 1849)

1444. Isaac Jones of Penn Yan, Yates Co., is searching for his lost son Phillip Jones. He was last seen 17 May 1849, when he attended the Circus. He is 12 yrs. old, ordinary size, black hair, large blue eyes, healthy, and can read and write. (25 Oct 1849)

1445. Henry Bennett and Cornelia Bradley, daughter of Henry Bradley, both of Penn Yan, Yates Co., were married 18 Oct 1849 by Rev. Silas Hawley, in Penn Yan. (25 Oct 1849)

1446. Harvey D. Pratt and Caroline V. Pearce, both of Penn Yan, Yates Co., were married 18 Oct 1849 by Rev. Wright in of Penn Yan. (25 Oct 1849)

1447. Christopher Spink and Esther Jones, both of Bellona, Yates Co., were married 21 Oct 1849 by Rev. Playsted in Bellona. (25 Oct 1849)

1448. Stephen Clark age 43 yrs., died 28 Oct 1849 in Jerusalem, Yates Co. (1 Nov 1849)

1449. __?__ Milburn (illegible) age 43 yrs., died 27 Oct 1849 in Geneva, Ontario Co., formerly of Penn Yan, Yates Co. (1 Nov 1849)

1450. Thomas E. Garvin Esq. of Evansville, IN. and Cornelia M. Morris of Penn Yan, Yates Co., were married 11 Nov 1849 by Rev. Starkey in Penn Yan. (15 Nov 1849)

1451. Thomas C. Casey and Rebecca Putney, both of Potter, Yates Co., were married 14 Nov 1849 by Rev. Gelston in Potter. (15 Nov 1849)

1452. William Schenck of Potter, Yates Co., and Sarah Det__?__ (illegible), daughter of John Det__?__ (illegible) of Gorham, Ontario Co., were married 23 Oct 1849 by Mr. Borden Esq. in Gorham. (15 Nov 1849)

1453. Horace Underwood and Ruth Warner, daughter of Nathan Warner, both of Potter, Yates Co., were married 29 Oct 1849 Rev. Nutting in Potter. (15 Nov 1849)

1454. Josiah Hawley age 41 yrs., died 9 Nov 1849 in Potter, Yates Co. (15 Nov 1849)

1455. Mrs. Butler died 9 Nov 1849 in Potter, Yates Co., wife of Davidson Butler. (15 Nov 1849)

1456. Mrs. Eleanor Householder died 28 Oct 1849 in Potter, Yates Co., wife of Jacob Householder, and daughter of Jacob Lazarus. (15 Nov 1849)

1457. Peter Dinturff of Potter, Yates Co., and Emily Hobart of Italy, Yates Co., were married 13 Nov 1849 by Rev. Coleman in Potter. (22 Nov 1849)

1458. Andrew J. Cadmus of Potter, Yates Co., and Caroline Williams, daughter of John Williams of Middlesex, Yates Co., were married 13 Nov 1849 by Rev. Coleman in Potter. (22 Nov 1849)

1459. Mrs. Elcey Reddout died 18 Nov 1849 in Potter, Yates Co., wife of William Reddout. (22 Nov 1849)

1460. Hezekiah Davis age 53 yrs., died 1_? Nov 1849 (illegible) in Jerusalem, Yates Co. (22 Nov 1849)

1461. Mrs. Charity VanZant died suddenly 20 Nov 1849 in Bethel, Ontario Co., wife of Garret VanZant of Potter, Yates Co. (22 Nov 1849)

1462. Daniel Frazier age 70 yrs., died 26 Nov 1849 in Benton, Yates Co., killed by his son Daniel

Frazier age 35 yrs., over an argument concerning the feeding of a cow. (29 Nov 1849)

1463. Hiram Nash age 34 or 54 yrs. (blurred), died 18 Nov 1849 in Penn Yan, Yates Co. (29 Nov 1849)

1464. Jonathan Ogden age 35 yrs., killed 30 Nov 1849 in Fulton, Oswego Co., at a planing and morticing mill where he worked. He was oiling a machine and was accidently caught up in the shaft. He leaves a wife and children. (6 Dec 1849)

1465. Theodore F. Sharpe of Penn Yan, Yates Co., and Maria Lathrop, daughter of Rev. Lathrop of Auburn, Cayuga Co., were married 27 Nov 1849 by Rev. Lathrop in Auburn. (6 Dec 1849)

1466. Myron Pulver of Milo, Yates Co., and Mary Miller of Newport, Wayne Co. were married 27 Nov 1849 by Rev. Chase in Newport. (6 Dec 1849)

1467. Mrs. Walbridge age 42 yrs., a mother of nine children, who with her husband and family were traveling west on the canal, drowned at Bushnell's basin near Rochester, Monroe Co., no date given. (13 Dec 1849)

1468. Hon. William Hunter age 76 yrs., died 10 Dec 1849 at Newport, RI., late Senator of that state. (13 Dec 1849)

1469. S.C. Goodwin of Hammondsport, Steuben Co., and Mary Ann K_?_elm ? (illegible) of Milo, Yates Co., were married 17 Dec 1849 by Rev. Robinson in Milo. (20 Dec 1849)

1470. Floyd McDaniels and Nancy Page, daughter of Abraham Page, were married 13 Dec 1849 by Rev. Tucker in Potter, Yates Co. (20 Dec 1849)

1471. Joseph Roots and Drusilla Tipple, both of Potter, Yates Co., were married 20 Dec 1849 in Middlesex, Yates Co., by Elder Bacon. (27 Dec 1849)

1472. William Miller age 68 yrs., died 20 Dec 1849 at his home in Kompton, Washington Co. A native of Pittsfield, MA. and a Captain of volunteers during the last war with England. (3 Jan 1850)

1473. Frederick Rowe of Wayne Co. and Nancy L. Robinson of Milo, Yates Co., were married 29 Dec 1849 by Rev. Wright in Milo. (3 Jan 1850)

1474. Calvin Stone and Mary A. Keeler, both of Milo, Yates Co., were married 30 Dec 1849 by Rev. Smith in Penn Yan, Yates Co. (3 Jan 1850)

1475. James Bucklin of Gerry, Chautauqua Co. and Sarah French, formerly of Geneva, Ontario Co., were married 4 Nov 1849 by Rev. Manier in Gerry. (3 Jan 1850)

1476. William Totten and Sarah M. Buck, both of Orange, Steuben Co., were married 31 Dec 1849 by Rev. Douglas in Penn Yan, Yates Co. (3 Jan 1850)

1477. James Staunton and Caroline A. Hall, both of Penn Yan, Yates Co., were married 1 Jan 1850 by Rev. Douglas in Penn Yan. (3 Jan 1850)

1478. Hiram Traver and Margaret Cooper, both of Penn Yan, Yates Co., were married 31 Dec 1849 by Rev. Robinson in Penn Yan. (3 Jan 1850)

1479. Jonas Wickes died 28 Dec 1849 in Albany, Albany Co., brother of Mrs. James Taylor of Penn Yan, Yates Co. (3 Jan 1850)

1480. Leroy G. Walters and Susannah Foster, daughter of William Foster, both of Middlesex, Yates Co., were married 3 Jan 1850 by Rev. Homes in Benton, Yates Co. (10 Jan 1850)

1481. James Savage of Potter, Yates Co., and Sarah Reynolds, daughter of Thomas Reynolds of Middlesex, Yates Co., were married 28 Dec 1849 by Rev. Homes in Potter. (10 Jan 1850)

1482. Staats Green and Rachel Wilcox, daughter of Steward Wilcox, both of Jerusalem, Yates Co., were married 7 Jan 1850 by Robert Buel Esq. in Jerusalem. (10 Jan 1850)

1483. Frances Briggs age 87 yrs., died 5 Jan 1850 in Potter, Yates Co. One of the first settlers of Yates Co. He resided 65 yrs. on the farm where he died. (17 Jan 1850)

1484. Jerome Cady and Mrs. Amanda Cowles, both of Penn Yan, Yates Co., were married 14 Jan 1850 by Rev. Wright in Penn Yan. (17 Jan 1850)

1485. Helen M. Halsted age 7 yrs., died 7 Jan 1850 in Potter, Yates Co., daughter of John Halsted. (17 Jan 1850)

1486. Oliver H.P. Pembrooke age 32 yrs., died 11 Jan 1850 in Benton, Yates Co., of consumption. (17 Jan 1850)

1487. Rev. Silas Hawley and Harriet J. Reddy, the daughter of Leander Reddy, both of Penn Yan, Yates Co., were married 24 Jan 1850 by Rev. Robinson in Penn Yan. (31 Jan 1850)

1488. Z.C. Swarthout of Benton, Yates Co., and Hester A. Southerland of Seneca, Ontario Co., were married 22 Jan 1850 by Rev. Litchfield in Seneca. (31 Jan 1850)

1489. James Brown and Amanda Slitor, the daughter of Richard V. Slitor, both of Burton, Geauga Co., Ohio, were married 23 Dec 1849 in Burton, no pastor named. (31 Jan 1850)

1490. Tiffana Durkee age 9 yrs. 6 mos., died 24 Jan 1850 in Milo, Yates Co. (31 Jan 1850)

1491. Mrs. Amanda Lown age 27 yrs., died 20 Jan 1850 in Potter, Yates Co., wife of Henry Lown. (31 Jan 1850)

1492. Warren L. Sholes and Abby Anderson, both of Penn Yan, Yates Co., were married 16 Jan 1850 by Rev. Wright in Penn Yan. (7 Feb 1850)

1493. Robert C. Nichols of Geneva, Ontario Co., and Eliza McGowan, daughter of the late Terence McGowan were married 25 Jan 1850 at Frederick, MD., no pastor given. (7 Feb 1850)

1494. TABLE OF MORTALITY FOR TOWN OF BENTON 1849; furnished for the "Yates Co. Whig" by S.G. Gage,

Jan...	1	Charles C. Youngs age 2 yrs.
"	2	Zenus Canfield age 58 yrs.
"	8	Sarah Garrison age 57 yrs.
Feb...	8	Sarah Day (colored) age 57 yrs.
Mar...	7	Daniel Brown age 89 yrs.
"	15	Lydia Brown age 48 yrs.
"	23	Lydia Might age 13 yrs.
"	23	Lydia Banks age 41 yrs.
"	23	Inf' dau. of S. Banks age under 1 yr.
"	30	John Pembrooke age 21 yrs.
Apr...	1	Mary Young age 16 yrs.
"	2	Ezekial B. Heilner age 7 yrs.
"	17	Charles Potter (colored) age 21 yrs.
"	28	Henry O. Chapman age 1 yr.

May...3 Mary E. Jewett age 14 yrs.
" 25 Lester A. Secor age 2 yrs.
" 25 Inf' of Mr. Smith age under 1 yr.
" 27 Myron Lester age 2 yrs.
" 27 James Watkins (colored) age 40 yrs.
" 25 Lydia McKean age abt. 25 yrs.
" 27 A colored boy, Wigdon age under 1 yr.
" 29 Marion Lester age 2 yrs.
Jun..15 William Barnes age 82 yrs.
" 16 Andrew M. Cronk age 6 yrs.
" 19 Eleanor M. Jewett age 22 yrs.
Jul...9 Charles Mingo (colored) age 21 yrs.
" 11 Agnes E. Perry age 27 yrs.
" 20 William Scofield age 63 yrs.
" 21 Alice Holmes age 4 yrs.
" 28 Cyrus S. Shoemaker age under 1 yr.
Aug...7 Robert Mingo (colored) age 1 yr.
" 13 Wilson Shaw age 18 yrs.
" 14 Frederick M. Veazie age 1 yr.
" 16 Ransom T. Olney age 65 yrs.
" 17 Scott A. Cornwell age under 1 yr.
" 21 Anna W. Hayden age 1 yr.
Sep...4 John B. Cornell age 18 yrs.
" 4 James Mingo (colored) age 22 yrs.
" 18 James B. Spencer age 33 yrs.
" 29 Sally Barden age 51 yrs.
" 29 Arthur Hazen age 1 yr.
" 30 Caleb Briggs age 6 yrs.
Oct..11 Thomas Rudd age 61 yrs.
" 12 Sarah Plattman age 52 yrs.
" 15 Ruth Parke, no age given.
" 26 Andrew M. Rector, no age given.
" 29 Sarah N. Gaylord age 26 yrs.
Nov...1 Nathaniel R. Cady age 47 yrs.
Dec..15 John L. Swarthout age 65 yrs.
" 21 George McMillen age 18 yrs.
" 26 John Voak age 84 yr.
" 29 Mary Daughtery age 24 yrs.
(7 Feb 1850)

1495. Zadock Hersley age 98 yrs., died at his home in Pembroke, MA. A soldier of the Revolution, no date given. (14 Feb 1850)

1496. Joshua Hull and Jennett Thomas, daughter of Abial Thomas Esq. of Potter, Yates Co., were married 30 Jan 1850 by Rev. Ackley in Geneva, Ontario Co. (14 Feb 1850)

1497. Stephen W. Briggs and Helen Shoemaker, both of Potter, Yates Co., were married 9 Feb 1850 in by Rev. Abner Chase in Penn Yan, Yates Co.
(14 Feb 1850)

1498. Consider Bordwell age 66 yrs., died 5 Feb 1850 in Potter, Yates Co. One of the early settlers in that town, having lived there over 40 yrs. (14 Feb 1850)

1499. George H. Vail age 30 yrs., died 25 Dec 1849 in San Francisco, CA., late of Troy, Rensselaer Co. (14 Feb 1850)

1500. Major C.G. Bryant of Corpus Christi, Texas. Formerly of Galveston, killed 6 Jan 1850 by a party of Indians. (28 Feb 1850)

1501. Albert F. Randall and Emeline McAlfin were married 18 Feb 1850 by Rev. Daniel Litchfield in Benton, Yates Co. (28 Feb 1850)

1502. William H. Rogers of Potter, Yates Co., and Celesta A. Loomis of Middlesex, Yates Co., were married 25 Feb 1850 by Rev. McGraham at Gorham, Ontario Co. (28 Feb 1850)

1503. Charles H. Randall and Laura Jane Smith, both of Benton, Yates Co., were married 28 Feb 1850 by Rev. Goldsmith in Benton. (7 Mar 1850)

1504. Orren S. Bonsteel and Mary Kenyon, both of Penn Yan, Yates Co., were married 2 Mar 1850 by Rev. Wright in Penn Yan. (7 Mar 1850)

1505. Benjamin Folson of Kent Co., Michigan, and Susan A. Finch, daughter of Theron Finch of Potter, Yates Co., were married 28 Feb 1850 by F. Crakes Esq. in Potter. (7 Mar 1850)

1506. Charles Whitaker age 4 mos., died 23 Feb 1850 in Benton, Yates Co., son of Gen. A.F. Whitaker. (7 Mar 1850)

1507. George A. Sheppard of Benton, Yates Co., and Anna Pettibone, daughter of Oliver Pettibone Esq. of Steuben, Oneida Co., were married 9 Mar 1850 by Robert Buel Esq. in Penn Yan, Yates Co. (14 Mar 1850)

1508. Rev. Truman Gillett age 79 yrs., died 8 Feb 1850 in Camden, Oneida Co. (14 Mar 1850)

1509. Rev. Porter Clay age 71 yrs., died 16 Feb 1850 at Camden, Arkansas, brother of Hon. Henry Clay. (14 Mar 1850)

1510. John Allen, committed to trial for the murder of a peddler, near the city of Utica, Oneida Co., a few weeks since. (21 Mar 1850)

1511. Caroline F. Kroger died in Boston, a friend to the poor at the North End. She contacted smallpox on a charitable mission, to a black family, no date given. (21 Mar 1850)

1512. Charles Angel age 25 yrs., perished 16 Mar 1850 in the house fire of Mr. S.L. Nye at Pharsulia, Chenango Co. (21 Mar 1850)

1513. Samuel L. Cole and Ann Cu__?__ (illegible), both of Benton, Yates Co., were married 22 Mar 1850 by S.G. Gage Esq. in Benton. (28 Mar 1850)

1514. William Coon of Jerusalem, Yates Co., and Jane Hawley, daughter of Josiah Hawley Jr. of Potter, Yates Co., were married 23 Mar 1850 by Rev. Robinson in Potter. (28 Mar 1850)

1515. Abiel Thomas and Minerva N. Holton, daughter of James Holton, both of Potter, Yates Co., were married 22 Mar 1850 by Rev.__?__ (illegible) in Benton, Yates Co. (28 Mar 1850)

1516. Samuel Dintruff age 23 yrs., died 17 Mar 1850 in Potter, Yates Co. (28 Mar 1850)

1517. George W. Andrews died 26 Mar 1850 in Potter, Yates Co., son of Peleg Andrews. (28 Mar 1850)

1518. Justin M. Simmons age 24 yrs., died 22 Mar 1850 in Potter, Yates Co. (28 Mar 1850)

1519. Dennison Butler and Lydia Paine Galigher, daughter of Simeon Galigher, all of Potter, Yates Co., were married 21 Mar 1850 by Rev. Park in Middlesex, Yates Co. (4 Apr 1850)

1520. Sarah Taylor age 22 yrs., died 1 Apr 1850, and Maria Jane Taylor age 18 yrs., died last 7 Jan 1850. The daughters of David S. Taylor, of Penn Yan, Yates Co., both died of consumption, services from the Baptist Church. (4 Apr 1850)

1521. Nathaniel Townsend of Starkey, Yates Co., and Austa Ross of Reading, Schuyler Co., were married 28 Mar 1850 by Rev. Andrews in Reading. (11 Apr 1850)

1522. Mrs. Rebecca Trask aged 56 yrs., died 2 Apr 1850 in Potter, Yates Co. (11 Apr 1850)

1523. Daniel McConnel aged 19 yrs., died 27 Mar 1850 in Starkey, Yates Co. (11 Apr 1850)

1524. Gabriel Bruen aged 82 yrs., died 9 Apr 1850 in Penn Yan, Yates Co., at the home of his son in-law James Cooley, formerly of Newark, NJ. (11 Apr 1850)

1525. Mrs. Julia Ann Walker died 26 Mar 1850 in Barrington, Yates Co., widow of Joseph Walker, sister of the late George Goundry. (11 Apr 1850)

1526. Mrs. Harriet C. Gillett aged 21 yrs., died 4 Apr 1850 in Benton, wife of John N. Gillett Esq. (18 Apr 1850)

1527. Mrs. Deborah Malin aged 84 yrs., died 13 Apr 1850 in Jerusalem, Yates Co. The widow of Elijah Malin, and only remaining relic of the Friends Society. (25 Apr 1850)

1528. H.M. Romeyn Esq. died 28 Apr 1850 at Kingston, Ulster Co., a lawyer and late member of the Assembly. (2 May 1850)

1529. STEAMBOAT ACCIDENT, an explosion aboard the steamboat "Wayne" occurred 28 Apr 1850, under Capt. Gore. The boat left Toledo and was just below Vermillion, when the boiler exploded, killed were J. Ellore 1st. engineer and Edward Beecher 2nd. engineer. (2 May 1850)

1530. John Brown and Emily Freer, both of Benton, Yates Co., were married 25 Apr 1850 by S.G. Gage Esq. in Benton. The same administrator married both parents of the above parties years ago. (2 May 1850)

1531. Edward P. Potter of Yatesville, Orleans Co., and Elizabeth A. Moore of Hartford, CT., were married 18 Apr 1850 by Rev. D.D. Buck in Rochester, Monroe Co. (2 May 1850)

1532. Horace Bailey age 17 yrs., a brother of Dr. G.D. Bailey of Havana, Schuyler Co., was taking down a shanty on the doctors property, which had been abandoned by some Irishmen. He found an auger under the floor, which several Irishmen claimed. A dispute arose and Bailey was attacked by three of the Irishmen, who were well intoxicated. Bailey warned Andrew Sullivan and Simon Hickey to let him alone, but they pursued, seriously threatening his life. Bailey eventually shot and killed both of them. He has turned himself in for examination, no date given. (9 May 1850)

1533. Mrs. Sally Vorce age 27 yrs., died 29 Apr 1850 in Milo, Yates Co., wife of Volney Vorce. (9 May 1850)

1534. Chauncy Hoyt and Electa Porter, both of Middlesex, Co., were married 1 May 1850 in Orleans Ontario Co., by Rev. Holmes. (16 May 1850)

1535. Elnathan Botsford Esq. age 82 yrs., died 11 May 1850 in Jerusalem, Yates Co. (16 May 1850)

1536. Edgar Burton Perry age 3 mos. 10 days, died 10 May 1850 in Potter, Yates Co., son of Franklin and Maria Perry. (16 May 1850)

1537. Charlotte Porter, formerly of Dansbury, CT., died 30 Apr 1850 in Benton, Yates Co., at the home of Mr. McFarren. (23 May 1850)

1538. A young man Mr. Hurley, his wife and 4 month old child were burned to death 20 May 1850 when their home was consumed by fire at Sheeshequin Township, Bradford Co., PA. (6 Jun 1850)

1539. Hon. John Knox of C___?__ (illegible) and Mrs. Catharine Ellis of Penn Yan, Yates Co., were married 4 Jun 1850 by Rev. Clarke in the Congregational Church at Penn Yan. (6 Jun 1850)

1540. Steward Wilcox and Emma Scofield, daughter of Aaron Scofield, both of Jerusalem, Yates Co., were married 12 May 1850 by Rev. Moshier in Jerusalem. (6 Jun 1850)

1541. John Lynn and Susan Ann Sutherland were married 2 Jun 1850 by Rev. Smith in the Baptist Church at Penn Yan, Yates Co. (6 Jun 1850)

1542. Aaron Swarthout and Jemima Trimmer, both of Benton, Yates Co., were married 9 May 1850 by Rev. Litchfield in Benton. (6 Jun 1850)

1543. Peter Bush of Benton, Yates Co., and Julia Hall of Potter, Yates Co., were married 23 May 1850 by Rev. Litchfield, no town given. (6 Jun 1850)

1544. A young man Thomas Malone, killed 10 Jun 1850 at the railroad station in Manlius, Onondaga Co. As the train was approaching the station, he told the conductor he wanted to get off, but was informed the train was an express, and not scheduled to stop there. It was traveling at a very fast speed, and Malone jumped off, catching his arm on the platform. His arm was torn off, and he was thrown beneath the train. His remains taken to Syracuse, Onondaga Co., for interment. (13 Jun 1850)

1545. Samuel Perry of Jerusalem, Yates Co., and Mary Dinehart, daughter of Peter J. Dinehart of Geneva, Ontario Co., were married 1 Jun 1850 by Rev. Remington in Geneva. (20 Jun 1850)

1546. Samuel Taylor Esq. of Dundee, Yates Co., and Mary E. Millieus of Barrington, Yates Co., were married 13 Jun 1850 by Rev. Bridgeman in Barrington. (20 Jun 1850)

1547. Mrs. Rose Robinson age 77 yrs., died 1 Jun 1850 in Jerusalem, Yates Co., wife of Jeremy Robinson. (20 Jun 1850)

1548. Jacob Oakley age 24 yrs., died 15 Jun 1850 of consumption, in Potter, Yates Co. (20 Jun 1850)

1549. Mrs. Mary Chidsey age 50 yrs., died 16 Jun 1850 in Penn Yan, Yates Co. (20 Jun 1850)

1550. Mrs. Hannah Briggs age 84 yrs., died 23 Jun 1850 at the home of Hamilton J. Briggs in Potter, Yates Co. (27 Jun 1850)

1551. Samuel Jeffreys, killed 11 Jun 1850 at Cameron, Steuben Co., leaving a wife and five children. Two Irishmen have been charged, one named Hollaran and the other Neugent. (27 Jun 1850)

1552. Mrs. Roxana Lee age 30 yrs., died 13 Jun 1850 in Italy, Yates Co. The wife of Roswell Lee, and daughter of Charles and Vesta Clark. (27 Jun 1850)

1553. Peter Finger and Mary Ann Barnes, daughter of S. Barnes Esq., all of Jerusalem, Yates Co., were married 18 Jun 1850 by Rev. D.B. Douglas in Penn Yan, Yates Co. (4 Jul 1850)

1554. Elijah Brown and Elizabeth Eddy, both of Benton, Yates Co., were married 29 Jun 1850 by Rev. Simon Southerland at Hopeton, Yates Co. (4 Jul 1850)

1555. Margaret Maria White age 22 yrs., died 29 Jun 1850 in Benton, Yates Co. (4 Jul 1850)

1556. George W. Stanton and Mary A. Hudson, both of Milo, Yates Co., were married 28 Jun 1850 in Milo, no pastor given. (11 Jul 1850)

1557. Philena Osgood died 9 Jul 1850 in Penn Yan, Yates Co. (11 Jul 1850)

1558. Gilbert Brownell Jr., committed suicide 18 Jul 1850 at Elmira, Chemung Co., formerly of Cayuga Co. He and his wife had been separated about nine years, but seemed to have worked out their differences. He left a considerable amount of property, and about fifteen or twenty thousand dollars cash to his wife. (18 Jul 1850)

1559. William Pickle of Ontario Co., and Mary Litchfield of Benton, Yates Co., were married 18 Jul 1850 by Rev. Daniel W. Litchfield in Benton. (18 Jul 1850)

1560. William Francis and Elizabeth Davis, both of Jerusalem, Yates Co., were married 5 Jul 1850 by S.G. Gage Esq. in Benton, Yates Co. (18 Jul 1850)

1561. Francis Page Esq. age 43 yrs., died 18 Jul 1850 in Penn Yan, Yates Co. (25 Jul 1850)

1562. David Oakley age 18 yrs., killed by lightning 29 Jul 1850 while drawing hay for his employer, Mr. Singer at Royalton, Niagara Co. (1 Aug 1850)

1563. Daniel H. Pearson, executed 26 Jul 1850 at East Cambridge, MA., for the murder of his wife and twin daughters last May 1850, at Wilmington, MA. (1 Aug 1850)

1564. Hiram Morrison of Penn Yan, Yates Co., and Lydia Caroline Sheppard, daughter of John Sheppard Esq. of Jerusalem, Yates Co., were married 4 Aug 1850 by Rev. D.B. Douglas in Jerusalem. (8 Aug 1850)

1565. Dr. Henry Gratton Wirt died 29 Jul 1850 at "Wirtland", Monticello, Florida, youngest son of the late William Wirt of Maryland. (8 Aug 1850)

1566. Julia Sartwell age 24 yrs., died 4 Aug 1850 in Milwaukee, Wisconsin. The eldest daughter of Dr. Henry Sartwell of Penn Yan, Yates Co. (15 Aug 1850)

1567. Isaac Hall of Potter, Yates Co., and Caroline Wheeler of Benton, Yates Co., were married 20 Aug 1850 by S.G. Gage Esq. in Benton. (29 Aug 1850)

1568. Joseph Arden and Charlotte Ellsworth, both of Penn Yan, Yates Co., were married 23 Aug 1850 by Rev. Smith in Penn Yan. (29 Aug 1850)

1569. Mrs. Harriet Spencer of Rome, Oneida Co., and her mother Mrs. Chapman of Clarksville, Madison Co. both died recently. Their deaths caused from the effects of an excessive amount of camphine they had used in washing, this past March. They both became seriously ill, and had spells of temporary insanity prior to their deaths, no date given. (5 Sep 1850)

1570. John Waddle and Hannah Williams, both of Penn Yan, Yates Co., were married 2 Sep 1850 by Rev. Abner Chase in Penn Yan. (5 Sep 1850)

1571. James Morgan Chapman and Mary Catherine Huntington, both of Penn Yan, Yates Co., were married 2 Sep 1850 by Rev. Clarke in Penn Yan. (5 Sep 1850)

1572. Henry Sutton of Penn Yan, Yates Co., and Emeranda Canderman of Howard, Steuben Co., were married 9 Sep 1850 by Rev. Bartholomew in Howard. (12 Sep 1850)

1573. W.G. Wood and Helen Matthias, both of Penn Yan, Yates Co., were married 5 Sep 1850 by Rev. Smith in Penn Yan. (12 Sep 1850)

1574. Oliver P. Guthrie of Benton, Yates Co., and Mary P. Rugg, daughter of Nathan Rugg of Potter, Yates Co., were married 3 Sep 1850 by Rev. Latimer in Potter. (19 Sep 1850)

1575. George D. Wells and Mary C. Tomlinson, both of Penn Yan, Yates Co., were married 12 Sep 1850 by Rev. Stryker in Penn Yan. (19 Sep 1850)

1576. The five member family of Phillip Kauffmann, left Germany several months ago, and embarked at Havre for the U.S. The oldest son, who had just finished his education for the practice of medicine, fell over board and drowned. Three or four weeks later, as the vessel neared New Orleans, the father died of ship fever. When they reached the city, the mother took her 12 year old son to the hospital for the same disease, she buried him the next day. Three weeks later, the mother took sick and died last Saturday, leaving a little girl aged about 5 or 6 yrs. old orphaned. A man named Samuel Lumsden has agreed to adopt her. Copied from the "St. Louis Int.", no dates given. (26 Sep 1850)

1577. Ira Clark found murdered 18 Sep 1850 in a field not far from his home in Orange, CT. His wife had harbored a man named Rowan, who with the woman had abused the deceased to such an extent, he had expressed fears for his life to his neighbors. Rowan was immediately suspected and fled. (26 Sep 1850)

1578. Mrs. Sarah Greene age 21 yrs., died 26 Sep 1850 in Penn Yan, Yates Co., wife of J.F. Greene. (3 Oct 1850)

1579. Mrs Clarissa Chadwick died 23 Sep 1850 at Genoa, Cayuga Co. The wife of Dr. Ansel Chadwick, formerly of Penn Yan, Yates Co. (3 Oct 1850)

1580. Alfred W. Hewitt and Helen Sutherland, daughter of William Sutherland Esq., all of Milo, Yates Co., were married 1 Oct 1850 by Rev. D.B. Douglas in Milo. (3 Oct 1850)

1581. Henry Clark, son of W.N. Clark of Geneva, Ontario Co., accidentally shot and killed himself 9 Oct 1850 at Angelica, Allegany Co. (10 Oct 1850)

1582. William Lowden of Ridgeway, Orleans Co., to be executed 23 Nov 1850 for the murder of his wife by poisoning. A brutal husband, and father of 13 children. His daughter was one of the chief witnesses against him. (10 Oct 1850)

1583. Peter Boots, son of the late Benjamin Boots, of Potter, Yates Co., was killed 2 Oct 1850 by two trains coming together at Seneca Falls, Seneca Co., he leaves a wife and three children. (10 Oct 1850)

1584. Hon. Chester Butler died 4 Oct 1850 of typhus fever in Philadelphia, PA. A member of Congress from the 11th district there. (10 Oct 1850)

1585. Samuel Boots and Nancy Hawley, daughter of Cyrus Hawley, all of Potter, Yates Co., were married 21 Sep 1850 in Bethel, Sullivan Co., no pastor given. (10 Oct 1850)

1586. Mrs. Polly Slitor age 65 or 85 yrs. (blurred), died 17 Sep 1850 at Buffalo, Erie Co., widow of Enoch Slitor, formerly of Gorham, Ontario Co. (10 Oct 1850)

1587. Charles Brown age 43 yrs., died 30 Aug 1850 at Dresden, Yates Co. (10 Oct 1850)

1588. Robert Chissom age 44 yrs., died 26 Sep 1850 in Jerusalem, Yates Co. (10 Oct 1850)

1589. Mrs. Elizabeth Lathrop age 74 yrs., died 5 Oct 1850 at the home of her son in-law, Dr. Greene, in Michigan. The mother of Rev. Lathrop of Auburn, Onondaga Co., NY., no town given. (17 Oct 1850)

1590. Samuel Wilbur Sackett age 8 mos., died 3 Oct 1850 in Potter, Yates Co., infant son of Richard and Lydia Sackett. (24 Oct 1850)

1591. Llewellyen J. Weaver and Almeda Barden, daughter of J.P. Barden Esq. of Branchport, Yates Co., were married 21 Oct 1850 by Rev. Carpenter in Branchport. (24 Oct 1850)

1592. Samuel Jennings of Waverly, Tioga Co., and Ann Nicholas Jones, daughter of the late Joseph Jones of Penn Yan, Yates Co., were married 21 Oct 1850 by Rev. Clark in Milo, Yates Co. (24 Oct 1850)

1593. Abel Briggs and Mary E. Smith, both of Jerusalem, Yates Co., were married 2 Nov 1850 by Rev. D.B. Douglas in Jerusalem. (7 Nov 1850)

1594. Hon. Cornelius Masten age 64 yrs., died 31 Oct 1850 in Penn Yan, Yates Co. Born at Kingston, Ulster Co. 17 Aug 1789, he married in 1832 Maria Vosburgh, daughter of Gen. Peter S. Vosburgh. He studied law at Kingston, was an officer in the last war, and buried 3 Nov 1850 with Masonic honors. (14 Nov 1850)

1595. Ex-Gov. Ford of Illinois, died 19 Oct 1850 in Peoria, IL. (14 Nov 1850)

1596. Carlton Legg Jr. of Benton, Yates Co., and Louisa Rappelye, daughter of Joseph Rappelye of Milo, Yates Co., were married 13 Nov 1850 by Rev. Bardon in Milo. (14 Nov 1850)

1597. James Watson of Potter, Yates Co., late of California, and Jane Clark of Potter, were married 3 Nov 1850 by T.H. Locke Esq. in Penn Yan, Yates Co. (14 Nov 1850)

1598. Oliver M. Martin of Dundee, Yates Co., and Harriet Calkins of Geneva, Ontario Co., were married 7 Nov 1850 by Rev. Shearer in Geneva. (14 Nov 1850)

1599. Thomas Brown of Chittenango, Madison Co., and Sarah Spurbeck of Jerusalem, Yates Co., were married 12 Nov 1850 by Rev. Mosher at Kinneys Corner, Yates Co. (14 Nov 1850)

1600. Mrs. Eliza A. Johnson age 2_ yrs. (blurred), died 27 Oct 1850 in Potter, Yates Co., the wife of Elder Leander Johnson. (14 Nov 1850)

1601. Mrs. Anna Tucker age 92 yrs., died 25 Oct 1850 in Potter, Yates Co. A resident of Maryland, she came to Potter over 50 yrs. ago, and has been a widow for 47 yrs. (14 Nov 1850)

1602. Henry Welles Hamilton age 6 yrs. 5 mos. 6 days, died 10 Nov 1850 at the home of his grandfather Hon. Henry Welles in Penn Yan, Yates Co. The son of Theodore and Emily Hamilton of Rochester, Monroe Co. (21 Nov 1850)

1603. Rev. W.W. Robinson age 31 yrs., died 14 Nov 1850 in Penn Yan, Yates Co., pastor of the Presbyterian Church. (21 Nov 1850)

1604. Hon. John Richardson died 20 Nov 1850 at Union Springs, Cayuga Co., a member of the Assembly last winter. (28 Nov 1850)

1605. Freeland Wheeler of Potter, Yates Co., and Calista Wing of Italy, Yates Co., were married in Naples, Ontario Co., no date or pastor given. (28 Nov 1850)

1606. Betsy Hamilton age 18 yrs., died 13 Nov 1850 in Penn Yan, Yates Co. (28 Nov 1850)

1607. Mrs. Hannah James age 36 or 56 Yrs. (blurred), died 21 Nov 1850 in Potter, Yates Co., wife of Waterman James. (28 Nov 1850)

1608. Capt. Bernardus VanZant age 82 yrs., died 7 Nov 1850 at his home in Biawenberg, New Jersey. (28 Nov 1850)

1609. John Lewis and Margaret E. Owen, both of Milo, Yates Co., were married 5 Dec 1850 by Rev. Clarke in Milo. (12 Dec 1850)

1610. William Cowan and Elizabeth Burns, both of Prattsburgh, Steuben Co., were married 6 Dec 1850 by Rev. Clarke in Milo, Yates Co. (12 Dec 1850)

1611. George Deusler of Lodi, Seneca Co., Ohio, formerly of Potter, Yates Co., New York, and Hannah Boots of Potter, were married 10 Nov 1850 in Noble Co., Indiana, no pastor named. (12 Dec 1850)

1612. Zachariah Poulson died in Philadelphia, PA., one of the oldest printers and publishers in the U.S., no date given. (19 Dec 1850)

1613. Chester A. Putney of Middlesex, Yates Co., and Mary Augusta Pratt of Rushville, Yates Co., were married 5 Dec 1850 by Rev. Homes in Geneva, Ontario Co. (19 Dec 1850)

1614. Capt. William E. Shannon died 3 Oct 1850 in California, formerly of Steuben Co., no town given. (26 Dec 1850)

1615. Lucinda Sackett died 29 Dec 1850 in Potter, Yates, Co., daughter of Thomas Sackett. (2 Jan 1851)

1616. Robert Brown and Margaret Finger, both of Benton, Yates Co., were married 23 Dec 1850 by S.G. Gage Esq. in Benton. (9 Jan 1851)

1617. Joseph Wells and Hannah Briggs, both of Potter, Yates Co., were married 1 Jan 1851 by S.G. Gage in Potter. (9 Jan 1851)

1618. John Henry VanAllen and Charlotte Cole, both of Geneva, Ontario Co., were married 1 Jan 1851 in the Presbyterian Church at Dresden, Yates Co. by Rev. Petrie. (9 Jan 1851)

1619. G.W. Taylor of Benton, Yates Co., and Frances Rappleye of Farmersville, Seneca Co., were married 1 Jan 1851 by Rev. Besler at Farmersville. (9 Jan 1851)

1620. P.H. Graham and M.L. VanDerlip, both of Penn Yan, Yates Co., were married 31 Dec 1850 Rev. Kellogg in Penn Yan. (9 Jan 1850)

1621. John Slitor and _?_alena Parsons (illegible), were married 15 Jan 1851 at Burton, Ohio. (6 Feb 1851)

1622. Mrs. Martha Mayers age 89 yrs., died 3 Feb 1851 at Kingston, Luzerne Co., PA. The last survivor of the "Wyoming Massacre" in PA. Her father Thomas Bennett was one of the 40 men who built the stockade called "Forty Fort". (13 Feb 1851)

1623. Samuel Holliday and Mrs. Nancy Pembroke, both of Benton, Yates Co., were married 25 Jan 1851 by Rev. Daniel Litchfield in Gorham, Ontario Co. (13 Feb 1851)

1624. D.C. Richards of Springport, Cayuga Co., and Mary Suydam of Fleming, Cayuga Co., were married 6 Feb 1851 by Rev. O. Miner in Fleming. (13 Feb 1851)

1625. Alice Tuell age 20 mos., died 8 Feb 1851 in Penn Yan, Yates Co., daughter of Amasa and Susan Tuell. (13 Feb 1851)

1626. Mary A. VanBuren age 7 mos. 3 days, died 23 Feb 1851 in Penn Yan, Yates Co., daughter of James and Harriet VanBuren. (27 Feb 1851)

1627. James Reed age 86 yrs., died 19 Feb 1851 at the home of his son David Reed in Potter, Yates Co. (27 Feb 1851)

1628. Mrs. Roxana Bordwell age 72 yrs., died 15 Feb 1851 in Potter, Yates Co., widow of Enoch Bordwell. She was one of the first settlers of that place. (27 Feb 1851)

1629. Edson Daniels of West Bloomfield, Ontario Co., and Mary Jane Plimpton, late of Penn Yan, Yates Co., were married 5 Feb 1851 by Rev. Fisher at West Bloomfield. (6 Mar 1851)

1630. Robert B. Howland of Union Springs, Cayuga Co., and Susannah Robinson, daughter of Dr. Daniel Robinson of Farmington, Ontario Co., were married 25 Feb 1851 in Friends Meeting House at Farmington. (6 Mar 1851)

1631. Leander Lane and Almira Hobart, both of Potter, Yates Co., were married 18 Feb 1851 by Rev. Nortine in Potter. (13 Mar 1851)

1632. Jeremiah Hewett age 73 yrs., died 3 Mar 1851 at the home of his son William Hewett, no town given. (13 Mar 1851)

1633. Amos Hawes died 12 Mar 1851 of consumption,

in Rushville, Yates Co. (20 Mar 1851)

1634. Ferdinand Suydam Esq. died at Buffalo, Erie Co., formerly of New York city, of the firm Suydam, Sage & Co., no date given. (27 Mar 1851)

1635. Major Noah died 22 Mar 1851 in New York city. The senior Editor of the "Sunday Times", connected with the press for over 40 yrs. (27 Mar 1851)

1636. Jacob C. Hovey of Bath, Steuben Co. and Mary E. Olmsted of Wayne, Schuyler Co., were married 13 Mar 1851 by Rev. Russell in Wayne. (27 Mar 1851)

1637. Henry L. Kendig and Joanna Casner, daughter of Hon. E. Casner of Penn Yan, Yates Co., were married 2 Apr 1851 by Rev. Kellogg in Penn Yan. (3 Apr 1851)

1638. William Nichols age 95 yrs., died 13 Mar 1851 at Weathersfield, VT. A native of Holden, MA., he moved to Vermont about 62 yrs. ago. A soldier of the Revolution. (10 Apr 1851)

1639. Andrew Hyslop and Mary Jane Pruner, both of Penn Yan, Yates Co., were married 8 Apr 1851 by Rev. D.B. Douglas in Penn Yan. (10 Apr 1851)

1640. Moses Woods of Newburgh, Orange Co., and Jane M. Jacobus of Benton, Yates Co., were married 16 Apr 1851 by Rev. Goldsmith in Benton. (17 Apr 1851)

1641. John Merritt of Jerusalem, Yates Co., and Lydia Osgood of Penn Yan, Yates Co., were married 17 Apr 1851 by Rev. Douglas in Penn Yan. (24 Apr 1851)

1642. Robert Dunn and Margaret McKee, both of Penn Yan, Yates Co., were married 18 Apr 1851 by Rev. Clarke in Penn Yan. (24 Apr 1851)

1643. Robert Griner and Margaret Miller, both of Benton, Yates Co., were married 12 Apr 1851 by S.G. Gage Esq. in Benton. (1 May 1851)

1644. Caroline Spencer age 23 yrs., died 29 Apr 1851 in Benton, Yates Co., of consumption. (22 May 1851)

1645. Thomas Clarke age 102 yrs., died 17 May 1851 in Starkey, Yates Co. (22 May 1851)

1646. Elijah Bigley age 62 yrs., died 7 May 1851 in Penn Yan, Yates Co. (22 May 1851)

1647. Capt. Jeremiah Barber age 26 yrs., died in Potter, Yates Co. (22 May 1851)

1648. Mrs. Fanny Slitor age 85 yrs., died 17 Apr 1851 at Barton, Geauga Co. Ohio. The widow of James Slitor, formerly of Gorham, Ontario Co. NY. (22 May 1851)

1649. Samuel Watkins age 94 yrs., died 10 May 1851 at his residence in Jefferson, Chemung Co. (22 May 1851)

1650. Caroline Spencer age 33 yrs., died 13 May 1851 of consumption in Benton, Yates Co. (29 May 1851)

1651. Ichabod Buel age 78 yrs., died 6 May 1851 in Milo, Yates Co. He was born 14 Jul 1772 in Queensbury, Warren Co., and came to Yates Co. the spring of 1792 in the company of the late Matthew Cole. (29 May 1851)

1652. Mrs. Marla Meets age 29 yrs., died 30 May 1851 in Penn Yan, Yates Co. (5 Jun 1851)

1653. George B. Kinney age 45 yrs., died 24 May 1851 in Penn Yan, Yates Co. (5 Jun 1851)

1654. Laroy Greene and Augusta Sage, daughter of W.F. Sage, were married by Rev. Stacy in Dundee, Yates Co., no date given. (12 Jun 1851)

1655. Mrs. Melinda Canda Clark age 57 yrs., killed when she was thrown from a wagon 31 May 1851 at Peoria, Illinois. The wife of Horace Clark Esq. of Buffalo, Erie Co., and mother of Mrs. Abram F. Hazen of Penn Yan, Yates Co. (12 Jun 1851)

1656. Jabez Bradley age 38 or 58 yrs. (blurred), died 7 Jun 1851 of apoplexy at Pine Valley, Chemung Co., brother of Henry Bradley Penn Yan, Yates Co. (12 Jun 1851)

1657. Daniel Johnson Jr. age 19 yrs., killed 17 Jun 1851 at Jerusalem, Yates Co. He was helping his father raise a barn, when a piece of timber slipped from the frame, striking him on the back of the neck, causing instant death. His family moved from Rome, Oneida Co., in the spring of 1849. (19 Jun 1851)

1658. Elizabeth Wolfinger age 90 yrs., died last week in Upper Dublin, Montgomery Co., PA., no date given. (26 Jun 1851)

1659. Henry Ellis age 12 yrs., drowned 30 Jun 1851 while bathing in the Big Stream near Dunn's Mill. He was the son of S.H.R. Ellis of Dundee, Yates Co. (3 Jul 1851)

1660. Rev. James Eells Jr. and Emma M. Page were married 1 Jul 1851 by Rev. Lathrop in the Second Presbyterian Church at Auburn, Cayuga Co. (3 Jul 1851)

1661. Rodney M. Taylor, a merchant in Buffalo, Erie Co., and Mary C. Beers, only daughter of Rev. Ashbel Beers of Jerusalem, Yates Co., were married 25 Jun 1851 by Rev. Sceening at Niagara Falls, Niagara Co. NY. (3 Jul 1851)

1662. Elder Tooker age 60 yrs., died 4 Jul 1851 in Lansing, Michigan. Born Oct 1791 in Orange Co. New york. He moved to Washtenaw Co. Michigan in 1835, where he lived for several years, moved to Shaiwassee Co. for 6 years, and then to Lansing. (10 Jul 1851)

1663. Joseph Van_?_ (illegible) and Ann Butterworth both of Penn Yan, Yates Co., were married 13 Jul 1851 by Rev. Kellogg in Penn Yan. (24 Jul 1851)

1664. Harvey Cu_?_ (illegible) and Amanda Barrett, both of Penn Yan, Yates Co., were married 12 Jul 1851 by Rev. Douglas in Penn Yan. (24 Jul 1851)

1665. Mrs. Elizabeth Underwood age 28 or 38 yrs. (blurred), died 17 Jul 1851 at Avon Springs, wife of James Underwood of Potter, Yates Co. (31 Jul 1851)

1666. Russell R. Fargo Esq. of Penn Yan, Yates Co., and Mrs. Mary St. John of Pulteney, Steuben Co., were married 2 Aug 1851 at Pulteney, no pastor named. (7 Aug 1851)

1667. Emily M. Youngs age 9 yrs. 9 mos. 22 days, died 6 Aug 1851 in Penn Yan, Yates Co., only child of Malav C. and Lois A. Youngs. (7 Aug 1851)

1668. George B. Chapman age 22 yrs., died 16 Jul 1851 at the home of his father, Samuel Chapman, near Penn Yan, Yates Co. (7 Aug 1851)

1669. D.O. Bradley late of Penn Yan, Yates Co., and Elizabeth Neeley, daughter of Albert Neeley Esq. of Chicago, Illinois, were married 7 Aug 1851 in by Rev. Swaner in Chicago. (14 Aug 1851)

1670. Mrs. Jane Millspaugh age 72 yrs., died 9 Aug 1851 in Milo, Yates Co., widow of David Millspaugh. (14 Aug 1851)

1671. Mrs. Anna Stone age 92 yrs., died 17 Jul 1851 in Jerusalem, Yates Co. One of the oldest resident and member of the M.E. Church. (14 Aug 1851)

1672. Charles Leland of New York city, and Ann Eliza Clark, daughter of Alva Clark Esq. of Penn Yan, Yates Co., were married 10 Aug 1851 by Rev. Eells at the Presbyterian Church in Penn Yan. (21 Aug 1851)

1673. Bradley P. Dunning age 23 yrs. 8 mos., died 16 Aug 1851 at the residence of his father near Hammondsport, Steuben Co., brother of L. Dunning of Penn Yan, Yates Co. (21 Aug 1851)

1674. A 6 yr., old child of Jonathan Ayres of Canterbury, NH., was sent out to the pasture 20 Aug 1851. When the child did not return, a search followed. The body was found mostly eaten, supposed by wolves. The father is a member of the NH Legislature, no date given. (28 Aug 1851)

1675. William Champlain and Theodosia Gilbert were married 12 Aug 1851 in Jerusalem, Yates Co., by Rev. _?_ (illegible). (28 Aug 1851)

1676. Mrs. Anna Sutton age 46 yrs., died 19 Aug 1851 in Benton, Yates Co. The wife of Daniel Sutton, and a member of the M.E. Church. (28 Aug 1851)

1677. Gen. George McClure age 80 yrs., died 15 Aug 1851 at Elgin, Illinois. The brother in-law of Judge Henry Welles of Penn Yan, Yates Co. (28 Aug 1851)

1678. Edward S. Morris and Mary Ann Brandon were married 2 Sep 1851 by Rev. Wilson in Milo, Yates Co. (4 Sep 1851)

1679. Darius Feagles and Rachel Lovejoy were married 29 Aug 1851 by Rev. Daniel W. Litchfield in Benton, Yates Co. (4 Sep 1851)

1680. Mrs. Sally Lewis age 76 yrs., died 3 Sep 1851 in Penn Yan, Yates Co. (11 Sep 1851)

1681. __?__ G. Weaver (illegible) of Cleveland, Ohio, and Ann Eliza Sunderlin of Tyrone, Schuyler Co., were married 3 Sep 1851 by Rev. Williams in Tyrone. (18 Sep 1851)

1682. J. Fennimore Cooper died 14 Sep 1851 at Cooperstown, Otsego Co. (18 Sep 1851)

1683. Hon. Frederick Whittelsey died 19 Sep 1851 of typhus fever, in Rochester, Monroe Co. The judge served in Congress from 1831 to 1835, * a brief biography printed. (25 Sep 1851)

1684. John Little of New Jersey, and Deborah Hall, daughter of J.A. Hall of Benton, Yates Co., were married 23 Sep 1851 by Rev. James Eells in Benton. (25 Sep 1851)

1685. Joseph L. Bellis of Eddytown, Yates Co. and Adelaide Hathaway, only daughter of Gilbert Hathaway of Barrington, Yates Co., were married 14 Sep 1851 by Rev. Wilson at Hammondsport, Steuben Co. (25 Sep 1851)

1686. Rev. James Hotchkiss age 70 yrs., died 21 Sep 1851 in Prattsburgh, Steuben Co. (25 Sep 1851)

1687. Mrs. Catharine J. Brown died 20 Sep 1851 in Benton, Yates Co., wife of James Rodney Brown. (25 Sep 1851)

1688. DREADFUL ACCIDENT on the Cleveland & Columbia Railroad. A freight train had passed Walworth Run abt. 2 miles from Cleveland, when the engine of the Delaware exploded and landed on the Lorain, killing the engineer of the Lorain Samuel Boothby of Cleveland. The engineer of the Delaware, Mr. Bryant was discovered, crawling upon the fence road, his skin almost completely frayed, and his clothing badly torn, he was not expected to live. Two firemen, a Mr. Sterns of the Delaware and Mr. Cotton of the Lorain, were dreadfully scalded, both of Berea, Ohio. (2 Oct 1851)

1689. Asa Gregory of Flint, MI., and Mary Sophia Pratt of Gorham, Ontario Co. NY., were married 23 Sep 1851 by Rev. McGlover in Gorham. (2 Oct 1851)

1690. Claudius B. Brace and Harriet N. Taylor,

daughter of James Taylor Esq. of Penn Yan, Yates Co., were married 1 Oct 1851 by Rev. James Eells in Penn Yan. (9 Oct 1851)

1691. N. Weed Gould of Montreal, Canada, formerly of Penn Yan, Yates Co., and Jenny S. Innes, only daughter of the late Dr. Robert Innes of Aberdeen, Scotland, were married 23 Sep 1851 by Rev. Hull in Trinity Church at Elmira, Chemung Co. NY. (9 Oct 1851)

1692. Phillip Roland age 65 yrs., died 3 Oct 1851 in Benton, Yates Co. He was harvesting corn in the field with a boy, when the boy noticed him in distress, Mr. Roland died almost immediately. (9 Oct 1851)

1693. Mrs. Emily Morse died 12 Oct 1851 in Barrington, Yates Co., of consumption. The wife of Dr. Roscius Morse of Starkey, Yates Co. (16 Oct 1851)

* * * SEVERAL PAPERS MISSING * * *

1694. Hosea C. Williams age 30 or 50 yrs. (blurred), died 19 Nov 1851 in Jerusalem, Yates Co. (27 Nov 1851)

1695. Caroline D. Day age 18 yrs., died 19 Nov 1851 in Middlesex, Yates Co. The wife of Dr. Fisk H. Day, and daughter of Edward Perry. (27 Nov 1851)

1696. Heman Peck of Dansville, Livingston Co., and Helen Root of Penn Yan, Yates Co., were married 3 Dec 1851 by Rev. H.K. Stimson in Penn Yan. (4 Dec 1851)

1697. Frank R. Masten age 9 mos. 11 days, died 28 Nov 1851 at Andover, Allegany Co., son of Peter Masten Esq. (4 Dec 1851)

1698. John Wilkinson of Penn Yan, Yates Co., and Harriet Whitney of Rochester, Monroe Co., were married 2 Dec 1851 by Rev. Hall in Rochester. (11 Dec 1851)

1699. Stephen Whittaker age 28 yrs., died 6 Dec 1851 at Toledo, Ohio. Buried in Cleveland, Ohio, the home of his parents. (11 Dec 1851)

1700. David Sprague of Milo, Yates Co., and Aradel Peckins of Benton, Yates Co., were married 11 Dec 1851 by Rev. Solomon in Benton. (18 Dec 1851)

1701. Maxwell W. Rhoda and Lucy Green, both of Penn Yan, Yates Co., were married 17 Dec 1851 by Rev. D.B. Douglas in Penn Yan. (18 Dec 1851)

1702. David Aspell and Helen R. Way, both of Milo, Yates Co., were married 14 Dec 1851, by Rev. Chase at the home of M.H. Lawrence in Milo. (18 Dec 1851)

1703. Amos V. Carr age 64 yrs., died 18 Dec 1851 in Milo, Yates Co. (18 Dec 1851)

1704. John S. Underwood age 66 yrs., died 29 Dec 1851 in Potter, Yates Co. (1 Jan 1852)

1705. Lewis Sunderlin of Penn Yan, Yates Co., and Mary A. Sutherland of Milo, Yates Co., were married 8 Jan 1852 by Rev. Shell in Milo. (15 Jan 1852)

1706. Levi Millspaugh and Betsey Quick, both of Branchport, Yates Co., were married 29 Dec 1851 by Rev. Colgrove in Branchport. (15 Jan 1852)

1707. Edward L. Jacobus age 3 mos. 5 days, died 13 Jan 1852 in Penn Yan, Yates Co. The son of Edward L. and Susan M. Jacobus. (15 Jan 1852)

1708. Frederick Fargo age 2 yrs. 2 mos. 2 days, died 4 Jan 1852 in New York city. The son of Elisha W. and Harriet Fargo, formerly of Penn Yan, Yates Co. (15 Jan 1852)

1709. John Clevas ? (blurred) age 84 yrs., died 6 Jan 1852 at Caledonia, Livingston Co. A native of Inverness, Scotland and the second settler in the town of York. (22 Jan 1852)

1710. William Gardiner died 15 Jan 1852 in Penn Yan, Yates Co. (22 Jan 1852)

1711. James Rowdy, killed 23 Jan 1852 at Potsdam, St. Lawrence Co., by John Dennison. (12 Feb 1852)

1712. Samuel Botsford Esq. and Esther Spangler, both of Jerusalem, Yates Co., were married 10 Feb 1852 by Rev. Kellogg in Penn Yan, Yates Co. (12 Feb 1852)

1713. Oliver S. Underwood of Potter, Yates Co., and Emily Harrison of Shrewsbury, New Jersey, were married 29 Jan 1852 by Rev. Taylor in Shrewsbury. (12 Feb 1852)

1714. George W. Spencer and Martha E. Wheeler of Potter, Yates Co., were married 13 Jan 1852 by Rev. Abner Chase in Potter. (12 Feb 1852)

1715. Benjamin Coddington age 84 yrs., died 29 Dec 1851 in Benton, Yates Co. (4 Mar 1852)

1716. Mrs. Jane E. Coddington age 28 yrs., died 29 Feb 1852 of consumption. The wife of Benjamin Coddington Jr. of Benton, Yates Co. and daughter of Horace and Jane Taylor of Benton. (4 Mar 1852)

1717. John Peabody age 42 yrs., died 6 Feb 1852 in Rushville, Yates Co. (4 Mar 1852)

1718. Nelson Welder age 44 yrs., died 29 Feb 1852 in Rushville, Yates Co. (4 Mar 1852)

1719. Jesse Nelson Brown age 15 yrs., died 12 Feb 1852 in Benton, Yates Co., son of James Brown. (4 Mar 1852)

1720. Luman Wakeman of Bergen, Genesee Co., and Sarah Bradbury of Penn Yan, Yates Co., were married 14 Mar 1852 by Rev. H.K. Stimson in the Baptist Church at Penn Yan. (18 Mar 1852)

1721. Henry Gillett and Emily Ladue, both of Bergen, Genesee Co. were married 14 Mar 1852 by Rev. H.K. Stimson in the Baptist Church at Penn Yan, Yates Co. (18 Mar 1852)

1722. Henry Brown and Mrs. Elizabeth Card, were married 15 Mar 1852 by Rev. Clark in Jerusalem, Yates Co. (18 Mar 1852)

1723. Eliza Conger age 17 yrs., died 25 Feb 1852 in Penn Yan, Yates Co., daughter of Jacob Conger. (18 Mar 1852)

1724. TABLE OF MORTALITY FOR THE TOWN OF BENTON 1851; furnished for the "Yates Co. Whig" by S.G. Gage Esq..

Jan..14	Mary F. Lamport age 1 yr.
" 20	Inf'dau. of Elder Clapp age under 1 yr.
" 24	Allen Bruce age 3 yrs.
Feb...3	Inf'son of H. Gedder age under 1 yr.
" 6	Rosetta Moon age 3 yrs.
" 16	Inf'dau. of L. Voorhees age under 1 yr.
Mar...1	John C. Jacobus age 7 yrs.
" 4	Fidelia A. Rector age under 1 yr.
" 20	Sarah Carr age 13 yrs.

Mar..	20	Delilah Feagles age 35 yrs.
"	28	William Smalley age under 1 yr.
May	__	Inf'son of H. Canfield age under 1 yr.
"	12	Caroline Spencer age 33 yrs.
"	13	Robert Robinson age 81 yrs.
"	27	John Scott age 51 yrs.
Jul..	__	Inf'son of S. Babcock (col'd) age 1 yr.
"	16	George B. Chapman age 22 yrs.
"	20	Deborah Roy age 69 yrs.
"	67	Nathaniel C. Kniffin age 67 yrs.
Aug..	10	Anna Sutton age 46 yrs.
"	26	Mary Rentoin age 25 yrs.
"	27	Susan Hazard age 53 yrs.
"	28	Jane McGlocklin age 27 yrs.
Sep..	__	Twin infants of C. Wyllys, a son and daughter age under 1 yr.
"	__	Alice Carr age 1 yr.
"	16	William Ardery age 15 yrs.
"	20	Catharine J. Brown age 43 yrs.
Oct...	3	Anson Warren age 77 yrs.
"	3	Phillip Roland age 65 yrs.
"	15	James Pembrooke age 12 yrs.
"	16	Boynton Groves age 65 yrs.
"	27	Inf' son of T. Norton age under 1 yr.
Nov...	5	John Agan age 26 yrs.
"	14	Maria Sandles age 57 yrs.
"	17	John Mittour age abt. 71 yrs.
"	28	Sylvia Mingo (colored) age 32 yrs.
Dec...	1	William Belt age 81 yrs.
"	5	James Scott age 83 yrs.
"	20	Benjamin Coddington age 84 yrs.

(23 Mar 1852)

1725. Mrs. Sarah Pettingill age 66 yrs., died 6 Mar 1852 in Dresden, Yates Co., wife of John Pettinggill. (23 Mar 1852)

1726. John Powell age 58 yrs., died 23 Mar 1852 in Penn Yan, Yates Co. (23 Mar 1852)

1727. Joseph C. Miller of West Nottingham, Chester Co., PA., killed near Baltimore, MD. 29 Dec 1851. A gang had forcibly entered Millers home to kidnap a free negro woman Rachel Parker, to be sold into slavery. Miller and several other men, pursued the gang to Baltimore, where the killing took place. (1 Apr 1852)

1728. Franklin S. Briggs age 2 yrs. 2 mos. 20 days, died 14 Mar 1852 in Potter, Yates Co. son of Peleg and Sarah M. Briggs. (8 Apr 1852)

1729. Mrs. Betsey Winans age 70 yrs., died 3 Apr 1852 in Potter, Yates Co., wife of David Winans. (8 Apr 1852)

1730. D. Warren Adams a merchant of Penn Yan, Yates Co., and Mrs. Harriet Ogden Slocum of Genoa, Cayuga Co., were married 8 Apr 1852 Rev. Franklin in Genoa. (15 Apr 1852)

1731. William H. Olin of Milo, Yates Co., and Mary L. Benton, only daughter of L.B. Benton of Penn Yan, Yates Co., were married 8 Apr 1852 by Rev. D.B. Douglas in Penn Yan. (15 Apr 1852)

1732. William P. Durrant of Geneva, Ontario Co., and Mary Brizzee of Penn Yan, Yates Co., were married 8 Apr 1852 by Rev. James Eells in Penn Yan. (15 Apr 1852)

1733. Samuel Bason and Margaret Lown, both of Potter, Yates Co., were married 11 Mar 1852 by Rev. William Bradley in Potter. (15 Apr 1852)

1734. Nelson Rector of Potter, Yates Co., and Caroline Coons of Naples, Ontario Co., were married 4 Mar 1852 by Rev. Baker in Naples. (15 Apr 1852)

1735. Catharine Judd age 32 yrs., died 13 Apr 1852 in Penn Yan, Yates Co., of typhus fever, daughter of Dr. Uri Judd. (15 Apr 1852)

1736. Hannah M. Savage age 16 yrs. 11 mos., died 1 Mar 1852 in Potter, Yates Co. (15 Apr 1852)

1737. Mrs. Sarah Reynolds age 57 yrs., died 16 Mar 1852 in Potter, Yates Co. (15 Apr 1852)

1738. Mrs. Huldah Sparling age 110 yrs., died 8 Apr 1852 in Owego, Tioga Co. (22 Apr 1852)

1739. George H. Ely of Rochester, Monroe Co., and Hannah Welles, daughter of Hon. Henry Welles of Penn Yan, Yates Co., were married 28 Apr 1852 by Rev. James Eells in Penn Yan. (29 Apr 1852)

1740. John Telfair, found murdered 27 Mar 1852 at Saw Mill Flat, about 3 miles above Knight's Ferry in the San Joaquin country. He was on a cattle drive for the firm of Ward and Visher. It is supposed he had about $1,200 to $1,400 dollars on him, when he was last seen in the company of a

Mexican, who is believed to be his killer. Telfair was from Schuylerville, Saratoga Co., NY. (6 May 1852)

1741. Mrs. Seth Swain, killed 1 May 1852 by a train at Macedon, Wayne Co. Her husband had stopped their one horse buggy on the railroad track, just before the Eastern Express train came through. The engineer blew the whistle, but was unable to avoid hitting the buggy, which also contained their one yr. old baby. Mrs. Swain was killed instantly, Mr. Swain was slightly injured, and miraculously the child was thrown free and uninjured. Mr. Swain is being question in this incident. (6 May 1852)

1742. Almond B. Sutton and Juliet Mather, both of Benton, Yates Co., were married 4 May 1852 by Rev. Northway in Benton. (6 May 1852)

1743. Julia Fowle age 7 yrs., died 2 May 1852 in Penn Yan, Yates Co., daughter of Edward J. Fowle Esq. (6 May 1852)

1744. John D. Castner died 6 May 1852 in Torrey, Yates Co. One of the oldest residents of this county, he settled 47 years ago near Dresden, Yates Co. (6 May 1852)

1745. Thomas Stafford age 77 yrs., and Polly Goben age 19 yrs., were married 15 Apr 1852 by Rev. Cunningham at Floyd's Fork, Jefferson Co., copied from the "Louisville Cour". (* Note ages copied as printed.) (13 May 1852)

1746. Mrs. Mershon, killed 5 May 1852 while crossing the railroad tracks at Waterloo, Seneca Co. She observed a freight train at the station backing towards her. In an attempt to avoid it, and while retreating, she was knocked down by another person, and run over by a passenger train coming on another track. (13 May 1852)

1747. Mrs. Lue Bradley North age 23 yrs., died 9 May 1852 at Elmira, Chemung Co., of consumption. The niece of Henry Bradley of Penn Yan, Yates Co. (13 May 1852)

1748. John C. Quick age 31 yrs., died 11 May 1852 in Penn Yan, Yates Co. (13 May 1852)

1749. Harriet Beecher Stowe, author of "Uncle Tom's Cabin", is the wife of Prof. Stowe of Bowdoin

College, daughter of Dr. Lyman Beecher, and sister of Rev. H.W. Beecher. (20 May 1852)

1750. Isaac T. Hopper died recently in New York city, well known for his unceasing philanthropy, no date given. (20 May 1852)

1751. Howard R. Miller of Penn Yan, Yates Co., and Mary Bower of Lansing, Tompkins Co., were married 17 May 1852 by Rev. Franklin in Lansing. (20 May 1852)

1752. David Winans age 70 yrs., died 13 May 1852 in Potter, Yates Co. (20 May 1852)

1753. Mr. Webster age 27 yrs., died last week at Poughkeepsie, Dutchess Co. He had been suffering from a toothache, and had it extracted. However he continued to suffer and died a few days later, no date given. (27 May 1852)

1754. Silvanus Spencer Ennis age 6 yrs., died 20 May 1852 in Penn Yan, Yates Co., son of Silvanus and Caroline Ennis. (27 May 1852)

1755. Mrs. Martha Beard age 61 yrs. 9 mos. 12 days, died 23 May 1852 at the home of her son in Benton, Yates Co., where she had gone for a visit, wife of Joshua Beard. (27 May 1852)

1756. Mr. Barber of Hebron, Washington Co., killed 31 May 1852. He had attempted to cross the railroad track near Salem, with a span of horses attached to his wagon. The train was within a few rods of him at the time, and unable to stop. Mr. Barber was killed instantly. (3 Jun 1852)

1757. John W. Nixon of Springwater, Livingston Co., committed suicide 1 Jun 1852 by cutting his own throat. (3 Jun 1852)

1758. Mary Ann Megrath age 20 or 29 yrs. (blurred), died 25 May 1852 at Greenfield, MA. (3 Jun 1852)

1759. Dr. Samuel Nott age 99 yrs., died 26 May 1852 at his home in Franklin, CT. About a week before his death, his gown had caught fire, badly burning his hand. The injury and excitement probably hastened his death. A resident of Franklin for over 70 yrs., and one of the oldest pastors of a parish in New England. The elder brother of Eliphalett Nott of Union College. (10 Jun 1852)

1760. Mrs. Caroline A. Townsend age 31 yrs., died 7 Jun 1852 in Penn Yan, Yates Co. The wife of Homer M. Townsend, daughter of Luther and Pamela Winants of Benton, Yates Co. (10 Jun 1852)

1761. Nathan P. Cole Esq. age 71 yrs., died 1 Jun 1852 in Benton, Yates Co. He was born 4 Mar 1782 in Litchfield, CT., and moved here with his father in 1792. In 1808, he married Sally Woodworth, a sister of Judge Woodworth of Penn Yan, Yates Co., and settled upon the farm where he died, less than a half mile from his fathers cabin. In 1844, he buried his wife, and remarried in 1846 to Charlotte Shay who survives him. His funeral from the M.E. Church. (10 Jun 1852)

1762. Hiram M. Townsend of Dundee, Yates Co., age 38 yrs., died 6 Jun 1852 from internal bleeding, brother of Elias Townsend. (10 Jun 1852)

1763. Mrs. Betsey Squires age 84 yrs., died 19 Apr 1852 in Potter, Yates Co. (10 Jun 1852)

1764. Jacob Lyons age 42 yrs., of Canandaigua, Ontario Co., drowned 13 Jun 1852, when he capsized a boat on the Canandaigua Lake. (24 Jun 1852)

1765. Silas Perry age 89 yrs., died 2 Jun 1852 at Keene, NH. A patriot of the Revolution, one of a detachment assigned to guard Major Andre and escort him to the gallows on 2 Oct 1780. (24 Jun 1852)

1766. Mrs. Eliza Ann Hicks age 43 yrs. 7 mos., died 22 Jun 1852 in Benton, Yates Co. The wife of Henry Hicks Esq., funeral from the Benton Baptist Church. (24 Jun 1852)

1767. Joseph Hartman, a grocer on E. Genesee St. in Buffalo, Erie Co., murdered 19 Aug 1852. Three men broke into his store, then robbed and killed him. His wife was stabbed and both of her arms broken, she is not expected to live. (19 Aug 1852)

1768. J.M. Burton of New York city, and Lucin Clark, daughter of Horace Clark Esq. of Buffalo, Erie Co., were married 11 Aug 1852 by Rev. Lord in Buffalo. (19 Aug 1852)

1769. Morgan D. Tracy of Pulteney, Steuben Co., and Deborah Curtiss of Torrey, Yates Co., were married 17 Aug 1852 Rev. James Eells in Torrey.
(19 Aug 1852)

1770. C.C. Humphrey and Amelia M. Wentz, both of Geneva, Ontario Co., were married 15 Aug 1852 by Rev. Gulick in Geneva. (19 Aug 1852)

1771. Mrs. Ann Wolcott age 40 yrs., died 12 Aug 1852 in Penn Yan, Yates Co., wife of Chauncey Wolcott. (19 Aug 1852)

1772. Jenny Allen died 15 Aug 1852, infant daughter of George M. and Emily S. Allen, no town given. (19 Aug 1852)

1773. Samuel Wise age 66 yrs., died 7 Aug 1852 at his home in New York city, formerly of Penn Yan, Yates Co. (19 Aug 1852)

1774. George Loree and Elizabeth M. Wiley, both of Steuben, Oneida Co., were married 16 Aug 1852 by Rev. Goldsmith in Benton, Yates Co. (26 Aug 1852)

1775. Silas Gayton and Sarah Ann Boley, both of Penn Yan, Yates Co., were married 19 Aug 1852 by Rev. Jones in Penn Yan. (26 Aug 1852)

1776. Mrs. Ann T. Kitridge age 40 yrs., died 13 Aug 1852 at Somerset, Niagara Co. The wife of R. Kitridge. (26 Aug 1852)

1777. Mrs. Subrine Campbell age 42 yrs., died 14 Aug 1852 at Somerset, Niagara Co., wife of John Campbell. (26 Aug 1852)

1778. Ex-Governor Joseph Vance of Ohio, died 24 Aug 1852 at Urbana. He had also served in Congress from that state. (2 Sep 1852)

1779. John Norman of Torrey, Yates Co., and Mrs. Eliza Jane Scofield of Penn Yan, Yates Co., were married 27 Aug 1852 by Rev. Jones in Penn Yan. (2 Sep 1852)

1780. David L. Hempstead of Geneva, Ontario Co., died 28 Aug 1852 of cholera in Canandaigua, Ontario Co. A contractor for the Canandaigua & Niagara Railroad. (2 Sep 1852)

1781. Stephen Dicks age 90 yrs., lives in Clarksburg, VA. He heard the original Declaration of Independence read from the State House in Phila., when he was 14 yrs. old. He moved to Clarksburg when there were but two shingled houses there. (9 Sep 1852)

1782. Thomas Bassett a bachelor age 45 yrs., died suddenly 3 Sep 1852 in Milo, Yates Co. He was milking, and mentioned to his brother he wasn't feeling well, took his pail and started for the cellar. In descending the steps, he either slipped or fainted, striking his head on a stone, which fractured his skull, he died soon after.
(9 Sep 1852)

1783. Miles V. Bush and Elizabeth Shearman were married 2 Sep 1852 by Rev. Abner Chase in Milo, Yates Co. (9 Sep 1852)

1784. Corydon Wheat and Emilie A. Lacy, both of Geneva, Ontario Co., were married 1 Sep 1852 by Rev. Curry in Geneva. (9 Sep 1852)

1785. Samuel Tuton of Dundee, Yates Co., and Cornelia D. Gilsen of Penn Yan, Yates Co., were married 19 Aug 1852 by Rev. H.K. Stimson in Penn Yan. (9 Sep 1852)

1786. Alanson Hopkins of Barrington, Yates co., and Elizabeth Layton, daughter of Allen G. Layton of Dundee, Yates Co., were married 28 Aug 1852 at Dundee, no pastor named. (9 Sep 1852)

1787. John P. Castner of Milo, Yates Co., and Sarah Bennett of Mt. Washington, Steuben Co., were married 22 Aug 1852 by Rev. Hull at Urbana, Steuben Co. (9 Sep 1852)

1788. Holmes W. Haveland and Ruby Hatburt, both of Rushville, Yates Co., were married 30 Aug 1852 by Rev. Ira Fairbanks in Benton, Yates Co.
(9 Sep 1852)

1789. Jonathan Taylor Esq. and Mrs. Betsey Boyes, both of Barrington, Yates Co., were married 2 Sep 1852 by Rev. D.B. Olney in Barrington. (9 Sep 1852)

1790. Stephen King and Louisa Keefer, both of Barrington, were married 26 Aug 1852 by Rev. Sunderlin at the home of Daniel Disbrow in Barrington.
(9 Sep 1852)

1791. Henry M. Smith of Vermont, and Mrs. Cynthia Pembrooke of Benton, Yates Co., were married 13 Sep 1852 by Rev. Abner Chase in Benton. (16 Sep 1852)

1792. Mrs. Helen Hackney age 40 yrs., died 31 Aug 1852 at Aurora, Illinois. The wife of Benjamin

Hackney Esq., daughter of the late James Bradley of Pine Valley, Chemung Co. NY. (16 Sep 1852)

1793. Mrs. Susan Lawson Dox age 29 yrs., died 4 Sep 1852 at Hopeton, Yates Co. The wife of Dr. George N. Dox, and daughter of the late Rev. Orrin Clark. (16 Sep 1852)

1794. The inf. son of Dennis Smith age 6 mos., died 10 Sep 1852 in Starkey, Yates Co. (16 Sep 1852)

1795. Some years ago, the daughter of Rev. John Cross of New Jersey, ran away with William Patterson, her father's gardener. Her relations separated the couple, and declared the lady insane. He put her in a mad house and procured a divorce. The couple were remarried 21 Aug 1852, no town or name for wife given. (23 Sep 1852)

1796. Elijah Castaline and Sarah Andrews, both of Starkey, Yates Co., were married 21 Sep 1852 by Rev. Brown in Starkey. (23 Sep 1852)

1797. Richard A. Bassett of Penn Yan, Yates Co., and Mary A. Hendrickson of Odessa, Schuyler Co., were married 19 Sep 1852 by Rev. Clarke in Havana, Schuyler Co. (23 Sep 1852)

1798. Willis Gregory of Penn Yan, Yates Co., and Jane Bell of Milo, Yates Co., were married 8 Sep 1852 by Rev. H.K. Stimson in Milo. (23 Sep 1852)

1799. John S. Jenkins Esq. of Auburn, Cayuga Co., died 22 Sep 1852 at Syracuse, Onondaga Co. (23 Sep 1852)

1800. Joseph Hover of Tyrone, Steuben Co. and Julia A. Taylor of Benton, Yates Co., were married 25 Sep 1852 by Rev. A.C. Mallory in Benton. (30 Sep 1852)

1801. Rufus Scofield died 23 Sep 1852 of dysentery, in Penn Yan, Yates Co., leaving a wife and four children. (30 Sep 1852)

1802. Richard Torrance age 66 yrs., died 11 Sep 1852 at Avon, Livingston Co., formerly of Starkey, Yates Co. (30 Sep 1852)

1803. W.D. McAllaster age 38 yrs., died 27 Sep 1852 in Penn Yan, Yates Co., his funeral from the M.E. Church. (30 Sep 1852)

1804. A female child, age about 3 mos., was left at the door of Michael J. Francisco in Middlesex, Yates Co., 3 Oct 1852. Having no children of their own, Mr. and Mrs. Francisco will adopt the healthy child. (7 Oct 1852)

1805. Hon. Benjamin Thompson died 24 Sep 1852 at his residence in Charlestown, MA. A member of Congress from the 4th district of that state. (7 Oct 1852)

1806. Daniel Fulton and Mrs. Menty Pierce, both of Benton, Yates Co., were married 22 Sep 1852 by Rev. Abner Chase in Penn Yan, Yates Co. (7 Oct 1852)

1807. Nicholas Turner and Waty Ann Andress, both of Potter, Yates Co., were married 3 Oct 1852 by Rev. Abner Chase in Penn Yan, Yates Co. (7 Oct 1852)

1808. Harvie C. Dean of Torrey, Yates Co., and Eveline A. Bush of Penn Yan, Yates Co., were married 25 Sep 1852 by Rev. F.G. Howard in Penn Yan. (7 Oct 1852)

1809. Lewis Danes age 13 mos. 17 days, died 28 Sep 1852 in Penn Yan, Yates Co., son of Francis and Mary Jane Danes. (7 Oct 1852)

1810. Joseph Forsyth of Parksburg, VA., died 11 Oct 1852 at Wheeling, VA., from a small eruption caused by the bite of a gnat or mosquito. (14 Oct 1852)

1811. James E. Coovert of Potter, Yates Co., and Elizabeth Clicker of Wayne, Steuben Co., both mutes, were married 13 Oct 1852 by Rev. Wilkins at Wayne. (14 Oct 1852)

1812. Silas A. Andrews and Elizabeth A. Smith, eldest daughter of David W. Smith, both of Jerusalem, Yates Co., were married 28 Sep 1852 by Rev. William Bradley in Jerusalem. (14 Oct 1852)

1813. Lot W. Rogers and Hannah Runnells, both of Potter, Yates Co., were married 6 Oct 1852 in Bethel, Sullivan Co., by Rev. Titus of Bethel. (14 Oct 1852)

1814. Henry Cook of Geneva, Ontario Co., and Mary Delano, eldest daughter of Elisha Delano Esq. of Penn Yan, Yates Co., were married 7 Oct 1852 by Rev. William Hogarth in Penn Yan. (14 Oct 1852)

1815. Robert Sweet and Emily Murdock, both of Penn Yan, Yates Co., were married 28 Sep 1852 by Rev. James Eells in Penn Yan. (14 Oct 1852)

1816. William Hause and Maria L. Kinne, daughter of Henry Kinne Esq., all of Dundee, Yates Co., were married 29 Sep 1852 by Rev. J.T. Seeley in Dundee. (14 Oct 1852)

1817. Stephen A. McCoy and Mary E. Jessup, both of Tyrone, Steuben Co., were married 6 Oct 1852 by Rev. A. Wilkins in Wayne, Schuyler Co. (14 Oct 1852)

1818. Floyd Florence and Elizabeth Swarts were married 30 Sep 1852 by Rev. J.T. Seeley in Starkey, Yates Co. (14 Oct 1852)

1819. Mrs. Margaret Torrey age 60 yrs., died 15 Sep 1852 in Potter, Yates Co., widow of Nathan Torrey. (14 Oct 1852)

1820. Mrs. Margaret Wheaton age 82 yrs., died 7 Oct 1852 in Penn Yan, Yates Co., formerly of Hornby, Steuben Co. (14 Oct 1852)

1821. Sarah A. Pelham age 11 yrs. 10 mos., died in Middlesex, Yates Co., from injuries received when she fell from a swing, no date given. (14 Oct 1852)

1822. John Watkins age 23 yrs., died 1 Oct 1852 aboard ship, on his way home from California. The son of Benjamin Watkins of Potter, Yates Co. (14 Oct 1852)

1823. Benjamin Hobart age 32 yrs., died recently while going to California on the "Isthmus". The son of William L. Hobart of Potter, Yates Co. (14 Oct 1852)

1824. Baron Von Humboldt celebrated his 83rd birthday 14 Oct 1852 at Berlin, by giving his friends a feast. The "Nestor of Science" is in excellent health. (21 Oct 1852)

1825. A.C. Lazelear and M.A. Tubbs, both of Geneva, Ontario Co., were married 14 Oct 1852 by Rev. William Hogarth in Geneva. (21 Oct 1852)

1826. Chester H. Stump of Geneva, Ontario Co., and Mary E. Sterrett of Lyons, Wayne Co., were married 18 Oct 1852 by Rev. Holly in Lyons. (21 Oct 1852)

1827. Daniel H. Pryor of Attica, Wyoming Co., and Mary Louisa Zimmar of Geneva, Ontario Co., were married 19 Oct 1852 at the home of L.K. Shulingbargar, by Gen. M. Horton Esq., no town given. (21 Oct 1852)

1828. Mrs. Sarah Emily Allen age 36 yrs., died 18 Oct 1852 in Penn Yan, Yates Co., of consumption. The wife of George M. Allen of Detroit, Michigan, and daughter of the late Dr. William Cornwell. (21 Oct 1852)

1829. Horace M. Towns age 38 yrs., died 2 Oct 1852 at Ottawa, Illinois, of cholera. He moved from Penn Yan, Yates Co., about a year and a half ago. (21 Oct 1852)

1830. L. McConnell of Horseheads, Chemung Co., and Ruba A. Barden of Seneca, Ontario Co., were married 14 Oct 1852 by Rev. B.M. Goldsmith in Seneca. (28 Oct 1852)

1831. Franklin Beard and Susan Ann Reynals, both of Benton, Yates Co., were married 21 Oct 1852 by Rev. H.K. Stimson in Benton. (28 Oct 1852)

1832. E. Davis of Barrington, Yates Co., and R.A. Terriss Shedd, eldest daughter of Rev. Philander Shedd, were married 24 Oct 1852 by her father in the Baptist Church of Milo, Yates Co. (28 Oct 1852)

1833. In Benton, after a severe but brief illness of two days, the following children of Reuben M. and Ann Gage died on the 15th and 16th of Oct 1852, Mary J. Gage age 3 yrs., Jesse T. Gage age 5 yrs., and Eleanor Ann Gage age 15 yrs. (28 Oct 1852)

1834. Mrs. Elizabeth Topping age 28 yrs., died 31 Oct 1852 in Bath, Steuben Co., of consumption. The wife of Perry Topping, and daughter of Nathaniel Bundy Esq. of Cameron, Steuben Co. (4 Nov 1852)

1835. Mary Helen Gage age 16 yrs., died 24 Oct 1852 of dysentery in Benton, Yates Co., daughter of Jesse T. and Mary Gage. (4 Nov 1852)

1836. Horace Clark Esq. of Buffalo, Erie Co., age 57 yrs., died 24 Oct 1852 in Pulteney, Onondaga Co. The father of Mrs. Abram F. Hazen of Penn Yan, Yates Co. (11 Nov 1852)

1837. Dr. Fitch Howes of Vernon, Oneida Co., and Mrs. Cornelia M. Crane of Penn Yan, Yates Co., were married 17 Nov 1852 by Rev. Clark in Penn Yan. (18 Nov 1852)

1838. Nelson Dimick and Amanda Branch, both of Hector, Schuyler Co., were married 31 Oct 1852 by Rev. O. Fraser at Eddytown, Yates Co. (25 Nov 1852)

1839. Mark Seeley age 2 yrs. 2 mos., died 25 Oct 1852 at Eddytown, Yates Co., son of Henry and Mary Seeley. (25 Nov 1852)

1840. W.W. McCay age 72 yrs., died 28 Nov 1852 at his residence in Bath, Steuben Co. For years, he was the agent of the Pulteney Estate. (2 Dec 1852)

1841. Thomas Watkins and Mrs. Ann Jacobus were married 28 Nov 1852 by Rev. A.C. Mallory in Seneca, Ontario Co. (2 Dec 1852)

1842. Andrew J. Shannon and Margaret Dunham, both of Geneva, Ontario Co., were married 7 Dec 1852 by Rev. William Hogarth in Geneva. (9 Dec 1852)

1843. George V. Hitchcock of Havana, Schuyler Co., and Lydia M. Ely of Hector, Schuyler Co., were married 25 Nov 1852 by Rev. Huggins in Hector. (9 Dec 1852)

1844. Mary Elizabeth Hartshorn age 7 mos. 7 days, died 21 Nov 1852 in Iowa, of inflamation of the brain. The infant daughter of Isaac and Sarah Hartshorn, no town given. (9 Dec 1852)

1845. Abraham Mather and Elizabeth Low, both of Middlesex, Yates Co., were married 16 Nov 1852 by Rev. Wilson in Middlesex. (16 Dec 1852)

1846. Charles Baggerly of Orleans, Ontario Co., and Mary Putney of Middlesex, Yates Co., were married 8 Dec 1852 by Rev. M. Gilston in Middlesex. (16 Dec 1852)

1847. Sterling Blair and Lucinia Bates, both of Middlesex, Yates Co., were married 9 Dec 1852 by Rev. Jacob F. Wager in Middlesex. (16 Dec 1852)

1848. John E. Stewart age 50 yrs., died 14 Dec 1852 in Penn Yan, Yates Co. (16 Dec 1852)

1849. Ebenezer Brown age 60 yrs., died 7 Dec 1852 in Goshen, Indiana. The former sheriff of Yates Co., NY., and postmaster of Penn Yan. (16 Dec 1852)

1850. William Japhet McAllister age 16 yrs., died 8 Dec 1852 at the home of his uncle F.P. McAllister in Penn Yan, Yates Co. The cause of his death was a hemmorrhage of the nose. (16 Dec 1852)

1851. Robert Shearman age 58 yrs., died 10 Dec 1852 in Milo, Yates Co. A native of Ireland, and resident of this town for more than 40 yrs. (16 Dec 1852)

1852. Ferdinand Parker Hamilton age 5 yrs., died 11 Dec 1852 at the residence of Hon. Henry Welles in Penn Yan, Yates Co., eldest son of Theodore B. and Emily Hamilton of Brooklyn, NY. He had been visiting for two weeks with his grandparents, when taken ill with the croup, and died the second day. His parents heard of his death, before the news of his illness had reached them. Two years ago they lost their oldest son aged 6 yrs., to the same affliction. (16 Dec 1852)

1853. Mrs. Polly Legg age 69 yrs. 7 mos. 17 days, died 8 Dec 1852 in Penn Yan, Yates Co., wife of Carlton Legg Esq. (16 Dec 1852)

1854. Margaret Lott age 18 yrs., died 16 Dec 1852 at the residence of her father in Lodi, Seneca Co. (23 Dec 1852)

1855. Hon. Elijah Spencer age 77 yrs., died 15 Dec 1852 at his residence in Benton, Yates Co. Born in Columbia Co., his family moved to Ontario Co. in his early years. He served in many public offices. * a brief biography printed. (23 Dec 1852)

1856. D.C. Gile of Boston, MA., and Margaret A. Weir of Havana, Schuyler Co., were married 16 Dec 1852 by Rev. M. Huggin in Havana. (23 Dec 1852)

1857. Richard Petherick of Canandaigua, Ontario Co., and Esther Franklin of Penn Yan, Yates Co., were married 15 Dec 1852 by Rev. George Cheeney at the residence of B.W. Franklin Esq. in Penn Yan. (23 Dec 1852)

1858. Isaac W. Conklin and Nancy L. Sperbeck, both of Jerusalem, Yates Co., were married 16 Dec 1852 by Rev. Abner Chase in Penn Yan, Yates Co. (23 Dec 1852)

1859. S.B. Whitaker and Mary L. Olmsted, both of Benton, Yates Co., were married 14 Dec 1852 by Rev. B.M. Goldsmith in Benton. (23 Dec 1852)

1860. Robert Watson and Ruth Webb, both of Barrington, Yates Co., were married 15 Dec 1852 by Rev. O. Montague in Barrington. (23 Dec 1852)

1861. J.H. Raplee and Eliza Ann Huson, daughter of N. Huson, both of Barrington, Yates Co., were married 15 Dec 1852 by Rev. O. Montague in Barrington. (23 Dec 1852)

1862. Frances Goodwin age 13 yrs. 2 mos. 7 days, died 16 Dec 1852 in Elmira, Chemung Co., daughter of Rev. W.H. Goodwin. (23 Dec 1852)

1863. Adelia Hopkins age 2 yrs., died 18 Dec 1852 in Penn Yan, Yates Co. (23 Dec 1852)

1864. Joseph C. Gillam age 34 yrs., died 15 Dec 1852 in Geneva, Ontario Co. (23 Dec 1852)

1865. Mrs. Eva Finger age 58 yrs. 7 mos. 5 days, died 20 Dec 1852 in Benton, Yates Co., wife of Jeremiah Finger. (23 Dec 1852)

1866. John Dawson Jr., late of Yorkshire, England, age 21 yrs., died 21 Dec 1852 at the residence of J.J. Burton in Milo, Yates Co. (23 Dec 1852)

1867. The wife of Elizur Wright has again blessed her husband with twins, a girl and a boy. This makes 18 children for this couple, one regularly every 11 mos., no date or town given. (30 Dec 1852)

1868. Alexander Patten of Barrington, Yates Co., and Emily Bishop of Penn Yan, Yates Co., were married 28 Dec 1852 by Rev. James Eells in Penn Yan. (30 Dec 1852)

1869. E.P. Spencer of Benton, Yates Co.,and Lizzie W. Hyer, daughter of A.C. Hyer Esq. of Phila., PA., were married 15 Dec 1852 by Rev. David Malin, no town given. (30 Dec 1852)

1870. Andrew Turner and Sarah A. Bates, both of Benton, Yates Co., were married 24 Nov 1852 by Rev. A.E. Chubbuck in Benton. (30 Dec 1852)

1871. Mead Sutherland age 69 yrs., died 30 Nov 1852 in Milo, Yates Co. (30 Dec 1852)

1872. Peter G. Dox age 34 yrs., died 22 Dec 1852 at Hopeton, Yates Co., son of the late Gerrit L. Dox of Albany. (30 Dec 1852)

1873. Arathusa Dutton age 27 yrs., died 20 Dec 1852 in Seneca, Ontario Co. of consumption, daughter of Austin and Sarah Dutton. (30 Dec 1852)

1874. John P. Hogarth and Sarah E. Field, both of Geneva, Ontario Co., were married 29 Dec 1852 by Rev. William Hogarth in Geneva. (6 Jan 1853)

1875. Darwin S. Peck of Benton, Yates Co., son of Hon. Abel Peck, and Rebecca Miller, daughter of David Miller Esq. of Seneca, Ontario Co., were married 30 Dec 1852 by Rev. B.M. Goldsmith in Seneca. (6 Jan 1853)

1876. Andrew Bullock and Phebe McCain, both of Barrington, Yates Co., were married 22 Dec 1852 by Rev. D.B. Olney in Barrington. (6 Jan 1853)

1877. George Wilson 2nd. Esq., age 32 yrs., died 29 Dec 1852 in Canandaigua, Ontario Co., the Surrogate of that county. (6 Jan 1853)

1878. Mrs. Mary Jones age 56 yrs., died 28 Dec 1852 in Hopewell, Ontario Co. The wife of Judge Amos Jones. (6 Jan 1853)

1879. Mrs. Bogart age 77 yrs., died 2 Jan 1853 in Geneva, Ontario Co., wife of the late Herman H. Bogart. (6 Jan 1853)

1880. Stephen Purdy age 65 yrs., died 4 Jan 1853 in Benton, Yates Co. A native of Dutchess Co., and a resident of Benton for over 40 yrs. (6 Jan 1853)

1881. The son of Gen. Franklin Pierce was killed about 6 Jan 1853 in a train accident near Lawrence, MA. (13 Jan 1853)

1882. 1852 TABLE OF MORTALITY for the town of Middlesex, Yates Co. prepared for the "Yates County Whig" by John Mather Esq.

Feb...6	Lyman H. Green age 42 yrs.
Mar..16	Mrs. Sarah Reynolds age 57 yrs.
" 26	Cuyler Collins age under 1 yr.
Apr...3	John Franklin Mather age under 1 yr.
" 15	Jesse Kilpatrick age 85 yrs.
" 26	Mrs. Ellen Smith age 28 yrs.
" 26	John Arnett age 59 yrs.

May..16 Mrs. Seamans age 72 yrs.
Jun..15 Mrs. Ann Maria Christie age 21 yrs.
Jul..19 Mary Seamans age 20 yrs.
Aug..15 James M. Underwood age 44 yrs.
Nov..25 Elizabeth Putney age 1 yr.
Dec..15 Mrs. Lydia Christie age 58 yrs.
" 22 Clarrisa Adams age 26 yrs.
(13 Jan 1853)

1883. Deloss Frink and Mary A. Hedger, both of Rushville, Yates Co., were married 25 Dec 1852 by Rev. Ira Fairbanks in Benton, Yates Co. (13 Jan 1853)

1884. Shubael C. Babcock and Rebeckah Gould, both of Penn Yan, Yates Co., were married 6 Jan 1853 by Rev. Abner Chase in Penn Yan. (13 Jan 1853)

1885. William Reynolds and L.J. Holly, both of Potter, Yates Co., were married 29 Dec 1852 by Rev. J.W. Wilson in Potter. (13 Jan 1853)

1886. Lovell Arnold and Caroline Clark, both of Potter, Yates Co., were married 6 Jan 1853 by Rev. J.W. Wilson in Potter. (13 Jan 1853)

1887. Joseph Peak of Rushville, Yates Co., and Mrs. Laura Loop of Elmira, Chemung Co., were married 23 Dec 1852 by Abner Wells Esq. in Wellsburg, Chemung Co. (13 Jan 1853)

1888. Benjamin Marvin of Fairport, Monroe Co., and Elizabeth S. Reeder, were married 29 Dec 1852 by Rev. O. Fraser in Eddytown, Yates Co. (13 Jan 1853)

1889. James Finch of Milo, Yates Co., and Mary Ann Long of Torrey, Yates Co., were married 1 Jan 1853 by Elder David F. Randolph in Torrey. (13 Jan 1853)

1890. Mrs. Rachel Sheppard age 78 yrs., died 16 Jan 1853 in Penn Yan, Yates Co., wife of the late Morris F. Sheppard. She was one of the early settlers of this county, emigrating with her father's family from PA., in the latter part of the 1700's. She married in Penn Yan, and reared five children who reached adulthood, three preceded her in death. It is believed she is the last female, of the original Friends Society. (20 Jan 1853)

1891. O. Kenyon and Lucy A. Hedges were married 13 Jan 1853 by Rev. H.K. Stimson in Milo, Yates Co. (20 Jan 1853)

1892. Ezekial C. Benedict and Martha Jane Sutton, both of Jerusalem, Yates Co., were married 30 Dec 1852 by Rev. D.D. Buck in Jerusalem. (20 Jan 1853)

1893. Azariah Finch and Mary Lewis, both of Milo, Yates Co., were married 1 Jan 1853 by Rev. J.T. Seeley in Milo. (20 Jan 1853)

1894. George P. Rose of Dundee, Yates Co., and Lenorah H. Seely, daughter of Jonathan Seely Esq. of Ypsilanti, Michigan, were married 5 Jan 1853 at Horseheads, Chemung Co., NY., no pastor named. (20 Jan 1853)

1895. Samuel C. Francisco and Mary A. Washburn, both of Gorham, Ontario Co., were married 6 Jan 1853 in by Rev. E.G. Townsend in Canandaigua, Ontario Co. (20 Jan 1853)

1896. Mrs. Hannah Bradley age 83 yrs. 5 mos. 25 days, died 8 Jan 1853 in Benton, Yates Co. The mother of the late Dr. Bradley, and grandmother of L.P. Holmes of Benton. Her death caused by the accidental fall through a cellar stairway. The death of her last surviving child, occurred on her 71st. birthday. A member of the Baptist Church for about 40 yrs. (20 Jan 1853)

1897. Hon. William Upham died 19 Jan 1853 in Washington, a U.S. Senator from Vermont. (20 Jan 1853)

1898. SOME OF THE DISTINGUISHED DEAD OF 1852, prepared for the "Yates County Whig" by S.G. Gage Esq., are as follows:

a. John Dixon, lawyer and ex-member of Congress died at West Bloomfield, Ontario Co., no date given. (27 Jan 1853)

b. John Howard Payne Esq. died at Tunis, American Consul at Tunis, author of the popular song "Home Sweet Home", no date given. (27 Jan 1853)

c. Hon. Dudley Marvin age 66 yrs., died at Ripley, Chautaqua Co., ex-member of Congress from Canandaigua, Ontario Co., no date given. (27 Jan 1853)

d. George Green age 90 yrs., died 15 Jan 1852 in Potter, Yates Co. A soldier of the Revolution, and relative of the celebrated Gen. Green of the Revolution. He settled on the farm where he died, in 1790. (27 Jan 1853)

e. Jonathan Pierpont died 29 Jan 1852 at New Haven, CT. A soldier of the Revolution, present at the surrender of Cornwall. * brief biography printed (27 Jan1853)

f. David Kennison age 115 yrs., died 24 Feb 1852 at Chicago, IL. He is thought to be the last survivor of the "Boston Tea Party", and a soldier of the Revolution. * a brief biography printed. (27 Jan 1853)

g. Dr. Isaac Thompson died __ Mar 1852 at New London, CT. The celebrated proprietor of the "Thompson's Eye Water". (27 Jan 1853)

h. Sir John Harvey died __ Mar 1852 at Halifax, NS, the Lieut. Governor of that place. (27 Jan 1853)

i. Hon. James Burt age 96 yrs., died 17 Mar 1852 at Watervliet, Albany Co., a soldier of the Revolution. (27 Jan 1853)

j. Huldah Sparling age 110 yrs., died 8 Apr 1852 at Owego, Tioga Co. (27 Jan 1853)

k. Bishop Hedding died 9 Apr 1852 at Poughkeepsie, Dutchess Co., of the Methodist Episcopal Church. (27 Jan 1853)

l. Charles Boucher age 106 yrs., died 10 Apr 1852 near Montreal, Canada. He was married to 3 wives, with whom he had 60 children. He leaves 43 children to deplore his loss, 66 grandchildren, and 13 great grandchildren. (27 Jan 1853)

m. Gen. Solomon Van Renselaer age 78 yrs., died 23 Apr 1852 at Cherry Hill near Albany, Albany Co., of apoplexy. He entered the army in 1792, and distinguished himself for skill and bravery in the Battle of Queenston in 1812. He held many public offices in this state and nation. (27 Jan 1853)

n. Hon. John Young age 50 yrs., died 23 Apr 1852 in New York city of consumption. An ex-member of Congresss, ex-Governor, and sub-Treasurer of New York city. (27 Jan 1853)

o. Joseph Johnson age 93 yrs., died __ May 1852 at Pleasant Mills, NY. A soldier of the Revolution, he entered the service in 1776, when only 16 yrs. old. (27 Jan 1853)

p. Isaac J. Hopper a well known philanthropist, died 7 May 1852 in New York city. (27 Jan 1853)

q. Hon. Charles Andrews age 38 yrs., died 7 May 1852 at Paris, Maine, a member of Congress. (27 Jan 1853)

r. Mrs. Louisa Adams died 15 May 1852 in Washington, wife of the late ex-President John Quincy Adams. (27 Jan 1853)

s. Peleg Redfield age 91 yrs., died 26 May 1852 at at Manchester, Ontario Co. A soldier of the Revolution under Gen. Washington, and in his retreat from Long Island. He was present at Yorktown and Valley Forge. He had smallpox while in the army, yet died of the same disease. One of the first settlers of Manchester, moving there in 1800. He was a member of the Baptist Church. (27 Jan 1853)

t. William Wilkison age 92 yrs., died 30 May 1852 at Providence, Rhode Island. The oldest living graduate of Brown University, a soldier of the Revolution, and was engaged in Sullivan's expedition. (27 Jan 1853)

u. Hosea Ballou age 81 yrs., died __ Jun 1852 at Boston, MA. The most prominent preacher of Universal Salvation. (27 Jan 1853)

v. Benjamin Burgess age 101 yrs., died 18 Jun 1852 at Wayne, ME. Born 17 Mar 1751 at Rochester, MA. In early years, he followed the seas, and in 1794 he moved to Wayne, ME, then an unbroken wilderness. He leaves 11 children, 67 grandchildren, and 90 great grandchildren. (27 Jan 1853)

w. "Tommy" an old negro, age 110 yrs., died 17 Jun 1852 at Jefferson, Schoharie Co. (27 Jan 1853)

x. B.R. Wormley age 67 yrs., died 26 Jun 1852 at Newport, RI. A Rear Admiral in the British Navy. (27 Jan 1853)

y. Samuel Nichols age 89 yrs., died __ Jul 1852 at Southport, Chemung Co. A soldier of the Revolution. (27 Jan 1853)

z. Hon Lewis Sanford died __ Jul 1852 at Toledo. A Justices of the Supreme Court of Albany, Albany Co. and former vice-Chancellor of that district. (27 Jan 1853)

1899. Asahel Stone Esq. age 69 yrs., died 21 Dec 1852 in Athens, Calhoun Co., Michigan. Formerly of Jerusalem, Yates Co. NY, in 1837 he moved to Athens and homestead where he remained until his death, he leaves a widow. (27 Jan 1853)

1900. Benjamin W. Wooster Esq. and Catharine Wright, daughter of T.S. Wright, were married 18 Jan 1853 in Elmira, Chemung Co., no pastor given. (27 Jan 18530

1901. Tewalt Swarts and Huldah Hair, both of Dundee, Yates Co., were married 19 Jan 1853 by Rev. J.T. Seeley in Tyrone, Schuyler Co. (27 Jan 1853)

1902. Asa Green of Potter, Yates Co., and Ellen Bennett of Middlesex, Yates Co., were married 19 Jan 1853 by Rev. Spinks in Middlesex. (27 Jan 1853)

1903. Ezra Fuller and Mrs. Rachel W. Peters, both of Middlesex, Yates Co., were married 20 Jan 1853 by Rev. Samuel Parker at Hopewell, Ontario Co. (27 Jan 1853)

1904. Caleb Fletcher Smith of Hector, Schuyler Co., and Mary Seeley of Ovid, Steuben Co., were married 12 Jan 1853 by Rev. T. Stacey in Ovid. (27 Jan 1853)

1905. Samuel G. Boots and Christiana Simmons, both of Potter, Yates Co., were married 16 Nov 1852 by Rev. William Bradley in Potter. (27 Jan 1853)

1906. Ezekial M. Coons of Naples, Ontario Co., and Phila A. Wheeler of Potter, Yates Co., were married 25 Dec 1852, no town or pastor given. (27 Jan 1853)

1907. Riley Wells of Potter, Yates Co., and Sophia Davis of Jerusalem, Yates Co., were married 30 Dec 1852, no town or pastor given. (27 Jan 1853)

1908. John Underwood Esq. and Mary E. Gardner, both of Potter, Yates Co., were married 4 Jan 1853, no town or pastor given.(27 Jan 1853)

1909. Mary Elizabeth Thompson age 15 mos., died 31 Dec 1852 in Penn Yan, Yates Co., the daughter of Nelson and Renette Thompson. (27 Jan 1853)

1910. Hon. Alexander H. Buell died 30 Jan 1853 in Washington city, a member of Congress from the Herkimer District of this state. (3 Feb 1853)

1911. TABLE OF MORTALITY FOR THE TOWN OF BENTON 1852, prepared for the "Yates County Whig, by S.G. Gage Esq., (Note, this list is identical with entry # 646 for 1831, and copied as printed.)

Jan...6	Buel Mariner age 77 yrs.
" 9	Peter Bain age 66 yrs.
" 17	Abigail Burgduff age 23 yrs.
Feb...5	Frances M. Moon age under 1 yr.
" 19	Mary Nichols age 71 yrs.
" 23	Thomas Chrysler age 60 yrs.
" 29	Jane E. Coddington age 26 yrs.
Mar..15	Sylvester N. Ketcham age 37 yrs.
" 19	Ann M. Scott age 38 yrs.
" 23	John Powell age 58 yrs.
Apr...1	Margaret Z. Earl age 18 yrs.
" 17	Sarah Brown age 88 yrs.
May...2	Julia Fowle age 7 Yrs.
" 3	Martha Beard age 62 yrs.
Jun...1	Nathan P. Cole age over 70 yrs.
" 1	Henry Andrews age 35 yrs.
" 2	Harriet Moon age 3 yrs.
" 7	Caroline A. Townsend age 31 yrs.
" 21	Anthony Griffin age 24 yrs., killed by lightning.
" 22	Eliza A. Hicks age 45 yrs.
Jul..20	Garret E. Crank age 11 yrs.
" 28	Charles R. Kelsey age 31 yrs.
Aug..14	Elizabeth Meeker age 66 yrs.
Oct..15	Mary S. Gage age 4 yrs.
" 15	Jesse T. Gage age 5 yrs.
" 16	Eleanor M. Gage age 15 yrs.
" 24	Mary H. Gage age 16 yrs.
Nov...2	Nancy Patchen age 74 yrs.
" 24	Inf'son of D. Feagles age under 1 yr.
" 28	DeWitt C. Chrysler age 37 yrs.
Dec..15	Hon. Elijah Spencer age 76 yrs.
" 20	Eva Finger age 59 yrs.
" 31	Ann King age 24 yrs.

(3 Feb 1853)

1912. Joshua Legg and Ellen Jane Rappelye, both of Milo, Yates Co., were married 27 Jan 1853 by Rev. James Eells in Milo. (3 Feb 1853)

1913. George P. McKay and Adelaide M. Ruckel were married 26 Jan 1853 by Rev. Bissell in Geneva, Ontario Co. (3 Feb 1853)

1914. Samuel F. Paddock of Rochester, Monroe Co., and Hannah M. Schermerhorn of Geneva, Ontario Co., were married 20 Jan 1853 by Rev. M. Tooker in Phelps (Oak's Corner), Ontario Co. (3 Feb 1853)

1915. William C. Swarts and Mary Jane Raplee, eldest daughter of Daniel Raplee Esq., were married 26 Jan 1853 by Rev. J.T. Seeley in Dundee, Yates Co. (3 Feb 1853)

1916. William Augustus Simonson age 14 yrs. 23 days, died 13 Jan 1853 in Starkey, Yates Co. The eldest son of Joel G. and Julia Simonson. (3 Feb 1853)

1917. Mrs. Cynthia Booth age 76 yrs., died 25 Jan 1853 in Dundee, Yates Co. The wife of Abijah Booth, late of Cameron, Steuben Co. (3 Feb 1853)

1918. Seth Stanly, fatally injured on the Chemung Railroad last Friday, at Horseheads, Chemung Co. He was in the act of coupling cars, when he was caught just above the thighs, crushing him in a horrible manner. The son of Lucius Stanly Esq. of Geneva, Ontario Co., he is not expected to live. (3 Feb 1853)

1919. INTERESTING DATA, a six year old boy was stolen from his parents at Adrian, Michigan, by a party of Chippewa Indians. They traded him off for a pony, with another Indian tribe farther west. He was finally adopted and raised among the Blackfeet, and married a daughter of one of the chiefs. After 14 yrs. of living with the natives. A white physician among the Blackfeet disclosed the secret. The young man paid a visit to his father near Detroit, but preferred to live the Indian life. The information stated, he was the grandson of Ira Chubb, formerly of Chubbs Hollow in Barrington, Yates Co. His parents had moved to Michigan in 1838 or 1839, no names given for the boy, or his parents. (10 Feb 1853)

1920. Sears C. Walker Esq., the eminent Astronomer and Mathematician, died 30 Jan 1853 at the home of his brother, Judge Walker near Cincinnati, Ohio. (10 Feb 1853)

1921. John S. Allen of Dansville, Livingston Co., and Mary Jane Tooker of Jerusalem, Yates Co., were married 8 Feb 1853 by Rev. Abner Chase in Penn Yan, Yates Co. (10 Feb 1853)

1922. William V.R. Sloan of Chicago, IL., and Arna A. Olmstead of Bethany, PA., were married 2 Feb 1853 by Rev. Kellogg in Bethany. (10 Feb 1853)

1923. William Pettengill of West Dresden, Yates Co., and Ellen Struble of Milo, Yates Co., were married 26 Dec 1852 by Rev. B.S. Borden in Milo. (10 Feb 1853)

1924. Obedia Allington age 41 yrs., died 29 Jan 1853 of consumption in Torrey, Yates Co. (10 Feb 1853)

1925. Mrs. Rebecca McHinch age 74 yrs., died 14 Feb 1853 in Penn Yan, Yates Co. of paralysis. She was born near Belfast, Ireland, and soon after her marriage, came with her husband to New York. He was a merchant for some years on Wall St. in New York. After the death of her husband, she lived in Brooklyn with her three daughters, till about 17 yrs. ago, when they moved to Penn Yan. She was the last of nine sisters, and a member of the Episcopal Church. (17 Feb 1853)

1926. Floyd D. Torrance of Rochester, Monroe Co., and Caroline Upton of Victor, Ontario Co., were married 26 Jan 1853 at Jacksonville, Florida, no pastor given. (17 Feb 1853)

1927. Jacob Conklin age 81 yrs., died 1 Feb 1853 at his home in Jerusalem, Yates Co., a resident of that town for 27 yrs. (17 Feb 1853)

1928. Mrs. Louisa Perry died 29 Jan 1853 at Monterey, Steuben Co. The wife of Dr. Levi Perry Jr. of Penn Yan, Yates Co. (17 Feb 1853)

1929. John Savage age 53 yrs., died 16 Feb 1853 in Penn Yan, Yates Co. (17 Feb 1853)

1930. Smith Meek age 16 yrs. 5 mos., died 1 Jan 1853 in Torrey, Yates Co. (17 Feb 1853)

1931. Daniel Benton age 80 yrs., died 11 Feb 1853 in Pulteney, Steuben Co. (17 Feb 1853)

1932. William H. Seward born 16 May 1801 in Florida, Orange Co., NY. * brief biography printed. (17 Feb 1853)

1933. Charles Willey age 106 yrs., died 23 Jan 1853 in Nottingham, NH. The oldest inhabitant of that town, born there 25 Mar 1746. A soldier of the Revolution, his son Jonathan Willey age between 70 and 80 yrs., is a pensioner of the War of 1812. (24 Feb 1853)

1934. Peter French of Naples, Ontario Co., and Phebe Gardner of Milo, Yates Co., were married 15 Feb 1853 by Rev. A.N. Fillmore in Milo. (24 Feb 1853)

1935. Henry Moshier and Harriet Carpenter, both of Milo, Yates Co., were married 26 Jan 1853 by J.V. VanAllen Esq. in Milo. (24 Feb 1853)

1936. Alonzo Murdough age 25 yrs. 6 mos. 22 days, died 31 Dec 1852 within 12 days sail of San Francisco, on board the steamship Cortes off St. Lucas Bay, of cholera. The son of William and Elizabeth Murdough of Benton, Yates Co., NY. (24 Feb 1853)

1937. Thomas Fitzgerald age 60 yrs., died 12 Feb 1853 at Gorham, Ontario Co. He fell through the railroad bridge, and died from his injuries. (24 Feb 1853)

1938. Kate Wight age 11 yrs., died 18 Feb 1853 at the home of her uncle, Nelson Thompson in Penn Yan, Yates Co. (24 Feb 1853)

1939. SOME OF THE DISTINGUISHED DEAD OF 1852, prepared for the "Yates County Whig" by S.G. Gage Esq. (continued from entry # 1896).

a. Hon. John McKinley died 8 Jul 1852 at Lexington, KY., a Judge of the U.S. Supreme Court.

b. Seth Sturtevant died 11 Jul 1852 at Hartford, ME., a soldier of the Revolution, present with Gen. Washington at Valley Forge, and the Battles of Stillwater and Monmouth. (3 Mar 1853)

c. A.J. Downing died 28 Jul 1852 aboard the ill fated steamer "Henry Clay" on the Hudson River, NY. (3 Mar 1853)

d. Stephen Allen age 85 yrs., died 28 Jul 1852 aboard the ill fated steamer "Henry Clay" on the Hudson River, NY. (3 Mar 1853)

e. Levi Buckingham age 87 yrs., died 28 Jul 1852 at Symmes, CT. He was with St. Clair at his defeat. (3 Mar 1853)

f. Major Joy, age 90 yrs., died __ Aug 1852 at Clayton, Jefferson Co., a soldier of the Revolution. (3 Mar 1853)

g. Dr. Thomas Richardson age 86 yrs., died 8 Aug 1852 at Fitzwilliam, NH. On the same day, his brother John Richardson age 82 yrs., died at Leominster, MA. Also, in the same place last 27 Jun 1852, a sister age 91 yrs., died. (3 Mar 1853)

h. Isaac Rice age 87 yrs., a soldier of the Revolution, died 11 Aug 1852 at Ticonderoga, and will be remembered by all visitors of that celebrated place as the old guide. (3 Mar 1853)

i. Col. William Wardworth age 48 yrs., died 21 Aug 1852 at Genesco, Livingston Co. (3 Mar 1853)

j. Benjamin Matthews died 21 Aug 1852, president of the PA state Senate. (3 Mar 1853)

k. Amos Raymond age 95 yrs. died 22 Aug 1852 at Allegany, PA. A soldier of the Revolution, and for the last 63 yrs., a soldier of the Cross and an explemplary member of the Baptist Church. (3 Mar 1853)

l. Joseph Vance died 24 Aug 1852 at Urbana, Ohio, ex-member of Congress and ex-Governor of that state. (3 Mar 1853)

m. Mrs. Lois Peck age 100 yrs. 8 mos. 6 days, died __Sep 1852 at Hampden, CT., for 75 yrs., a member of the Congregational Church. (3 Mar 1853)

n. Hon. Orrin Fowler died 3 Sep 1852 at Washington city, a member of Congress from MA. (3 Mar 1853)

o. Hon. Edward McGaughey died 6 Sep 1852 a member of Congress from IN. (3 Mar 1853)

p. Hon. Mark H. Sibley died 8 Sep 1852 at Canandaigua, Ontario Co. Late Judge and Surrogate of that county, a member of the Whig Party, by which he was chosen to the Senate and Congress. (3 Mar 1853)

q. Hon. William Badger age 74 yrs., died 11 Sep 1852 at Gilmartin, NH., ex-Govenor of that state. (3 Mar 1853)

r. Hon. Berry Thompson died 24 Sep 1852 at Charlestown, MA., a member of Congress from that state. (3 Mar 1853)

s. Bishop Chase died 29 Sep 1852 in New York city, of the Protestant Episcopal Church. (3 Mar 1853)

t. Hon. Whitcomb of NY., died 4 Oct 1852 in New York city, ex-Governor and Senator of this state. (3 Mar 1853)

u. John L. Stephens age 47 yrs., died 13 Oct 1852 at New York city, well known author and traveler. (3 Mar 1853)

v. John Wadleigh age 85 yrs. 7 mos. 23 days, died 23 Oct 1852 at Shaker Village, NH. A soldier of the Revolution, he was at the Battle of Bunker Hill and one of the last to leave the scene of action. He was one of the founders of the Shaker Society, having been a member for over 75 yrs. (3 Mar 1853)

w. Hon. Daniel Webster age 76 yrs., died 24 Oct 1852 at Marshfield, the U.S. Secretary of State. (3 Mar 1853)

x. Hon. J.C. Clark died 25 Oct 1852 at Chemung, Chemung Co. Solicitor of the U.S. Treasury and ex-member Congress for Chenango Co. (3 Mar 1853)

y. Ex-Govenor Schultz died __Nov 1852 in Lancaster, PA. (3 Mar 1853)

z. Hon. Walter Forward age 65 yrs., died 24 Nov 1852 at Pittsburg, PA. He had filled many public offices, a member of Congress, Secretary of the Treasury under President Tyler, Minister to Denmark and up to his death, a Judge of the District Court. (3 Mar 1853)

aa. Hon. John W. Crockett age 45 yrs., died 24 Nov 1852 at Memphis, TN. The son of the renowned Col. Crockett, a member of Congress. (3 Mar 1853)

bb. Mrs. Abigail Guilford age 88 yrs., died 29 Nov 1852 at Lynn, MA. At the time of her death, she had 54 great-grandchildren. (3 Mar 1853)

cc. Fanny Wright Darusmont age 57 yrs., died 13 Dec 1852 in Cincinnati, OH., from the effects of a severe fall last winter, she was worth $150,000. (3 Mar 1853)

dd. Hon. Elijah Spencer age 76 yrs., died 15 Dec 1852 in Benton, Yates Co. A distinguished citizen of this county. He has served in the Legislature, Congress and was a member of the Convention which adopted the Constitution of the United States. (3 Mar 1853) ee. James Lafoon age 90 yrs., died 27 Dec 1852 in Fayette, KY., a soldier of the Revolution. (3 Mar 1853)

ff. Hon. Thomas J. Marvin age 50 yrs., died 29 Dec 1852 at Saratoga Springs, Saratoga Co. (3 Mar 1853)

gg. Stephen Spaulding age 97 yrs., died 30 Dec 1852 at Monroe, ME. One of the veterans who composed the "Life Guard" of Gen. George Washington. (3 Mar 1853)

1940. The "Wayne Co., Whig" notices the death of Dr. James Bemis Adams age 27 yrs., son of Gen. William H. Adams of that village. The deceased was at Curracoa, in the Caribbean Sea, having gone there with an invalid sister, he died of yellow fever, no date or town given. (3 Mar 1853)

1941. Thomas J. Mattison of Pulteney, Steuben Co., and Bethiah Sutton of Torrey, Yates Co., were married 27 Feb 1853 by Rev. A.C. Mallory in Torrey. (3 Mar 1853)

1942. Albert Ellis of Watkins, Schuyler Co., and Caroline M. Voak of Reading, Steuben Co., were married 23 Feb 1853 by Rev. C.M. Gardner in Reading. (3 Mar 1853)

1943. John D. VanGorder of Barrington, Yates Co., and Elizabeth Rowles of Bradford, Steuben Co., were married 31 Jan 1853 by Rev. P. Olney in Wayne, Steuben Co. (3 Mar 1853)

1944. Joel A. Taylor of Starkey, Yates Co., and Lola Thomas of Reading, Steuben Co., were married 20 Feb 1853 by Rev. S. White, no town given. (3 Mar 1853)

1945. Wilson Ayres age 73 yrs. 1 mo., died 22 Feb 1853 in Milo, Yates Co. (3 Mar 1853)

1946. John DeWitt age 71 yrs., died 8 Feb 1853 at Bath, Steuben Co., formerly of Starkey, Yates Co. (3 Mar 1853)

1947. Dr. Lewis Sleight died 5 Jan 1853 at Martinez, California, late of Alloway, Wayne Co., New York. He was married just previous to his departure for California to Catharine Staats of Geneva, Ontario Co., NY. (3 Mar 1853)

1948. Capt. Stephen Chase age 71 yrs., died 21 Feb 1852 in Seneca, Ontario Co., at the home of his son in-law J.H. Tuttle. The deceased was for many years a resident of Benton, Yates Co. (3 Mar 1853)

1949. Mrs. Caroline H. Torrance died 9 Feb 1853 in Syracuse, Onondaga Co., wife of Floyd D. Torrance of Rochester, Monroe Co. The deceased was returning from Florida with her husband, and had been married just two weeks. Buried in Victor, Ontario Co. (3 Mar 1853)

1950. Rufus L. Adams age 29 yrs., died 27 Feb 1853 in Middlesex, Yates Co. (3 Mar 1853)

1951. James E. Seaver died 6 Mar 1853 at Batavia,, Genesee Co., an Editor and publisher of the "Spirit of The Times". (10 Mar 1853)

1952. P.P. Thayer a druggist at Rochester, Monroe Co., committed suicide 5 Mar 1853 by cutting his throat. He was suffering from insanity caused by intemperance. (10 Mar 1853)

1953. David Sutherland and Charlotte Cole were married in Potter, Yates Co., no date or pastor given. (10 Mar 1853)

1954. Hiram Witter of Gorham, Ontario Co., and Emily Page of Middlesex, Yates Co., were married 24 Feb 1853 in Middlesex, no pastor named. (10 Mar 1853)

1955. Mr. Plattman and Miss E.A. VanWort, both of Benton, Yates Co., were married 10 Dec 1852 in Benton, no pastor given. (10 Mar 1853)

1956. Robert Crittenden and Catharine Briggs were married 23 Feb 1853 by Rev. James L. Edson in Gorham, Ontario Co. (10 Mar 1853)

1957. George B. Richardson a printer, and E.R. Willour, both of Bath, Steuben Co., were married 27 Feb 1853 by Rev. G.D. Stewart in Bath. (10 Mar 1853)

1958. Arthur Wintermute and Amelia Seeley, both of Pulteney, Steuben Co., were married 17 Feb 1853 by Rev. J. Ainsworth in Pulteney. (10 Mar 1853)

1959. Friend D. Pitts, formerly of Penn Yan, Yates Co., and Mary C. Baldwin, daughter of the late

Judge Baldwin of Glenn's Falls, were married 24 Feb 1853 by Rev. S.T. Sewar in Brooklyn, NY. (10 Mar 1853)

1960. Norman Holmes age 32 yrs., died 20 Jan 1853 in Benton, Yates Co. (10 Mar 1853)

1961. Samuel Reed age 79 yrs., died 27 Feb 1853 in Seneca, Ontario Co. (10 Mar 1853)

1962. Mrs. Catharine Ansly age 42 yrs., died 18 Jan 1853 in Potter, Yates Co., wife of William Ansly. (10 Mar 1853)

1963. Noah A. Hoze age 24 yrs., died 18 Feb 1853 at the residence of his sister in Benton, Yates Co. (10 Mar 1853)

1964. Margaretta S. Wilder age 27 yrs., died 1 Mar 1853 in Geneva, Ontario Co., wife of Dr. L.V. Wilder, of consumption. (10 Mar 1853)

1965. Rev. John Baggerly age 75 yrs., died 18 Feb 1853 at Phelps, Ontario Co., his wife Mrs. Ruth Baggerly age 79 yrs., died 1 Mar 1853 in Phelps. (10 Mar 1853)

1966. Morris B. Ovenshire and Matilda E. Fenton were married 2 Mar 1853 in Barrington, Yates Co., no pastor given. (17 Mar 1853)

1967. Henry Lamareaux and Ann Harkness were married 8 Mar 1853 in Middlesex, Yates Co., no pastor given. (17 Mar 1853)

1968. Lemuel Dwelle and Mary Raplee were married 3 Mar 1853 by Rev. J.W. Wilson in Gorham, Ontario Co. (17 Mar 1853)

1969. Gilbert J. Snyder of Potter, Yates Co., and Clarrisa Briggs of Urbana, Steuben Co., were married 7 Mar 1853 by Henry Chickester Esq. in Wheeler, Steuben Co. (17 Mar 1853)

1970. Mrs. Jane Fox age 65 yrs., died 11 Mar 1853 in Italy, Yates Co., wife of James Fox Esq. (17 Mar 1853)

1971. Mrs. Julia Townsend age 50 yrs., died 8 Mar 1853 in Geneva, Ontario Co., wife of L.G. Townsend formerly of Big Stream, Yates Co. (17 Mar 1853)

1972. Mrs. Sarah Welles age 20 yrs.,died 23 Feb 1853 in Geneva, Ontario Co. (17 Mar 1853)

1973. The wife of Hon. William S. Hubbell died 18 Mar 1853 in Bath, Steuben Co. (24 Mar 1853)

1974. George T. Millspaugh of Milo, Yates Co., and Alma Perry, daughter of Amos Perry Esq. of Jerusalem, Yates Co., were married 17 Mar 1853 at the Congregational Church in Penn Yan, Yates Co. by Rev. S.S. Hughson. (24 Mar 1853)

1975. Cyrenius Townsend of Branchport, Yates Co., and Mary Jane Perry, daughter of Amos Perry Esq. of Jerusalem, Yates Co., were married 17 Mar 1853 at the Congregational Church in Penn Yan, Yates Co. by Rev. S.S. Hughson. (24 Mar 1853)

1976. Henry L. Edwards of Waterloo, Seneca Co., and Julia McCane of Penn Yan, Yates Co., were married 4 Mar 1853 by William H. Burton Esq. in Waterloo. (24 Mar 1853)

1977. Freeman Frits and Catharine Berry, both of West Dresden, Yates Co., were married 9 Mar 1853 by Rev. B.S. Borden in West Dresden. (24 Mar 1853)

1978. Fanny Davison was born 11 Mar 1821 in Ridgebury, Bradford Co. PA. She convert to God and the Methodist Church in Mar 1834 at Hector, Tompkins Co. NY., She went with her husband to Painted Post, and after a few months they moved to Milton, Northumberland, Co. PA. Later moving to Wells, Bradford Co. Pa., in Dec 1844, and she died there 6 Feb 1853. (24 Mar 1853)

1979. Deacon Hart Massey and Deacon Moses Bacon, both of the First Presbyterian Church in Watertown, Jefferson Co., one age 86 yrs., and the other age 76 yrs., both died 27 Mar 1853 in the same hour. (31 Mar 1853)

1980. Almon L. Read of Potter, Yates Co., and Harriet A. Legg, second daughter of M.A. Legg Esq., of Torrey, Yates Co., were married 29 Mar 1853 by Rev. Colson in Torrey. (31 Mar 1853)

1981. Albert S. Grosvenor of Elmira, Chemung Co., and Lucy Hoyt of Penn Yan, Yates Co., were married 28 Mar 1853 in the First Congregational Church at Penn Yan by Rev. S.S. Hughson. (31 Mar 1853)

1982. Orison Howe and Sarah Hurd, both of Elmira, Chemung Co., were married 26 Mar 1853 by Rev. B.W. Capron in Starkey, Yates Co. (31 Mar 1853)

1983. William B. Hunter of Watkins, Schuyler Co., and Lola F. Walling of Reading, Schuyler Co., were married 24 Mar 1853 in Elmira, Chemung Co., no pastor given. (31 Mar 1853)

1984. Azariah Finch age 60 yrs., died 20 Mar 1853 in Milo, Yates Co. (31 Mar 1853)

1985. Mrs. Cornelia S. Dillon age 27 yrs., died 20 Mar 1853 in Phelps, Ontario Co., wife of William Dillon, Editor of the "Phelps Atlas". (31 Mar 1853)

1986. Jane Glann age 22 yrs., died 18 Mar 1853 in Potter, Yates Co. (31 Mar 1853)

1987. The son of William R. Kelsey age 11 yrs., died several days ago at Dresden, Yates Co., from injuries received, when two other boys, aged 15 yrs. and 17 yrs., severely beat him as a matter of cruel sport, no date given. The two boys were arrested and will stand trial. (31 Mar 1853)

1988. Rev. Silas Hawley has relinquished his charge of the Presbyterian Church at Phelps, Ontario Co., and is moving to Fond du Lac, Wisconsin, where he will resume his ministerial labors. (7 Apr 1853)

1989. Harriet Munroe Babcock age 7 yrs., died 2 Apr 1853 in Penn Yan, Yates Co., only daughter of John C. and Celestia Babcock. Five weeks ago her father left his home, under an appointment of the Government, as Mail Agent for San Francisco. (7 Apr 1853)

1990. The wife of Millard Fillmore, ex-President of the U.S., died 30 Apr 1853 in Washington city. (7 Apr 1853)

1991. O.T. Houston of Grand Traverse, MI., murdered one of his sister's children. He had tortured the child with a hot iron for several days, while he kept his wife and own children locked up. He left the door unlocked one day when he went in the woods and they escaped, no date given. (7 Apr 1853)

1992. After a courtship of 3 years, John Pearce and Hannah Cook, only daughter of B. Cook Esq., both of Branchport, Yates Co., were married 29 Mar 1853 in Hammondsport, Steuben Co. by Mr. Crammer Esq., (7 Apr 1853)

1993. Charles Westbrook of Bradford, Steuben Co., and Phebe A. Genung of Jerusalem, Yates Co., were married 24 Mar 1853 by Rev. J. Jones in Jerusalem. (7 Apr 1853)

1994. George D. Carpenter of Elmira, Chemung Co., and Lydia J. Higley of Penn Yan, Yates Co., were married 30 Mar 1853 by Rev. J. Jones in Penn Yan. 97 Apr 1853)

1995. Francis H. Rugar of Galesburg, Illinois., and Elizabeth Beers of Danby, Tompkins Co., NY., were married by Rev. J. Jones in Danby. (7 Apr 1853)

1996. Rily Kittredge and Samatha Elles, both of Penn Yan, Yates Co., were married 25 Mar 1853 by Rev. A.C. Mallory in Benton, Yates Co. (7 Apr 1853)

1997. Lathrop S. Henderson and Cornelia C. Bryant, both of Rock Stream, Yates Co., were married 7 Mar 1853 by Rev. A. Coburn at Rock Stream. (7 Apr 1853)

1998. Robert Baskins of Barrington, Yates Co., and Mrs. Delia Eaton, widow of the late L.M. Eaton, were married 24 Mar 1853 in Starkey, Yates Co., no pastor named. (7 Apr 1853)

1999. Ezra Loncoy of Milo, Yates Co., and Eliza Hathaway of Dresden, Yates Co., were married 23 Mar 1853 by Rev. O. Montaque in the Dundee House at Dundee, Yates Co. (7 Apr 1853)

2000. Theodore L. Owen of Geneva, Ontario Co., and Mary Page of West Dresden, Yates Co., were married 19 Mar 1853 by John Agar J.P. in West Dresden. (7 Apr 1853)

2001. Schuyler Sutherland of Seneca Falls, Seneca Co., and Elizabeth H. Hunt of Milo, Yates Co., were married 31 Mar 1853 by Rev. Abner Chase in Milo. (7 Apr 1853)

2002. Nathaniel M. Matthews and Helen Ann Ely were married 9 Mar 1853 by Rev. D. Hutchins in Hector, Schuyler Co. (7 Apr 1853)

2003. George C. Schwartz of Philadelphia, PA., and Eliza Lathrop of Penn Yan, Yates Co., were married 20 Mar 1853 by Rev. William Hogarth in Geneva, Ontario Co. (7 Apr 1853)

2004. Mrs. Martha Henries age 48 yrs., died 21 Mar 1853 in Penn Yan, Yates Co. (7 Apr 1853)

2005. Mrs. Margaret Green age 36 yrs., died at the Elmira Water Cure, Chemung Co. The wife of John R. Green, and daughter of Isaac Hedges of Milo, Yates Co., no date given. (7 Apr 1853)

2006. Edward Alexander Kelley age 11 yrs. 3 days, died 25 Mar 1853 at Dresden, Yates Co., son of William R. and Eliza Kelley, formerly of Geneva, Ontario Co. (7 Apr 1853)

2007. Calvin Mead age 17 yrs., died 21 Mar 1853 from injuries received in a fall at his fathers residence in Penn Yan, Yates Co. He had indulges in a playful exercise with his friends, and dislocated his ribs. (7 Apr 1853)

2008. Mrs. Ester Ann Green age 29 yrs., died 22 Mar 1853 at Cincinnati, Ohio. The wife of J.B. Green Esq., buried in the Woodland Cemetery at Dayton. (7 Apr 1853)

2009. Asbury Harpending age 39 yrs., died 3 Apr 1853 at his home in Dundee, Yates Co. (14 Apr 1853)

2010. William H. Deyo of Waterloo, Seneca Co., has been appointed Postmaster at Kalamazoo, Michigan. (14 Apr 1853)

2011. Willard C. Morse of Painted Post, Steuben Co., and Mary E. Cooper, daughter of J. Cooper Jr., of Cooper's Plains, Steuben Co., were married 6 Apr 1853 by Rev. John VanDeventer in Cooper's Plains. (14 Apr 1853)

2012. Samuel T. Gunn and Mary E. Dubois, both of Geneva, Ontario Co., were married 6 Apr 1853 by Rev. Cheeney in Penn Yan, Yates Co. (14 Apr 1853)

2013. Mrs. Sarah A. Hartshorn age 26 yrs., died 5 Apr 1853 in Jerusalem, Yates Co., wife of I.W. Hartshorn, and daughter of Ashbel and Elizabeth Beers. (14 Apr 1853)

2014. Mary Louisa Spears age 4 yrs. 10 mos. 1 day, died 29 Mar 1853 in Geneva, Ontario Co., daughter of Smith and Sarah Spears. (14 Apr 1853)

2015. William Knight age 111 yrs. 11 mos. 8 days, died 11 Mar 1853 in Farmington, Ontario Co. (14 Apr 1853)

2016. Mrs. Henrietta B. Gregg age 30 yrs. 8 mos., died 22 Mar 1853 in Elmira, Chemung Co., wife of Isaac B. Gregg, and daughter of the late Mordecai Ogden Esq. (14 Apr 1853)

2017. Dr. Lewis A. Birdsall, formerly of Penn Yan, Yates Co., has been appointed Superintendent of the U.S. Mint in California. (14 Apr 1853)

2018. Hon. William R. King died 18 Apr 1853 in Cahawba, AL., vice-President of the U.S. (21 Apr 1853)

2019. The body of an inebrate named Clute, was found on the wayside last week, near Mt. Morris, Livingston Co., where he had died in a fit of intoxication. (21 Apr 1853)

2020. James Travis of Torrey, Yates Co., and Mrs. Eliza Warner of Havana, Schuyler Co., were married 31 Mar 1853 by Rev. Huggins in Havana. (21 Apr 1853)

2021. Phillip Kinney and Catharine Riker were married 5 Apr 1853 by A. Sawyer Esq. in Dundee, Yates Co. (21 Apr 1853)

2022. Samuel Seymour of New York city, and Mary Jane Crawford of Penn Yan, Yates Co., were married by Rev. Cheeney in Penn Yan, no date given. (21 Apr 1853)

2023. George T. Stevens and Jane M. Harris, both of Jerusalem, Yates Co., were married 3 Mar 1853 by Rev. William Bradley in Jerusalem. (21 Apr 1853)

2024. Robert Boyd age 73 yrs., died 18 Apr 1853 at his home in Benton, Yates Co. (21 Apr 1853)

2025. Samuel Jayne age 90 yrs., died 8 Apr 1853 in Benton, Yates Co. (21 Apr 1853)

2026. Stephen Collins age 26 yrs., died 29 Mar 1853 in Middlesex, Yates Co. (21 Apr 1853)

2027. Alonzo C. Jackson of the U.S. Navy, age 23 yrs., died 31 Mar 1853 at Clifton Springs, Ontario Co., of a disease of the brain, brought on by a too arduous application to the scientific duties of his profession. (21 Apr 1853)

2028. Emily Ann Gage age 23 yrs., died 20 Jan 1853 last, in Middlesex, Yates Co. (21 Apr 1853)

2029. Adam H. Houghtaling and Margaret Travis, both of Jerusalem, Yates Co., were married 24 Apr 1853 by Rev. J.L. Smith in Milo, Yates Co. (28 Apr 1853)

2030. Thomas J. Conklin and Mary Ann Titsworth, both of Starkey, Yates Co., were married 17 Apr 1853 in Dundee, Yates Co., no pastor given. (28 Apr 1853)

2031. Michael B. Misner and Minerva E. Shannon, both of Starkey, Yates Co., were married 17 Apr 1853 by Elder Sunderlin in Milo, Yates Co. (28 Apr 1853)

2032. Charles W. Barnes of Rock Stream, Yates Co., and Mary S. Simmons of Reading, Steuben Co., were married at the residence of Alonzo Simmons Esq., in Reading, no date given. (28 Apr 1853)

2033. Eugene Susop Washburn a young Chief, and Alazuma Cummick, both of the Walaitpee tribe of southern Oregon, were married 7 Mar 1853 in Stafford, Genesee Co. NY., by Rev. D. Field. (28 Apr 1853)

2034. Abramham N. Wagener age 40 yrs. 7 mos. 7 days, died 26 Apr 1853 at his home in Penn Yan, Yates Co. Born in Penn Yan, the son of Abraham Wagener Esq. (28 Apr 1853)

2035. The infant son of Ezra and Martha Spink age 7 mos., died 17 Apr 1853 in Starkey, Yates Co., no name given for the child. (28 Apr 1853)

2036. John Fitzwater age 72 yrs., died 12 Apr 1853 in Jerusalem, Yates Co. (28 Apr 1853)

2037. Hon. Jacob Burney age 82 yrs., died 27 Apr 1853 in Cincinnati, Ohio. A native of Newark, New Jersey, he moved to Cincinatti in 1797. A former Judge of the Ohio Supreme Court, and a Senator for that state. (5 May 1853)

2038. Jerome Doubleday and Mary E. Neff, both of Penn Yan, Yates Co., were married 21 Apr 1853 by Rev. F.W. Purington in Prattsburgh, Steuben Co. (5 May 1853)

2039. William H. Booth of Dundee, Yates co., and Almira Arnold of Cameron, Steuben, Co., were married 14 Apr 1853 by Esq. Aldrich in Cameron. (5 May 1853)

2040. M.J. Hedges a conductor on the "New York and Erie Railroad", and Henrietta Converse of Elmira, Chemung Co., were married 28 Apr 1853 by Rev. Murdock in Elmira. (5 May 1853)

2041. Mrs. Lydia Parkman age 81 yrs., died 22 Apr 1853 at Oak Orchard, Orleans Co., wife of Alexander Parkman, one of the early settlers of Potter, Yates Co. (5 May 1853)

2042. Col. M.H.N. Kendig, formerly of Penn Yan, Yates Co., has a comfortable situation with the San Francisco Custom House in California. (12 May 1853)

2043. Peter I. Waggoner of Columbia Co., and Mrs. Polly Bain of Potter, Yates Co., were married 4 May 1853 by John Sutherland Esq. in Benton, Yates Co. (12 May 1853)

2044. John Stanton age 79 yrs., died 4 May 1853 in Penn Yan, Yates Co., formerly of Gorham, Ontario Co. (12 May 1853)

2045. Moses Hurd age 67 yrs., died 29 Apr 1853 at Rock Stream, Yates Co. (12 May 1853)

2046. Frances F. Crane age 1 yr. 6 mos. 27 days, died 6 May 1853, only daughter of Joel W. and Mariette Crane of Penn Yan, Yates Co. (12 May 1853)

2047. Rev. Edwin C. Brown of Bath, Steuben Co., and Theresa Spencer of Penn Yan, Yates Co., were married 17 May 1853 by Rev. Horace Spencer in Penn Yan. (19 May 1853)

2048. Wortman Sherwood of Dundee, Yates Co., and Harriet Drake of Southport, Chemung Co., were married last 27 Mar 1853 in Elmira, Chemung Co., no pastor given. (19 May 1853)

2049. A.D. Bloss of Dresden, Yates Co., and Mary Welch of Ireland, were married 2 May 1853 by Henry Tuthill Esq. in Starkey, Yates Co. (19 May 1853)

2050. Daniel Bartholomew of Barrington, Yates Co., and Rachel Demoth of Tyrone, Schuyler Co., were married 8 May 1853 by Rev. J.T. Seeley in Barrington. (19 May 1853)

2051. Mrs. Sarah L. Hunt age 20 yrs., died 26 Apr 1853 in Milo, Yates Co., wife of Charles L. Hunt. (19 May 1853)

2052. H.H. Lawrence Esq. of Napa City, California, formerly of Penn Yan, Yates Co., and Sarah A. Mack of Ludlowville, Tompkins Co., were married 30 Apr 1853 by Rev. Cook in Ludlowville. (26 May 1853)

2053. Seymour French of Milo, Yates Co., and Ann Horn of Dundee, Yates Co., were married 17 May 1853 by Rev. J.H. Currier in Dundee. (26 May 1853)

2054. Hiram Fowler of Starkey, Yates Co., and Sarah Marie Culver of Dundee, Yates Co., were married 17 May 1853 by John T. Andrews Esq. in Dundee. (26 May 1853)

2055. J.R. Bronson of Waterbury, CT., and Louisa M. Bronson of Geneva, Ontario Co., were married 18 May 1853 by Rev. J.B. Richardson in Geneva. (26 May 1853)

2056. John Rippey and Elizabeth Black, both of Seneca, Ontario Co., were married 18 May 1853 by Rev. S. Tippley at the residence of Moses Black in Seneca. (26 May 1853)

2057. George D. Bowman of St. Anthony, Minnesota, and Jane P. Derby of Elmira, Chemung Co., were married 23 May 1853 by Rev. G. Hood in Elmira. (26 May 1853)

2058. Thomas Hathaway age 81 yr., died 22 May 1853 at his residence in Torrey, Yates Co., where he has lived for the last 64 yrs. (26 May 1853)

2059. Maria Johnson age 38 yrs., died 12 May 1853 in Starkey, Yates Co., late of Honeoye, Monroe Co. (26 May 1853)

2060. Mrs. Lydia Ackley age 31 yrs. 3 mos. 29 days, died 18 May 1853 in Geneva, Ontario Co., wife of John Ackley. (26 May 1853)

2061. Mrs. Lenantia Bennett age 32 yrs. 9 mos., died 13 May 1853 in Geneva, Ontario Co., of consumption, wife of Daniel Bennett. (26 May 1853)

2062. Mrs. Anna Phillips age 69 yrs., died 5 May 1853 in Gorham, Ontario Co., wife of Isaac Phillips. (26 May 1853)

2063. Joshua Hallock age 83 yrs., died 22 May 1853 in Bath, Steuben Co. (26 May 1853)

2064. Abraham Wagener age 78 yrs., died 21 May 1853 at his residence in Penn Yan, Yates Co. (26 May 1853)

2065. William Gray age 16 yrs., died 30 May 1853 in New York city, of hydrophobia from a dog bite. (2 Jun 1853)

2066. Robert Chapin Esq. of Hopewell, Ontario Co., and Eliza Derman of Seneca, Ontario Co., were married 10 May 1853 by Rev. Goldsmith in Seneca. (2 Jun 1853)

2067. Charles S. Collins and Sophy F. Southworth, both of Rochester, Monroe Co., were married 25 May 1853 by Rev. William G. Howard in Rochester. (2 Jun 1853)

2068. William E. Sill, Counsellor at Law, and Anna Sutherland, daughter of the late Jacob Sutherland, were married 25 May 1853 by Rev. William Hogarth in Geneva, Ontario Co. (2 Jun 1853)

2069. William Callaham an Irishman, was shot and killed 8 Jun 1853 in Havana, Chemung Co., by Asa Winton, at the home of Dr. Winton. Callaham was under the employed of the doctor, and Asa Winton of Ohio, the doctor's brother, had been under medical treatment for about a year for depression. He was being held in the Elmira jail. (9 Jun 1853)

2070. Dionysia Tucker age 100 yrs., died 2 May 1853 in Warwick, near Hamilton, Bermuda. (16 Jun 1853)

2071. Stephen Tobey Sr. W.M. of the Reading Masonic Lodge # 123, age 72 yrs., died 7 Jun 1853. A large number of the Masonic Fraternity assembled on the 8th, and services were conducted by Charles G. Judd P.M. of the Milo Lodge # 108. Mr. Tobey had been a member for nearly 50 yrs. (16 Jun 1853)

2072. Jonathan D. Merce and Mary Benedict, both of Jerusalem, Yates Co., were married 9 Jun 1853 by Rev. A.C. Mallory in Jerusalem. (16 Jun 1853)

2073. Samuel W. Salisbury and Agnes Walker, both of Canandaigua, Ontario Co., were married 4 Jun 1853 by Rev. George N. Cheeney in Canandaigua. (16 Jun 1853)

2074. Frances Caroline Parsons age about 8 yrs., died 12 Jun 1853 in Penn Yan, poisoned by the phosphorus from matches. A twin daughter of William C. Parsons Esq. (16 Jun 1853)

2075.Mrs. Nancy Voak age 47 yrs., died 18 Apr 1853 in Benton, Yates Co., wife of the late Samuel Voak. (16 Jun 1853)

2076. Mrs. Ida VanZant age 76 yrs. 2 mos. 17 days, died 8 Jun 1853 in Potter, Yates Co. (16 Jun 1853)

2077. Jonathan Phelps age 78 yrs., died 3 Jun 1853 in Canandaigua, Ontario Co. One of the earlest settlers in that village, having moved there over 50 years ago from Massachusetts. (16 Jun 1853)

2078. Walter Luce killed in a powder mill explosion at Enfield, CT., last week. The only remnant of his body that could be found, was the lower part of one leg, blow over 90 rods away. * The "Hartford Times" says Mrs. Luce has lost three husbands by powder and explosions. (23 Jun 1853)

2079. Perry Babcock of Havana, Chemung Co., and Margaret A. Darling, daughter of Andrew Darling Esq., of Hector, Schuyler Co., were married 7 Jun 1853 by Rev. Joel Jewell in Ithaca, Tompkins Co. (23 Jun 1853)

2080. S.S. Catlin and Elizabeth Reddout, both of Rushville, Yates Co., were married 16 Jun 1853 by Rev. E.G. Townsend in Rushville. (23 Jun 1853)

2081. Dr. Joseph S. Hart of Fairfax Co. Virginia, and Jane Pierce, daughter of Abner Pierce, formerly of Penn Yan, Yates Co., were married 20 Jun 1853 by Rev. Brown in Dundee, Yates Co. (23 Jun 1853)

2082. Erastus Raplee and Christiana Knapp, both of Barrington, Yates Co., were married 27 May 1853 by J.C. Knapp Esq. in Barrington. (26 Jun 1853)

2083. Mrs. Mariah Bogert age 70 yrs., died 24 May 1853 at the residence of M.H. Lawrence in Milo, Yates Co., wife of the late Isaac Bogert. She was a long time resident of Dresden, Yates Co., her husband being one of the early, and most prominent settlers of that village. (26 Jun 1853)

2084. The body of George S. Clark of Jerusalem, Yates Co., was brought home from New York city, where he had gone for a visit, but became ill and died. His wife died some months ago, two children survive him. A member of the Friends Society, no date given. (30 Jun 1853)

2085. Jonathan Overton a colored man, age 101 yrs., died 14 Jun 1853 in Edenton, North Carolina, a soldier of the Revolution, served under Gen. Washington, and was in the Battle of Yorktown. (30 Jun 1853)

2086. Frederick Buckeridge Esq. of London, England, and Margaret Anne Hodgins, youngest daughter of the late William Hodgins Esq. of Penboke Park, Dublin, Ireland, were married 8 Jun 1853 in Canandaigua, Ontario Co. by Rev. George Cheeney. (30 Jun 1853)

2087. James T. Norton, Editor of the "Livingston Republican", Genesco, Livingston Co., and Sarah A. Phelps, second daughter of Lester Phelps Esq. of Mt. Morris, Livingston Co., were married 14 Jun 1853 by Rev. O.I. Sprague at Mt. Morris. (30 Jun 1853)

2088. Charles L. Morris of Vienna, Oneida Co., and Isabella Esther Platt, daughter of Isaac Platt of Geneva, Ontario, Co., were married 22 Jun 1853 by Rev. Raines in Geneva. (30 Jun 1853)

2089. Hiram E. Tooker of Sacramento, California, and Martha A. Clark of Middlesex, Yates Co., were married 6 Jun 1853 by Rev. James Wilson in Middlesex. (30 Jun 1853)

2090. John Caward of Prattsburgh, Steuben Co., and Mrs. Sarah Jane Emerson of Canandaigua, Ontario Co., were married 17 Jun 1853 by Rev. Ira Fairbanks in Potter, Yates Co. (30 Jun 1853)

2091. Clinton Camp age 24 yrs., died 17 May 1853 in Pisa, near Leghorn, son of Col. H. Camp of Trumansburg, Tompkins Co. (30 Jun 1853)

2092. Lorenzo Murdough age 24 yrs. 1 mo. 1 day, died 30 Apr 1853 at Marysville, California, late of Penn Yan, Yates Co., son of William and Elizabeth Murdough of Benton, Yates Co. (30 Jun 1853)

2093. Caroline Brown, daughter of Samuel Brown of Utica, Oneida Co., recevied a diploma to practice medicine from the Eclectic College, Cincinnati, Ohio, and was one of the most through and accomplished students, no date given. (30 Jun 1853)

2094. Francis Scott Lampson age 19 mos., drowned 1 Jul 1853 in the Crooked Lake, son of Zebulon Lampson, no town given. (7 Jul 1853)

2095. Mr. Simonson, killed his wife 5 Jul 1853 in Pulteney, Steuben Co., in a fit of jealousy, he beat her severely, then took an axe and cut off her head. (7 Jul 1853)

2096. John C. Merrill age 44 yrs., died 5 Jul 1853 at Rochester, Monroe Co., publisher of the "Genesee Evangelist". The son of Ira Merrill, who for many years was the Editor and publisher of the "Geneva Courier". (7 Jul 1853)

2097. Charles Carroll McTavish of Carroll Hall, Baltimore, Maryland, and Marcella Scott, youngest daughter of Gen. Scott were married 29 Jun 1853 in New York city by Archbishop Hughes. (7 Jul 1853)

2098. William Fraser of Ogdensburg, St. Lawrence Co., and Sarah Chidsey of Penn Yan, Yates Co., were married 3 Jul 1853 by Rev. J. Jones in Penn Yan. (7 Jul 1853)

2099. James Decker and Mrs. Lucratia P. Keefer, both of Milo, Yates Co., were married 27 Jun 1853 in Milo, no pastor named. (7 Jun 1853)

2100. John D. Davis and Sarah Marie Davis, both of Benton, Yates Co., were married 4 Jul 1853 by J.V. VanAllen Esq. in Penn Yan, Yates Co. (7 Jul 1853)

2101. Edward Graham and Rhoda Ann Graham, both of Italy, Yates Co., were married 4 Jul 1853 by J.V. VanAllen in Penn Yan, Yates Co. (7 Jul 1853)

2102. Mrs. Elizabeth VanGorden age 80 or 89 yrs. (blurred), died 26 Jun 1853 in Tyrone, Schuyler Co. (7 Jul 1853)

2103. The wife of Samuel Pierce, age 49 yrs., died 27 Jun 1853 in Starkey, Yates Co. (7 Jul 1853)

2104. Deacon Caleb Case age 79 yrs., died 11 Jun 1853 in Phelps, Ontario Co. (7 Jul 1853)

2105. Alida Schermerhorn age 52 yrs. died 19 Jun 1853 in Phelps, Ontario Co. (7 Jul 1853)

2106. James Holmes age 99 yrs., died 27 Jun 1853 in Owego, Tioga Co., a soldier of the Revolution. (14 Jul 1853)

2107. James V. VanAllen and Sarah Smith, daughter of Eben Smith, all of Penn Yan, Yates Co., were married 18 Jun 1853 by Rev. James Eells Jr. in Penn Yan. (24 Jul 1853)

2108. Thomas Morrel of Williamsburgh, Long Island, and Cordelia Hicks, daughter of Henry Hicks Esq., of Benton, Yates Co., were married 6 Jul 1853 by Rev. A.C. Mallory in Benton. (14 Jul 1853)

2109. S.M. Pettengill, a newspaper and advertising agent of New York and Boston, and Sarah E. Kendall of Boston, MA., were married 22 Jun 1853 by Rev. Wines in Boston. (14 Jul 1853)

2110. Marshall A. Hunt and Elizabeth P. Powers, both of Rushville, Yates Co., were married 5 Jul 1853 by Rev. J.W. Wilson in Rushville. (14 Jul 1853)

2111. Rev. Asa Story age 51 yrs., died 18 Nov 1852 last, at Pine Bluff, Arkansas. (14 Jul 1853)

2112. Judge Hubbel, formerly of Ithaca, Tompkins Co., had been on trial in Wisconsin for malfeasance in office, but acquited, no town given. (21 Jul 1853)

2113. Mary Jane Hazen age 21 yrs., died 16 Jul 1853 at the home of her parents, Caleb and Laura Hazen, in Penn Yan, Yates Co. She was born 1828 in Carmel, Putnam Co., and became a member of the Baptist Church, her funeral preached by Rev. C. Morton, and Rev. J. Jones who had been her attending physician. (21 Jul 1853)

2114. Enos Head age 77 yrs., died 18 Jul 1853 in Penn Yan, Yates Co. (21 Jul 1853)

2115. Mrs. Elizabeth Rice age 52 yrs., died 1 Jul 1853 in Seneca, Ontario Co. (21 Jul 1853)

2116. Mrs. Isabella Crosier age 94 yrs., died 1 Jul 1853 at the residence of Thomas Wilson in Seneca, Ontario Co. (21 Jul 1853)

2117. From the "Ontario Repository"., The son of James M. Palmer, age 8 yrs., drowned in that village. He had been playing with several friends on the bridge of the Canandaigua & Elmira Railroad, crossing the Canandaigua Outlet, when he fell in the water. All efforts were made to revive him, but failed. His remains were interred 24 Jul 1853, no date or town given. (28 Jul 1853)

2118. The son of Alvan Lansing age 4 yrs., drowned 20 Jul 1853, his body found about two and a half rods from the shore, near the Sulfar Springs, Yates Co. (28 Jul 1853)

2119. Major General Jonathan P. Couch, Commander of the 7th Division of the New York State Militia, died 24 Jul 1853 at his residence in Havana, Chemung Co. He was interred in Havana, with full Military and Masonic honors. (28 Jul 1853)

2120. Hon. Hezekiah C. Seymour, late State Engineer and Surveyor, died last week at Piermont, Rockland Co., no date given. (28 Jul 1853)

2121. Z.E.B. Nash, formerly of Penn Yan, Yates Co., and Octavia M. Mills of St. Anthony, Minnesota, were married 3 Jul 1853 by Rev. C. Seccombe in St. Anthony. (28 Jul 1853)

2122. William W. Perry, formerly of West Dresden, Yates Co., and Susan J. Wheeler, daughter of the Hon. Jonathan F. Wheeler of Fort Smith, Arkansas, were married 2 Jun 1853 by Rev. C. Washbourne at Fort Smith. (28 Jul 1853)

2123. G.W. Lathrop of Geneva, Ontario Co., and Mrs. Margaret James of Elmira, Chemung Co., were married 16 Jul 1853 by Rev. William B. Goodwin in Elmira. (28 Jul 1853)

2124. Samuel Sprowls age 74 yrs., died 23 Jul 1853 in Starkey, Yates Co. (4 Aug 1853)

2125. James Carmichael age 65 yrs., died 26 Jul 1853 in Starkey, Yates Co. (4 Aug 1853)

2126. James Townsend age 80 yrs., died in Seneca, Ontario Co., no date given. (4 Aug 1853)

2127. Edwin A. Palmeter age 37 or 87 yrs. (blurred), died in Lyons, Wayne Co., no date given. (4 Aug 1853)

2128. William O. Burton and Harriet O. Shory, both of Benton, Yates Co., were married 4 Aug 1853 by S.G. Gage Esq. in Benton. (11 Aug 1853)

2129. Byron S. Sunderlin of Barrington, Yates Co., and Rachel Ellis of Starkey, Yates Co., were married 7 Aug 1853 by Rev. A.C. Mallory in Benton, Yates Co. (11 Aug 1853)

2130. Prof. James E. Latimer of Northfield, New Hampshire, and Anna E. Ross of Elmira, Chemung Co., were married 3 Aug 1853 by Rev. A. Hull in Elmira. (11 Aug 1853)

2131. Mary Abigail Spears age 10 mos., died very suddenly of brain fever, 26 Jul 1853 in Geneva, Ontario Co., daughter of Sarah and Smith Spears. (11 Aug 1853)

2132. Mrs. Tuton died 22 Jul 1853 in Canandaigua, Ontario Co., mother of Samuel Tuton of Dundee, Yates Co., (11 Aug 1853)

2133. Mrs. Cornelia Tuton age 18 yrs., died 28 Jul 1853 in Dundee, Yates Co., wife of Samuel Tuton. (11 Aug 1853)

2134. Mrs. Julia Lord age 45 yrs., died 30 Jul 1853 in Dundee, Yates Co., wife of Ralph L. Lord. (11 Aug 1853)

2135. Hon. John Knox age 71 yrs., died 31 Jul 1853 in Waterloo, Seneca Co. (11 Aug 1853)

2136. Thomas Heber Chapin age 21 yrs. 9 mos., died 5 Aug 1853 at the Franklin House in Geneva, Ontario Co. The son of William Chapin of Philadelphia, PA., formerly of Yates Co. His service from the Presbyterian Church, conducted by Rev. James Eells Jr. (11 Aug 1853)

2137. Dr. Matthew Brown age 80 yrs., died 5 Aug 1853 at Pittsburg, president of Jefferson College. (11 Aug 1853)

2138. Benjamin Houghtaling of LaSalle, Illinois, and Jane Cleveland of Lodi, Seneca Co. NY., were married 14 Aug 1853 at the home of E. Cleveland in Lodi, by Rev. Elijah Wood. (18 Aug 1853)

2139. Norman Cole of Three Rivers, Michigan, and Lucy Jane Lewis of Benton Centre, Yates Co. NY., were married 13 Aug 1853 by S.G. Gage in Benton Centre. (18 Aug 1853)

2140. Capt. George S. Dodge of Geneva, Ontario Co.,

and Miss A.S. Babcock of Sherburne, Chenango Co., were married 6 Jul 1853 by Rev. A.C. Tuttle in Sherburne. (18 Aug 1853)

2141. Peter VanZant age 96 yrs., died at the home of George V. Miller, in Lodi, Seneca Co., no date given. (18 Aug 1853)

2142. Mrs. Ida VanZant age 76 yrs., died 8 Jun 1853 in Potter, Yates Co., wife of Nicholas VanZant. (18 Aug 1853)

2143. John M. Thurston, whose trial concluded last week at Ithaca, Tompkins Co., for the murder of Anson Garrison of Owego, Tioga Co., was acquited on the ground of insanity. He was sent to the Lunatic Asylum at Utica, Oneida Co. (25 Aug 1853)

2144. Benjamin Coddington, postmaster of Bellona, Yates Co., died at his home there, 8 or 10 days ago. A middle aged man, his illness was brief and his death quite unexpected. (25 Aug 1853)

2145. Rev. G.J. Garretson died in New York city, no date given, formerly of Seneca Co. (25 Aug 1853)

2146. John Casterlin and Catherine Light, both of Penn Yan, Yates Co., were married 10 Aug 1853 by Rev. J. Jones in Penn Yan. (25 Aug 1853)

2147. Sylvester Tibbetts and Ruth E. Lampson, both of Milo, Yates Co., were married 21 Aug 1853 by Rev. J. Jones in Milo. (25 Aug 1853)

2148. Caster Shorts and Rachel Ann Prater, both of Benton, Yates Co., were married 18 Aug 1853 by S.G. Gage Esq. in Benton. (25 Aug 1853)

2149. Christian Granholtz and Eliza Hoofman, both of Penn, Yates Co., were married 21 Aug 1853 by John Southerland Esq. in Potter, Yates Co. (25 Aug 1853)

2150. John T. Noble of Glen's Falls, Warren Co., and Anna J. Godard of Macon, Georgia, were married 11 Aug 1853 by Rev. Seeley in Saratoga, Saratoga Co. (25 Aug 1853)

2151. Col. W.A. Dutcher age 45 yrs., died 10 Aug 1853 in Chicago, Illinois, formerly of Penn Yan, Yates Co. (25 Aug 1853)

2152. Anthony Snyder age 71 yrs., died 2 Aug 1853 at Bethel, Ontario Co. (25 Aug 1853)

2153. Major John R. Hull of Columbus, Georgia, and Mary E. Fishburn of Charleston, South Carolina, were married 2 Aug 1853 in St. Peters Church, Charleston, no pastor given. (1 Sep 1853)

2154. The wife of Russell Skiff died 20 Aug 1853 in Reading, Schuyler Co. (1 Sep 1853)

2155. William Dunham age 85 yrs., died 21 Aug 1853 in Altay, formerly of Reynoldsville. (1 Sep 1853)

2156. Mrs. Catharine Wormlet age 77 yrs., died 10 Jul 1853 at Hopewell, Ontario Co. (1 Sep 1853)

2157. George Bryan age 77 yrs., died 11 Aug 1853 in Bath, Steuben Co. (1 Sep 1853)

2158. Mary Adell Ewing age 2 yrs. 2 mos. 9 days, died 19 Aug 1853 at Dresden, Yates Co., youngest daughter of James and M.A. Ewing. (1 Sep 1853)

2159. Mary Jane Rice age 19 yrs., died 27 Aug 1853 in Penn Yan, Yates Co., daughter of the late Stephen Rice. A member of the Congregational Church, where her service was given by Rev. Hughson. (1 Sep 1853)

2160. David H. Johnson, formerly of Benton, Yates Co., killed 22 Aug 1853. He was going from his home in Oak Hill, to Painted Post, in Steuben Co. For some unknown reason, he had stopped and somehow caught his foot in the wheel of the wagon, when his horses took fright, dragging him about 80 rods. (8 Sep 1853)

2161. Henry Ogden age 29 yrs., died 30 Aug 1853 in Bath, Steuben, Co., of consumption. (15 Sep 1853)

2162. Reuben Abbott Varick, Steuben Co., and Sarah A. Potter of Starkey, Yates Co., were married 12 Sep 1853 by Rev. Higgins in Havana, Steuben Co. (15 Sep 1853)

2163. Richard Lanning of Woodhull, Steuben Co., and Susan Showit of Belfast, Allegany Co., were married 19 Jul 1853 by Rev. J. Ketchill in Allen, Allegany Co. (15 Sep 1853)

2164. Annie A. Loveless age 15 yrs., died 25 Aug

1853 at the home of her parents in Dundee, Yates Co., only daughter of George W. and Sarah A. Loveless. (15 Sep 1853)

2165. George Huntington age 96 yrs., died 22 Aug 1853 in Mobile, Alabama, of yellow fever. (15 Sep 1853)

2166. Frederic Schaffner age 59 yrs., died 8 Sep 1853 in New York city, Buffalo papers please copy. (15 Sep 1853)

2167. Mary Simondson age 126 yrs., died last week at Shipensburg, PA., no date given. (22 Sep 1853)

2168. Hon. Victory Birdseye age 70 yrs., died 17 Sep 1853 in Pompey, Onondaga Co., an ex-Senator, Congressman, and ardent member of the Whig party. (22 Sep 1853)

2169. Orlando Hurd of Watkins, Schuyler Co., and Julia A. Townsend, daughter of L.G. Townsend of Geneva, Ontario Co., were married 12 Sep 1853 by Rev. William Hogarth in Geneva. (22 Sep 1853)

2170. Rev. Harris V. Teall of New York city, and Mrs. Polly Bishop of Tyrone, Schuyler Co., were married at the residence of Allen Bassett in Barrington, Yates Co., by Rev. J.H. Currier, no date given. (29 Sep 1853)

2171. Hiram H. Gasper and Merilla Foster, both of Barrington, Yates Co., were married 21 Sep 1853 by Rev. J. Landreth in Barrington. (29 Sep 1853)

2172. Elias Fraser age 68 yrs., died 22 Sep 1853 in Ithaca, Tompkins Co., of stomach cancer. A native of Columbia Co., but lived his early years in Montgomery Co. The last 25 yrs., of his life he lived in Hector, Schuyler Co. He was the father of one son and two daughters, who survive him. (29 Sep 1853)

2173. Henry Decker of Lima, Livingston Co., and Catharine Hall of Havana, Schuyler Co., were married 28 Sep 1853 by Rev. William Goodwin at the residence of Major F.D. Goodwin in Havana. (6 Oct 1853)

2174. Mrs. Mary J. Smith age 61 yrs., died 5 Sep 1853 in Hector, Tompkins Co., wife of Caleb Smith. (6 Oct 1853)

2175. Mrs. George G. Freer died 1 Oct 1853 in Watkins, Schuyler Co., the late widow of Dr. Samuel Watkins. (13 Oct 1853)

2176. Edmund Wright and Sarah Walton, both of Penn Yan, Yates Co., were married 5 Oct 1853 by Rev. J. Jones in Penn Yan. (13 Oct 1853)

2177. Evert M. Doubleday of Batavia, Genesee Co., and Sarah A. Gload of Pulteney, Steuben Co., were married 6 Oct 1853 by Rev. H.R. Dakin in Pulteney. (13 Oct 1853)

2178. Selah Crosby and Elcy McDowell, both of Barrington, Yates Co., were married 25 Sep 1853 by Rev. Olsen in Wayne, Steuben Co. (13 Sep 1853)

2179. Lorenzo Stanton of Barrington, Yates Co., and Martha A. VanGordon of Starkey, Yates Co., were married 25 Sep 1853 by Rev. Olsen in Wayne, Steuben Co. (13 Oct 1853)

2180. Amasa Griffith of Prattsburg, Steuben Co., and Phebe E. Raymond of Boston, were married 17 Oct 1853 by Rev. Abner Chase in Penn Yan, Yates Co. (20 Oct 1853)

2181. Giles F. Adams and Anna M. Underwood, both of Middlesex, Yates Co., were married 12 Oct 1853 by Rev. J.E. Wager in Middlesex. (20 Oct 1853)

2182. Darwin P. VanAllen and Emma Ellis, both of Starkey, Yates Co., were married 17 Sep 1853 by Rev. Sunderlin in Starkey. (20 Oct 1853)

2183. William M. Platt of St. Louis, and Frances L. Barnard, daughter of E. Barnard of Geneva, Ontario Co., were married 11 Oct 1853 Rev. Hogarth in Geneva. (20 Oct 1853)

2184. Vroman Decker of Geneva, Ontario Co., and Cornelia B. Dodge of Middleburgh, Schoharie Co., were married 12 Oct 1853 by Rev. Isaac Lee in Middleborough. (20 Oct 1853)

2185. Mrs. H. Randvilla Jones age 28 yrs., died 12 Oct 1853 in Middlesex, Yates Co., wife of Joshua Jones, and daughter of John and Rebecca Adams. She leaves three children. (20 Oct 1853)

2186. Betsey Coolbaugh age 36 yrs., died 17 Oct 1853 in Barrington, Yates Co. (20 Oct 1853)

2187. Mrs. Malinda Frost age 42 yrs., died 15 Oct 1853 Catherine, Chemung Co., wife of Col. E.C. Frost. (20 Oct 1853)

2188. A young man named McAdam, who had been a resident of Canandaigua, Ontario Co. but a few months was accidentally shot while gunning in a boat on the lake. In drawing his fowling piece toward him, the charge exploded and entered his head causing instant death. (27 Oct 1853)

2189. John Delafield died 22 Oct 1853 at his residence near Geneva, Ontario Co. A distinguished citizen of Seneca Co., and president of the Board of Trustees of the Agricultural College. (27 Oct 1853)

2190. The negro "Jerry", whose rescue from the U.S. Officers had made him a celebrated character, died 8 Oct 1853 at Kingston, C.W., where he had resided since his escape and rescue. About a year since he became converted. (27 Oct 1853)

2191. E.D. Tuthill of Starkey, Yates Co., and Mary P. Hazard of Milo, Yates Co., were married 20 Oct 1853 by Rev. J. Landreth, no town given. (27 Oct 1853)

2192. Mrs. Sophia Lee age 63 or 68 yrs. (blurred), died 24 Oct 1853 in Penn Yan, Yates Co., wife of the late Dr. Joshua Lee. (27 Oct 1853)

2193. Otis A. Bullard age 37 or 87 yrs. (blurred), died 13 Oct 1853 in New York city of epilepsy. (27 Oct 1853)

2194. Hon. Colin M. Ingersoll of New Haven, CT., and Julia H. Pratt, only daughter of Hon. Zadoc Pratt, of Prattsville, Greene Co., were married recently in Prattsville, no date given. (3 Nov 1853)

2195. James L. Wicks of Reading, Schuyler Co., and Matilda Gulick of Hector, Schuyler Co., were married 22 Sep 1853 by Rev. Platt in Hector. (3 Nov 1853)

2196. William Dillion an Editor of the "Western Atlas", and Charlotte Jones, both of Vienna, Oneida Co., were married 20 Oct 1853 by Rev. Tooker in Vienna. (3 Nov 1853)

2197. Mrs. Lydia Lanning age 48 yrs., died 30 Oct 1853 in Starkey, Yates Co., of consumption. The wife of Isaac Lanning, and member of the Christian Church in Starkey. (3 Nov 1853)

2198. Mrs. Joanna W. Hale age 32 yrs., died 29 Oct 1853 in Penn Yan, Yates Co. The wife of Chancey H. Hale of the American Hotel. She leaves behind six children. (3 Nov 1853)

2199. Fanny B. Pettengill age 43 yrs., died 12 Oct 1853 at her fathers residence in Dresden, Yates Co. (3 Nov 1853)

2200. The powder mill of Lewis Bemis, known as the Corning Mill in Spencer, Tioga Co. blew up 4 Nov 1853 killing five men. Henry Avis age 22 yrs., an Englishman and foreman, no family. Richard Avis his brother, age 33 yrs., had a wife and one child. Robert Perkins age 30 yrs., an Englishman, and no family. George Swallow age 25 yrs., an Englishman, had a wife. John Latlin age 25 yrs., teamster and an Irishman, had no family and was blow into fragments. (10 Nov 1853)

2201. Sally McGonnegals age 68 yrs. killed 4 Nov 1853 in Penn Yan, Yates Co. As the Mail Train South was coming into town, she had just crossed the track and dropped some apples. She turned back to pick them up and was struck by the engine. She has no relatives here, a brother lives near Bath, Steuben Co. (10 Nov 1853)

2202. Barnet West of Jerusalem, Yates Co., and Hannah S. Goodrich of Penn Yan, Yates Co., were married 2 Nov 1853 by Rev. Abner Chase in Penn Yan. (10 Nov 1853)

2203. William A. Carr of Italy, Yates Co., and Mary Holliday of Jerusalem, Yates Co., were married 7 Nov 1853 by Rev. Abner Chase in Penn Yan, Yates Co. (10 Nov 1853)

2204. James H. Minisee and Maria Ray, both of Jerusalem, Yates Co., were married 26 Oct 1853 by Rev. J. Jones in Branchport, Yates Co. (10 Nov 1853)

2205. Silas R. Elder and Maria Cravens, both of Benton, Yates Co., were married 29 Oct 1853 by Rev. J. Jones in Penn Yan, Yates Co. (10 Nov 1853)

2206. Mrs. Sarah Blanset age 49 yrs., died 11 Oct

1853 in Jerusalem, Yates Co. The wife of Thomas Blanset, and mother of his children. A member of the Baptist Church in Penn Yan. (10 Nov 1853)

2207. John L. Remer of Dresden, Yates Co., and Rachel A. Legg, daughter of M.A. Legg of Torrey, Yates Co., were married 14 Nov 1853 by Rev. F.G. Hibbard in Torrey. (17 Nov 1853)

2208. W.M. Horton of Cameron, Steuben Co., and Nancy M. Bancroft of Orange, Schuyler Co., were married 13 Nov 1853 by Rev. A.C. Mallory in Benton Centre, Yates Co. (17 Nov 1853)

2209. Rev. Asa Countryman of Rushville, Yates Co., and Sabra A. Lapham of Penn Yan, Yates Co., were married 30 Oct 1853 in the Methodist Episcopal Church by Rev. D.D. Buck in Penn Yan. (17 Nov 1853)

2210. Jackson J. Miller of Lodi, Seneca Co., and Martha A. Smith of Dundee, Yates Co., were married 26 Oct 1853 by Rev. Moses in Dundee. (17 Nov 1853)

2211. William T. Prosser of Torrey, Yates Co., and Margaret Ann Riker of Dundee, Yates Co., were married 27 Oct 1853 by Rev. Goodwin in Elmira, Chemung Co. (17 Nov 1853)

2212. Harriet Elizabeth Miller age 6 mos., died 13 Nov 1853 in Penn Yan, Yates Co., daughter of Mary and Howard R. Miller. (17 Nov 1853)

2213. Leman Dunning age 72 yrs., died 2 Nov 1853 near Hammondsport, Steuben Co., father of Levi O. Dunning of Penn Yan, Yates Co. (17 Nov 1853)

2214. Mrs. Jane Jewel age 38 yrs., died 25 Oct 1853 in Hector, Schuyler Co., wife of Edward Jewel. (17 Nov 1853)

2215. Mrs. Mary Hudson age 76 yrs., died 22 Oct 1853 at her home in Jerusalem, Yates Co., wife of the late Reuben Hudson. One of the first settlers there, and a member Friends Society. (17 Nov 1853)

2216. James Henry Knapp age 9 yrs. 3 mos. 24 days, died 28 Oct 1853 in Starkey, Yates Co. The son of John W. and Rebecca Knapp. (17 Nov 1853)

2217. Mary Eliza Cheever age 7 yrs., died 27 Oct 1853 in Starkey, Yates Co., daughter of Benjamin G. Cheever. (17 Nov 1853)

2218. A Mr. Moss was killed several days ago while excavating a well in Farmington, Ontario Co. He had prepared for blasting a rock on the side of the excavation site. When he looked down to watch its progress, and was instantly killed by a premature explosion, no date or first name given.
(24 Nov 1853)

2219. Chauncey Wolcott and Mrs. Elizabeth Slaughter, both of Penn Yan, Yates Co., were married 23 Nov 1853 by Rev. J. Jones in Penn Yan.
(24 Nov 1853)

2220. N.J. Milliken an Editor with the "Ontario County Times", and Orline O. Sutton, both of Canandaigua, Ontario Co., were married 21 Nov 1853 at the home of S. McDonald in Canandaigua, by Rev. Chandler. (24 Nov 1853)

2221. George B. Treman and Ann Grant, both of Mecklenberg, Schuyler Co., were married 8 Nov 1853 by Rev. H. West in Mecklenberg. (24 Nov 1853)

2222. T.W. Hanes of Benton, Yates Co., and Louisa A. Wagener of Fort Plains, Montgomery Co., were married 7 Nov 1853 by Rev. Shank at Fort Plains.
(24 Nov 1853)

2223. David H. Rosencronse of Hamburgh, Suffolk Co. New Jersey, and Louisa V. Perry of Potter, Yates Co., were married 17 Nov 1853 by Rev. Goshen in Potter. (24 Nov 1853)

2224. Robert Shannon age 32 or 82 yrs. (blurred), died 3 Nov 1853 in Bath, Steuben Co. (24 Nov 1853)

2225. George Messenger an Editor and publisher of the "Weekly Trojan", and Caroline H. Davies, formerly of Athens, Greene Co. New York, were married 6 Oct 1853 by Rev. Wagner in Troy, PA.
(1 Dec 1853)

2226. Daniel Bates age 76 yrs., died 22 Nov 1853 in Ithaca, Tompkins Co., one of the wealthiest men of that village. (8 Dec 1853)

2227. D.A. Demming of Syracuse, Onondaga Co., and Catharine King, daughter of Daniel King Esq. of West Dresden, Yates Co., were married by Rev. Borden in West Dresden, no date given. (8 Dec 1853)

2228. George B. Parshall and Ann E. Saunders, both of Potter, Yates Co., were married 16 Dec 1853 by Rev. J.W. Wilson in Rushville, Yates Co. (8 Dec 1853)

2229. Delafield Dwelle and Adessa Arnold were married 16 Nov 1853 by Rev. J.W. Wilson in Rushville, Yates Co. (8 Dec 1853)

2230. John A. Higgins of Tyrone, Schuyler Co., and Fanny A. Gleason of Ithaca, Tompkins Co., were married 28 Nov 1853 by Rev. J.M. Harris in Ithaca. (8 Dec 1853)

2231. P.R. Sellon of Reading, Schuyler Co., and Loyal Marvin of Tyrone, Schuyler Co., were married 16 Nov 1853 by Rev. Ezra Marvin in Tyrone. (8 Dec 1853)

2232. Mrs. Mary Richards age 31 yrs., died 3 Dec 1853 in Springport, Cayuga Co. The sister of N.D. Suydam of Penn Yan, Yates Co. (8 Dec 1853)

2233. Walsteen C. Howe age 59 yrs., died 28 Sep 1853 in Houston, Texas, of yellow fever. Formerly of Penn Yan, and Branchport, Yates Co. He leaves a wife, but no children. (8 Dec 1853)

2234. One of the employees of the Troy and Boston Railroad, James Dickerson age 30 yrs., was killed 10 Dec 1853. A teamster, employed to draw cars from the depot to the city limits. On Saturday afternoon, being desirous of spending the Sabbath with his friends, he employed a substitute. The Conductor of the train objected to his leaving the city, and as the train was under way, pushed him off the platform. Dickerson fell beneath the wheels of the train and was crushed to death. The Conductor passed on with the train, but will doubtless be arrested. The deceased was from East Bennington, and had no family, no town given. (15 Dec 1853)

2235. Ebenezer M.W. Nye and Margaret Sharp, both of Hector, Schuyler Co., were married 7 Dec 1853 by Rev. F.G. Hubbard in Torrey, Yates Co. (15 Dec 1853)

2236. Kiamesia Townsend age 2 yrs. six mos., died 8 Dec 1853 in Benton, Yates Co., daughter of Homer Townsend. (15 Dec 1853)

2237. Nathaniel Ayres age 66 yrs., died 21 Nov 1853 in Ulyses, Tompkins Co. (15 Dec 1853)

2238. Mrs. Sarah A. Rugar age 24 yrs., died 17 Nov 1853 at the home of her father in-law Thomas Rugar Esq. in Potter, Yates Co. The wife of Elisa V. Rugar. (15 Dec 1853)

2239. Rev. George N. Cheeney, Rector of St. Mark's Church in Penn Yan, Yates Co., and Helen Elizabeth Whayer, only daughter of Solomon D. Whayer Esq. of Branchport, Yates Co., were married 21 Dec 1853 in St. Mark's Church at Penn Yan by Rev. Schuyler of Oswego. (22 Dec 1853)

2240. George Johnson of Jerusalem, Yates Co., and Samaria Smith of Salisbury, Herkimer Co., were married 8 Dec 1853 at Augusta Center, Oneida Co., no pastor named. (22 Dec 1853)

2241. Matthew Anderson of Gaines, Orleans Co., and Mrs. Harriet Drew of Barre, Orleans Co., were married 14 Dec 1853 by Rev. A.C. Mallory in Benton, Yates Co. (22 Dec 1853)

2242. Raphael Hall and Hannah Moon, both of Potter Yates Co., were married 15 Dec 1853 by J.D. Bordwell Esq. in Potter. (22 Dec 1853)

2243. Levi Walker age 22 or 32 yrs. (blurred), died 17 Dec 1853 in Jerusalem, Yates Co. (22 Dec 1853)

2244. Hon. Brookins Campbell of TN., age 45 yrs., died 25 Dec 1853 in Washington. (29 Dec 1853)

2245. John B. Beard and Susan M. Trayer, daughter of Jacob Trayer, all of Milo, Yates Co., were married 26 Dec 1853 by Rev. J.L. Smith in Milo. (29 Dec 1853)

2246. Dr. Henry S. Lovell age 44 yrs., died 8 Dec 1853 in Benton, Yates Co. (29 Dec 1853)

2247. J. Francis Bates of the Granite Insurance Co. in New York city, and Sarah E. Bacon, eldest daughter of Rev. J.B. Bacon of Penn Yan, Yates Co., were married 21 Dec 1853 by Rev. S.S. Hughson in Penn Yan. (29 Dec 1853)

2248. Charles H. Hobart and Polly Wells, both of Potter, Yates Co., were married 21 Dec 1853 by Rev. C.S. Coats in Potter. (29 Dec 1853)

2249. G.V. Scott age 32 yrs., died 23 Dec 1853 in Benton, Yates Co. (29 Dec 1853)

2250. As the new propeller "Watkins" lay at the wharf in Geneva, Ontario Co., 29 Dec 1853, a few minutes before the starting time. One of her boiler flues exploded severely scalding Thomas Fish a fireman, and Captain Edmund Davis, a passenger, who had stopped in for a chat. Both died later that day. Mr. Fish leaves a wife and 3 young children, Capt. Davis age 45 yrs., was unmarried. (5 Jan 1854)

2251. James Carley died 3 Jan 1854 in Hudson, Columbia Co., from eating putrid, or carrion meat. (5 Jan 1853)

2252. George Burden and Ann Shoemaker, both of Penn Yan, Yates Co., were married 29 Dec 1853 by Rev. Abner Chase in Penn Yan. (5 Jan 1854)

2253. A.W. Stout of Amity, Allegany Co., and Catharine Davis of Milo, Yates Co., were married 2 Jan 1854 at the Canandaigua Hotel by Rev. S.W. Alden in Canandaigua, Ontario Co. (5 Jan 1854)

2254. Henry Harrower of Lawrenceville, PA., and Elizabeth Donley, step-daughter of Dr. Spence of Starkey, Yates Co., were married 25 Dec 1853 by Rev. O. Fraser in Starkey. (5 Jan 1853)

2255. David Kidder Esq. age 76 yrs., died 17 Nov 1853 at his home in Benton, Yates Co. (5 Jan 1854)

2256. John Huson age 7 yrs. 2 mos., died 24 Dec 1853 in Dundee, Yates Co. Only son of Samuel Huson, a merchant of that village. (5 Jan 1854)

2257. Harriet A. Hays age 24 yrs., died 29 Dec 1853 in Prattsburg, Steuben Co. The eldest daughter of Cassom Hays, of consumption. (5 Jan 1854)

2258. Rev. David Harrower age 81 yrs., died 29 Dec 1853 in Lawrenceville, PA. (5 Jan 1854)

2259. Frances Jane Daboll age 26 yrs., died 17 Dec 1853 in Prattsburg, Steuben Co., only daughter of Auren Daboll. (5 Jan 1854)

2260. Mrs. Naomi Steere age 76 yrs., died 30 Dec 1853 in Bath, Steuben Co. at the residence of her son in-law L.V. Church. (5 Jan 1854)

2261. Walstien H. Pettingill aged 3 yrs., this past July 25th, died 5 Dec 1853. His brother George W. Pettingill age 11 mos. 9 days, died 9 Dec 1853, Both of Dresden, Yates Co., both died of scarlet fever. (12 Jan 1854)

2262. Mrs. Joanna Wagener age 73 yrs., died 16 Jan 1854 at the home of her son George Wagener Esq.in Penn Yan, Yates Co., wife of the late Abraham Wagener Sr.. (19 Jan 1854)

2263. Jonathan Kinney age 43 yrs., died 13 Jan 1854 of small pox, in Benton, Yates Co. (19 Jan 1854)

2264. Samuel Johnson and Ann Perry, both of Barrington, Yates Co., were married last 9 Aug 1853 by J. Taylor Esq. in Barrington. (19 Jan 1854)

2265. John Polleston and Phebe Potter, both of Barrington, Yates Co., were married 4 Jan 1854 by Rev. James Landreth in Barrington. (19 Jan 1854)

2266. M. Wellington Marshall of Rock Stream, Yates Co., and Ellen Flint, eldest daughter of Jacob Flint of Lockport, Niagara Co., were married 29 Dec 1853 by Rev. O. Fraser at the home of Ralph Allen Esq., no town given. (19 Jan 1854)

2267. Edward Majors of Port Perry, C.W.., and Maria E. Morrison of Penn Yan, Yates Co., were married 18 Jan 1854 by Rev. Eells in Penn Yan. (19 Jan 1854)

2268. Marvin Parks of Penn Yan, Yates Co., and Mary R. Swarthout, fourth daughter of Henry Swarthout Esq., all of Hammondsport, Steuben Co., were married 17 Jan 1854 by Rev. S.S. Hughson in Milo, Yates Co. (19 Jan 1854)

2269. Wortman Sherwood age 24 yrs., died 16 Jan 1854 in Elmira, Chemung Co., formerly of Penn Yan, Yates Co. (19 Jan 1854)

2270. Samuel Beach Jr. and Mary Bell, both of Hammondsport, Steuben Co., were married 2 Jan 1854 by Rev. William R. Downs in Monterey, Schuyler Co. (19 Jan 1854)

2271. Job Ward and Frances A. Hopkins, both of Barrington, Yates Co., were married 29 Dec 1853 by Rev. D.B. Olney in Barrington. (19 Jan 1854)

2272. William VanOrsdoll age 21 yrs. 4 days, died 14 Dec 1853 at Himrods Corners, Yates Co. (19 Jan 1854)

2273. Mrs. Susan Sprowls age 74 yrs., died 9 Jan 1854 in Starkey, Yates Co., wife of the late James Sprowls. (19 Jan 1854)

2274. Mrs. Elizabeth Chapin age 78 yrs., died 14 Jan 1854 at the home of her son in-law Joseph Rappelye in Milo, Yates Co. A native of Philadelphia, she moved to Yates Co. in 1828, where she has since resided. (19 Jan 1854)

2275. Moses Black age 60 yrs., died 13 Jan 1854 in Geneva, Ontario Co. by the fall of a tree. He was standing by while his men were chopping, and giving orders as to the direction the tree should fall, when the accident occurred. (26 Jan 1854)

2276. THE 1853 TABLE OF MORTALITY FOR THE TOWN OF BENTON, prepared for the "Yates County Whig" by S.G. Gage Esq.

Jan...4	Stephen Purdy age 67 yrs., from an ulct'd throat.
" 8	Hannah Bradley age 83 yrs., from a fall.
" 16	Rachel Sheppard age 78 yrs.
" 20	Norman Holmes age 32 yrs., from cons.
" 25	Miner W. Herrmance age under 1 yr., from a sore throat.
" 25	Inf'son of R.N. McFarren age und' 1 yr.
Feb...4	Bridget Kinney age 35 yrs., from childbirth.
" 14	Rebecca McHinch age 74 yrs.
" 18	Noah A. Rose age 24 yrs.
Mar...5	Melissa J. Hatch age 3 yrs.
" 5	Mary A. Pressler age 6 yrs., ran over.
" 12	Andrew Eldridge age over 1 yr.
" 21	Rodney Lamport age 17 yrs., from cons.
Apr..11	Samuel Jayne age over 90 yrs.
Apr..13	Nancy Voak age 47 yrs., from cons.
" 18	Robert Boyd age 73 yrs.
Jun..12	Frances C. Parsons age 3 yrs.
" 16	Inf' son of W.A. Jones age under 1 yr.
Jul..16	Mary Jane Hazen age 24 yrs.
" 19	Sibbell Throckmorton age 55 yrs.
Aug..12	Margaret Haines age 38 yrs.
" 13	Inf' son of W.L. Smith age under 1 yr.
" 15	Benjamin Coddington age 38 yrs.
Sep...7	Jonathan Slayton age 45 yrs., found dead.

Sep 22 Elisha Clark age 84 yrs.
Oct..15 Selim Barringer age 11 yrs., from fever.
" 19 Thomas H. Trimmer age 17 yrs., from fever.
Nov..15 Susan Riche age 42 yrs.
" 17 David Ridder age 76 yrs.
" 20 Franklin Dean age 8 yrs.
Dec...8 Kiamesia Townsend age 2 yrs.
" 9 Dr. Henry S. Lovell age 44 yrs.
" 16 Garrett V. Scott age 32 yrs.
(26 Jan 1854)

2277. Bayard Taylor is a fine looking man, six feet in height. His eyes and hair, beard and moustache are light brown. His age 29 yrs., and looks every inch a gentleman and poet. (26 Jan 1854)

2278. William Dean of Tyrone, Schuyler Co., and Ann Maria Ketchum of Barrington, Yates Co., were married 12 Jan 1854 by Rev. P. Olney in Barrington. (26 Jan 1854)

2279. Backett Wixon of Wayne, Steuben Co., and Belinda Ketchum of Barrington, Yates Co., were married 12 Jan 1854 by Rev. P. Olney in Barrington. (26 Jan 1854)

2280. James Norman and Isabella Emmett, both of Torrey, Yates Co., were married 19 Jan 1854 by P.M. Dox J.P. in Geneva, Ontario Co. (26 Jan 1854)

2281. John C. Rippey age 39 yrs., died 18 Jan 1854 in Gorham, Ontario Co. (26 Jan 1854)

2282. Mrs. Margaret O'Neil age 31 or 91 yrs. (blurred), died 14 Jan 1854 in Seneca, Ontario Co. (26 Jan 1854)

2283. Betsy Ann Squier age 19 yrs., died 13 Jan 1854 in Gorham, Ontario Co., at the residence of William Monicle. (26 Jan 1854)

2284. Wilmot H. Depue age 5 yrs. 5 mos. 7 days, died 6 Jan 1854 in Milo, Yates Co., only son of Myron and Cynthia Jane Depue. (26 Jan 1854)

2285. George Fletcher of London, England, will be 107 yrs. old in February. He recently preached at the Methodist Chapel in Nottingham. Mr. Fletcher served in the British Army during the Revolution, and has been a class leader for 80 yrs. (2 Feb 1854)

2286. THE 1853 TABLE OF MORTALITY FOR THE TOWN OF MIDDLESEX, prepared for the "Yates County Whig" by John Mather Esq.

Jan..20 Emily Gage age 23 yrs.
" 24 Lawrence Lambertson age 80 yrs.
Feb...3 Mrs. Cyntha Adams age 66 yrs.
" 5 Mrs. Eleanor VanHouten age 61 yrs.
" 27 Rufus J. Adams age 28 yrs.
Mar..25 Emma A. Allen age under 1 yr.
" 28 Mrs. Mary Francisco age 35 yrs.
" 30 Stephen Collins age 26 yrs.
Apr...8 Mrs. Mary Brewer age 59 yrs.
" 10 Myron Bates age 28 yrs.
" 20 Mrs. Jane Mather age 60 yrs.
Jun..13 Nathan Emory age 14 yrs.
" __ Inf' son of David Eddy age under 1 yr.
Jul..28 Mary Jane Brown age 12 yrs.
Aug...2 Henry Lamoreux age 23 yrs.
" 14 Jane Hunter age 30 yrs.
" 22 Henry Wood age 24 yrs.
Sep..12 Inf' son of Thomas Seamans Esq. age under 1 yr.
Oct..12 Mrs. Randilla Jones age 27 yrs.
" 20 Mrs. Mahala Ellick age 28 yrs.
Nov...1 Emeline Adams age 21 yrs.
" 11 John Aldrich age 34 yrs.
(2 Feb 1854)

2287. _zera M. Stead ? (illegible) of Penn Yan, Yates Co., and Mary Jane Rogers of Jerusalem, Yates Co., were married 28 Jan 1854 by Rev. Abner Chase in Penn Yan. (2 Feb 1854)

2288. J.C. Sheppard of Stockton, California, formerly of Rochester, Monroe Co., NY., and Melissa Lyons were married 25 Jan 1854 by Rev. Kellogg in Penn Yan, Yates Co. (2 Feb 1854)

2289. Mary P. Robinson died 21 Jan 1854 in Mishawaka, LA. or IA. (illegible), at the residence of her brother in-law Jacob Mearifield ? (blurred). The youngest daughter of the late Hon. James Robinson of Potter, Yates Co., NY. (2 Feb 1854)

2290. SOME OF THE DISTINGUISHED DEAD OF 1853, prepared for the "Yates County Whig" by S.G.Gage.

a. Violet Proctor a colored woman, age 108 yrs., died at the Alms House, New Bedford, MA. A former slave, she retained most of her mental and physical faculties to the last, no date given. (9 Feb 1854)

b. William Waugh age 95 yrs., died at Derring, New Hampshire. A soldier of the Revolution, no date given. (9 Feb 1854)

c. David Wilson age 107 yrs. 2 mos. 10 days died in Dearborn, Co. PA. A soldier of the Revolution, and a native of New York. He had been married five times, and at the time of his death, was the father of 47 children. While residing near the old Redstone Post, PA., his wife gave birth to 5 children in 11 mos. Mr. Wilson was about five and a half feet tall. He served throughout the entire Revolution under Gen. Washington, and served in most of the Indian Wars since. He was a companion of Marion and Rodgers, as well as other pioneers of our Western and Southern wilds. His son Alexander Wilson of North Madison, the forty fifth child of the subject verified this information, no date given. (9 Feb 1854)

d. John Grissenger age 98 yrs., died at Lewisburg, PA. A soldier of the Revolution, he leaves 14 children, 123 grandchildren and 242 great grandchildren, no date given. (9 Feb 1854)

e. Sears C. Walker age 107 died in Cincinnati, OH. Born in 1746, a famous astronomer, no date given. (9 Feb 1854)

f. Hon. John Thompson age 75 yrs., died 2 Jan 1853 at New Lisbon, Ohio. A member of Congress from 1829 to 1837. (9 Feb 1854)

g. Benjamin Pierce age 12 yrs., died 6 Jan 1853 near Andover, MA. Killed by the cars, son of the President elect of the U.S. (9 Feb 1854)

h. Hon. William Upham age 60 yrs., died 14 Jan 1853 in Washington city. A U.S. Senator from Vermont. (9 Feb 1854)

i. Charles Willey age 107 yrs., died 23 Jan 1853 in Nottingham, NH. Born 25 Feb 1746 in that town, a soldier of the Revolution and pensioner. He has a son Jonathan Willey aged between 70 and 80 yrs., who is also a pensioner from the War of 1812. (9 Feb 1854)

j. Abigail Fillmore age 55 yrs., died 30 Mar 1853 in Washington city. The wife of ex-President Millard Filmore. (9 Feb 1854)

k. Samuel Jayne age 90 yrs. died 11 Apr 1853 in Benton, Yates Co. A soldier of the Revolution. (9 Feb 1854)

l. Hon. Judge Burnett a native of Newark, Tioga Co., died 27 Apr 1853 in Cincinnati, OH. He moved to Cincinnati in 1797 when only a cluster of log cabins were there. Former Judge of the Ohio Supreme Court, and a Senator in Congress. (9 Feb 1854)

m. Joshua McQueen age 106 yrs., died __ May 1853 in Frankfort, KY. A sergeant in the army of Gen. Washington during the Revolution. (9 Feb 1854)

n. Major Thomas Stearns age 90 yrs., died 7 May 1853 in Brooksville, ME. A soldier of the Revolution. (9 Feb 1854)

o. William Cobb age 83 yrs., died 12 Jun 1853 at Warwick, MA. Appointed Postmaster under Pres. Jefferson in 1800, he held that office until his death. Also Treasurer of that town. (9 Feb 1854)

p. Jonathan Overton age 101 yrs., died 14 Jun 1853 at Edenton, NC. A colored man and soldier of the Revolution. He served under Gen. Washington, and was at the Battle of Yorktown. (9 Feb 1854)

q. Richard Taylor died 19 Jun 1853 in Arkansas. Chief of the Cherokee Nation, and Captain of a company of Cherokees under Gen. Jackson in the Creek War. (9 Feb 1854)

r. Hon. Henry Vail age 70 yrs., died 25 Jun 1853 at Troy, Rensselaer Co. A ex-member of Congress. (9 Feb 1854)

s. James Holmes age 99 yrs., died 27 Jun 1853 at Owego, Tioga Co. A soldier of the Revolution, he fought in the Battles of Monmouth, Germantown, and Brandywine. (9 Feb 1854)

t. Hon. Hezekiah C. Seymour died __ Jul 1853 at Piermont, Rockland Co. Late state engineer and surveyor. (9 Feb 1854)

u. Major Gen. Jonathan P. Couch died 24 Jul 1853 in Havana, Chemung Co. A resident of that county for the last 30 years. (9 Feb 1854)

v. Hon. John Knox age 70 yrs., died 31 Jul 1853 in Watertown, Jefferson Co. A late Judge of Seneca Co., NY. (9 Feb 1854)

w. Asa Holden age 91 yrs., died 3 Aug 1853 in New York city. The last surviving soldier of the Revolution from that city. (9 Feb 1854)

x. Benjamin Mallory died 9 Aug 1853 in Lockport, Niagara Co. A soldier of the Revolution and one of Gen. Scott's right hand men in the War of 1812. (9 Feb 1854)

y. Hon. John Taliafero age 85 yrs., died 25 Aug 1853. A member of Congress from Westmoreland Co., VA. (9 Feb 1854)

z. Mary Simondson age 126 yrs., died __Sep 1853 near Shippenburg, PA. (9 Feb 1854)

aa. Hon. Victory Birdseye age 70 yrs., died __ Sep 1853 at Pompey, Onondaga Co. An ex-member of Congress from this state. (9 Feb 1854)

bb. Hon. Thomas C. Love died __ Sep 1853 at Buffalo, Erie Co. An ex-member of Congress from this state. (9 Feb 1854)

cc. Joseph Bimelar died 20 Sep 1853 in Tuscarawas Co., Ohio. The founder of the Zoarite Socialist Community. (9 Feb 1854)

dd. Gen. Tallmadge died 29 Sep 1853 at Metropolitan Hall, NY. Ex-Senator, and a Minister to Russia. (9 Feb 1854)

ee. Tristan Burgess died 13 Oct 1853 at Providence, RI., an ex-member of Congress. (9 Feb 1854)

ff. Gen. Felix Lacoste died 14 Nov 1853 in New York city, Consul General to France. (9 Feb 1854)

gg. Hon. Charles G. Atherson age 49 yrs., died 15 Nov 1853, a Senator from NH. (9 Feb 1854)

hh. Daniel Benjamin age 95 yrs., died 24 Nov 1853 in Washington, Orange Co. A soldier of the Revolution. (9 Feb 1854)

2291. James W. Sunderlin and Margaret Swarthout, both of Wayne, Steuben Co., were married 25 Jan 1854 by Rev. P. Olney in Wayne. (9 Feb 1854)

2292. William VanCamp, Editor of the "Lyons Gazette", and Mary S. Tenney, both of Lyons, Wayne Co., were married 1 Feb 1854 by Rev. C. Hawley in Lyons. (9 Feb 1854)

2293. Mrs. Caroline Coleman age 48 yrs., died 3 Feb 1854 in Bellona, Yates Co., wife of Henry Coleman. (9 Feb 1854)

2294. Amelia M. Tyler age 13 yrs. 12 days, died 24 Jan 1854 of scarlet fever, in Dresden, Yates Co., only daughter of Hiram and Ruth Ann Goff. * Copied as printed. (9 Feb 1854)

2295. Charles Kinney age 45 yrs., died 28 Jan 1854 in Starkey, Yates Co. (9 Feb 1854)

2296. John H. Rumney Esq. age 66 yrs., died 20 Jan 1854 at the residence of his son Rev. Theodore S. Rumney in Uniontown, PA. For many years a resident of Geneva, Ontario Co., NY. (9 Feb 1854)

2297. Roger Haskell age 77 yrs., died 18 Jan 1854 at Peninsula, Summit Co., Ohio. Formerly of Geneva, Ontario Co., NY. (9 Feb 1854)

2298. Jacob M. Howard of Shafishery, Bennington Co. Vermont, and Hannah H. Almy of Potter, Yates Co., were married 12 Feb 1854 by Rev. J. Jones in Penn Yan, Yates Co. (16 Feb 1854)

2299. Abraham Cole of Benton, Yates Co., and Sarah A. Hammond of Penn Yan, Yates Co., were married 12 Feb 1854 by Rev. J. Jones in Penn Yan. (16 Feb 1854)

2300. Prof. William Marvin, Principle of the Dundee Academy in Dundee, Yates Co., New York, and Harriet N. Ewer of Bedford, Ohio, were married 31 Jan 1854 by Rev. S.B. Ewer in Bedford. (16 Feb 1854)

2301. C.G. Wheat of Tioga, PA., and Mrs. Isabella Howell of Barrington, Yates Co., were married 31 Jan 1854 by Rev. A.W. Sunderlin in Barrington. (16 Feb 1854)

2302. Edmund Boyce of Barrington, Yates Co., and Susan Baskin of Milo, Yates Co., were married 2 Jan 1854 by Rev. A.W. Sunderlin in Milo. (16 Feb 1854)

2303. Stephen R. Bean of Canadice, Ontario Co., and Sarah M. Coykendall of Starkey, Yates Co., were married 29 Jan 1854 by Rev. J. Hudgin in Dundee, Yates Co. (16 Feb 1854)

2304. S.G. McKane of Geneva, Ontario Co., and Melissa D. Hicks, formerly of Grand Rapids, Michigan, were married 8 Feb 1854 by Rev. B.M. Goldsmith in Torrey, Yates Co. (16 Feb 1854)

2305. James Johnstone age 54 yrs., died 1 Feb 1854 in Canandaigua, Ontario Co. Son of the late John Johnstone Esq. of Geneva, Ontario Co., and former agent of the Hornby Estate. (16 Feb 1854)

2306. The only son of Henry Bennett Esq., age 3 yrs., died 18 Feb 1854 from accidental scalding in Ontario, Wayne Co. (23 Feb 1854)

2307. Mrs. Helen M. Rohde age 34 yrs. 16 days, died 26 Jan 1854 in Benton, Yates Co. The wife of Lewis Rohde of Penn Yan, Yates Co. (23 Feb 1854)

2308. William Henry Ackley age 4 yrs., died 15 Feb 1854 in Penn Yan, Yates Co. Only son of William and Emily Ackley. (23 Feb 1854)

2309. Mrs. Elizabeth Wait age 72 yrs., died 31 Jan 1854 at her home in Bluff Point, Yates Co. Wife of the late Benjamin Wait, and a member of the Baptist Church for over 50 yrs. (23 Feb 1854)

2310. Mrs. Catharine Dunn now residing in Nunda, Livingston Co., was born 15 Oct 1753. She came to the Chemung Valley from Orange Co., about 70 yrs. ago, and from there moved to Nunda. She is the grandmother of John Carpenter of Elmira, Chemung, Co. (23 Feb 1854)

2311. Mrs. Margaret Purdy age about 103 yrs., of Spencer, Tioga Co., is the grandmother of Dr. Jothan Purdy of Elmira, Chemung Co. She retains her natural mental abilities in a remarkable degree, and during the summer walks to church without a cane. A native of Westchester Co., where her husband was killed in the Revolutionary War, at which time, she dragged his body from the combat scene. She came to this part of the country about 50 yrs. ago. (23 Feb 1854)

2312. Joseph Tanner and Esther Tubbs, both of Branchport, Yates Co., were married 23 Feb 1854 by Judge Laramore in the Mansion House at Bath, Steuben Co. (2 Mar 1854)

2313. George Hayes of Buffalo, Erie Co., and Mary Weeks of Prattsburg, Steuben Co., were married 20 Feb 1854 by Rev. B.C. Smith in the Presbyterian Church in Prattsburg. (2 Mar 1854)

2314. E. VanVolkenburgh, former Editor and owner of the "Geneva Courier", and Jane A. Blackman, daughter of E. Blackman of Newark, Wayne Co., were married 8 Feb 1854, no town or pastor given. (2 Mar 1854)

2315. Waterman Park and Mary Baker, both of Dundee, Yates Co., were married 5 Feb 1854 by Rev. J.N. Brown in Dundee. (2 Mar 1854)

2316. Arnold Stowell of Orange Co., and Eliza Barrack of Wayne, Steuben Co., were married 10 Feb 1854 by H. Baker Esq. in Wayne. (2 Mar 1854)

2317. Addison Wambaugh of Addison, Steuben Co., and E. Velnette Chase of Wayne, Steuben Co., were married 14 Feb 1854 by Rev. Russel in Wayne. (2 Mar 1854)

2318. Samuel S. Baldwin age 72 yrs., died at the home of his daughter, Mrs. Titus in Geneva, Ontario Co., no date given. (2 Mar 1854)

2319. Nathan Parke Esq. age 61 or 67 yrs.?(blurred) died 22 Feb 1854 at the home of his son in-law John H. Tillman in Geneva, Ontario Co. (2 Mar 1854)

2320. Patrick Maguir and Ann Russels of Dundee, Yates Co., were married 28 Feb 1854 by Hon. J.L. Lewis Jr. Esq. in Penn Yan, Yates Co. (9 Mar 1854)

2321. Col. Eli C. Frost of Catharine, Schuyler Co., and Sarah McConnell were married 2 Mar 1854 by Rev. S.W. Alden in Canandaigua, Ontario Co. (9 Mar 1854)

2322. Charles H. Carpenter of Starkey, Yates Co., and Harriet E. Drake of Reading, Schuyler Co., were married 22 Feb 1854 by Rev. J.T. Seeley in Reading. (9 Mar 1854)

2323. Cyrus Chubb age 39 yrs., died 21 Feb 1854 in Chubbs Hollow, near Barrington, Yates Co. (9 Mar 1854)

2324. Lydia Shannon age 72 yrs., died 22 Feb 1854 in Dundee, Yates Co. (9 Mar 1854)

2325. Lewis Raplee age 6 yrs., died 23 Feb 1854, and his brother Emmet Raplee age 9 yrs., died 25 Feb 1854. Both sons of Joshua and Hannah Raplee of Milo, Yates Co. (9 Mar 1854)

2326. Mrs. Dean age 91 yrs., died 24 Feb 1854 in Starkey, Yates Co. She had been blind for nearly 20 yrs. (9 Mar 1854)

2327. Mrs. Sally Clark age 26 yrs., died 26 Feb 1854 in Tyrone, Schuyler Co., wife of Edmund Clark. (9 Mar 1854)

2328. Nathaniel Berry of Poughkeepsie, Dutchess Co., and Emily A. Sunderlin of Barrington, Yates Co., were married 6 Mar 1854 by Rev. J.B. Brown in Barrington. (16 Mar 1854)

2329. A daughter of Mr. Seamans, age 8 yrs., died 3 Mar 1854 in Milo, Yates Co. (16 Mar 1854)

2330. Carlton Legg Esq. age 72 yrs., died 14 Mar 1854 at the home of his son in-law in Penn Yan, Yates Co. (16 Mar 1854)

2331. Mary C. Griswold age 5 yrs. 8 mos., died 25 Feb 1854 in Penn Yan, Yates Co., daughter of David and Hannah Griswold. (16 Mar 1854)

2332. Mrs. Olive D. Smith age 34 yrs., died 15 Mar 1854 in Benton, Yates Co. Wife of Job T. Smith, and youngest daughter of the late Henry Townsend. (16 Mar 1854)

2333. Edward Raplee age 14 mos., died 3 Mar 1854 in Starkey, Yates Co., son of Rochester and Lydia Raplee. (16 Mar 1854)

2334. David Hays age 20 yrs., died 4 Mar 1854 in Starkey, Yates Co., son of Joel Hays. (16 Mar 1854)

2335. A son of Wheeler Randall, age 18 mos., died 4 Mar 1854 in Milo, Yates Co. (16 Mar 1854)

2336. Mrs. Elsie Jefferson age 84 yrs., died 3 Mar 1854 at the home of her grandson, J. Fraser, in Elmira, Chemung Co. (16 Mar 1854)

2337. Mrs. Maria Bean age 30 yrs., died 7 Mar 1854 from paralysis of the spine at Geneva, Ontario Co., wife of John E. Bean. (16 Mar 1854)

2338. Mrs. Charlotte Garner died 17 Mar 1854 from apoplexy, while engaged at work in Sheldon's Hall. The wife of H.H. Garner, no town given. (23 Mar 1854)

2339. Edward Sunderlin of Wayne, Steuben Co., and Naomi Hopkins of Barrington, Yates Co., were married 7 Mar 1854 by Rev. D.B. Olney in Barrington. (23 Mar 1854)

2340. A.T. Crego of Elmira, Chemung Co., and Lola Annie LaFever, daughter of Reuben LaFever of Reading, Steuben Co., were married 9 Mar 1854 by Rev. J.T. Seeley in Elmira, Chemung Co. (23 Mar 1854)

2341. Mrs. Mary D. Jackson age 40 yrs., died 12 Mar 1854 in Havana, Schuyler Co., wife of the Hon. William T. Jackson. (23 Mar 1854)

2342. Lloyd M. Goodrich age 40 yrs., died 28 Mar 1854 in Penn Yan, Yates Co. (30 Mar 1854)

2343. Frank Wheeler age 4 yrs. 5 mos., died 23 Mar 1854 of Scarlet Fever. The son of Freeman G. and Catharine Wheeler of Penn Yan, Yates Co. (30 Mar 1854)

2344. Peter Ayres age 64 yrs., died 26 Mar 1854 at his home in Milo, Yates Co. (30 Mar 1854)

2345. Mary Ann Blake age 13 or 15 yrs.? 5 mos. 26 days (blurred), died 11 Mar 1854 in Starkey, Yates Co., oldest daughter of Franklin Blake. (30 Mar 1854)

2346. William Stark and Abbie Hatmaker, both of Torrey, Yates Co., were married 23 Mar 1854 by Rev. Abner Chase in Torrey. (30 Mar 1854)

2347. Thomas Jennings and Anna Maria Wheat, both of Benton, Yates Co., were married 28 Mar 1854 by Rev. Ira Fairbanks in Benton. (6 Apr 1854)

2348. Norton Swarthout of Milo, Yates Co., and Mary Ann Raymond of Jerusalem, Yates Co., were married 28 Mar 1854 by Rev. C. Morton in Jerusalem. (6 Apr 1854)

2349. Aaron Potter and Amanda M. Ely, both of Peach Orchard, NY., were married 26 Mar 1854 by Rev. Mann in Peach Orchard. (6 Apr 1854)

2350. John VanOrsdol age 84 yrs., died 25 Mar 1854 at the home of his brother in Ohio, no town given. (6 Apr 1854)

2351. Mrs. Susan Dunn age 80 yrs., died 8 Mar 1854

at the home of her son, Col. Terrill in Starkey, Yates Co. (6 Apr 1854)

2352. A young man John D. Whipple from Clinton, NY. A porter with the Cresent City Hotel in San Francisco, CA., was killed by an accidental shot from a pistol while playing with a fellow servant, no date given. (13 Apr 1854)

2353. John P. Playsted of Barrington, Yates Co., and Martha Ann Bayard of Milo, Yates Co., were married 6 Apr 1854 by Rev. C. Morton in Milo. (13 Apr 1854)

2354. Phebe Ann W. Miller age 26 yrs., died 7 Apr 1854 at the home of her father in Milo, Yates Co. (13 Apr 1854)

2355. Mrs. Mary C. Hurd age 27 yrs., died 30 Jan 1854 at Madras, India of typhoid fever. The former Mary C. Bassett of Hector, Tompkins Co., NY. She was the wife of Rev. Hurd, formerly of the Presbyterian Church at Big Flatts, Chemung Co., NY. In the Spring of 1852, they had sailed to India as missionaries. (20 Apr 1854)

2356. George Catlin and Elizabeth Gano, both of Dix, Chemung Co., were married 12 Apr 1854 by Rev. C.S. Davis in Dix. (20 Apr 1854)

2357. Mary R. Young age 10 or 19 yrs.? (blurred), died 24 Mar 1854 in Potter, Yates Co. (20 Apr 1854)

2358. Ebenezer Hurd age 95 yrs., died 10 Apr 1854 at the home of his son in Benton, Yates Co. A former resident of Dutchess Co., NY. (20 Apr 1854)

2359. Hon. John Knox age 84 yrs., died 18 Apr 1854 at his home in Knoxville, near Corning, Steuben Co. One of the early settlers of that place, he served in the State Legislature and other offices for NY. (27 Apr 1854)

2360. Hon. John Davis died 19 Apr 1854 at his home in Worcester, MA. A statesman from that place. (27 Apr 1854)

2361. Charles R. Ludlow of Tyrone, Schuyler Co., and Tacey M. Randolph of Milo, Yates Co., were married 25 Apr 1854 by Rev. D.D. Bank in Penn Yan, Yates Co. (27 Apr 1854)

2362. Mrs. Catharine Rector age 28 yrs., died 21 Apr 1854 of inflammatory rheumatism, in Benton, Yates Co. The wife of William J. Rector and youngest daughter of Gillett Kelsey. (27 Apr 1854)

2363. George William Huntington age 3 yrs. 8 mos. 28 days, died 12 Apr 1854, and his brother, Edward Harvey Huntington age 5 mos., died 24 Apr 1854. Both sons of Charles and Amelia Huntington of Penn Yan, Yates Co. (27 Apr 1854)

2364. Harriet A. Laire age 4 yrs. 5 mos. 2 days, died 14 Apr 1854, daughter of Absalom and Phebe Laire of Italy Hill, Yates Co. (27 Apr 1854)

2365. William S. Sutton age 41 yrs., died 16 Apr 1854 at his home in Jerusalem, Yates Co. (27 Apr 1854)

2366. Mrs. Hannah H. Ely age 24 yrs., died 23 Apr 1854 of consumption, at the home of her father, Hon. Henry Welles, in Penn Yan, Yates Co. The wife of George H. Ely of Rochester, Monroe Co. (27 Apr 1854)

2367. Rev. Abner Chase age 71 yrs., died 27 Apr 1854 at his home in Penn Yan, Yates Co. One of the earliest pioneers of Methodism in Western New York. (4 May 1854)

2368. Jonathan Pitney age 60 yrs., has been missing for two weeks. A resident of Torrey, Yates Co., he was last seen in an aberanted state of mind. Please contact A.R. Pitney of Dresden, Yates Co. if you have any information. (4 May 1854)

2369. Dr. Darius Ketchum age 28 yrs., died 14 Apr 1854 of inflammation of the lungs, in Penn Yan, Yates Co. The son of Jonathan Ketchum Esq. (4 May 1854)

2370. Florence Augusta Gooding age 12 yrs., died in Bristol, Ontario Co., no date given. (4 May 1854)

2371. Mrs. Sarah Jane Fuller age 18 yrs. 6 mos., died 22 Apr 1854 in Barrington, Yates Co. (4 May 1854)

2372. Andrew J. Cole and Mary Lafler, daughter of Sydney Lafler, were married 27 Apr 1854 in Middlesex, Yates Co. by Rev. Sydney Lafler. (11 May 1854)

2373. Edward H. Silsby of Alexander, Wisconsin, and Laura A. Scofield of Starkey, Yates Co., were married 30 Apr 1854 by Rev. J.H. Currier in Starkey. (11 May 1854)

2374. Samuel Hartshorn age 82 yrs., died 6 May 1854 in Jerusalem, Yates Co. (11 May 1854)

2375. Mrs. Sarah Mallory age 63 yrs., died 17 Apr 1854 in Reading, Hillsdale Co., Michigan. The wife of Matthew Mallory, formerly of Barrington, Yates Co., NY. (11 May 1854)

2376. Sarah Francisco age 18 yrs., died 29 Apr 1854 in Barrington, Yates Co. (11 May 1854)

2377. Dr. Israel Howe age 90 yrs., died in Rushville, Yates Co., no date given. (11 May 1854)

2378. Hon. Robert Nicholas died on Staten Island, NY. A ex-Senator, and former resident of Ontario Co., no date given. (18 May 1854)

2379. Silas Chapin died 11 May 1854, an old citizen of Geneva, Ontario Co., killed instantly by being thrown from his wagon. (18 May 1854)

2380. Kate Masten age 1 yr. 8 mos., died 14 May 1854, only daughter of A.V. and Calista Masten of Penn Yan, Yates Co. (18 May 1854)

2381. Margaret Patten age 4 yrs. 3 mos. 18 days, died 26 Apr 1854, and her brother, William Alexander Patten age 2 yrs. 2 mos. 5 days, died 4 May 1854. The only children of Sherburne and Jane Patten of Barrington, Yates Co., both of typhoid fever. (18 May 1854)

2382. J. Wells Taylor of Rochester, Monroe Co., and Elizabeth T. Hunt, daughter of Major Russel Hunt of Milo, Yates Co., were married 17 May 1854 by Rev. J. Landreth in Milo. (25 May 1854)

2383. Charles H. Hunt and Lydia A. Fillmore, daughter of Rev. A.N. Fillmore of the East Genesee Conference, were married 18 May 1854 by Rev. Hubbard at Milo Centre, Yates Co. (25 May 1854)

2384. Frank Lewis Gildersleeve age 9 yrs. 22 days, died 28 Apr 1854, youngest child of Romulus and Emeline Gildersleeve of Penn Yan, Yates Co. (25 May 1854)

2385. Simon S. Raymond of Benton, Yates Co., and Sarah A. Ardrey of Torrey, Yates Co., were married 21 May 1854 by Rev. A.C. Mallory in Benton. (1 Jun 1854)

2386. Joshua Jones and Ursula Case, both of Middlesex, Yates Co., were married by Rev. A.C. Mallory in Benton, Yates Co. (1 Jun 1854)

2387. James Hulso of Middletown, Orange Co., and Hannah J. Noble of Rock Stream, Yates Co., were married 27 May 1854 by Rev. O. Fraser at the home of Nathaniel Penny in Reading, Schuyler Co. (1 Jun 1854)

2388. Captain William E. Molthrop, emigrated from North Haven to Oregon, about 8 mos. ago. News has been received that his three daughters were all married 29 Mar 1854 in Wapato. (8 Jun 1854)

2389. Charles W. Noble Esq. of Cleveland, Ohio, and Caroline G. VanBuren, daughter of E. VanBuren Esq. of Penn Yan, Yates Co., NY., were married 31 May 1854 by Rev. James Eells in Penn Yan. (8 Jun 1854)

2390. Charles Secor of Torrey, Yates Co., and Cornelia Potter of Milo, Yates Co., were married 21 May 1854 by Rev. D.B. Olney in Barrington, Yates Co. (8 Jun 1854)

2391. Horace Freeman and Jenett Legg, both of Torrey, Yates Co., were married 14 May 1854 by Rev. B.S. Borden in Torrey. (8 Jun 1854)

2392. Miriam Parker age 94 yrs. 9 mos., died 22 May 1854 at the residence of Jesse T. Gage in Benton, Yates Co. (8 Jun 1854)

2393. Cornelius Ryan a lock tender, drowned the day before yesterday at the locks near Millport, Chemung Co. While closing one of the gates, something gave way, and he was precipatated into the surging water right under a boat. Copied from the "Elmira Advertiser", no date given. (15 Jun 1854)

2394. Willard F. Barden of New York city, and Mary L. Whitaker of Penn Yan, Yates Co., were married 8 Jun 1854 by Rev. S.S. Hughson in Penn Yan. (15 Jun 1854)

2395. Otis Avery of Canandaigua, Ontario Co., and Miss A. --nfield (illegible) of Himrods Corners,

Yates Co., were married 11 May 1854 by Rev. S.S. Hughson in Penn Yan, Yates Co. (15 Jun 1854)

2396. O.A. Pennoyer and Margaret L. Morris, both of Penn Yan, Yates Co., were married 13 Jun 1854 by Rev. James Eells in Penn Yan. (15 Jun 1854)

2397. Isaac Lanning Esq. and Emeline A. Palmer, both of Starkey, Yates Co., were married 1 Jun 1854 by Rev. Currier in Dundee, Yates Co. (15 Jun 1854)

2398. Melchoir Wagener age 75 yrs. 5 mos., died __ Jun 1854 in Pulteney, Steuben Co. (15 Jun 1854)

2399. Charles V. Winants age 27 yrs., died 17 Apr 1854 in San Francisco, CA., formerly of Yates Co. (15 Jun 1854)

2400. J.M. Chapman formerly of Penn Yan, Yates Co., is now the Railroad Ticket Agent at Peoria, IL. (22 Jun 1854)

2401. R.R. Dumas Esq. of the "Elmira Republican", and M. Henrietta Davidson of Elmira, Chemung Co., were married 6 Jun 1854 by Rev. W.H. Goodwin in Elmira. (22 Jun 1854)

2402. Calvin J. Harford and Susan J. Baker, both of Benton, Yates Co., were married 11 Jun 1854 by Peter M. Dox Esq. in Geneva, Ontario Co. (22 Jun 1854)

2403. Hon. Fred. Emerson of Tennessee, and Caroline Hodge of Bath, Steuben Co., were married 3 Jun 1854 by Rev. Potter in Avon, Steuben Co. (22 Jun 1854)

2404. J. Baxter, former foreman in the Havana Journal Office, and Mary A. Hyslop of Havana, Schuyler Co., were married 14 Jun 1854 by Rev. A.G. Laman in Havana. (22 Jun 1854)

2405. William Baxter age 42 yrs., died 17 Jun 1854 in Milo, Yates Co. (22 Jun 1854)

2406. Mary Barnes age 8 yrs., died 4 Jun 1854 in Dundee, Yates Co. Only daughter of George and Catherine Barns. * note the spelling of Barnes and Barns are as they appeared. (22 Jun 1854)

2407. Barnett Christie age 38 yrs., of Middlesex, Yates Co. committed suicide 22 Jun 1854 in Penn Yan, Yates Co. by hanging himself. (29 Jun 1854)

2408. Oscar Nutt of Torrey, Yates Co., and Rhoda E. Smith of Benton, Yates Co., were married 26 Jun 1854 by Rev. A.C. Mallory in the Baptist Meeting House in Benton. (29 Jun 1854)

2409. A.J. Wood of Virgil, Cortland Co., and E.M. Briggs of Starkey, Yates Co., were married in Starkey by Rev. S.R. Evens of Fabius, Onondaga Co., no date given. (29 Jun 1854)

2410. Mrs. Ann Storms, a widow age 82 yrs., died 11 Jun 1854 in Seneca, Ontario Co. (29 Jun 1854)

2411. Mrs. Eliza French age 47 yrs., died 19 Jun 1854 in Seneca, Ontario Co., wife of William H. French. (29 Jun 1854)

2412. Charles A. Gibbs of Ovid, Seneca Co., and Elizabeth R. Gibbs his wife, died recently from cholera, while on a visit in La Porte, Indiana. Mrs. Gibbs is the daughter of Upton Dorsey Esq. of Geneva, Ontario Co. (6 Jul 1854)

2413. W. Dean Mitchell and N. Barstow Coryell, both of Benton, Yates Co., were married 28 Jun 1854 by Rev. Goldsmith in Benton. (6 Jul 1854)

2414. The son of John Chambers, age 7 yrs., died 7 Jul 1854 in Penn Yan, Yates Co., from injuries received when he fell out of a tree while playing. (13 Jul 1854)

2415. George Goodrich of Barrington, Yates Co., and Mary Himrod of Tyrone, Schuyler Co., were married 4 Jul 1854 by Rev. C. Morton in Penn Yan, Yates Co. (13 Jul 1854)

2416. John Whitbeck and Helen Conklin, both of Jerusalem, Yates Co., were married 8 Jul 1854 by Isaac Purdy Esq. in Jerusalem. (13 Jul 1854)

2417. Mrs. Emily Hartshorn age 33 yrs., died 8 Jul 1854 of consumption, in Jerusalem, Yates Co., wife of James H. Hartshorn. (13 Jul 1854)

2418. William Riker of Dundee, Yates Co., and Sarah Tuell of Barrington, Yates Co., were married 3 Jul 1854 by Rev. Seeley in Barrington. (27 Jul 1854)

2419. Morris Loomis of Barrington, Yates Co., and Canadace Vance of Starkey, Yates Co., were married 16 Jul 1854 by Rev. D.B. Olney in Barrington. (27 Jul 1854)

2420. Hermon H. Clarke of Corning, Steuben Co., and Harriet E. Laire of Penn Yan, Yates Co., were married 3 Jul 1854 by Rev. Smith in Italy Hill, Yates Co. (27 Jul 1854)

2421. Mrs. Annie Winants died 9 Jul 1854 at the residence of her son in-law, F.P. Allen, in Malone, Franklin Co. Widow of the late James T. Winants of Prattsburgh, Steuben Co. (27 Jul 1854)

2422. Ebenezer Holcomb age 88 yrs., died 12 Jul 1854 in Benton, Yates Co. (27 Jul 1854)

2423. Daniel Raplee age 25 yrs., died 14 Jul 1854 in Savona, Steuben Co. (27 Jul 1854)

2424. Lynham E. Taylor age 7 yrs. 1 mo. 21 days, died 17 Jul 1854 in Branchport, Yates Co., son of James and Rebecca Taylor. (27 Jul 1854)

2425. William Wells, a professor of modern languages and literature at Genesee College, and Alice Yackley of Gorham, Ontario Co., were married 15 Jul 1854 by Rev. Joseph Cummings in Gorham. (3 Aug 1854)

2426. Darius A. Ogden, formerly of Penn Yan, Yates Co., has been appointed as Consul to Honolulu. (10 Aug 1854)

2427. Charles Rudges of Geneva, Ontario Co., and Adelia Holmes of Penn Yan, Yates Co., were married 1 Aug 1854 by Rev. George Cheeney in Penn Yan. (10 Aug 1854)

2428. Julia Welles Ely age 14 mos. 11 days, died 28 Jul 1854 at the home of her grandfather, Hon. Henry Welles in Penn Yan, Yates Co. Daughter of George H. Ely of Rochester, Monroe Co. (10 Aug 1854)

2429. Henry Heniore age 87 yrs., died in West Fayette, Seneca Co. A resident of that county for about 50 yrs., no date given. (17 Aug 1854)

2430. The "Milwaukee Sentinel" records the death of an unknown man at Oconsmonie, Wisconsin. A name marked on his arm was F.C. Cunn, and an envelope in his pocket was postmarked from Rushville, Yates Co., NY. (17 Aug 1854)

2431. Mr. John Potter age 72 yrs., died 10 Aug 1854 at his home in Potter, Yates Co. The father of Dr.

Hazzard A. Potter of Penn Yan, Yates Co. One of the pioneers of Western New York, having come from Genesee Co. 63 yrs. ago. (17 Aug 1854)

2432. William M. Patchin and Jane Winters, both of Penn Yan, Yates Co., were married 7 Aug 1854 by Rev. Joseph Clark at Niagara Falls, Niagara Co. (17 Aug 1854)

2433. Samuel Tuton of Dundee, Yates Co., and Mary Ann Hannibal of Barrington, Yates Co., were married 3 Aug 1854 by Rev. J.N. Brown in Barrington. (17 Aug 1854)

2434. Peter Decker of Torrey, Yates Co., and Margaret Bruce of Bellona, Yates Co., were married 1 Aug 1854 by Rev. A.E. Chubbuck in Bellona. (17 Aug 1854)

2435. The adopted son of Anson Hall, age 21 yrs., drowned 22 Aug 1854 in the lake near Penn Yan, Yates Co., no name given. (24 Aug 1854)

2436. W.F. Thompson of Penn Yan, Yates Co., and Sarah E. Chapman, daughter of Hon. Heman Chapman of Torrey, Yates Co., were married 23 Aug 1854 by Rev. A.W. Sunderlin in Torrey. (24 Aug 1854)

2437. Lucy Williams age 19 yrs., died 18 Aug 1854 of consumption in Jerusalem, Yates Co. (24 Aug 1854)

2438. The Rev. D.D. Buck pastor of the Methodist Church in Penn Yan, Yates Co., has been appointed to the First Church at Elmira, Chemung Co. The Rev. Thomas Tousey of Trumansburg, Tompkins Co. will take his place. (31 Aug 1854)

2439. Rev. J.B. Brown, pastor of the Methodist Church in Dundee, Yates Co. has been appointed at Penfield, Monroe Co. (31 Aug 1854)

2440. Dewitt Clinton Benham has been elected as a candidate for Member of the Assembly from Yuba Co., California. Formerly of Penn Yan, Yates Co., NY., and a son of Hon. Miles Benham, now of Syracuse, Onondaga Co. (31 Aug 1854)

2441. William Johnson of Penn Yan, Yates Co., and Helen M. Canfield of Danby, Tompkins Co., were married 26 Aug 1854 by Rev. E.F. Hadley in Danby. (31 Aug 1854)

2442. F.L. French of Chittenango, Madison Co., and Eva L. Wheaton of Prattsburgh, Steuben Co., were married 17 Aug 1854 by Rev. James Eells in Penn Yan, Yates Co. (31 Aug 1854)

2443. Mrs. Sarah Jane Randall age 29 yrs., died 17 Aug 1854 in Penn Yan, Yates Co., wife of Charles H. Randall. (31 Aug 1854)

2444. Mary Chamberlain age 3 yrs. 7 mos. 16 days, died 18 Aug 1854, and her sister Emma Chamberlain age 2 yrs. 3 mos. 19 days, died 19 Aug 1854, only daughters of George W. and E.J. Chamberlain of Dundee, Yates Co. (31 Aug 1854)

2445. James Townsend and Millicent Ann Griffin, both of Dresden, Yates Co., were married 30 Aug 1854 by Rev. B.M. Goldsmith in Bellona, Yates Co. (7 Sep 1854)

2446. David Robson and Sarah Johnson, both of Italy Hollow, Yates Co., were married there 3 Sep 1854, no pastor given. (7 Sep 1854)

2447. Hon. William T. Jackson and Elma Aylworth, both of Havana, Schuyler Co., were married 31 Aug 1854 by Rev. Huggins in Havana. (7 Sep 1854)

2448. Andrew Lovejot age 45 yrs., died 2 Aug 1854 at LaGrange, Indiana, formerly of Penn Yan, Yates Co., NY. (7 Sep 1854)

2449. Rev. George N. Cheeney, Pastor of the Episcopal Church in Penn Yan, Yates Co., has been given charge of a church in Rochester, Monroe Co. (28 Sep 1854)

2450. William E. Potter and Susan Austin, both of Jerusalem, Yates Co., were married 27 Sep 1854 by Isaac Purdy Esq. in Jerusalem. (28 Sep 1854)

2451. John D. Walds of Prattsburgh, Steuben Co., and Charlotte Stewart of Jerusalem, Yates Co., were married 21 Sep 1854 by Rev. Smith in Jerusalem. (28 Sep 1854)

2452. William Waters and Jane Strowbridge, both of Potter, Yates Co., were married 21 Sep 1854 by Rev. M. Foster in Potter. (28 Sep 1854)

2453. Joseph Colton Esq. of New Orleans, LA., and Caroline A. Garrison, eldest daughter of Stephen

Garrison Esq. of Bellona, Yates Co., NY., were married 21 Sep 1854 by Rev. B.M. Goldsmith in Bellona. (28 Sep 1854)

2454. E.T. Judd and Virginia A. Lilley, both of Geneva, Ontario Co., were married 23 Sep 1854 by Rev. William Hogarth in Geneva. (28 Sep 1854)

2455. Dr. W.T. Swart and Jane Stearns, both of Gorham, Ontario Co., were married there 31 Aug 1854, no pastor given. (28 Sep 1854)

2456. Charles Senteel, Editor of the "Waterloo Observer", and Susan H. Hathaway, both of Waterloo, Seneca Co., were married 14 Sep 1854 by Rev. E. Livermore in Waterloo. (28 Sep 1854)

2457. Nehemiah Leach of Dundee, Yates Co., and Emily Stone of Penn Yan, Yates Co., were married 2 Oct 1854 by Rev. S.S. Hughson in Penn Yan. (5 Oct 1854)

2458. A.B. Morgan and Sarah Look, both of Prattsburgh, Steuben Co., were married 25 Sep 1854 by Rev. W.F. Purington in Prattsburgh. (12 Oct 1854)

2459. Homer M. Townsend of Penn Yan, Yates Co., NY. and Marilla Morgan of Geneva, Ohio., were married 28 Sep 1854 by Rev. Andrews in Geneva, Ohio. (12 Oct 1854)

2460. J.H. Cooley of Wayne, Steuben Co., and Huldah Miles of Barrington, Yates Co., were married 4 Oct 1854 by Rev. D. Olney in Barrington. (12 Oct 1854)

2461. John N. Smith age 56 yrs., died 28 Sep 1854 in Hector, Schuyler Co. (12 Oct 1854)

2462. Dr. William Kimble died 12 Oct 1854 of cholera, in Geneva, Ontario Co. (19 Oct 1854)

2463. Rev. William H. Channing and family sailed for Liverpool, England, where he will take charge of the Second Unitarian Society. (19 Oct 1854)

2464. Allen T. Farwell and Caroline A. Grady, both of Penn Yan, Yates Co., were married 11 Oct 1854 by Rev. Thomas Tousey in Penn Yan. (19 Oct 1854)

2465. George Wilson Nicholas of Chicago, Illinois, and Olivia Murray Gallagher, daughter of the late George Gallagher, were married 12 Oct 1854 by Rev.

Mason Gallagher in the Trinity Church at Geneva, Ontario Co., NY. (19 Oct 1854)

2466. Edward Jewell and Sarah Ann Carley, both of Hector, Schuyler Co., were married 9 Oct 1854 by Rev. Shearer in Watkins, Schuyler Co. (19 Oct 1854)

2467. Mrs. Esta Noltrup age 83 yrs., died 13 Oct 1854 in Penn Yan, Yates Co. (19 Oct 1854)

2468. John T. Johnson of Italy, Yates Co., and Catharine Coons of Jerusalem, Yates Co., were married 30 Jul 1854 by Rev. C. Gould at the parsonage in Potter, Yates Co. (19 Oct 1854)

2469. David Swarthout of Wayne, Steuben Co., and Emily Huson of Barrington, Yates Co., were married 10 Oct 1854 by Rev. D.B. Olney in Barrington. (19 Oct 1854)

2470. Samuel Welles Parker age 1 yr., died 16 Oct 1854 in Detroit, Michigan. The son of Ferdinand F. and Sarah W. Parker, and grandson of Hon. Henry Welles of Penn Yan, Yates Co., NY. (19 Oct 1854)

2471. Dr. James H. Merritt and Antoinette Brown, the clergy-woman, were married 17 Oct 1854 at Mt. Carmel, NY., no pastor named. (26 Oct 1854)

2472. A young man Abram D. Fowler of Hamburgh, Erie Co., killed by breathing the foul gas of a well, which he was engaged in digging, and into which he descended soon after a blast had exploded, all efforts to save him failed. (26 Oct 1854)

2473. Johannes ___eilel (illegible) and Magdalena Blac, both of Germany, were married 18 Oct 1854 on the Watertown and _____ne Railroad (illegible) by Elder Judd through an interpreter. The passengers made up a purse and presented it as a gift to the happy couple. (26 Oct 1854)

2474. Egswell Clark of Canisteo, Steuben Co., and Mrs. Electa B. Clark of Jerusalem, Yates Co., were married 16 Oct 1854 by Rev. A.H. Starkweather in Corning, Steuben Co. (26 Oct 1854)

2475. Charles S. Brotker of Seneca, Ontario Co., and Francis M. Whalins, only daughter of John G. Whalins of Ithaca, Tompkins Co., were married 18 Oct 1854 by Rev. Schuyler in Ithaca. (26 Oct 1854)

2476. Charles Hill of Ithaca, Tompkins Co., A conductor on the Cayuga and Susquehanna Railroad, was killed 26 Oct 1854. He was on top of the car, making arrangements to switch off some freight cars, with his face turned away from an approaching bridge. He either forgot, or was so occupied with his task, his head struck the bridge with such a force as to break his neck, causing instant death. (2 Nov 1854)

2477. J.H.C. Blades of Flint, Michigan, and Helen A. Chambers of Syracuse, Onondaga Co., were married 20 Oct 1854 by Rev. J.W. Wiggins in Penn Yan, Yates Co. (2 Nov 1854)

2478. James Johnson of Torrey, Yates Co., and Nancy J. Brown of Port Byron, Cayuga Co., were married 24 Oct 1854 by Rev. E.H. Cranner in Benton, Yates Co. (2 Nov 1854)

2479. William Crighton of Buffalo, Erie Co., and Mary Kennedy, daughter of John Kennedy, were married 24 Oct 1854 by Rev. B.C. Smith at Italy Hill, Yates Co. (2 Nov 1854)

2480. Peter M. Dox Esq. of Geneva, Ontario Co., and Matilda Wyatt Pope, youngest daughter of B.S. Pope Esq. of Anille ? (blurred) nr. Huntsville, Alabama, were married 12 Oct 1854 by Rev. P.B. Robinson in Anille (?). (2 Nov 1854)

2481. Eliza Adams died 28 Oct 1854 of cholera, in Penn Yan, Yates Co. The infant daughter of D.W. Adams. (2 Nov 1854)

2482. Sarah Kinney age 45 yrs., died 23 Oct 1854 at the home of E.C. Robbins in Penn Yan, Yates Co. (2 Nov 1854)

2483. A collision 22 Oct 1854 on the Great Western Railroad, about 20 miles west of Chatham, Columbia Co., killed about 50 people, and injured about 41. The following are from this area:

Yates Co......	Mary Gallagher of Penn Yan.
" "	Patrick Gallagher " "
" "	John Gallagher " "
" "	Edward Barrows of Benton.
" "	Samuel Davis of Starkey.
" "	Irvin J. Beach, no town given.
Livingston Co.	Elizabeth Kingston of Mt. Morris.
" "	Thomas Kingston (dead) " "
Allegany Co...	Thomas Allen of Burns Co.

Monroe Co.....	George Irlay of Rochester.
" "	Patrick Tracey "
" "	George Hitzler "
" "	Angelina Hitzler "
Cortland Co...	Isaac Watson of Virgil.
" "	Margaret Walton "
" "	Harriet M. Walton "
Steuben Co....	Royal Sawin of Corning.
" "	Thomas Sawin "
" "	Freeland Sawin "

(9 Nov 1854)

2484. P.S. Blackman of Painsville, and Julia Hurlburt, daughter of Dr. Hurlburt of Kirtland, Oneida Co., were "spiritually" married 15 Oct 1854 in Kirtland. The ceremony consisted of the matrimonial declaration made by themselves in the presence of about 50 friends. (9 Nov 1854)

2485. Rev. James Eells Jr. has left the Presbyterian Church of Penn Yan, and has taken charge of a flourishing church in Cleveland, Ohio. (16 Nov 1854)

2486. William G. Ackley of Geneva, Ontario Co., and Catharine Arnold of Gorham, Ontario Co., were married 31 Oct 1854 by Rev. J.J. Brayton in Clifton Springs, Ontario Co. (16 Nov 1854)

2487. Philo Brown and Mary Ann Lane were married 2 Oct 1854 by Rev. Olney in Barrington, Yates Co. (16 Nov 1854)

2488. Andrew E. Tenbroeck and Mary Jane Bullock were married 8 Nov 1854 by Rev. Olney in Barrington, Yates Co. (16 Nov 1854)

2489. Robert Buel age 51 yrs., died 2 Nov 1854 at Plainfield, Michigan. Formerly of Penn Yan, Yates Co. (16 Nov 1854)

2490. Judith Sutherland age 61 yrs., died 12 Nov 1854 at the home of L. Sunderlin in Penn Yan, Yates Co. (16 Nov 1854)

2491. Jacob Hager age 67 yrs., died 13 Oct 1854 in Hector, Schuyler Co. (16 Nov 1854)

2492. Samuel H. Welles of Penn Yan, Yates Co., and C. Adell Wilkie, daughter of Frederick Wilkie of Branchport, Yates Co., were married 31 Oct 1854 by Rev. A.W. Cowles in Branchport. (23 Nov 1854)

2493. Andrew Finger of Benton, Yates Co., and Rosetta Barnes of Jerusalem, Yates Co., were married 16 Nov 1854 by Rev. A.C. Mallory in Benton. (23 Nov 1854)

2494. Hiram Brown of Benton, Yates Co., and Susan Perkins of Seneca, Ontario Co., were married 11 Nov 1854 by S.G. Gage Esq. in Benton. Hiram, is the youngest of three brothers married by S.G. Gage, who married their parents, and the parents of the eldest brothers wife. (23 Nov 1854)

2495. Frederick W. Seward, an assistant Editor of the "Albany Journal", son of Gov. Seward, and Anna M. Wharton, daughter of William A. Wharton, all of Albany, Albany Co., were married 21 Oct 1854 by Rev. Campbell in Albany. (23 Nov 1854)

2496. Isaac _?_witt (illegible) and Eliza Ann Eddy, both of Milo, Yates Co., were married 28 Oct 1854 by Rev. Ira Brown in Corning, Steuben Co. (30 Nov 1854)

2497. John F. Hazen age 20 yrs., died 13 Nov 1854 of consumption in Benton, Yates Co. Son of Caleb and Laura Hazen. (30 Nov 1854)

2498. A young man Michael Doughtery committed suicide 9 Dec 1854 by hanging himself in Penn Yan, Yates Co. (14 Dec 1854)

2499. J.M. Chapman formerly of Penn Yan, Yates Co., is now a Freight Agent for one of the Illinois Railroads in St. Louis, MO. (14 Dec 1854)

2500. Joseph R. Cortell and Sarah A. Spink, both of Starkey, Yates Co., were married 29 Nov 1854 by Rev. C. Morton in Penn Yan, Yates Co. (14 Dec 1854)

2501. Myron Peckens and Sarah J. Taylor, both of Benton, Yates Co., were married 9 Nov 1854 by Rev. C. Morton in Benton. (14 Dec 1854)

2502. Dennis D. Bray of Elmira, Chemung Co., and Ellen Hendrick of Penn Yan, Yates Co., were married 4 Nov 1854 by Rev. J.F. Dean at St. Michaels Catholic Church in Penn Yan. (14 Dec 1854)

2503. Emma Moore mysteriously disappeared several weeks ago from her home in Rochester, Monroe Co., and no clue has not been found. (21 Dec 1854)

2504. Thomas N. Boardman and Susan A. Overshire, both of Barrington, Yates Co., were married 29 Nov 1854 by Rev E.D. Ross in Barrington. (21 Dec 1854)

2505. Deacon C.C. Wheeler and Sarah Ann Shultz were married 2 Nov 1854 by Rev. A.W. Sunderlin in Avoca, Steuben Co. (21 Dec 1854)

2506. A.S. Allen and Sarah Griggs, both of Avoca, Steuben Co., were married 4 Dec 1854 by Rev. A.W. Sunderlin in Avoca. (21 Dec 1854)

2507. Morvalden McMonegal of Cuba, Allegany Co., and Helen Asable of Middlesex, Yates Co., were Married 22 Nov 1854 by Rev. M. Wheeler in Middlesex, Yates Co. (21 Dec 1854)

2508. Anson Dolph of Marion, Wayne Co., and Susan Bordwell of Potter, Yates Co., were married 4 Dec 1854 by Rev. John H. Day in Potter. (21 Dec 1854)

2509. Cornelia Anna Roof age 4 yrs. 6 mos. 1 day, died 4 Dec 1854. The daughter of Phillip and Catharine Roof of Starkey, Yates Co. (21 Dec 1854)

2510. Francis O'Daniels and Mary Jane Ketchum, both of Starkey, Yates Co., were married 14 Dec 1854 by Rev. J. Landredth at Lodi, Seneca Co. (28 Dec 1854)

2511. Dr. L. Per___ (illegible) of Penn Yan, Yates Co., and Martha A. Briggs of Potter, Yates Co., were married 21 Dec 1854 by Rev. Jones in Potter. (28 Dec 1854)

2512. Mrs. Lucy Lazell age 69 yrs., died 7 Dec 1854 at the residence of her son in-law, A. Olmsted, in Wheeler, Steuben Co. Wife of the late Rev. Lazell. (28 Dec 1854)

2513. Andrew J. Guile and Sarah Castner, both of Milo, Yates Co., were married 31 Dec 1854 by Rev. D.B. Olney in the Baptist Church at Barrington, Yates Co. (4 Jan 1855)

2514. John M. McNiel of Penn Yan, Yates Co., and Sarah J. Spencer, daughter of the late Hon. Elijah Spencer of Benton, Yates Co., were married 3 Jan 1855 by Rev. Tousey in Benton. (4 Jan 1855)

2515. Homes G. Elwood of Barrington, Yates Co., and Charlotte A. Insco of Starkey, Yates Co., were married 1 Jan 1855 by Rev. S.S. Hughson in Starkey. (4 Jan 1855)

2516. Mrs. Mary McClure age 75 yrs., died 26 Dec 1854 at the home of her son, William McClure, in Canandaigua, Ontario Co. In 1818, she was left a widow with five small children to rear, a member of the Associate Reformed Church. (4 Jan 1855)

2517. THE 1854 TABLE OF MORTALITY FOR THE TOWN OF MIDDLESEX, prepared for the "Yates County Whig" by John Mather Esq.

Feb..15	Lucy Gage age 48 yrs.
Mar..18	Garret Lyons age 1 yr.
" 26	Eunice Seamons age 3 yrs.
Apr...8	Elizabeth L. Hobart age 6 yrs.
May...4	Laura A. Pierce age 6 yrs.
" 13	Benjamin Lindsley age 72 yrs.
Jun..23	Barnet Christie age 38 yrs.
Jul..28	Mary A. Mothersell age 19 Yrs.
Aug..18	Emma Ingram age 1 yr.
Oct...6	Thomas Reynolds age 74 yrs.
" 7	Marshal Hurd age 2 yrs.
Nov...2	Lucy Jane Cochrane age 10 yrs.
" 29	Wesley F. Brinkundee age 1 yr.

(11 Jan 1855)

2518. Abram Wolfe and Emma Layton, both of Dundee, Yates Co., were married 23 Dec 1854 by Rev. T. McElheny in Dundee. (11 Jan 1855)

2519. Joseph E. Hopkins and Louisa Knapp, both of Barrington, Yates Co., were married 25 Dec 1854 by Rev. T. Olney in Barrington. (11 Jan 1855)

2520. Tunis West of Jerusalem, Yates Co., and Catharine Smith of Dundee, Yates Co., were married 1 Jan 1855 by H. Ogden Esq. in Watkins, Schuyler Co. (11 Jan 1855)

2521. Squire L. Coolbaugh of Barrington, Yates Co., and Fanny S. Gray of Wayne, Steuben Co., were married 19 Dec 1854 by Rev. W.C. Matison in Wayne. (11 Jan 1855)

2522. Winthrop Atwill, former Editor of the "Geneva Courier" in Ontario Co., has moved to Iowa and taken charge of the "Davenport Courier". (18 Jan 1855)

2523. Lewis Frey and Salome Schwrickhart, both of Potter, Yates Co., were married 7 Jan 1855 by S.G. Gage in Benton, Yates Co. (18 Jan 1855)

2524. George W. Smith and Lydia A. Davidson, both of Jerusalem, Yates Co., were married 11 Jan 1855 by Rev. Morton in Penn Yan, Yates Co. (18 Jan 1855)

2525. William McConnell and Sarah R. Byington, both of Dundee, Yates Co., were married 9 Jan 1855 by Rev. J.C. Moses in Dundee. (18 Jan 1855)

2526. Samuel M. Sheppard of London, Ohio, and Cynthia D. Adams of Middlesex, Yates Co., NY., were married 19 Dec 1854 by Rev. D. Hutchinson in Middlesex. (18 Jan 1855)

2527. J.F. Garton of Delaware, Ohio, and Mary Burger of Waterloo, Seneca Co., were married 15 Dec 1854 by Rev. M. Wheeler in Potter, Yates Co. (18 Jan 1855)

2528. Hannah Elizabeth Dunn age 11 yrs. 10 mos., died 10 Jan 1855 in Milo, Yates Co., daughter of Andrew and Elizabeth Dunn. (18 Jan 1855)

2529. Mrs. Amelia Jones Goodrich died 10 Jan 1855 at the home of her son in-law, Charles Judd Esq. in Penn Yan, Yates Co. The wife of Rev. Charles Goodrich. She was born 21 Aug 1780 in New Haven, CT., and married 17 Sep 1797. They lived in Pittsfield, MA. until June 1831, when they removed to Havana, Schuyler, Co., NY., and in Nov 1852 removed to Penn Yan. (18 Jan 1855)

2530. THE 1854 MORTALITY TABLE FOR BENTON, prepared for the "Yates County Whig" by S.G. Gage Esq.

Jan..13	Jonathan Kinney age 43 yrs., small pox.
" 21	Isaac D. Gage age 81 yrs.
" 26	Mary Kinney age 83 yrs., small pox.
" 26	Helen M. Rohde age 34 yrs.
Feb...2	Elizabeth Jennings age 49 yrs., cancer.
" 4	Caroline Coleman age 47 yrs., cancer.
" 11	Willard B. Lucas age 52 yrs.
Mar..11	Kesiah Rosenkrantz age 79 yrs.
" 15	Olive D. Smith age 34 yrs., fever.
" 16	Eliza Peck age under 40 yrs. cons.
Apr...1	Sarah Brown age 81 yrs.
" 3	John Crank age 88 yrs.
" 6	William H. Jacobus age under 1 yr.
" 6	Andrew O. Carroll age 2 yrs.
" 7	Thomas H. Trimmer age 57 yrs.
" 10	Ebenezer Hurd age 95 yrs.
" 21	Catharine Rector age 28 yrs. rheu'tism.
" 26	Elizabeth Finger age under 1 yr.
May..22	Miriam (Gage) Parker age 95 yrs.

May..28 Dea. Charles Angus age 52 yrs.
Jun..12 George Turner age 51 yrs.
Jul..12 Ebenezer Holcomb age 88 yrs.
" 22 William Michels age 44 yrs.
Aug..17 Lydia Baker age 68 yrs.
" 27 Mary Whitaker age 70 yrs. (on her birthday).
Sep...3 Cornelia Andrews age 4 yrs. dysen'ty.
" 11 Millard F. Jones age 3 yrs. dysen'ty.
Sep..24 Mary E. Jones age 7 yrs. dysen'ty.
Oct..12 William W. Haines age 14 yrs.
Nov..10 Catherine Hoxter age 65 yrs.
" 13 John Hazen age 20 yrs., cons.
" 15 John Bailey age 17 yrs. fever.
" 16 Aaron Remer age 3 yrs.
Dec...3 John S. Wheat age 58 yrs., fall.
" 7 Ophalia Scott age 6 yrs.
(25 Jan 1855)

2531. Mrs. George Shearman of Penn Yan, Yates Co., age 61 yrs., died 14 Jan 1855 in New York city. (25 Jan 1855)

2532. Lizzie Hoag age 4 yrs., died 19 Jan 1855 in Penn Yan, Yates Co. The daughter of George and Jane Hoag, and adopted daughter of John and Lucy Bruen. (25 Jan 1855)

2533. Charles Pumpelly age 76 yrs., died 6 Jan 1855 in Owego, Tioga Co. He settled in Owego in 1808 when this section of the state was an unbroken wilderness. A member of the 1821 Convention and later a member of the Legislature. (25 Jan 1855)

2534. THE 1854 MORTALITY TABLE FOR THE TOWN OF ITALY, prepared for the "Yates County Whig" by William S. Green Esq.
Jan...1 Elzur B. Reed age 4 yrs., cons.
" 16 Mrs. Sloven age 66 yrs.
" 26 Charles Mumford age 17 yrs., fever.
Feb..20 Mr. Gregory age over 80 yrs.
Mar..11 Obadiah Geer age 60 yrs., cons.
Apr..14 Harriet A. Laire age 4 yrs.
May...1 Eveline Gillett age 3 yrs.
" 17 Olive Clark age 32 yrs., cons.
Jun...5 child of V. Northrup age under 1 yr.
" 5 David Barclay age 60 yrs.
Jul..17 Edward Markham age 75 yrs.
" 19 Annette Green age 3 yrs.
" 20 William Mower age 16 yrs.
Aug...4 Nancy Green age 31 yrs., cons.
Sep...8 Mrs. Lather age unknown.

Oct...1 child of Eli Quick age under 1 yr.
" 15 Nancy Scott age 21 yrs., cons.
" 21 Mrs. Stoddard age 21 yrs.
Nov...1 child of G. Doubleday age 3 yrs.
Dec...4 Ellen Mumford age 53 yrs., typh'd fever.
" 12 Mrs. D. Taylor age 53 yrs., typh'd fever
" 30 son of A. Flint age 3 yrs.
" 30 David Servis age 60 yrs.
(1 Feb 1855)

2535. Caleb Brinton Jr. and Hattie M. Granger, daughter of Gen. John A. Granger, were married 17 Jan 1855 by Rev. Daggett in Canandaigua, Ontario Co. (1 Feb 1855)

2536. Laman Smith and Mary Jane Culver, both of Tyrone, Schuyler Co., were married 20 Jan 1855 by Rev. J.H. Currier at the Dundee House in Dundee, Yates Co. (1 Feb 1855)

2537. Joel Minard age 22 yrs., died 30 Jan 1855 near Monterey, Schuyler Co. On 8 Jan 1855 his mother died, and 12 days after, her eldest son was buried ? * These are clearly the dates given. (1 Feb 1855)

2538. J. Beers killed 7 Feb 1855 in Hornellsville, Steuben Co. The keeper of a bowling saloon, died instantly when he was hit in the head with a bottle. (8 Feb 1855)

2539. Eli Simonds of Milo, Yates Co., and Hattie M. Kidder of Penn Yan, Yates Co., were married 6 Feb 1855 by Rev. C. Morton in Penn Yan. (8 Feb 1855)

2540. Lewis Keeper and Mary Ann Decker were married 4 Feb 1855 by Rev. D.B. Olney in Barrington, Yates Co. (8 Feb 1855)

2541. John Leonard and Mary Weeks were married 1 Feb 1855 by Rev. D.B. Olney in Barrington, Yates Co. (8 Feb 1855)

2542. Mrs. Eliza Lathrop Schwartz age 83 yrs., died 26 Jan 1855 in Philadelphia, PA. Formerly of Penn Yan, Yates Co., NY. (8 Feb 1855)

2543. A young daughter of Lucas Smith, age 8 yrs., accidentally killed at a saw mill in Painted Post, Steuben Co. on Saturday __ Jan 1855, date torn off. (8 Feb 1855)

2544. Rev. William Hogarth of the Presbyterian Church of Geneva, Ontario Co., has accepted the call of the First Presbyterian Church in Brooklyn, NY. (15 Feb 1855)

2545. An inquest was held 2 Feb 1855 on the body of Daniel Haight at Lyons, Wayne Co. He had started drinking with a friend at Galen, and they were on their way to Geneva. After consuming a good amount of drink along the way, his traveling companion decided to stop at the Wayne County Hotel to rest, and thinking Haight was asleep, tried to wake him, but found him dead. The coroner stated his death was from intoxication. Haight was formerly of Dresden, Yates Co. (15 Feb 1855)

2546. George Dusinberre of Penn Yan, Yates Co., and Catharine Hazzard of Jerusalem, Yates Co., were married 7 Feb 1855 by Rev. Thomas Tousey in Penn Yan. (15 Feb 1855)

2547. Mrs. Abbie R. Stark age 27 yrs., died 7 Feb 1855 at the residence of her father, Dr. John Hatmaker in Torrey, Yates Co. The wife of William Stark. (15 Feb 1855)

2548. P.H. Williams age 22 yrs. committed suicide 19 Feb 1855 by taking morphine, in Elmira, Chemung Co. A printer with the "Daily Republican". (22 Feb 1855)

2549. Jerome P. Southerland of Seneca, Ontario Co., and Sarah C. Clark of Benton, Yates Co., were married 6 Feb 1855 by Rev. H. Mallory in Benton. (22 Feb 1855)

2550. F.R. Raplee of Farmer, Seneca Co., and Sarah E. Taylor, only daughter of William Taylor Esq. of Benton, Yates Co., were married 14 Feb 1855 by Rev. S.S. Hughson in Benton. (22 Feb 1855)

2551. Hon. David D. Spencer age 56 yrs., died 18 Feb 1855 at his home in Ithaca, Tompkins Co. Born 17 Feb 1799 in Bristol, Ontario Co. where he lived until 1810, then removed with his parents to Canandaigua, Ontario Co. An Editor, and an active member of the Whig Party. * A brief biography printed. (1 Mar 1855)

2552. Col. C.P. Babcock is one of the proprietors of a new hotel erected in Grand Rapids, Michigan. Formerly of Penn Yan, Yates Co., NY. (1 Mar 1855)

2553. George W. Voorhies of Romulus, Seneca Co., and Mary C. Coleman of Bellona, Yates Co., were married 25 Feb 1855 by Rev. D. Crow in Bellona. (1 Mar 1855)

2554. Thomas Orton of the book firm "Prince, Orton and Miller" in Geneva, Ontario Co., and Sarah C. Orton, daughter of Rev. Samuel G. Orton of Gowanda, Erie Co., were married 20 Jan 1855, no town or pastor given. (1 Mar 1855)

2555. Thomas Ledgerwood and Margaret Anne McCandish both of Seneca, Ontario Co., were married 15 Feb 1855 by Rev. S. Topping at the home of Alexander McCandish in Seneca. (1 Mar 1855)

2556. John Hager age 61 yrs., died 18 Jan 1855 in Reynoldsville, Schuyler Co. (1 Mar 1855)

2557. Seth V. DeGraff age 18 yrs., died 17 Feb 1855 of consumption in Gorham, Ontario Co. The son of Deacon S.V. DeGraff. (1 Mar 1855)

2558. Mrs. Lucinda Cone age 32 yrs., died 31 Jan 1855 of consumption in Gorham, Ontario Co. The wife of Pitt Cone, and daughter of Lewis P. Witter. (1 Mar 1855)

2559. Stephen B. Ayres of Penn Yan, Yates Co., and Artemisia J. Dunlap of Ovid, Seneca Co., were married 28 Feb 1855 by Rev. F.C. Hubbard in Ovid. (8 Mar 1855)

2560. George E. Crozier and Fannie H. Becker were married 28 Feb 1855 by Rev. A.C. Mallory in Benton, Yates Co. (8 Mar 1855)

2561. Walter P. Hobart of Potter, Yates Co., and Loana Randall of Benton, Yates Co., were married 20 Feb 1855 by Rev. E.H. Cranmer in Benton. (8 Mar 1855)

2562. David H. Clark of Benton, Yates Co., and Harriet H. Robertson of Potter, Yates Co., were married 10 Mar 1855 by Rev. A.C. Mallory in Benton. (15 Mar 1855)

2563. Jarad W. Sleeper and Jannett S. Hurd were married 15 Feb 1855 by Rev. O. Fraser in Starkey, Yates Co. (15 Mar 1855)

2564. Robert Forshee of Tyrone, Schuyler Co., and

Mary Bradner of Orange Co., were married 25 Feb 1855 by Rev. B.C. Hurd in Reading, Schuyler Co. (15 Mar 1855)

2565. John R. Drake and O.A. LaFever, daughter of Deacon LaFever, both of Reading, Schuyler Co., were married 7 Mar 1855 by Rev. J.T. Seeley in Reading. (15 Mar 1855)

2566. Nahan Clark age 72 yrs., died 8 Mar 1855 in Middlesex, Yates Co. * note name as spelled. (15 Mar 1855)

2567. Mrs. Patience Terrel age 65 yrs.? (blurred), died 8 Mar 1855 in Dundee, Yates Co., wife of Jon. S. Terrel. (15 Mar 1855)

2568. The body of Emma Moore who disappeared a few months ago in Rochester, Monroe Co., was found in a mill race, and the coroner states she was enciente. Whether she voluntarily drowned herself, or was placed there is yet a mystery. The young man she was engaged to marry, has been taken into custody. (22 Mar 1855)

2569. Jeptha Lee age 91 yrs. 10 days, died 11 Mar 1855 in Ulysses, Tompkins Co. A soldier of the Revolution in Col. Lane's Regiment of Artillery. He was at Fort Montgomery when it was taken by the British and escaped out of the fort with Col. James Clinton. He was in the Battles of Short Hills, Germantown, Monmouth, Brandywine, and was at the taking of Cornwallis. He has lived the last 50 yrs. on lot 14 in Ulysses. (22 Mar 1855)

2570. Stephen W. Miller and Julia A. Baskin, both of Milo, Yates Co., were married 20 Mar 1855 by Rev. D.D. Buck in Milo. (22 Mar 1855)

2571. John Sutherland age 88 yrs., died 3 Mar 1855 of apoplexy in Benton, Yates Co. A resident of that village for upwards of 42 yrs. (22 Mar 1855)

2572. Charles H. Swarthout age 34 yrs., died 14 Feb 1855 in Sacramento, CA., formerly of Benton, Yates Co., NY. (22 Mar 1855)

2573. Mrs. Harriet C. St.John age 29 yrs., died 28 Feb 1855 in Avon, Livingston Co. The wife of C.H. St.John and youngest daughter of Richard Torrence, formerly of Yates Co. (22 Mar 1855)

2574. Dr. J.B. Breck died 25 Mar 1855 in Elmira, Chemung Co., leaving a wife and family. (29 Mar 1855)

2575. SOME OF THE DISTINGUISHED DEAD OF 1854, prepared for the "Yates County Whig" by S.G. Gage.

a. Comfort Smith age 87 yrs., died in ScottsVille, Monroe Co., NY. A soldier of the Revolution, no date given. (29 Mar 1855)

b. Mrs. Susan Bigler at Delaware, PA., mother of the present Governor's of PA and CA., no date given. (29 Mar 1855)

c. Dr. Avery Downer age 92 yrs., died at Preston, CT. The last survivor of the Battle of Fort Griswold in the Revolution. He was at the fort with his father, who was also a physician at the time of the massacre, and assisted in dressing the wounds of the soldiers, no date given. (29 Mar 1855)

d. Mrs. Elizabeth Stillwagon age 115 yrs. died __ Feb 1854 at Cornellsville, PA. She had two sons born before the Revolution, in which her husband was a soldier and one time prisoner. (29 Mar 1855)

e. Alfred Hovey age 76 yrs. died __ Mar 1854 at Syracuse, Onondaga Co., NY. One of the original contractors on the Erie Canal. (29 Mar 1855)

f. Mrs. Judith Town age 107 yrs. died at Marshall, NY. Her eldest daughter is living at the age of 86 yrs., no date given. (29 Mar 1855)

g. Hon. Friend Humphrey age 67 yrs., died 19 Mar 1854 at Albany, Albany Co. An ex-Senator, and past Chief Magistrate. (29 Mar 1855)

h. Dea. Daniel Clark a soldier of the Revolution died at Brooklyn, CT. For the last 50 yrs. a resident of Plymouth, CT., no date given. (29 Mar 1855)

i. Jonathan Harrington died 1 Apr 1855, the last survivor of the Battle of Lexington, no town given. (29 Mar 1855)

j. Lieut. John Reed age 90 yrs., died 4 Apr 1854 at Bluffton, LA., a soldier of the Revolution. (29 Mar 1855)

k. Hon. Nehemiah Knight died 18 Apr 1855 at Providence, RI., ex-Governor of RI., and for 20 yrs. a member of Congress. (29 Mar 1855)

l. Daniel Ross age 97 yrs., died 24 Apr 1854 at Ipswich, MA., a soldier of the Revolution. (29 Mar 1855)

m. Mrs. Emily Judson died 1 Jun 1855 at Hamilton, Madison Co. Widow of Dr. Judson, the missionary to Burmah. Mrs. Judson was known in the literary world as Fanny Forrester. (29 Mar 1855)

n. Durreil Williams age 90 yrs., died __ Jul 1854 at Albany, Albany Co. A soldier of the Revolution, he was with Gen. Washington at West Point and Newburg, and present at the evacuation of New York by the British. A resident of PA. when the war broke out, he has lived in Albany for the last 20 yrs. (29 Mar 1855)

o. Thomas Ritchie age 80 yrs., died 3 Jul 1854 at Richmond, VA. Editor of the "Richmond Enquirer" for 50 yrs. (29 Mar 1855)

p. Judge Daile died 15 Jul 1854, Chief Justice of Rhode Island. (29 Mar 1855)

q. Abby Filmore age 22 yrs., died 28 Jul 1854 at Aurora, NY., daughter of the ex-President. (29 Mar 1855)

r. Daniel Ames age 100 yrs. 1 mo. 10 days, died 29 Aug 1854 at Montville, CT. A soldier of the Revolution, wounded at the Battle of Bunker Hill. (29 Mar 1855)

s. Dr. R.M. Patterson age 68 yrs., died 5 Sep 1854. Former director of the U.S. Mint, President of the American Philosophical Society, and a Professor at the Universities of PA and VA. (29 Mar 1855)

t. Mrs. Elizabeth Fish age 80 yrs., died 6 Sep 1854 in New York city. Widow of Col. M. Fish and mother of ex-Governor Fish. She descends directly from Gov. Stuyvesant. (29 Mar 1855)

u. Hon. Samuel Stevens died 11 Sep 1854 at Rochester, Monroe Co. A lawyer and ex-Lieut. Governor of this state. (29 Mar 1855)

v. William Parrot age 109 yrs. 7 mos., died 20 Sep 1854 at Laura, VA. A soldier of the Revolution. (29 Mar 1855)

w. Jonathan M. Wainwright died 21 Sep 1854 at New York city, Episcopal Bishop of the Diocese of New York. (29 Mar 1855)

x. Alexander W. Stow died 22 Sep 1854 at Milwaukee, Wisconsin, Chief Justice of that state. (29 Mar 1855)

y. Samuel Dunham age 100 yrs. 10 mos. 25 days, died 12 Oct 1854 at Mansfield, CT. A soldier of the Revolution. (29 Mar 1855)

z. Samuel Moore age 105 yrs. 10 mos. 25 days, died 21 Oct 1854 at Albion, ME. (29 Mar 1855)

aa. Mrs. Sarah W. Karnes age 117 yrs. 3 mos. 16 days, died __ Nov 1854 in New York city. Born in this country, she was taken Ireland as an infant and lived in Cork. After her marriage she returned to the U.S. She was the mother of 22 children. (29 Mar 1855)

bb. John Howland died __ Dec 1854 at Providence, RI. A soldier of the Revolution. (29 Mar 1855)

cc. Aaron Abbott age 96 yrs., died 9 Dec 1854 at New Canaan, CT. A soldier of the Revolution. (29 Mar 1855)

dd. Thomas W. Dorr died 27 Dec 1854 at Providence RI. He headed the Revolutionary party in the little Johnny cake state. For the part Gov. Dorr took in resisting the regular authorities, he was tried for treason, and sent to the state prison. He was pardoned last year. (29 Mar 1855)

ee. Charles Sigourney Esq. died 31 Dec 1854 at Hartford, CT., husband of the poetess. (29 Mar 1855)

2576. James J. Perkins of Victor, Ontario Co., and Sarah A. Woodworth of Penn Yan, Yates Co., were married 14 Mar 1855 by Rev. J. Jones in Penn Yan. (29 Mar 1855)

2577. R. Gideon Townsend of Nunda, Livingston Co., and Elvira Nutt of Torrey, Yates Co., were married 10 Apr 1855 by Rev. A.C. Mallory in Torrey. (12 Apr 1855)

2578. Rev. John Crickmore an aged man, died in Barrington, Yates Co. Born in England, he had lived many years in this country. A member of the Methodist Church. He had also lived in Havana, Schuyler Co. (19 Apr 1855)

2579. Jesse Brown age 90 yrs. 7 mos. 20 days, died 14 Apr 1855 in Torrey, Yates Co. He moved from CT. to the head of the Seneca lake in 1788. A year or two later, he moved to the Friend's Settlement, and in 1792 to the farm where he died. He was Baptised into the Baptist Church 21 Jul 1806 and continued a faithful membership. (19 Apr 1855)

2580. Daniel Randolph of Torrey, Yates Co., and Achsah Jane Supplee of Milo, Yates Co., were married 8 Apr 1855 by Rev. Chubbuck in the M.E. Church at Milo. (19 Apr 1855)

2581. Mrs. Laura S. Ray age 24 yrs., died 11 Mar 1855 in Rochester, Monroe Co. Daughter of the late Mrs. VanDerlip of Penn Yan. (19 Apr 1855)

2582. ANOTHER DREADFUL RAILROAD ACCIDENT; Three men were standing on the tracks of the Niagara Falls Railroad, near the Canandaigua Hotel on Monday 23 Apr 1855. A freight train had just come in, and they stepped aside. Amidst the noise and confusion, they failed to see another engine backing towards them. They were struck down, and Mr. Hall was killed instantly. His head severed from his body. David Pillsbury was severely injured, and his ankle and collar bones broke. Mr. Nelson of Miller's Corner in Bloomfield, was scalped entirely, and rumor has it he has since died. (26 Apr 1855)

2583. Henry H. Beard of Milo, Yates Co., and Sarah A. Borden of Torrey, Yates Co., were married 12 Apr 1855 in Milo, no pastor given. (26 Apr 1855)

2584. Thomas Griffith of Canandaigua, Ontario Co., and Susan Friedenburgh of Penn Yan, Yates Co., were married 21 Apr 1855 by Rev. John Jones in Penn Yan. (26 Apr 1855)

2585. Lluellen Sones age 11 mos., died 21 Apr 1855 in Penn Yan, Yates Co. Son of James and Phebe Ann Sones. (26 Apr 1855)

2586. Mrs. Sarah Cobb age 59 yrs., died 2_ Mar 1855 (date as printed) in Canton, Ohio. (26 Apr 1855)

2587. Mrs. Catharine Graham age 76 yrs., died 7 Apr 1855 in Penn Yan, Yates Co. (26 Apr 1855)

2588. Ralph Chapin Esq. age 50 yrs., died yesterday in Canandaigua, Ontario Co. Copied from the Canandaigua Times, no date given. (3 May 1855)

2589. Rev. Charles Morton for two years, pastor of the Baptist Church in Penn Yan, Yates Co., will be taking charge of a church in Corning, Steuben Co. (3 May 1855)

2590. M.O. Wilder Esq., killed 30 Apr 1855 at Syracuse, Onondaga Co., when the train ran over his horse. (3 May 1855)

2591. J.M. Latimer of Penn Yan, Yates Co., and L.C. Story of Newburyport, MA., were married 21 Apr 1855 by Rev. Dimmick at Newburyport. (3 May 1855)

2592. William Hittle and Mary Jane Searles, both of Penn Yan, Yates Co., were married 16 Apr 1855 by James V. VanAllen Esq. in Penn Yan. (3 May 1855)

2593. Charles E. Jennings of Rochester, Monroe Co., and Harriet C. Schuyler of South Hingham, MA., were married 29 Apr 1855 by Rev. Charles Morton at the home of Jesse Coon Esq. in Penn Yan, Yates Co., NY. (3 May 1855)

2594. G.B. Westcott and Eliza B. Bishop, both of Barrington, Yates Co., were married 29 Apr 1855 by Rev. E.D. Ross in Barrington. (10 Apr 1855)

2595. Stephen Briggs age 2 yrs. 2 mos., died 6 May 1855 in Benton, Yates Co., son of Edward and Ann Briggs. (10 May 1855)

2596. Myron O. Wilder died 13 May 1855 on the train, no location given. He was late of Bristol, Ontario Co., and studied law with William H. Seward at Auburn. On his admission, he opened an office in Canandaigua, Ontario Co. (17 May 1855)

2597. Hon. John C. Spencer died last week in Albany, Albany Co. The eldest son of Chief Justice Spencer, no date given. (24 May 1855)

2598. Alexander McCaig of Benton, Yates Co., and Martha Deyo of Seneca, Ontario Co., were married 17 May 1855 by Rev. A.C. Mallory in Benton. (24 May 1855)

2599. Nathaniel Gay age 40 yrs., died 21 May 1855 in Penn Yan, Yates Co. (24 May 1855)

2600. Mrs. Caroline Rector age 24 yrs. 4 mos., died 21 May 1855 in Benton, Yates Co., wife of Nelson Rector. (31 May 1855)

2601. Hon. John Chadwick age 70 yrs., died 29 May 1855 at his home near Bangor, Maine. The father of Prof. Edmund Chadwick of the Starkey Seminary. A native of New Hampshire. (7 Jun 1855)

2602. Benjamin Franklin and Mrs. Clara Atwater, both of Havana, Schuyler Co., were married 29 May 1855 by Rev. A.C. Laman in Havana. (7 Jun 1855)

2603. Dr. E.S. Wright of Syracuse, Onondaga Co., and Mary Jackson, daughter of Hon. William T. Jackson of Havana, Schuyler Co., were married 30 May 1855 by Rev. M. Huggins in Havana. (7 Jun 1855)

2604. E.C. Winslow and Laura Thayer were married 26 May 1855 by Rev. D.B. Olney in Milo, Yates Co. (7 Jun 1855)

2605. Michael Corbit and Julia A. Northrup were married 30 May 1855 by Rev. D.B. Olney in Barrington, Yates Co. (14 Jun 1855)

2606. George W. Welles of Seneca Falls, Seneca Co., and Helen E. Parshall of Milo, Yates Co., were married 11 Jun 1855 by B.L. Hoyt Esq. in Penn Yan, Yates Co. (14 Jun 1855)

2607. Mrs. Gen. Clark died 14 Jun 1855 at Lyons, Wayne Co. A native of Ontario Co., and sister of Mrs. Mark H. Sibley. (21 Jun 1855)

2608. J. Fraser of Elmira, Chemung Co., and Anna M. Harrington of Westfield, Chautauqua Co., were married 12 Jun 1855 by Rev. Charles F. Munsey in Westfield. (21 Jun 1855)

2609. James Monroe Lane age 19 yrs. 3 mos., died 12 Jun 1855 in Dundee, Yates Co. The son of Jacob V. Lane. (21 Jun 1855)

2610. Z.E.B. Nash formerly of Penn Yan, Yates Co., is now a dealer in hardware at St. Anthony, Minnesota. (28 Jun 1855)

2611. Ebenezer Scofield of Benton, Yates Co., and Elizabeth Stokoe of Seneca, Ontario Co., were married by Rev. E.H. Cranmer in Benton, no date given. (28 Jun 1855)

2612. Mrs. Lucy Ann Bridgman died 12 Jun 1855 in Penn Yan, Yates Co., wife of Jacob F. Bridgman. (28 Jun 1855)

2613. Silas Walker age 49 yrs., died in Geneva, Ontario Co. of a heart disease, induced by inflamatory rheumatism. A former citizen of Gorham, Ontario Co. (5 Jul 1855)

2614. Chester Borden and Charity Youngs, both of Torrey, Yates Co., were married 21 Jun 1855 by Rev. A.E. Chubbuck in Torrey. (5 Jul 1855)

2615. Thomas Griffin, lock tender at Dresden, Yates Co., drowned 11 Jul 1855 in the canal. The line from a crib of timber, threw him into the water just forward of the timber in the lock. (12 Jul 1855)

2616. Thomas Delany drowned 8 Jul 1855 in the mill pond of Mr. B's in Rushville, Yates Co. It is thought he was seized with cramps. (12 Jul 1855)

2617. The wife of Gov. DeWitt Clinton died 2 Jul 1855 at the home of her step-daughter, Mrs. David S. Jones in Poughkeepsie, NY. (12 Jul 1855)

2618. George Chapman of Torrey, Yates Co., and Libbie A. Acker of West Fayette, Seneca Co., were married 2 Jul 1855 by Rev. James D. Stover in West Fayette. (12 Jul 1855)

2619. Jacob J. Schenck of Ada, Kent Co., Michigan, and Charity C. Brown of Benton, Yates Co., NY., were married 4 Jul 1855 by Rev. Francis Prescott in Grand Rapids, Michigan. (12 Jul 1855)

2620. Mrs. Mary S. Taylor age 23 yrs., died 9 Jul 1855 of consumption at the home of her father, Ashbel Beers Esq. in Jerusalem, Yates Co. The wife of Rodney M. Taylor of Buffalo, Erie Co. The last of three sisters and three brothers, who have died in the last 13 years, from the same disease, with the exception of one brother who died of a chill fever. (12 Jul 1855)

2621. The 1854 Census of Potter, Yates Co., giving the ages of persons living over the age of 80 yrs., submitted by Richard Warfield, Marshall.

age 97 yrs. Barbery Dutch b. PA.
90 " Elizabeth Shoemaker b. Dutchess Co.
89 " Nathaniel Wilson b. MA.
88 " Magdalena Caylor b. France.
87 " Dorcas Loomis b. VT.
85 " Annis James b. CT.
84 " Nicholas Hetzlar b. PA.
84 " Esther Slayton b. MA.
84 " Jared Foote b. CT., married 64 yrs.
83 " Lucinda Foote b. CT. wife of above.
83 " William Bassett b. MA.
83 " Nicholas VanZant b. NJ.
83 " Hannah Sackett b. MA.
83 " Mary Pierce b. Rensselaer Co.
82 " Luke Conley b. Ireland
80 " George Helsler b. France
80 " Nathan Warner b. MA.
80 " Gabriel Robinson b. Columbia Co.
80 " Joshua Green b. RI.

...and the length of time of the oldest persons born in, or having lived in Potter over 50 yrs.

63 yrs. Isaac Lain b. Yates Co.
63 " Hannah Robinson b. Yates Co.
61 " William Bassett b. MA.
61 " Benjamin French b. Yates Co.
61 " Dorcas Loomis b. VT.
60 " Peleg Bates b. RI.
60 " Isabel Bates b. Orange Co. wife of above.
59 " William L. Hobart b. MA.
59 " Joseph L. Hobart b. Yates Co.
58 " Edmund Perry b. Yates Co.
58 " Esther Hall b. Yates Co.
58 " Lydia Hollet b. Yates Co.
58 " Rebecca Voak b. Yates Co.
57 " Lindsey Warfield b. MD.
57 " James Voak b. NJ.
56 " Margaret Ruger b. Yates Co.
55 " Walter P. Hobart b. Yates Co.
54 " Jacob Dintruff b. PA.
54 " Barbery Bley b. Yates Co.
53 " Joshua Green b. RI.
53 " Elizabeth Wyman b. RI.
52 " Samuel W. Warner b. Yates Co.
52 " Calista Bardwell b. CT.
52 " Sarah Shoemaker b. Yates Co.
50 " Nathan Warner b. MA.
50 " Hamilton J. Briggs b. Yates Co.
50 " Barbery Dutch b. PA.

(19 Jul 1855)

2622. Charles W. Hobart, formerly of Yates Co., has started a paper in Adrian, Michigan, called the "Michigan Republican". (19 Jul 1855)

2623. Jacob G. Nurigan of Geneva, Ontario Co. was killed by lightning 18 Jul 1855 on the canal boat at Utica, Oneida Co. (19 Jul 1855)

2624. William T. Compton of Penn Yan, Yates Co., and Jane Bucher ? (blurred) of Catlin, Chemung Co., were married 4 Jul 1855 by Rev. Harrington in Watkins, Schuyler Co. (19 Jul 1855)

2625. Rev. J.B.K. Clayton of Bethel, Sullivan Co., and Ellen Bennett, youngest daughter of Sanford Bennett Esq. of Jerusalem, Yates Co., were married 20 Jun 1855 by Rev. C.S. Coats in Jerusalem. (19 Jul 1855)

2626. John A. Holmes of Penn Yan, Yates Co., and Elizabeth Woodward of Elmira, Chemung Co., were married 3 Jul 1855 by Rev. S.R. Jones in Southport, Chemung Co. (19 Jul 1855)

2627. Philander B. Lines of Grand Traverse, Michigan, and Mary E. Page of Dundee, Yates Co., were married 23 Jun 1855 by Rev. T. McElheny in Dundee. (26 Jul 1855)

2628. Eli Ross and Louisa Sheppard, both of Reading Centre, Schuyler Co., were married 28 Jun 1855 by Rev. Edward Royce at the home of the bride's father. (26 Jul 1855)

2629. M.M. Davis and Adaline Bewley, both of Reading Centre, Schuyler Co., were married 30 Jun 1855 by Rev. Edward Royce in Reading. (26 Jul 1855)

2630. James G. Stacy Esq. died 9 Jul 1855 at his home in Fayette, Seneca Co. (26 Jul 1855)

2631. Mrs. Anna Hall age 60 yrs.? (blurred), died at New Providence, New Jersey. Formerly of Penn Yan, Yates Co., NY., no date given. (2 Aug 1855)

2632. The mother of Horace Greeley died 27 Jul 1855 at Wayne, Erie Co. His father is still living. (9 Aug 1855)

2633. Winfield Scott Sheppard age 4 1/2 yrs., died 13 Aug 1855 in Benton, Yates Co. Son of George A. Sheppard. (16 Aug 1855)

2634. Sila Sprague age 17 yrs., died 9 Aug 1855 in Benton, Yates Co. (16 Aug 1855)

2635. Mary H. Bruen age 2 yrs. 4 mos. 14 days., died 10 Aug 1855 in Penn Yan, Yates Co. The son of George and Ann A. Bruen. (23 Aug 1855)

2636. Loyal C. Whewell Esq. of Rushville, Yates Co., and H. Amelia Field, daughter of Dea. Prentise Field of Potter, Yates Co., were married 28 Aug 1855 by Rev. S.S. Hughson in Rushville. (30 Aug 1855)

2637. Jane Lawson Nichols died 17 Aug 1855, daughter of John C. Nicholas, no town given. * note, names are as they appeared. (30 Aug 1855)

2638. Mrs. Reliance W. Lapham age 43 yrs., died 10 or 19 Aug 1855 (blurred), in Penn Yan, Yates Co., wife of Ludlow E. Lapham. (30 Aug 1855)

2639. Daniel Playsted of Milo, Yates Co., and Elizabeth Perry of Jerusalem, Yates Co., were married 30 Aug 1855 by Rev. Thomas Tousey in Jerusalem. (6 Sep 1855)

2640. Mrs. Orrilia Barrett age 36 yrs., died 25 Aug 1855 in Jerusalem, Yates Co. The wife of Josephus Barrett, and daughter of Johnathan and Nancy Danes. She leaves three children. (13 Sep 1855)

2641. Charles M. Curtis of Pulteney, Steuben Co., and Caroline Dingee of Penn Yan, Yates Co., were married 8 Sep 1855 by Rev. J. Jones in Penn Yan. (13 Sep 1855)

2642. Joseph Halladay and Sarah Jane Moon, both of Penn Yan, Yates Co., were married 28 Aug 1855 by Rev. J. Jones in Penn Yan. (13 Sep 1855)

2643. John Clapper and Jane Haight, both of Canandaigua, Ontario Co., were married 11 Sep 1855 by Rev. John Cunningham at the American Hotel in Penn Yan, Yates Co. (13 Sep 1855)

2644. George A. Smith and Sarah Ann Wright, only daughter of James Wright Esq., both of Dundee, Yates Co., were married by Rev. McElheny in Dundee, no date given. (13 Sep 1855)

2645. Mrs. Isabella Robson age 83 yrs., died 1 Sep 1855 in Torrey, Yates Co. (13 Sep 1855)

2646. Mrs. Elizabeth Woods age 82 yrs., died 1 Sep 1855 in Geneva, Ontario Co. The mother of James H. Woods Esq. of New York city. (13 Sep 1855)

2647. Rev. Spencer H. Cone age 71 yrs., died 18 Sep 1855 in New York city. Born 30 Apr 1775 in Princeton, NJ., he was admitted into Princeton College at the age of twelve. He married Sallie Wallage Morrell 10 May 1812, she died 15 Aug 1854. He leaves two sons, Spencer Wallace Cone a lawyer, and Edward Cone. * A brief biography printed. (20 Sep 1855)

2648. David Chapin of Havana, Schuyler Co., recently showed his Revolution pension papers to us. He was 94 yrs. when they were made out. His wife has reached the age of 88 yrs. If they live until the first of October, they will celebrate their 70th wedding anniversary. They live with their son Reuben Chapin in Havana. Mr. Chapin is a true member of the Whig party. (20 Sep 1855)

2649. Solomon Williams Jr. of Penn Yan, Yates Co., and Sarah Stocker of Pittstown, PA., were married 8 Sep 1855 by Rev. D.D. Buck in Elmira, Chemung Co. (20 Sep 1855)

2650. Thompson Dunn of the firm "Dunn and Cass" in Elmira, Chemung Co., and Mary E. Tuthill, daughter of C.G. Tuthill Esq. of Burdett, Schuyler Co., were married 18 Sep 1855 by Rev. Fellows in Burdett. (20 Sep 1855)

2651. William A. Little and Elizabeth White, both of Dundee, Yates Co., were married 19 Aug 1855 by Rev. Kennedy in Tyrone, Schuyler Co. (20 Sep 1855)

2652. Loren S. Loveless and Ann Clark, both of Dundee, Yates Co., were married 8 Sep 1855 by Rev. McElheny in Dundee. (20 Sep 1855)

2653. George A. Smith and Sarah Ann Wright, both of Starkey, Yates Co., were married 8 Sep 1855 by Rev. McElheny in Dundee, Yates Co. (20 Sep 1855)

2654. A.J. Swart, assistant teacher at the Starkey Seminary, and Maria Jennison of Eddytown, Yates Co., were married 8 Sep 1855 by Rev. J.H. Currier in Dundee, Yates Co. (20 Sep 1855)

2655. P. Prouty Jr. and Adelaide Cobleigh, daughter of Andrew M. Cobleigh, all of Geneva, Ontario Co., were married 18 Sep 1855 by Rev. Collier in Geneva. (27 Sep 1855)

2656. Ira C. Allen of Fairhaven, VT., and Mary E. Richardson of Geneva, Ontario Co., were married 19 Sep 1855 by Rev. Cannon in Geneva. (27 Sep 1855)

2657. William McAllister of Dundee, Yates Co., and Emily Stone of Milo, Yates Co., were married 22 Sep 1855 by Rev. Bainbridge in Milo. (27 Sep 1855)

2658. Gen. Hugh W. Dobbin age 89 yrs., died 19 Sep 1855 in Geneva, Ontario Co. (27 Sep 1855)

2659. J.E. Curtis of Adrian, Michigan, and Henriette A. Kidder, daughter of Dr. J.S. Kidder of Pekin, Niagara Co., were married 19 Sep 1855 by Rev. J.F. Taylor in Pekin. (4 Oct 1855)

2660. Orville Chaffee of Middlesex, Yates Co., and Helen Clark of Italy, Yates Co., were married 20 Sep 1855 by Rev. Hyle in Italy. (4 Oct 1855)

2661. Charles Green of Italy, Yates Co., and Polly Blair of Middlesex, Yates Co., were married 25 Sep 1855 by Rev. Foley in Middlesex. (4 Oct 1855)

2662. Dr. Philo K. Stoddard of Prattsburgh, Steuben Co., and Sarah Ida Cowing of Jerusalem, Yates Co., were married 29 Sep 1855 by Rev. Smith in Jerusalem. (4 Oct 1855)

2663. Elizabeth Brown age 2 yrs. 3 mos., died 16 Sep 1855 at the home of her parents James and Maria Brown in Jerusalem, Yates Co. (4 Oct 1855)

2664. Dr. George Z. Noble and Anna H. Hazen were married 10 Oct 1855 by Rev. S.M. Bainbridge at the home of Caleb Hazen in Penn Yan, Yates Co. (11 Oct 1855)

2665. Hon. Gaines H. Roberts of Warrick Co., IN., and Mrs. Susan Morris of Penn Yan, Yates Co., NY., were married 7 Oct 1855 by Rev. W.W. Taylor in Penn Yan. (11 Oct 1855)

2666. John W. Russell of New York city, and Mary, daughter of David Hu___ Esq. (illegible) of Geneva, Ontario Co., were married 3 Oct 1855 by Calvin Walker Esq. in Geneva. (11 Oct 1855)

2667. John Elliot Thayer of Boston, MA., and Cornelia Adeline Granger, only daughter of Hon. Francis Granger of Canandaigua, Ontario Co., were married 2 Oct 1855 by Rev. Daggett in Canandaigua. (11 Oct 1855)

2668. Richard Sutphen of Hector, Schuyler Co., and C.M. Frankenburger of Geneva, Ontario Co., were married 3 Oct 1855 by Rev. W.H. Goodwin in Geneva. (11 Oct 1855)

2669. George Hatley Dox age 6 yrs., died 1 Oct 1855 in Hopeton, Yates Co., son of the late Peter G. Dox. (11 Oct 1855)

2670. John McKinney, who murdered Conrad Bauer in a Lager Bier saloon 6 Aug 1855 in Newark, New Jersey, was arrested in New Orleans last Monday, no date given. (18 Oct 1855)

2671. E. Mason Lyon of Canandaigua, Ontario Co., killed 11 Oct 1855 near the Falls. A brakeman on the "Niagara Falls Railroad", had apparently fallen asleep in the caboose. When aroused for the purpose of applying the brakes, being half awake. He made a mis-step, which precipitated him from the platform onto the tracks. The wheels passed over him, and crushed him in a horrible manner. Mr. Lyon was his mother's only support, as his father drowned two years ago in Canandaigua Lake. (18 Oct 1855)

2672. Dr. Joel Shew the well known Hydropathic physician, died 15 Oct 1855 at Oyster Bay, L.I. (18 Oct 1855)

2673. Mr. Kilpatrick and Eunice Underwood, both of Middlesex, Yates Co., were married 7 Oct 1855 by Rev. Brown in Naples, Ontario Co. (18 Oct 1855)

2674. Horace H. Wheeler of Potter, Yates Co., and Elizabeth P. Lacy of Warren, PA., were married 11 Oct 1855 by Rev. Thomas Tousey in Benton, Yates Co. (18 Oct 1855)

2675. George C. Wheeler of Potter, Yates Co., and Jennie M. Welch of Lima, Livingston Co., were married 4 Sep 1855 by Rev. Arnold in Canandaigua, Ontario Co. (18 Oct 1855)

2676. Richard N. Warfield has moved from Rushville, Yates Co., to Rochester, Monroe Co., and entered into the drug trade. (25 Oct 1855)

2677. John T. Gary and Mariah Aldrich, both of Middlesex, Yates Co., were married 18 Oct 1855 by Rev. Merrill Ford in Middlesex. (25 Oct 1855)

2678. Walter D. Green of Italy, Yates Co., and Fanny Blair of Middlesex, Yates co., were married 23 Oct 1855 by Rev. S.S. Hughson in Middlesex. (25 Oct 1855)

2679. Eli A. Robinson Esq. and Amelia Kellogg, both of Geneva, Ontario Co., were married 18 Oct 1855 by Rev. J.B. Richardson in Geneva. (25 Oct 1855)

2680. H.A. Counrad of Ontario Co., and Martha Bates of Benton, Yates Co., were married 11 Oct 1855 by Rev. Goldsmith at the home of the brides father in Benton. (25 Oct 1855)

2681. Mrs. Lettice Hunter age 68 yrs., died 20 Oct 1855 at the home of Dashel Bostwick in Middlesex, Yates Co. (25 Oct 1855)

2682. Stephen P. Sherwood of Pawling, Dutchess Co., and Jerusha Stark of Dover, Dutchess Co., were married 10 Oct 1855 by Rev. A. Hunt in Jerusalem, Yates Co. (8 Nov 1855)

2683. Benoni Pearce of Jerusalem, Yates Co., and Rachel Stark of Dover, Dutchess Co., were married 24 Oct 1855 by Rev. A. Hunt in Jerusalem. (8 Nov 1855)

2684. Andrew J. Brown and Lillius H. Pearce , both of Jerusalem, Yates Co., were married 31 Oct 1855 by Rev. H. Boardman in Jerusalem. (8 Nov 1855)

2685. Melvin C. Hutches age 8 yrs. 5 mos. 8 days., died 7 Oct 1855. Only son of Morris and Malinda Hutches of Milo, Yates Co. During his illness he seemed to know he was about to die. One day he told his father to give all his things to his sister, and to bury him where he went to Sabbath School, meaning the grave yard of the Baptist Meeting House. A few days before he died, he told his mother he wanted to sing for them, yet he was so weak, it was even difficult for him to speak. He commenced to sing "The Little Traveler", a song found in his Sabbath School Book, about one day living with Jesus. (8 Nov 1855)

2686. William D. Squier of the firm Ayres & Squier in Penn Yan, Yates Co., and Emma Hermance, daughter of Dr. James Hermance of Potter, Yates Co., were married 14 Nov 1855 by Rev. Spink in Potter. (13 Nov 1855)

2687. Mrs. Louisa Williams age 35 yrs., died 31 Oct 1855 in Warren, PA., wife of DR. D.M. Williams Esq. (13 Nov 1855)

2688. Samuel Hart Wright of Dundee, Yates Co., and Mary Jane Burtch of Jerusalem, Yates Co., were married 14 Nov 1855 by Rev. S.M. Bainbridge in Jerusalem. (22 Nov 1855)

2689. Andrew Schuman, Editor of the "Syracuse Journal", and Lucy B. Dunlap, daughter of Joseph Dunlap Esq. of Ovid, Seneca Co., were married 13 Nov 1855 by Rev. Charles Votey in Ovid. (22 Nov 1855)

2690. Louis P. Millspaugh of Branchport, Yates Co., and Caroline S. Turner, daughter of F. Turner Esq. of Benton, Yates Co., were married 22 Nov 1855 by Rev. S.S. Hughson in Benton. (29 Nov 1855)

2691. Charles Sherman and Harriet Baxter, both of Milo, Yates co., were married 20 Nov 1855 by Rev. D.B. Olney in Milo. (29 Nov 1855)

2692. Daniel Westerfield of New York city, and Mary Durry, daughter of John Durry, were married 19 Nov 1855 by Rev. William W. Taylor at the brides home near Penn Yan, Yates Co. (29 Nov 1855)

2693. Carleton Foote of New York city, and Margaret Foote, daughter of Salmon Foote, were married 27 Nov 1855 by Rev. William W. Taylor at the brides home near Penn Yan, Yates Co. (29 Nov 1855)

2694. John Kennedy and Janett Cameron were married 15 Nov 1855 by Rev. William W. Taylor in Penn Yan, Yates Co. (29 Nov 1855)

2695. Mrs. Elizabeth Barden age 81 yrs., died in Penn Yan, Yates Co., widow of Otis Barden. She was born 25 Apr 1774 in Washington Co., RI. The daughter of James Barden, a soldier of the Revolution. She married in 1793, and immediately moved to Ontario Co., now Yates Co. (6 Dec 1855)

2696. N.H. Potter of Genoa, Cayuga Co., and Emilene Hewitt of Dundee, Yates Co., were married 20 Nov 1855 by Rev. T. McElheny in Dundee. (6 Dec 1855)

2697. Perry A. Poyneer of Penn Yan, Yates Co., and Phoebe Jane Culver of West Dresden, Yates Co., were married 22 Nov 1855 by Rev. D.A. Abbott in Dresden. (6 Dec 1855)

2698. Philemon Prindle and Mrs. Lovejoy, both of Penn Yan, Yates Co., were married __ Oct 1855 by Rev. S.M. Bainbridge in Penn Yan. (6 Dec 1855)

2699. Joseph C. Dean Esq. of Altay, Schuyler Co., and Nancy Hair of Jerusalem, Yates Co., were married 27 Oct 1855 by Rev. McFarrand in Jerusalem. (6 Dec 1855)

2700. Joseph Barrett and Hannah M. Rose, both of Jerusalem, Yates Co., were married 2 Dec 1855 by Rev. McFarrand in Jerusalem. (6 Dec 1855)

2701. Nathan Slawson of Potter, Yates Co., and Jane Cairns of Prattsburgh, Steuben Co., were married 22 Nov 1855 by Rev. McFarrand in Potter. (6 Dec 1855)

2702. William Henry Kelsy and Lusina A. Barnes, both of Middlesex, Yates Co., were married 25 Nov 1855 by Rev. Gibbs in Geneva, Ontario Co. (6 Dec 1855)

2703. Deacon Philo Bronson age 74 yrs., died 29 Nov 1855 at his home near Geneva, Ontario Co. (6 Dec 1855)

2704. Dyer B. Draper age 65 yrs., died 29 Nov 1855 in Geneva, Ontario Co. (6 Dec 1855)

2705. William Jerome Sabin and Caroline A. Francisco, daughter of Francis Francisco Esq., both of Gorham, Ontario Co., were married 12 Dec 1855 by Rev. S.S. Hughson in Rushville, Yates Co. (20 Dec 1855)

2706. Virgil Hixon and Olive M. Adams, fifth daughter of John Adams, both of Middlesex, Yates Co., were married 12 Dec 1855 by Rev. S.S. Hughson in Middlesex. (20 Dec 1855)

2707. S. Otis Livingston of the firm "W.H. Livingston & Co." in New York city, and S. Nellie Tuthill, daughter of C.G. Tuthill of Burdett, Schuyler Co., were married 19 Dec 1855 by Rev. Thomas Tousey in Burdett. (20 Dec 1855)

2708. James Dephew of Milo, Yates Co., and Mary Hutchess of Urbana, Steuben Co., were married 14 Nov 1855 by Rev. L. Johnson in Urbana. (20 Dec 1855)

2709. Mrs. William Whitney died 18 Nov 1855 in San Francisco, CA., formerly of Penn Yan, Yates Co., NY. (20 Dec 1855)

2710. Mrs. Mary B. Pierce age 38 yrs. 6 mos., died 15 Nov 1855 at the home of her uncle, Mr. Barnum in Bridgeport, CT. The wife of L.L. Pierce and daughter of the late Ammon Benedict of Penn Yan, Yates Co., formerly of Benton, Yates Co. (20 Dec 1855)

2711. Jacob F. Bridgeman and Ruth A. Sheppard, both of Penn Yan, Yates Co., were married 24 Dec 1855 by Rev. Thomas Tousey in Penn Yan. (27 Dec 1855)

* Found at the end of this film were several papers dating back to Aug 1855.

2712. The son of Robert N. McFarren age 3 yrs., was killed 10 Aug 1855 on the railroad tracks near his home. The engineer discovered the child on the track and did all in his power to stop the train, but was too late. (17 Aug 1855)

2713. The son of Mr. Sones of Penn Yan, Yates Co., age about 5 yrs., fell from the railroad bridge 14 Aug 1855. He fractured his skull and collar bone, and is not expected to live. (17 Aug 1855)

2714. Mrs. Amos Smith died 20 Aug 1855 in Geneva, Ontario Co, the former Miss Jane Cobb. Buried in Penn Yan, Yates Co. (23 Aug 1855)

SPECIAL INDEX OF INDIVIDUALS WITH REFERENCES TO THE REVOLUTIONARY WAR

* Please note..to use index, individuals are listed under the entry number and not the page number.

GENERAL INDEX

* Please note..to use index, individuals are listed under the entry number and not the page number.